LANDLORDS AND FARMERS IN

THE HUDSON–MOHAWK REGION

1790–1850

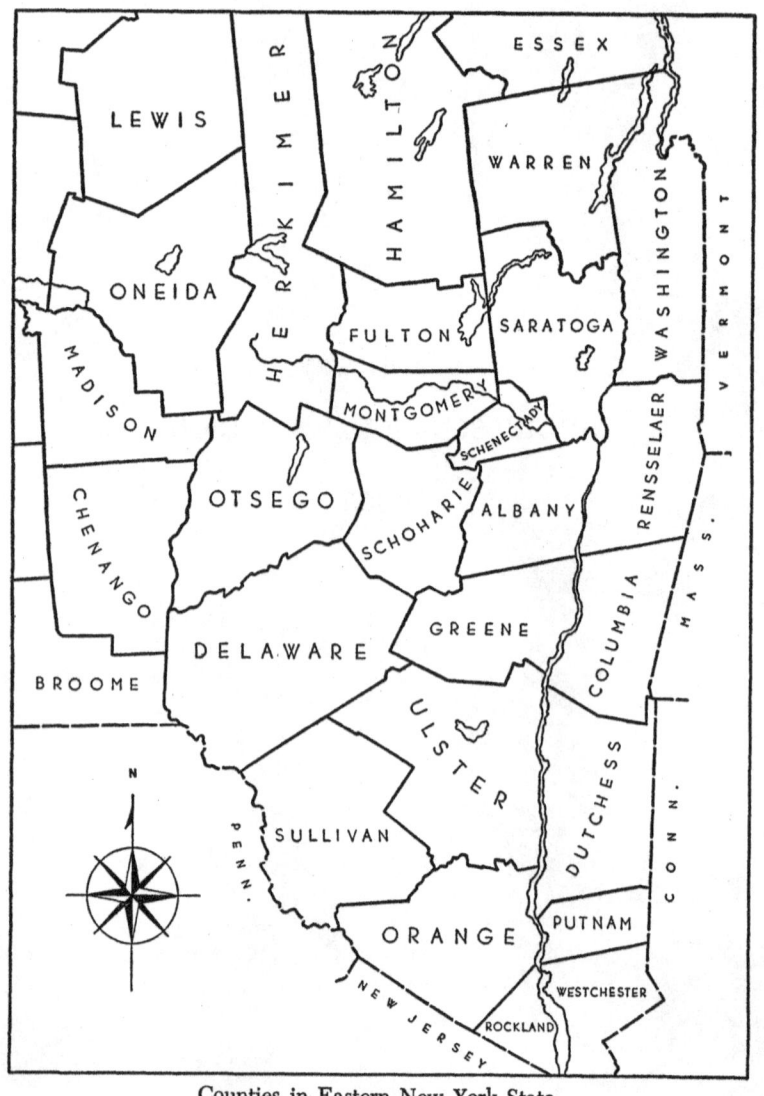

Counties in Eastern New York State.

LANDLORDS *and* FARMERS
in the
HUDSON-MOHAWK REGION
1790–1850

ભ

DAVID MALDWYN ELLIS

Fall Creek Books
AN IMPRINT OF
CORNELL UNIVERSITY PRESS
ITHACA AND LONDON

 Fall Creek Books is an imprint of Cornell University Press dedicated to making available again classic books that document the history, culture, natural history, and folkways of New York State. Presented in new paperback editions that faithfully reproduce the contents of the original editions, Fall Creek Books titles will appeal to all readers interested in New York and the state's rich past. For a complete listing of titles published under the Fall Creek Books imprint, please visit www.cornellpress.cornell.edu.

Copyright © 1946 by Cornell University

All rights reserved. Except for brief quotations in a review, this book, or parts thereof, must not be reproduced in any form without permission in writing from the publisher. For information, address Cornell University Press, Sage House, 512 East State Street, Ithaca, New York 14850.

First printing, Cornell University Press, 1946
First printing, Fall Creek Books, 2010

Printed in the United States of America

TO PAUL WALLACE GATES

PREFACE

WITHIN recent years several significant studies of regional development paying particular attention to agricultural history have attracted widespread interest despite the latent hostility of many historians to what is disparagingly called local history. Such studies as those by Joseph Schafer in the *Wisconsin Domesday Series*, Avery Craven's *Soil Exhaustion as a Factor in the Agricultural History of Virginia and Maryland, 1606–1860*, and Lewis Stillwell's *Emigration from Vermont, 1776–1860* illustrate most graphically the very real contribution which a careful study of a restricted area can add to our knowledge of American history. In fact, these monographs suggest the importance of making similar studies of other regions in the United States. My undertaking, it is hoped, will meet the need for an account of the striking readjustments which transformed the agrarian life of the Hudson-Mohawk region between 1790 and 1850.

Readjustment to changing conditions seemed to be the fate of the American farmer in that period as well as in the years that followed. The perplexing problems faced by those who struck out for the western prairies and plains have been frequently and ably described. Too often, however, has the significant fact been overlooked that those farmers who stayed at home faced a future fully as hazardous and unpredictable. The expansion of the

PREFACE

transportation network unleashed two of the most revolutionary forces in our agricultural history: the "pull" of the growing home market and the flood of cheap western produce. The transition from a predominantly self-sufficient economy to one primarily dependent on the market was to effect changes fully as far-reaching if not as spectacular as those accompanying the industrial revolution. In a certain sense farming as a way of life was yielding place to the concept of farming as a means of profit. No group of farmers in the country felt the impact of these revolutionary forces more directly than those of eastern New York. How they met this challenge is the central theme of this work.

The author has set before him certain major tasks: to describe the process of settlement, the growth of population, and the characteristics of pioneer agriculture; to trace the rapid shifts from grain culture to sheep raising and dairying; to point out the variety of individual and local adjustments caused by differences in soils, topography, accessibility to market, racial practices, and individual enterprise; to contrast the forces leading to rural decline with the beginnings of scientific husbandry and agricultural education; to evaluate the role of roads, canals, and railroads; and to outline the land pattern and the effect of the leasehold upon the agrarian development of eastern New York. In short, this work tries to describe the transformation of the pioneer farmer into the dairyman.

Of course the most striking, although by no means the most significant event, was the antirent episode of the 1840's, the last of a series of tenant uprisings originating from the peculiar land system of eastern New York. Considerable attention has been given to the background of tenant unrest, its periodic outbursts, and the political activities of the antirenters. Although the land pattern and the antirent war of the 1840's lend themselves to separate treatment, they cannot be divorced from the main current of agricultural history. The conditions under which land was acquired and held vitally affected the farmer. Furthermore, tenant

PREFACE

unrest was only one phase of the larger problem of agrarian discontent. Antirentism was often the channel through which much dissatisfaction expressed itself.

The breadth and scope of this subject make it impossible to explore entirely new ground. The general field of agricultural history has been surveyed on a national scale several times and recently has been intensively studied in a few states. Several writers have already investigated significant portions of this phase of New York history. Notable among these are E. Wilder Spaulding, whose *New York in the Critical Period, 1783–1789* furnishes an excellent introduction to the period; Edward P. Cheyney, who made the pioneer study of *Anti-Rent Agitation in the State of New York;* and Russell Anderson, author of "New York Agriculture Meets the West," which appeared in the *Wisconsin Magazine of History.* More recently Henry Christman has recreated the drama and color of the antirent struggle in his *Tin Horns and Calico.*

But many gaps have been left to be filled. The growth and influence of the urban market; the role of land speculation; the importance of waterways, turnpikes, and railroads in shaping the agricultural history of this region; the problem of rural decline; the relation of the National Reform movement to antirentism; the later phases of the antirent war; and a host of minor problems have never been adequately discussed. Furthermore, the scattered material has never before been synthesized into an integrated pattern.

Many persons and institutions have helped me in the preparation of this work. To Professor Paul Wallace Gates I owe a special debt of gratitude for his critical suggestions, advice, and encouragement. It is hardly necessary to add that responsibility for all errors and misinterpretations should be laid on my doorstep.

The staffs of various libraries have helped to lighten and to enliven the task of finding and collecting material. Most important among this number are the Cornell University Library, the New York State Library (especially Miss Edna L. Jacobsen), the New

PREFACE

York Historical Society, the New York Public Library, and the American Antiquarian Society.

I wish to take this opportunity to thank the members of the Cornell University Press for making substantial improvements in the final form of the manuscript. I also wish to thank Dr. Everett E. Edwards, editor of *Agricultural History*, for permission to use material which previously appeared in his publication. The chapters on the antirent movement received the benefit of Professor Harold W. Thompson's criticism. I should also like to acknowledge my indebtedness to Dean Harry S. Carman of Columbia University, whose friendly interest encouraged me to revise my doctoral dissertation for publication.

It is also my pleasant duty to thank those who have helped me in nonprofessional capacities. Their contribution if less tangible and specific has been no less real. My parents, Mr. and Mrs. Sam Ellis of Utica, have followed the progress of this enterprise with sympathy and encouragement. Mr. and Mrs. Robert G. Blabey of Albany and Dr. and Mrs. William Rankin Ward Jr. of Newark, New Jersey, have likewise extended every assistance. It is my hope that this undertaking will merit the confidence and justify the encouragement of all those who have had a hand in its preparation.

D. M. E.

April, 1946

CONTENTS

	Preface	vii
	List of Maps	xiii
I	The Background	1
II	Population Growth and the Land Pattern, 1790–1808	16
III	The Good Years, 1790–1808	66
IV	Years of Uncertainty, 1808–1825	118
V	The Transportation Network, 1825–1850	159
VI	The Rise of the Dairy State, 1825–1850	184
VII	The Antirent Movement, 1839–1845	225
VIII	Antirentism in Politics	268
	Appendixes	313
	Bibliography	318
	Index	335

LIST OF MAPS

Counties in Eastern New York State	ii
Increase in Population by Counties, 1790–1800	18
Changes in Population by Townships, 1800–1810	19
Turnpikes of Eastern New York	86
Changes in Population by Townships, 1810–1820	119
Changes in Population by Townships, 1820–1830	121
Changes in Population, 1830–1840	161
Sheep in Each Town in 1836 (Based on Benton and Barry)	162
Changes in Population, 1840–1850	164
Changes in Population, 1850–1860	165
Railroads and Canals of 1855	174

CHAPTER I

THE BACKGROUND

THE HUDSON-MOHAWK River has cut a channel in New York history as deep and lasting as its breach through the Appalachian barrier. Its history is much more than the colorful pageant of stirring events, such as Captain Hudson viewing the Palisades from the high-pooped "Half Moon," Benedict Arnold fleeing from West Point, or the "Clermont" belching black smoke on her maiden voyage. The history of this waterway is likewise a barometer of local, state, and national growth. To the Hudson River landings in colonial days came the wheat, flour, potash, and barreled meats of the farms fringing the river. After the Revolution wagons and later canalboats laden with cereals and lumber brought through the Mohawk gateway the products of central and western New York. By 1850 the flood of wheat, pork, and kindred products from the Lake states exceeded in tonnage that which originated within the state.[1] Railroad engineers discovered at an early date that the Mohawk route was the best pass through the Appalachian Mountains. Over the rails of the New York Central passed a large share of the country's freight and passenger traffic, which increased rapidly with the industrialization of the nation. Finally, in the twentieth century highway contractors built mag-

[1] See Table 28 in *New York Assembly Documents,* no. 31 (Albany, 1877).

nificent highways paralleling the Hudson-Mohawk waterway.[2]

The Revolution and its aftermath gave a violent wrench to the state's development. Confusion and unrest disorganized the older counties. British armies, Continental guerrillas, and Tory bushwhackers had laid waste large areas near the City as well as on the frontier. Victory did not end the problem of how to deal with the Tories. To be sure, thousands departed for Canada. The treatment of those who remained was to bedevil state politics for a decade. The struggle to ratify the Constitution reopened the controversy between the democratic farmers and the aristocratic landholders. Alexander Hamilton, who had married Elizabeth Schuyler, led the conservative forces. George Clinton became the champion of the debtor farmers. In the meantime the New York frontier was ablaze with activity. By 1783 the Iroquois menace had disappeared. Yankees by the thousands were crossing the border and taking up farms. Land jobbers were grabbing millions of acres of new land thrown on the market by the politicians of New York and Massachusetts.

These changes were sweeping; they were not revolutionary.[3] To be sure, Tory landholders saw their acres confiscated, but patriotic families such as the Van Rensselaers kept their holdings intact. Admittedly George Clinton broke the political monopoly of the landed aristocracy. Nevertheless, the aristocracy retained

---

[2] In 1930, 84 per cent of the population of the state lived in a narrow belt following the Hudson and Mohawk valleys and thence stretching across to Buffalo on Lake Erie. In this belt, which comprises only 16 per cent of the land area of the state, are the metropolitan centers of New York, Albany, Utica, Syracuse, Rochester, and Buffalo. Connecting these centers are the New York Central Railroad, the Barge Canal–Hudson River water route, and two of the state's main highways. See map of the valley belt in New York Planning Board's *A Graphic Compendium of Planning Studies* (Albany, 1935), p. 120.

[3] Dixon Ryan Fox in the Foreword to E. Wilder Spaulding's *New York in the Critical Period, 1783–1789* (New York, 1932) declares that no other state "underwent such striking and far-reaching social changes by means of the Revolution as did New York."

THE BACKGROUND

most of its original political power and was able to stop manhood suffrage until it was overridden by the constitution of 1821. The freehold became the prevailing form of land tenure, especially in the new areas opened to settlement. But the leasehold lingered on stubbornly in the Hudson Valley counties. In fact, tenancy was to exhibit enough vigor to survive transplantation to such pioneer regions as Delaware County and the Genesee Valley. The rapid growth of central and western New York, the social gains of the Revolutionary period, and the election of George Clinton as governor were changing the stable structure of colonial New York and pointed the way to more radical reforms in the future. Nevertheless, the aristocracy and the leasehold were twin legacies which survived the Revolution and were to complicate the agrarian life of eastern New York for the sixty years following 1790.

The area covered by the expression "Hudson-Mohawk region" requires more precise definition. It corresponds roughly with the drainage basin of the Hudson River and its tributaries. Historical considerations, however, have made it desirable to include additional areas, especially in the watershed of the Delaware and Susquehanna rivers. For convenience in statistical matters it has been found wise to follow political boundaries rather than to adhere rigidly to geographical divisions. We have therefore selected for our study the twenty-one counties in the southeastern part of the state.[4] The reader will note that the term "eastern New York" is used interchangeably with "Hudson-Mohawk region" throughout this book.

The Hudson-Mohawk region thus defined is not a political,

---

[4] We have excluded Long Island because geologically, culturally, and to a degree economically her history is more closely identified with New England than with New York. New York City must likewise be excluded, even though its significance on the surrounding hinterland has been deeply significant. Otherwise the southern and eastern boundaries of the "Hudson-Mohawk region" coincide with those of the state. The western boundary follows the western line of Delaware, Otsego, and Oneida counties. The Adirondacks hem in our area on the north.

physiographic, or an economic unity. It deserves close study if for no other reason than that it was a microcosm, so to speak, illustrating virtually every phase of agricultural development between 1790 and 1850. Land speculation, tenancy, rural decline, the rise of dairying, and the influence of the metropolitan market are only a few of the threads which give its history so variegated and rich a pattern. Moreover, the region does have a certain internal unity of its own. Almost the entire area does lie within the Hudson-Mohawk drainage basin. The important exceptions are Otsego, Delaware, and Sullivan counties. Furthermore, eastern New York covers roughly the region which had been partially settled and whose lands had been largely distributed before the Revolution. Leasehold tenure, which gave rise to periodic antirent wars, was almost completely confined to this region.

The twenty-one counties contain 9,028,000 acres, or approximately one third of the total area of the state. This figure seems more impressive when compared with the acreage of nearby states. Eastern New York is roughly one and one-half times the size of Vermont or New Hampshire, almost twice the size of New Jersey or Massachusetts, almost three times that of Connecticut, and thirteen times that of Rhode Island. The settlement of this region was indeed an achievement of the first order.

New York was a racial melting pot from the start.[5] The Dutch, by reason of their early settlement, left a deeper imprint on the social life than their relatively small numbers warranted. The region around Albany and Ulster County was their stronghold. About half of the white population was of English origin. They formed a strong element in New York City, Long Island, and along the eastern bank of the Hudson where they easily outnumbered the Dutch. Yankees had sailed across Long Island Sound and carried

---

[5] "Report of the Committee on Linguistic and National Stocks in the Population of the United States," *Annual Report of the American Historical Association, 1931*, I, 103–324.

THE BACKGROUND

all the hallmarks of their civilization to the eastern half of Long Island. The western tip of the island and New York, however, were cosmopolitan. Next in numbers to the English and Dutch was the German group. The Germans were largely the descendants of the Palatines who had scattered to the Schoharie Valley and the pioneer region of the upper Mohawk. Scots, Ulster Irish, Irish, and French in small numbers added flavor to the racial diversity. At the bottom of the economic and social ladder were the Negroes, who formed almost 8 per cent of the population.[6]

The main facts as to the settlement and expansion of the New York colony are fairly well known.[7] The most remarkable feature was its slow growth and small population. As late as 1790 New York had only 340,120 inhabitants, a figure surpassed by the four states of Massachusetts, Pennsylvania, Virginia, and North Carolina.[8] Upstaters were concentrated, or to use a more descriptive term dispersed, along the Hudson and Mohawk valleys with scattered settlements along the Schoharie, the Wallkill, and the upper reaches of the Susquehanna.[9] Few settlers cared to move more than a few miles from the riverbank. The hill country so characteristic of eastern New York remained almost unbroken wilderness at the time of the American Revolution, except along the east bank of the lower Hudson where Yankee farmers were pressing westward from Connecticut. Only a handful of hardy

---

[6] United States, Census Office, *First Census* (Philadelphia, 1791).

[7] Ruth Higgins' *Expansion in New York with Especial Reference to the Eighteenth Century* (Columbus, 1931) is the most recent study.

[8] U.S. Census Office, *First Census*. A large part of the population of 1790 had come into the state after 1783.

[9] Stella Sutherland, *Population Distribution in Colonial America* (New York, 1941), p. 75. For maps of the extent of settlement, see *ibid.*, p. 62; Higgins, *op. cit.*, rear papers; Edward Channing, *A History of the United States* (New York, 1905–1925), III, 528. One estimate has it that in 1784 only 1,000,000 acres out of approximately 29,000,000 acres of land had been improved (James Macauley, *The Natural, Statistical, and Civil History of the State of New York* [New York, 1829], II, 57).

LANDLORDS AND FARMERS

pioneers had invaded the hunting grounds of Uncas and Leatherstocking.

Contemporary observers and modern historians are in substantial agreement as to the major causes for the slow pace of New York's growth. These causes may be regarded as twofold: French and Indian attacks from the north and west, and the blighting effect of the land system.

The Mohawk Valley has become famous as the gateway to the West. But before 1783 this valley and its companion, the Champlain Valley, served more often as invasion routes for enemies than as highways for westward-pushing frontiersmen. As the rivalry between England and France grew in intensity, the strategic importance of these two waterways became more evident. Indian raiding parties, stiffened with French and during the Revolution with Tory and British officers, threaded the forest trails and paddled down the lakes and streams. The Champlain gateway witnessed a procession of invaders: Champlain, Montcalm, Burgoyne. Between the burning of Schenectady in 1691 and the battle of Oriskany in 1777 settlers along the Mohawk flats lived in fear of the dreaded tomahawk. Few places on the Continent have served as a battlefield for so long a time. Fear of bloodshed alone was enough to persuade many potential immigrants to settle in New Jersey or Pennsylvania, where land was not only cheaper but the mountain ranges gave greater safety from the Indians.

The fur trade of the Lake region was the chief prize sought by both English and French. The merchants of Montreal and Albany coveted the trade in pelts. The Dutch took advantage of the fine location of Albany to exploit the fur trade, even at the expense of discouraging settlement to the west.[10] The Iroquois served as middlemen between the Indians of the interior and the Albany traders. The government of New York naturally considered the Iroquois as allies. The Iroquois Confederacy was usually in a state of chronic

---

[10] Higgins, *op. cit.*, p. 11. Not until the founding of Oswego in 1725 did Albany relinquish even partial control of the fur trade (*ibid.*, p. 46).

THE BACKGROUND

warfare with the native allies of the French who likewise sought furs in the Lake country.[11]

The uneasy alliance between the government of New York and the Six Nations did help to screen the province from French attack, but it likewise deterred the government from ousting the Indians from central New York. Their mere presence, favored as they were by the colonial governors and ably supported after 1755 by Sir William Johnson, Superintendent for Indian Affairs, constituted a formidable obstacle to any westward advance.[12]

The "inequitable distribution" of landed wealth was equally important in retarding the growth of colonial New York.[13] A small, class-conscious, and closely knit aristocracy acquired huge tracts which they either held for speculation or leased in small units to actual farmers. The leases ran for perpetuity or for the life span of the two or three persons named in the document. Members of the aristocracy aped the genteel manners of their English compeers. They browbeat the royal governors to submission and excluded the majority of males from the suffrage by setting up high property qualifications.[14] Land jobbing, aided and abetted by corrupt and pliant officials, was the custom.[15]

---

[11] Arthur H. Buffinton, "The Colonial Wars and Their Result," in Alexander C. Flick, ed., *History of the State of New York* (New York, 1933–1937), II, 204 ff. In his Introduction to Peter Wraxall's *An Abridgement of the Indian Affairs, 1678–1751* (Cambridge, 1915), Charles H. McIlwain has a good account of the role of the Iroquois in the fur trade.

[12] Higgins, *op. cit.*, pp. 83–85. Sir William Johnson was on excellent terms with the Indians. He was also active in acquiring large tracts for himself.

[13] Irving Mark, *Agrarian Conflicts in Colonial New York, 1711–1775* (New York, 1940), p. 19. Dr. Mark gives an excellent description of the land grants of the colonial governors (*ibid.*, pp. 19–49). A list of the chief patents may be found in John H. French, *Gazetteer of the State of New York: Embracing a Comprehensive View of the Geography, Geology, and General History of the State* (Syracuse, 1860), pp. 50–52. Plate 3 in Joseph R. Bien's *Atlas of the State of New York* (New York, 1895) is a map showing the location of the original grants.

[14] Mark, *op. cit.*, pp. 19–49; Carl L. Becker, *The History of Political Parties in the Province of New York, 1760–1776* (Madison, 1909), pp. 8 ff.

[15] Higgins, *op. cit.*, p. 22; Edmund Burke O'Callaghan, ed., *Documen-*

LANDLORDS AND FARMERS

The patroonship of Rensselaerswyck is admittedly not typical of New Netherlands. Nevertheless, it did serve as a precedent for the great estates created under English auspices.[16] In 1685 Governor Dongan confirmed the title of the Van Rensselaer family. Their princely domain covered some 750,000 acres in present-day Albany and Rensselaer counties, and also more than 250,000 acres in northern Columbia County.[17] Six manors were set up in Westchester County, the three small manors of Morrisania, Pelham, and Fordham lying in the southern part of the county. Scarsdale, Cortlandt, and Philipsburgh were much larger manors and contained about 400 square miles of land.[18] The 160,000 acres of Livingston Manor stretched across the lower third of what is now Columbia County. Large patents such as the Highland Patent (205,000 acres) in Dutchess County filled in the gaps between Rensselaerswyck and Long Island Sound. During the last two decades of the seventeenth century most of the east bank of the Hudson south of Albany passed into the hands of large landholders.

Speculators likewise acquired tracts in the Catskill region, the Mohawk country, and the Green Mountain area. All too frequently colonial governors handed out grants to insiders and lined their own pockets. The rather complicated procedure by which patents were granted favored the speculator who had access to high officials and was able to pay the necessary fees.[19] The small farmer found it difficult to secure choice land.

---

tary History of the State of New-York (Albany, 1849–1851), I, 384. Hereafter the latter work will be referred to as *Doc. Hist. of N.Y.*

[16] Clarence W. Rife, "Land Tenure in New Netherlands," in *Essays in Colonial History Presented to Charles McLean Andrews* (New Haven, 1931), p. 64.

[17] S. G. Nissenson, *The Patroon's Domain* (New York, 1937), pp. 302–305.

[18] Becker, *op. cit.*, p. 9.

[19] Legal fees included those to the surveyor general, attorney general, the secretary, and the governor. Some governors also exacted a certain percentage of the lands granted. See Mark, *op. cit.*, p. 30 *et passim;* Higgins, *op. cit.*, pp. 28–31.

THE BACKGROUND

Governor Fletcher (1692–1698) and Governor Cornbury (1702–1708) were the most notorious offenders in squandering the landed wealth of the province. Some of Fletcher's grants, notably the more than 800 square miles which he gave to Captain John Evans, were subsequently annulled. In 1698 the Board of Trade, upon the recommendation of Governor Bellomont, a capable and honest public servant, issued instructions that henceforth 2,000 acres would be the maximum amount of land to be granted to any individual and that such lands should pay not only a quitrent of two shillings six pence per hundred acres but also should be improved within three years on pain of forfeiture. Landholders and officials easily evaded these instructions. The appointment of Governor Cornbury inaugurated another wave of extravagant grants. Companies of speculators banded together and secured control of virtually all the remaining lands.[20] Among these grants was the great Hardenburgh Patent of over 1,000,000 acres which embraced much of Ulster, Delaware, Sullivan, and Greene counties.

Speculation in land was encouraged by the failure of the English government to enforce strictly the collection of the quitrent. Early governors frequently exacted nominal and varied rents which complicated the task of collection. Furthermore, landholders resisted every effort to collect, not only because they wished to save the money but also because the revenue might make the governor more independent of the financial grants of the Assembly.[21] As a result the quitrents had little effect in discouraging speculation. Colonial officials condoned other injurious practices as well. Failure to mark out clearly the metes and bounds enabled scheming land jobbers to enlarge their holdings. It also cast a shadow over

---

[20] Cornbury granted the Kayeraderosseras Patent covering a good share of Saratoga County, the Wawayanda totaling 356,000 acres, the Little Nine Partners in Dutchess County, and several others (Charles Worthen Spencer, "The Land System of Colonial New York," *Proceedings of the New York State Historical Association*, XVI [1917], 154–157).

[21] Beverly Bond, *The Quit-Rent System in the American Colonies* (New Haven, 1919), pp. 254, 261–262.

land titles. Corruption in acquiring land titles from the Indians added to the confusion.

The concentration of landed wealth in the hands of a small group, coupled as it was with the policy of the proprietors to lease rather than to sell, greatly retarded the expansion of the upstate area. Most of the great patents remained virtually uninhabited.[22] Few farmers wished to become tenants when they could secure freeholds in neighboring states. Cadwallader Colden, an able official who knew intimately the land situation, stated the case in 1732:

> ... it is chiefly if not only where these large Grants are made where the Country remains uncultivated—tho they contain some of the best of the Lands, and the most conveniently situated. ... The reason of this is that the Grantees themselves are not, nor never were in a Capacity to improve such large Tracts and other People will not become their Vassals or Tenants for one great reason as peoples (the better sort especially) leaving their native Country, was to avoid the dependence on landlords, and to enjoy lands in fee to descend to their posterity that their children may reap the benefit of their labour and Industry.[23]

Agrarian discontent has had a long and venerable history in New York from the riots of the tenants against the colonial landlords to the violent milk strikes of the 1930's. The "spectre of insecurity of tenure" haunted the tenant farmer and the perpetual rents, tax burdens, and minor manorial incidents weighed heavily upon him. The thousands of tenant farmers who lived on the manors along the east bank of the Hudson staged several outbreaks against the landed aristocracy.[24]

The antirent leaders of the 1840's often protested that they were

---

[22] Edmund Burke O'Callaghan, ed., *Documents Relative to the Colonial History of the State of New York* (Albany, 1853–1887), VII, 654.

[23] *Doc. Hist. of N.Y.*, I, 384. See Mark, *op. cit.*, p. 74, for additional evidence.

[24] John Watts in 1777 estimated that six thousand tenant farmers could be persuaded to rise against the landlords (*The Penn. Ledger or the Weekly Advertiser*, Oct. 29, 1777 quoted by Mark, *op. cit.*, p. 13). Dr. Mark has the most careful and detailed account of unrest among the tenants.

THE BACKGROUND

merely trying to do away with the last vestiges of feudalism which the Dutch and the English had transplanted to the New York province. These declarations had a certain degree of validity, although historians and jurists are still in sharp disagreement as to whether the manors possessed genuine feudal powers.[25] Whatever the exact legal status of the manors may have been, the fact that the tenants were subject to certain manorial jurisdictions and that three large manors enjoyed direct representation in the Assembly gives color to the charge of feudalism. The contrast between the freeholds of New England and the leases of New York, the latter involving annual rent in kind or money, reservations by the landlord of mining and water privileges, a day's service with team or carriage, and the right of quarter sales, was too conspicuous to be long unnoticed by the tenantry.

The condition of the tenants on the patents was hardly preferable to that of the manorial tenants.[26] Whether the landed proprietor enjoyed the special political advantages belonging to the manor or whether he merely owned a large patent, he generally believed that the best way to develop an estate was to lease and not to sell. The aristocracy of New York hoped to build up estates comparable to those held by the English nobility. Throughout the colonial period ownership of land was the mark of gentility and social distinction. Like their English cousins the landed gentry of

---

[25] *Ibid.*, pp. 51–61; Spaulding, *op. cit.*, pp. 58–62. If New York were considered a conquered country, it is argued that the Crown was not limited by *Quia Emptores* and the statute of 1660 from granting feudal rights (Mark, *op. cit.*, pp. 52–54). Mark has an excellent discussion of the question. For a view which flatly states that the feudal system never existed in New York, see Edward Floyd DeLancey, "Origins and History of Manors in the County of Westchester," in J. Thomas Scharf, *History of Westchester County, New York* (Philadelphia, 1886), I, 80, *passim*. Spaulding (*op. cit.*, p. 60) concludes, "Yet the manors created a feudal system with lords and freemen, but without villeins."

[26] Tenants on patents usually paid cash rents and escaped clauses providing for quarter sales, services, and water reservations as well as the direct supervision of the landlord (Spaulding, *op. cit.*, p. 63).

LANDLORDS AND FARMERS

New York actively engaged in politics and dominated the government.[27]

The tenants resented their economic and political subservience and tried on every occasion to challenge their landlords. The fact that fraud and chicanery tainted many land titles was well known. It intensified the tenants' hatred of the leasehold and spurred them to set up rival claims. They eagerly seized upon land claims which were derived from unextinguished Indian claims and were dangled before them by Massachusetts speculators. Throughout the 1750's the tenants on Livingston Manor carried on a fierce antirent war. During the early years of the next decade the tenantry from Rensselaerswyck to Cortlandt Manor defied landlords, resisted enforcement officers, and engaged in sporadic violence. The great rebellion of 1766 was put down only because the landed gentry secured military aid and effectively controlled the courts and administration.[28] Scarcely had antirentism been put down in the Hudson Valley than the farmers of the New Hampshire grants began their campaign against the great land speculators from New York. The freeholders of Vermont gave the New York aristocracy its first defeat. The Green Mountain Boys, led by the turbulent Ethan Allen, took advantage of the general disorder accompanying the Revolutionary War and made good their defiance. But in New York the landlords were too firmly entrenched politically to be overturned. Not until the tenant farmers secured a decisive influence in politics were they able to throw off the landlord yoke.

The Revolutionary War, which in New York was also a civil war, did not fundamentally change the land system or the status of the small farmer. To be sure, a few breaches were made in the legal framework although the constitution of 1777 specifically confirmed all previous land grants made by the Crown. The elimination of entail and primogeniture foreshadowed the eventual partition of

---

[27] Mark, *op. cit.*, pp. 85–106.
[28] *Ibid.*, pp. 131–163. See also Oscar Handlin, "The Eastern Frontier of New York," *New York History*, XXXV (Jan., 1937), pp. 50–75.

THE BACKGROUND

the manors. Furthermore, the legislature in 1787 formally ended feudal obligations and banned all feudal tenures.[29] The landowner could also commute the quitrent by paying fourteen times the annual charge.[30]

On the east bank of the lower Hudson the disorders caused by the war and the confiscation of loyalist estates hastened the development of a more democratic land system. Despite the fact that most of the confiscated estates first passed through the hands of land speculators, the land did get into the hands of small farmers.[31] Westchester County is the best example of this trend. At one time at least five sixths of the inhabitants lived on manors.[32] After the Revolution the independent farmer was the predominant type. Farther upstream along the middle Hudson the holdings of such patriots as the Livingstons and Van Rensselaers emerged unscathed. Nevertheless, the increasing number of yeomen farmers, who were in the majority in 1785 even in those counties where the largest manors were located, foreshadowed the eventual eclipse of the aristocracy. The shift in political power was slow in coming; the final liquidation of the leasehold was still slower. Almost half a century was to elapse between the election of George Clinton as governor in 1777, the first shock to landlord pretensions, and the constitutional convention of 1821, where the introduction of manhood suffrage spelled the final decline of the aristocracy.[33]

Agriculture was of course the mainstay of colonial economy. It

---

[29] See law of February 20, 1787, *Laws of the State of New York*, II, 415–416.

[30] Spaulding, *op. cit.*, p. 70.

[31] J. Franklin Jameson, *The American Revolution Considered as a Social Movement* (Princeton, 1926), p. 62; Harry B. Yoshpe, *The Disposition of Loyalist Estates in the Southern District of the State of New York* (New York, 1939), pp. 111–117.

[32] Frederick Jackson Turner, "The Old West," *Proceedings of the Wisconsin Historical Society* (1908), p. 196.

[33] Dixon Ryan Fox (*The Decline of Aristocracy in the Politics of New York* [New York, 1919]), skillfully describes the declining influence of the aristocracy.

directly supported 80 per cent of the population. Moreover, handling the products of farm and forest absorbed most of the attention of merchants and shippers. The small farm was the basic unit. Whatever pretensions the large landlords may have had, they did not try to operate their estates on the plantation system. The tenant-operated farms were thus quite similar to those owned by the yeomen, who, it must be reiterated, were the most numerous element of the agricultural population.[34]

The colonial farmer of eastern New York soon became interested not only in grubbing out a living but also in producing for the export market. Unlike many New England farmers who found it difficult to transport their products to market, the New York farmer was singularly favored by nature. Ocean-going vessels could sail up the Hudson River and dock at the many landings. As early as 1678 Governor Andros reported wheat exports totaling 60,000 bushels, as well as considerable amounts of peas, beef, pork, furs, horses, and lumber.[35] The sharp contest between the city of New York and the upstate millers over the metropolitan monopoly of bolting flour illustrates the importance that wheat culture had attained by the last years of the seventeenth century. Lumber and livestock likewise were important items in the export trade.[36]

The condition of agriculture was "very low," as Sir William Johnson aptly described it in 1765.[37] Indeed, the tools and practices of eastern New York farmers would not have been unfamiliar to the farmers of ancient Rome and medieval France. Almanacs contained virtually all the information, both good and bad, which

---

[34] Samuel McKee ("The Economic Pattern of Colonial New York," in Flick, *History of N.Y.*, II, 280 ff.) has a good discussion. See also Lyman Carrier, *The Beginnings of Agriculture in America* (New York, 1923), p. 157.

[35] *Doc. Hist. of N.Y.*, I, 90.

[36] *American Husbandry* (London, 1775), I, 124. The author estimated that in 1763–1766 New York province exported 250,000 barrels of flour and biscuit (*ibid.*).

[37] *Doc. Hist. of N.Y.*, IV, 348–349.

was known. The principles of rotation and the use of fertilizers were universally ignored. The abundance of land and the scarcity of labor, two of the most compelling and persistent factors determining the course of American agriculture, operated with telling force. As a result, extensive cultivation was the general practice. An almost inevitable corollary was the custom of cropping the land until it was exhausted.[38] Unfortunately, farm implements were so primitive that they did not permit the farmer to make sufficient economies in the amount of labor which he put into the production of his crops to compensate him for his extensive cultivation. Consequently he derived little benefit from the low cost of land.

Of course, farming was not nearly so closely geared to the market as it is today. Instead, farming was a way of life. Self-sufficiency was the distinguishing feature. Each farm raised practically all its own foodstuffs and supplied its own fuel and clothing. The life of self-sufficiency tended to develop traits of thrift, resourcefulness, and independence. Furthermore, family welfare, not the caprice of the market, determined what should be produced. But the life of self-sufficiency, shed of the romantic coloring with which time has clothed it, was hard and merciless to the weak. It spelled drudgery for man and woman. Such a society was naturally one of limited cultural horizons. Schools, libraries, and art were as conspicuous by their absence as disease, poverty, and death were omnipresent.

In subsequent chapters we shall examine the forces which developed commercial agriculture and broke down the self-sufficient nature of rural life. In 1790 the New York farmer was on the threshold of a significant new era. If the life of the farmer were not as idyllic as that painted by Crèvecoeur in his famous *Letters from an American Farmer,* it did offer a livelihood and, what is more important, it gave promise of a bright and happy future.

---

[38] William H. Smith, *The History of the Late Province of New York from its Discovery to the Appointment of Governor Colden in 1762* (New York, 1829), I, 230.

CHAPTER II

POPULATION GROWTH AND THE LAND PATTERN

1790 - 1808

THE HOISTING of the Continental flag in 1783 was the signal for a quarter century of unprecedented growth for both metropolitan and upstate New York. The Iroquois Confederacy and the virtual land monopoly of the aristocracy, which had so seriously stunted the growth of the province, no longer stood in the way. Meanwhile, a combination of new factors was propelling New York toward her future position as Empire State. Yankees by the tens of thousands were crossing the border to seek their fortunes on frontier farms or behind store counters and workbenches. Land proprietors who had acquired millions of acres of land in northern and western New York were competing with one another and with the old landed gentry in selling land to new settlers. As a result, land was available to small farmers at reasonable prices. Old towns along the Hudson were booming; new towns such as Troy and Hudson were springing up overnight. Merchants were promoting turnpikes to the west and east in order to attract wheat and livestock to their wharves, from which ships set sail for Liverpool, Jamaica, and the Mediterranean. The demand for wheat, long the most important cash crop, kept rising, especially after the French Revolution plunged Europe into war. Eastern New York, except for some of the older rural areas along the lower Hudson, was in the forefront of this

POPULATION GROWTH AND LAND PATTERN

state-wide boom. A feeling of confidence and the spirit of enterprise infected the people, who were "all under the influence of a hope of better times."[1] These were indeed the good years, never to be equaled until the demand for fluid milk brought further prosperity to the farmers of eastern New York.

The story of this period of activity can best be traced in the population statistics.[2] From 1790 to 1800 population in the twenty-one counties designated as eastern New York jumped from 256,737 to 402,313, or more than 57 per cent. A 32 per cent increase in the following decade brought the number of inhabitants to 530,997. As we shall see in later chapters, the rate of increase steadily declined in the future, the percentage increase from 1810 to 1820 falling to the relatively low rate of 17 per cent.

The map showing population changes between 1790 and 1800 reveals that the counties in the west were gaining population at the greatest rate. Oneida, Herkimer, Otsego, Schoharie, and Delaware counties more than doubled their populations.[3] Sullivan, Greene, and Albany counties grew proportionally faster than the state as a whole. Most noticeable of all was the slow growth of Rockland, Westchester, Putnam, and Dutchess counties, which maintained an almost stationary population.

The map showing changes by townships between 1800 and 1810 clearly demonstrates that almost every part of eastern New York was gaining population at a rapid rate. Columbia County and a few of the towns along the New England border did not

---

[1] "Journal of Rev. John Taylor's Missionary Tour Through the Mohawk and Black River Countries in 1802," in *Doc. Hist. of N.Y.*, III, 1137.

[2] A convenient source for population statistics is the Introduction to the *Census of the State of New-York for 1855*, compiled by Franklin B. Hough, Superintendent of the Census (Albany, 1857). The Introduction contains a summary of preceding census returns, assigning the population to the towns as of 1855 without reference to the counties in which they were contained at the time of taking the various censuses. Hereafter this work will be cited as the *N.Y. Census for 1855*.

[3] The political units of the present are used as a basis for these population changes.

LANDLORDS AND FARMERS

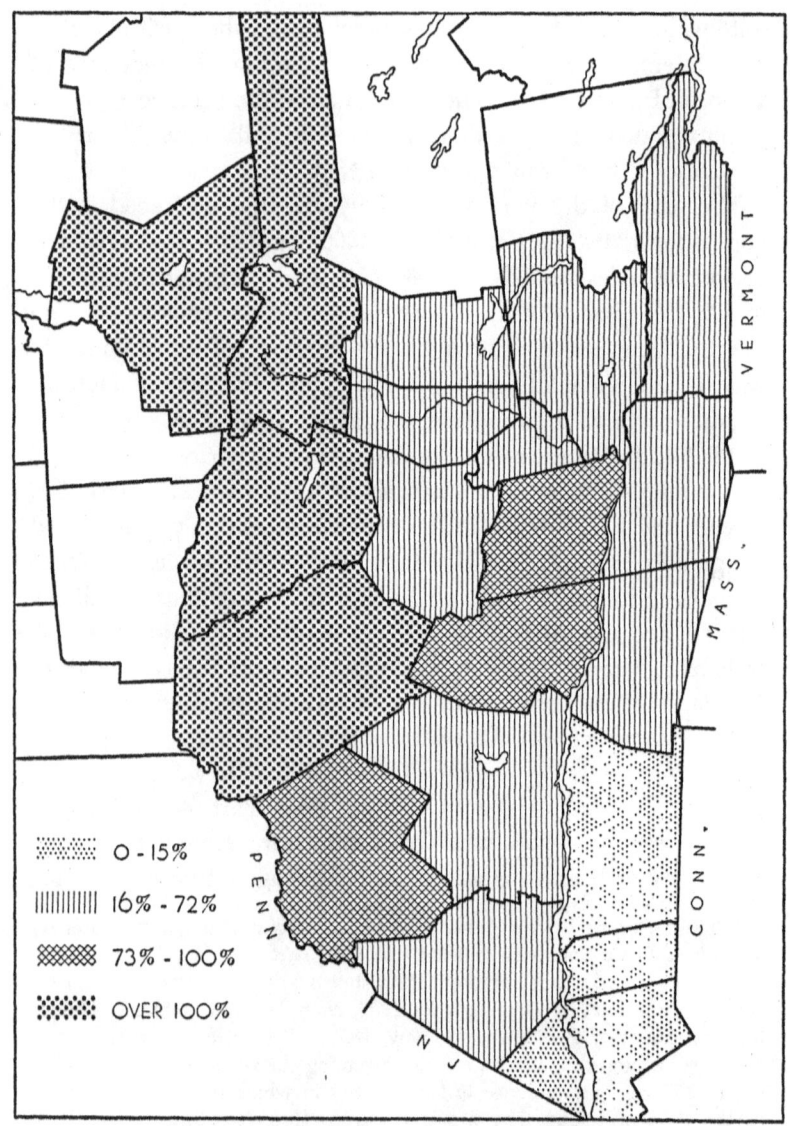

Increase in Population by Counties, 1790–1800.

POPULATION GROWTH AND LAND PATTERN

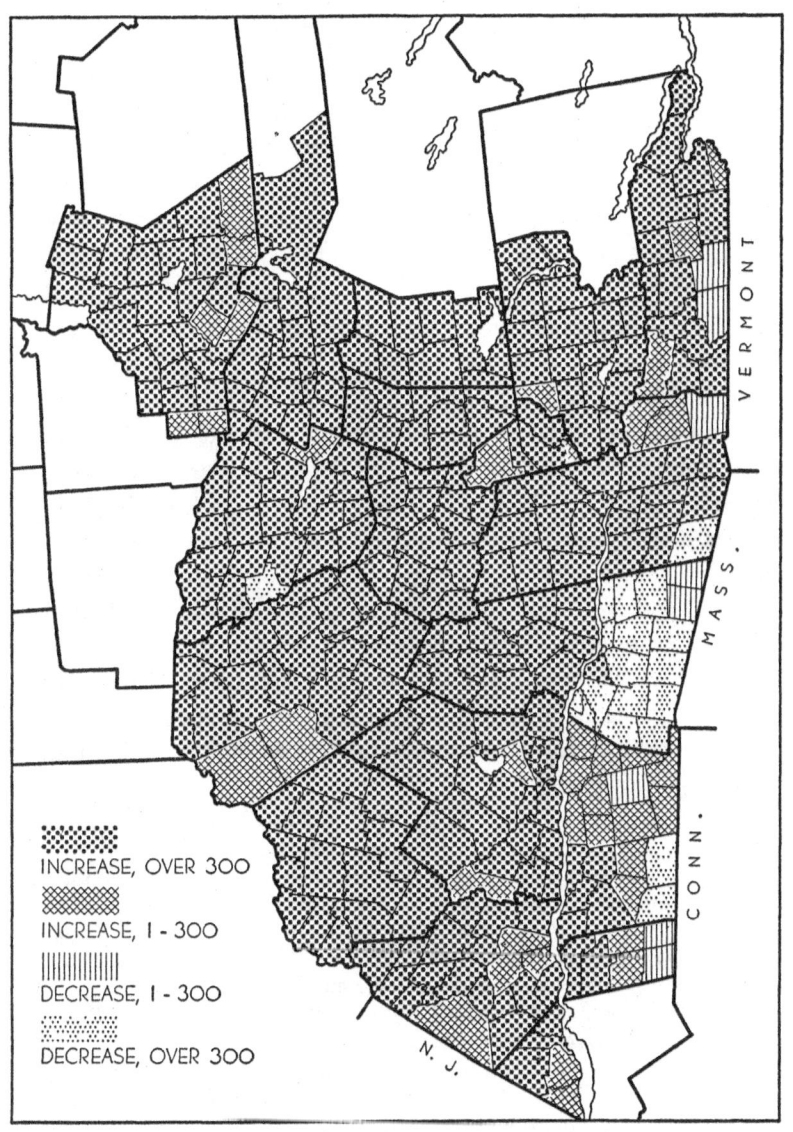

Changes in Population by Townships, 1800–1810.

LANDLORDS AND FARMERS

participate in this movement largely for local reasons which will be examined somewhat later in this chapter.

The high birth rate was responsible for a part of this growth. Early marriages and large families were common. In 1800 and in 1810 over one half of the white population of New York State was under sixteen years of age.[4] The fact that only 11 per cent of the population was forty-five years old and upwards merely emphasized the youthful character of the people. If the birth rate was high, so also was the death rate. The hazards of a hard life, the lack of proper care, and recurrent epidemics took a heavy toll.[5]

Immigration, and especially that from New England, accounted for the bulk of the population increase. Immigration from Europe increased after the Revolutionary War, and considerable numbers of Welsh, Scots, and Germans took up lands in the interior of New York.[6] Long Island likewise contributed thousands of her sons to the settlement of the back country. These sources, however, were relatively insignificant when compared with the vast outpourings from New England.

The story of the New England migration has been so often told and its significance so widely recognized that the main facts have become familiar. Even before the Revolution considerable num-

---

[4] *N.Y. Census for 1855*, xii–xiii.

[5] In the *Hudson Balance*, Feb. 2, 1802, p. 34, is a report of a plague taking forty to fifty people in the vicinity of Hudson. See also *Doc. Hist. of N.Y.*, III, 1140; *Albany Gazette*, Jan. 18, 1813; *Albany Argus*, Feb. 26, 1813. (No attempt will be made to show the variations in title of the latter newspaper, which will hereafter be cited merely as the *Argus*.) Jeremy Belknap (*Journal of a Tour From Boston to Oneida, June, 1796* [Cambridge, 1882]) calls Oneida County "fever and ague country."

[6] The Welsh settled in Oneida County shortly after 1795 (Paul Evans, *The Welsh in Oneida County* [Ithaca, 1914]). Benjamin Walker, aided by Baron Steuben, persuaded a shipload of Germans to settle on the Genesee lands of Charles Williamson (Benjamin Walker to Charles Williamson, Oct. 15, 1792, Oneida Historical Society). Timothy Dwight noted the tidy Scots Settlement in Cambridge, Washington County, in 1799 (*Travels in New-England and New-York* [New Haven, 1821–1822], III, 237).

POPULATION GROWTH AND LAND PATTERN

bers of Yankees had filtered into the eastern townships of Westchester County and across the Hudson River into Orange County. The main current, however, set in after 1783, carrying with it thousands of Yankees into all parts of the state.[7] They came by land and by water. Ships sailed up the Hudson laden with the household goods of families bound for the frontier. Sleighs and wagons came overland through the steep hills fringing the New England border. In the 1790's many immigrants were seeking the new settlements in the Champlain country as well as the richer lands of central and western New York.[8] So many Yankees moved to New York State that in 1820 Timothy Dwight believed that the state would become a "colony from New England," since he estimated that 60 to 67 per cent of its people were of New England origin.[9]

This migration had important political, economic, and social effects on the subsequent history of the state. Even the older communities in eastern New York felt its impact. Yankee farmers brought leveling ideas in regard to landed estates.[10] Yankee merchants established commercial and shipping towns such as Troy and Hudson, and so penetrated the economic and political life of Albany that in 1803 they succeeded in forcing the angry Dutch citizens to cut off their long rainspouts.[11] Yankee politicians forced the old aristocratic Dutch families to share the political offices and honors.[12] The ill-concealed contempt which the enterprising sons of New England felt toward the "churlish, ignorant, and unenter-

---

[7] Lois K. Mathews, *The Expansion of New England* (Boston, 1909), pp. 153 ff.

[8] *Albany Gazette*, March 4, 1796.

[9] *Op. cit.*, III, 266–267.

[10] Mrs. Anne Grant, *Memoirs of an American Lady* (London, 1808), II, 137. James Fenimore Cooper in *The Redskins* (New York, 1892), p. 457, has one of his characters assert that most of the antirent trouble was caused by New Englanders who desired to hold land only in fee simple.

[11] Joel Munsell, *The Annals of Albany* (Albany, 1850–1859), X, 196.

[12] D. R. Fox, *Decline of Aristocracy*, pp. 35 ff.

prising" Germans and Dutch [13] led to bitter racial prejudices which only the passage of time softened into a feeling of mutual good will.

The compelling drive behind the New England migration was land-hunger. The lack of a market for agricultural products prevented farmers from adopting intensive cultivation and forced the surplus population to seek new lands.[14] Before the Revolution the vacant lands in northern New England absorbed most of this surplus. From Connecticut, where pressure on the land was greatest, emigrated large numbers of farmers. So many of them poured into the present area of Vermont that it was sometimes called "New Connecticut." After the peace of 1783 the main current turned toward New York, where Connecticut Yankees were prominent on every frontier.[15] Before 1795 few immigrants moved into New York State from Vermont, but shortly thereafter "the people went in a flood." [16] One authority estimates that between the years 1790 and 1820 the three states of southern New England lost approximately eight hundred thousand persons through emigration.[17]

The desire to escape heavy taxes, thin stony soils, and the political and religious conservatism of New England also caused a feeling of restlessness among the rural population. In Massachusetts

---

[13] Remarks of Chancellor Kent, quoted by John Horton, *James Kent, A Study in Conservatism* (New York, 1939), p. 130. See also Elkanah Watson, *History of the Rise . . . of the Western Canals in the State of New York* (Albany, 1820), p. 27, for the mutual dislike of Germans and Yankees. Dwight, *op. cit.*, III, pp. 172 ff., also castigates the "low morals" and ignorance of the "Mohawk Dutch."

[14] Percy W. Bidwell, "Rural Economy in New England at the Beginning of the Nineteenth Century," *Transactions of the Connecticut Academy of Arts and Sciences*, XX (April, 1916), 352.

[15] Francis W. Halsey, *The Old New York Frontier* (New York, 1913). Mr. Halsey makes the interesting observation that in the New York constitutional convention of 1821 a majority of the 127 members were either born in Connecticut or were sons of fathers born there.

[16] Lewis Stillwell, "Migration from Vermont (1776–1860)," *Proceedings of the Vermont Historical Society*, V (1927), p. 120. Stillwell's study is an excellent analysis of economic and social conditions in Vermont.

[17] Bidwell, *op. cit.*, p. 387.

POPULATION GROWTH AND LAND PATTERN

the burden of taxation coming at a time of grinding deflation ruined thousands of farmers, whose attempt to secure public relief under the banner of Daniel Shays failed miserably. Settlers, braving the wild country near Lake George, confided to a traveler that they had emigrated to avoid the capitation tax they would be subject to in Rhode Island.[18] Farmers on small farms hoped that they would be able to secure enough land to provide for their numerous children.

Glowing reports of conditions in New York added to the general feeling of unrest. Missionaries to the Iroquois had sent back accounts of level and fertile lands, a report which veterans of Sullivan's expedition into central and western New York were quick to confirm. Pioneers wrote letters urging their friends and relatives to emigrate. Hugh White in Oneida County sent back to his friends in Middletown specimens of his wheat, corn, potatoes, and onions as proof of the fertility of central New York.[19] Agents distributed handbills offering new farms at tempting prices and on generous terms.[20] Many discontented Yankees abandoned their impoverished farms and set forth hopefully toward the west.

Before we discuss the land pattern in the counties of eastern New York, we must take note of the mania for land speculation which swept both the state and nation after the Revolutionary War. "Gentlemen" on the seaboard invested large sums of capital in wild lands.[21] Both the federal government and that of New York considered the vacant lands as a source of revenue and as suitable for settlement. The interest in land speculation became so

---

[18] *An Englishman in America, 1785, Being the Diary of Joseph Hadfield,* ed. by Douglas Robertson (Toronto, 1923), p. 26.

[19] Pomroy Jones, *Annals and Recollections of Oneida County* (Rome, 1851), p. 790.

[20] For an example of a land agent's activities, see letter of Samuel A. Law to Robert Johnson, Aug. 26, 1795, *Samuel Law Letter Book,* S. A. Law Papers, N.Y. State Library.

[21] Robert East, *Business Enterprise in the American Revolutionary Era* (New York, 1938), p. 315.

widespread that in 1796 a visitor called America a "land of speculation."[22]

The merchants of Albany and New York were actively engaged in buying large tracts of wild lands. By 1791 over 5,500,000 acres of land in northern and central New York had been sold, chiefly in large tracts.[23] The largest purchaser was Alexander Macomb, who acquired 3,635,000 acres at the rate of eight pence an acre.[24] In 1788 Massachusetts sold its right to the land west of Seneca Lake to Phelps and Gorham for less than three cents an acre. In both cases the original speculators overextended themselves and the lands passed into the hands of other speculators.

To be sure, most of the lands purchased from the state lay to the north and west of "eastern New York." Nevertheless, this wave of land speculation materially influenced the value and development of lands in the older counties. Cheap lands in the west prevented land values in the east from rising too abruptly. Discontented farmers and tenants sought relief by taking up cheaper and better lands in the west. Land agents in the east had to keep the value and advantages of western lands continually in mind when they sold or leased farms.

It is difficult to describe with any accuracy the market value of lands in eastern New York between the years 1790 and 1808. Climate, soil, nearness to market, density of population, and educational and social opportunities were factors of varying importance influencing the judgment of both landowners and buyers. Of particular importance was the ease with which a farmer could transport his produce to market. An intangible factor of great importance in subsequent American history was the desire of many Americans of all classes to harvest the unearned increment. The desire of Americans to seek new frontiers led to a great mobility of

---

[22] William Priest, *Travels in the United States of America, Commencing in the Year 1793 and Ending in 1797* (London, 1802), p. 132.
[23] *Doc. Hist. of N.Y.*, III, 1083.
[24] *Ibid.*, pp. 1069–1071.

POPULATION GROWTH AND LAND PATTERN

population which in turn tended to keep land values in a kind of precarious balance.[25]

Land values rose steadily during this period. In 1794 one observer stated that lands in the old settled country below Schenectady were worth £3 7s. 10d. per acre, while lands in the new settled country to the west brought 9s. 3¾d. per acre.[26] In contrast, land in Rhode Island, Connecticut, and Massachusetts usually brought £4 an acre.[27]

The alluvial flats bordering the Mohawk and to a lesser extent the Hudson were famous for their high yields of wheat, the most important crop in eastern New York. These lands sometimes brought as much as $125 an acre.[28] After years of constant cropping, the bottom land produced as high a yield as ever. Bottom land near Schenectady was considered more profitable at £30 to £40 an acre than good uplands at £8 an acre.[29] Not only were the alluvial soils highly fertile, but the products raised from them could be easily transported to market.

On the other hand, wild lands away from the river brought low prices. To take one example, wild lands in Oneida County between

---

[25] James Finlay Weir Johnston, in *Notes on North America* ([Boston, 1851], I, 163), said that almost "every farm from Eastport in Maine to Buffalo is for sale." Foreigners were often amazed at the restlessness of Americans, many of whom moved from frontier to frontier.

[26] Strickland, *op. cit.*, p. 13. Eight shillings equal one dollar.

[27] *Ibid.*, p. 7.

[28] John Maude, *Visit to the Falls of Niagara in 1800* (London, 1826), p. 29. Lands on the flats near Kingston sold for $90 an acre in 1797 (François Alexandre Frédéric de la Rochefoucault Liancourt [sic], *Travels Through the United States of North America* [2d ed.; London, 1799], II, 452). John Lincklaen in 1791 noted that lands on the Schoharie Flats sold for $62.50 an acre (*Travels in the Year 1791 and 1792 in Pennsylvania, New York, and Vermont; Journals of John Lincklaen, with a Biographical Sketch and Notes* [New York, 1897], p. 125). Lands at German Flats brought $60 an acre in 1800 (Maude, *op. cit.*, p. 32).

[29] John Harriott, *Struggles Through Life, Exemplified in the Various Travels and Adventures in Europe, Asia, Africa and America* (2d ed.; London, 1808), II, 141–142.

LANDLORDS AND FARMERS

1788 and 1791 usually sold for $1.00 an acre.[30] But by 1795 Gerrit Boon was selling lands in the Servis Patent for $4.50 an acre.[31] In the more remote Adgate tract he sold land for $1.50 to $2.00 an acre. By 1806 lands in the Servis Patent were valued at $10.00 an acre. A similar rise in the value of uncleared lands took place even in the isolated interior counties of Sullivan and Delaware, where wild lands brought $3.00 to $5.00 an acre between 1798 and 1800.[32]

The prospective settler or speculator, and often the two were not distinguishable, had only to open his newspaper to find lands of every description and in several localities offered to him.[33] If he had no money, he could squat on the land until the landholder either ejected him or else made an agreement satisfactory to both parties. In eastern New York this agreement often took the form of a lease, thus spreading a form of land tenure which had led to serious agrarian revolts in the colonial period.

The frontier of eastern New York was unusual in that a good share of the land was developed on the leasehold system. In other respects this frontier presented the same problems of transportation, scarcity of money, and the subjugation of the wilderness by the ax. Before we take up these problems, let us first examine in detail the land pattern of eastern New York, and the special institution of leasehold tenure.

---

[30] Jones, *op. cit.*, p. 172; Lincklaen, *op. cit.*, p. 71. Land in Richfield, Otsego County, sold for $1.25 an acre in 1789. See Levi Beardsley, *Reminiscences* (New York, 1852), p. 21.

[31] Paul Evans, *History of the Holland Land Company* (Buffalo, 1924), pp. 67 ff.

[32] "Statement of Accounts, Land, 1771–1816," Box 8, Samuel A. Law Papers; James Eldridge Quinlan, *History of Sullivan County* (Liberty, 1873), p. 336. Landholders of interior valleys offered lands at a lower price than in the Mohawk Valley. To encourage early settlement, the landholders often sold the first lands at a nominal cost (Almon Lauber, "The Valleys of the Susquehanna and the Delaware," in Flick, *History of N.Y.*, V, 133).

[33] *Albany Gazette*, Dec. 1, 1785, Oct. 26, 1795, April 11, 1796, May 1, 1798; *Albany Register*, Oct. 30, 1797, Dec. 19, 1800. See these issues for typical offers.

POPULATION GROWTH AND LAND PATTERN

Westchester County had become by 1790 a well-settled agricultural community of independent farmers. The destruction wrought by marching armies and the laws confiscating Tory estates and abolishing manors merely hastened the trend to freehold tenure which had already begun before the Revolution. Scharf has pointed out the favorable conditions of fixed tenure, low rents, good soil, and access to the New York market which brought great prosperity to Westchester farmers before the Revolution.[34] Moreover, the landlords were usually willing to sell the fee simple "whenever it was applied for." [35] By 1847 only 2,500 to 3,000 acres out of the original 86,000 acres of Cortlandt Manor remained in the hands of the family.[36] The great manor of Philipsburgh (156,000 acres) was confiscated by the state government because Colonel Frederick Philipse remained loyal to the British Crown. Despite the speculation in this estate, the land gradually found its way into the possession of small owners. Nevertheless, some of the tenants on these confiscated estates were evicted when they failed to use their pre-emption right to buy back the lands and improvements.[37]

During the two decades following 1790 Westchester County grew slowly. Its population was almost entirely rural and increased at less than 15 per cent each decade. The farmers seemed content to devote their energies to producing foodstuffs for the New York markets.

Turning northward to Dutchess County, which included in this period the present county of Putnam, we find conditions quite similar to those in Westchester. By 1790 the county had been well settled and, like its sister county to the south, it grew but slowly. Dutchess County farmers, however, enjoyed the reputation of fol-

---

[34] Scharf, *op. cit.*, I, 178–179.

[35] *Ibid.*, p. 177, n. 4. For the willingness of the Van Cortlandts to sell the fee, see Mark, *op. cit.*, p. 70.

[36] Scharf, *op. cit.*, p. 139.

[37] Yoshpe, *op. cit.*, pp. 32–35, 56–57. Dr. Yoshpe states that the farmers were well-to-do since they were able to pay large sums for their farms (*ibid.*, p. 54).

LANDLORDS AND FARMERS

lowing the most advanced agricultural methods.[38] In the southern part of the county the steep slopes of the highlands discouraged extensive settlement.

Farm tenancy persisted tenaciously, although there was a perceptible drift toward freeholds. By 1790 the large patents had been distributed among the owners. Some sold their lands; others leased farms on various terms. The Van Cortlandts and Madam Brett sold outright their lots in the Rombout Patent, while the Verplanck family, which owned a third interest wedged between the other parties, insisted on a policy of leasing the land.[39] When Daniel Verplanck died in 1834 he left thirty farms valued at $320,913, most of which were under life leases. The Little Nine Partners had been cut up into 63 parcels in 1744 and the holders had adopted several methods of land disposal in accordance with their own preferences.[40] In the northern township of Milan the leased lands of George C. Clarke, Jr., were marked by worn-out fields, dilapidated buildings, and poverty.[41] In the southern town of Phillipstown the tenant system was charged with retarding development as late as 1849.[42] Dutchess County thus presented a checkered pattern of land tenure with numerous leaseholds interspersed among the predominant freeholds.

That portion (approximately 50,000 acres) of the Highland Patent of Frederick Philipse, which in 1754 had passed to Roger Morris and his wife, was confiscated by the state government.[43]

---

[38] Dwight, *op. cit.*, III, 426; Horatio Gates Spafford, *A Gazetteer of the State of New York* (Albany, 1813), p. 74.

[39] Frank Hasbrouck, ed., *The History of Dutchess County, New York* (Poughkeepsie, 1909), pp. 310–312.

[40] Isaac Huntting, *History of Little Nine Partners, of North East Precinct and Pine Plains, New York, Dutchess County* (Amenia, N.Y., 1897), p. 31.

[41] Philip H. Smith, *General History of Dutchess County, from 1609 to 1876, Inclusive* (Pawling, N.Y., 1877), p. 240.

[42] William J. Blake, *The History of Putnam County, N.Y.* (New York, 1849), p. 146.

[43] For a good account of these lands in Putnam County, see Kenneth Porter, *John Jacob Astor, Business Man* (Cambridge, 1931), II, 876–892.

POPULATION GROWTH AND LAND PATTERN

Between 1782 and 1784 the property was sold chiefly to the former tenants. Such action merely dramatized the gradual shift away from farm tenancy. Probably the best evidence of the extent of this shift was the advanced state of agriculture.[44] As we shall point out in later chapters, tenancy and slovenly cultivation went hand in hand. During the antirent agitation the leaders of the movement often compared the agricultural backwardness of Columbia County with the advanced methods in Dutchess County. Invariably the blame was fastened on the tenancy system.[45]

Rockland, Orange, and Ulster counties grew more rapidly than Westchester and Dutchess across the Hudson. Vacant land in abundance was available. Considerable numbers of Yankees invaded this stronghold of Dutch colonization and brought new vigor to the river towns.[46] Perhaps the Yankee immigrant preferred to settle in a region where the small independent farmers were most numerous and politically the dominant social class.[47] Governor George Clinton and Jeffersonian democracy drew much of their political strength from the yeomen of this area. The small farmer instinctively distrusted the aristocratic pretensions of the large landowners, and eventually succeeded in wresting more political power from the small ruling clique. An example of this class consciousness among the farmers can be seen in a speech made by the president of the Orange County Agricultural Society in 1818.[48]

---

[44] Dwight, *op. cit.*, III, 426; Spafford, *op. cit.*, p. 74. Dwight commented on the excellent cultivation. Spafford (*op. cit.*, p. 281) linked the improvement in agricultural techniques in Rhinebeck with the increasing number of freeholds.

[45] *Anti-Renter*, Jan. 31, 1846; speech of Ira Harris quoted in *Albany Freeholder*, Feb. 11, 1846. Hereafter this paper will be cited as the *Freeholder*.

[46] For the extent of the New England settlement in New York in 1790, 1800, and 1810, see Mathews, *op. cit.*, pp. 150, 154, 158; and La Rochefoucault Liancourt, *Travels*, II, 461. The Duke was surprised at the number of Yankees between New Paltz and Newburgh.

[47] Spaulding, *op. cit.*, p. 52; Fox, *Decline of Aristocracy*, p. 48.

[48] Samuel Eager, *An Outline History of Orange County* (Newburgh, 1846–1847), p. 65.

LANDLORDS AND FARMERS

The speaker rejoiced that the representatives of the society were free and respectable farmers and not under the control of ambitious landlords as in some other counties.

Originally, large patents had covered great areas of Orange and Ulster counties, but fortunately most of these patents and particularly those in the settled areas near the river had been broken up and freely sold during the eighteenth century.[49] In Orange County a similar tendency for landowners to sell and not to lease was early manifested.[50] The annulment by Governor Bellomont of the notorious Evans Patent (350,000 acres), which had covered much of Ulster and Orange, paved the way for the granting of relatively small tracts averaging 2,000 acres.[51] According to the local historian, this repeal saved all of Ulster County below New Paltz and east of the mountains as well as a good share of Orange County from the "blighting effects" of landlordism.[52]

Many of the early settlements in these counties had been made by groups of associates similar to the town proprietors of New England. For a time the associates held the land in common but eventually partitioned their tracts. Many Dutch communities cultivated the arable land in common as well as holding woodland and pasture collectively. After 1793 a distinct movement, aided by legislative enactment, took place whereby the common tracts

---

[49] Frank B. Green, *The History of Rockland County* (New York, 1886), pp. 13–40 *et passim*.

[50] Eager, *op. cit.*, p. 451. Between 1807 and 1819 over 12,000 acres of confiscated Tory lands in the Minisink Patent were sold by the state for $9,508.95 (Alexander C. Flick, *Loyalism in New York During the American Revolution* [New York, 1901], pp. 257–261).

[51] Edward Ruttenber, *History of the County of Orange, with a History of the Town and City of Newburgh* (Newburgh, 1875), p. 28.

[52] Marius Schoonmaker, *The History of Kingston, New York* (New York, 1888), p. 100. Spafford specifically notes that the fee simple was the prevailing form of land tenure in the Ulster County towns of Rochester, Marbletown, Kingston, Hurley, and New Paltz, and the Orange County towns of Montgomery and Warwick (*op. cit.*, pp. 283, 230–231, 220, 212, 245, 239, 321 respectively).

POPULATION GROWTH AND LAND PATTERN

formerly held by the trustees were divided and allotted to the proprietors.[53]

The great Hardenburgh Patent covered the northwestern part of Ulster County. Later in this chapter we shall take up in detail the ownership of the lots into which the original tract had been divided. In the three towns of Shandaken, Shawangunk, and Woodstock, the system of three-life leases was the common form of land tenure.[54] Not until the antirent agitation of the 1840's had run its course did this part of Ulster County become a country of independent freeholding farmers.

Prior to 1790 the area which later became Greene County had failed to attract many settlers. We do not have to search far for the reason. Except for the townships fronting the river, where the bulk of the population was concentrated in 1790, the surface of Greene County is broken and mountainous. The steep slopes of the Catskill Mountains approach within ten miles of the river, providing an effective barrier to agricultural settlement. The stony soil underlain by hardpan was a further discouragement even to later generations.

Despite these handicaps Greene County grew rapidly, increasing its population from an estimated 7,208 in 1790 to 19,536 in 1810. Settlers pushed into the interior valleys and began to send out so much wheat that in 1804 the village of Catskill manufactured over 30,000 barrels of flour.[55] Stephen Day of Connecticut purchased a large tract containing the modern townships of Jewett, Durham, Windham, and Ashland, and induced his countrymen to leave their worn-out farms and take up lands among the foothills of the Catskills.[56] The lands near Freehold (now Durham) sold for $3.00 to $6.00 an acre, and land between Freehold and Catskill

---

[53] Irving Etling, *Dutch Village Communities on the Hudson River* (Baltimore, 1886), p. 40.
[54] Spafford, *op. cit.*, pp. 297, 331; Schoonmaker, *op. cit.*, p. 100.
[55] Dwight, *op. cit.*, IV, 16.
[56] French, *op. cit.*, p. 33.

brought $6.00 to $7.00 an acre in 1797.[57] Apparently the Yankees considered the land well worth the price, for in 1815 Timothy Dwight observed how rapidly the region near Cairo and Durham had been brought under cultivation since his previous visit of 1804.[58]

Few immigrants penetrated the mountain fastnesses in southwestern Greene County until the tanning industry found a profitable use for the heavy stands of virgin hemlock. Furthermore, the great Hardenburgh Patent covered most of this region, and the proprietors had not yet attempted to develop their tracts on any large scale. Their attempts to introduce the leasehold contrasted with the freehold tenure prevailing in the Day purchase and the older townships along the river.

For over a century fierce agrarian revolts marred the history of Columbia County. Probably no other section of the United States has witnessed a struggle of such duration between landlords and tenants. Insecurity of tenure and burdensome obligations led to bitter hatred and periodic revolts. In 1755 and again in 1766 the tenants rose only to be forcibly put down.[59] In the 1790's hostility to the landlords resulted in riots and the killing of Sheriff Hogeboom. In the 1840's the antirent lecturers fanned the smoldering resentment into flames once more. It was only after 1850 that the tenants of the Van Rensselaers and the Livingstons succeeded in throwing off the claims of the landlords to the soil.

Livingston Manor was the estate of the famous family which contributed so many influential leaders to the political life of the colony, state, and nation. Embracing some 160,000 acres in all, it stretched across the lower third of Columbia County. The family leased out farms on various terms, but estates for the life of two persons in being (two-life leases) were the most numerous.[60]

---

[57] La Rochefoucault Liancourt, *Travels,* II, 438–439.

[58] Dwight, *op. cit.,* IV, 17, 180.

[59] Mark, *op. cit.,* pp. 122–128, 131–163.

[60] *Ibid.,* p. 69; *New York Assembly Documents,* no. 156 (1846), pp. 60–68.

POPULATION GROWTH AND LAND PATTERN

Originally the tenants agreed to pay rent at the rate of 14 bushels of wheat per hundred acres, but in later years this rent was commuted to roughly $18 per hundred acres. In addition, the tenant labored under other obligations and restrictions, some of which were most galling.[61] Failure to meet the terms usually led to speedy eviction, for the Livingstons did not trifle with recalcitrant tenants.[62]

The Claverack lands of the Van Rensselaer family adjoined Livingston Manor to the north. Originally this tract contained some 250,000 acres, but subsequent patents such as the Jan von Hoesen purchase and Kinderhook Patent were carved out of it.[63] Unfortunately, the boundaries were so vaguely drawn that endless litigation between rival claimants resulted. In 1812 the state legislature appointed commissioners to determine the rights and titles of all parties. Naturally, these lawsuits prevented orderly development and added to the feeling of insecurity among the tenants.[64]

---

[61] *Ibid.* For example, a lease in 1772 by Robert Livingston to Jacob Rosman and his wife called for an annual payment of 30 shipples of good, merchantable, winter wheat, four fat fowls, and two days' labor with wagon or team and an able man. This last requirement in case of default had to be paid at the rate of 12 shillings a day. Further provisions required Rosman to clear 2 acres of land a year until all the farm was plowed, sow on the farm at least 12 bushels of winter wheat a year, spread on the farm all manure, set up an orchard of 100 trees, build a barn (30 by 20 feet) within five years, pay all taxes and assessments besides 6 shillings a year to a Protestant clergyman, and keep no stranger more than forty-eight hours on the farm. Perhaps the most annoying of all were the provisions requiring Rosman to give his lord the pre-emption to buy all his fruits, stock, and grain, to have his corn and grain ground at Livingston's mill, and to give his lord one third of the sale price of his farm in case he should sell out his rights in the farm. Another lease of 1797 called for similar payments but required only one fifth the sale price to be paid to the lord (*ibid.*, pp. 67 ff.).

[62] Spaulding, *op. cit.*, p. 64. In 1792 the estate of Robert L. Livingston lying east of the post road was divided among four sons, Walter, Robert C., John, and Henry. On April 14, 1792, Walter sold his share (amounting to over 20,000 acres) to his brother, Henry, for £24,900 (*Columbia County at the End of the Century* [Hudson, 1900], I, 17).

[63] Nissenson, *op. cit.*, p. 305.

[64] Spafford, *op. cit.*, p. 208. Spafford stated that several lives had been

LANDLORDS AND FARMERS

Perpetual leases calling for 16 bushels of wheat per hundred acres were ordinarily granted on the John I. Van Rensselaer tract.

When we examine the population map from 1800 to 1810, we find that every township in the county except the urban township of Hudson was losing population. This decline is all the more startling because the state's population was increasing at a tremendous rate, and even the counties on the east bank of the Hudson were showing moderate gains.

The explanation for the decline lies in the fierce antirent war waged by the Livingston and Van Rensselaer tenants. The small farmers desperately sought to prevent the eviction of tenants who had refused or failed to pay the rent.[65] At Nobletown an armed mob forced the deputy sheriff to adjourn an auction at the Arnold farm. A week later, on October 27, 1791, Sheriff Cornelius Hogeboom arrived at the farm where a large band of determined tenants had likewise assembled. Seventeen men disguised as Indians interrupted the proceedings and followed the sheriff. Mr. Arnold took

---

lost in these controversies. Horace Greeley in the *New-York Weekly Tribune*, April 12, 1847, stated that a lawyer retained by the landlords told him that Columbia County leases were the worst since the various landlords had conflicting titles.

[65] Elizabeth Gebhard, *The Parsonage Between Two Manors; Annals of Clover-Reach* (Hudson, 1925), pp. 185 ff.; *Albany Gazette*, Oct. 31, 1791; Franklin Ellis, *History of Columbia County, New York* (Philadelphia, 1878), p. 42. In passing, we may note that General Philip Schuyler made an appeal in 1790 to the tenants of his wife, the daughter of John Van Rensselaer. Unless they would agree to his "concessions," he threatened "to institute suits for the recovery of his property." He offered the following terms: The original lessee or his assign was assured possession. Occupants were also assured possession even if they had no lease. Schuyler offered to remit all arrears of rent from those lots which were purchased. He would sell the land in fee at the rate of $2.25 an acre, to be secured by a mortgage which was to be retired in five years. Those who did not buy the fee were to pay one year's rent before January 1, 1791. Apparently it was his effort to oust his recalcitrant tenants that added to the agrarian unrest in Columbia County. See *Address of Gen. Philip Schuyler to the Tenants of Lands at Hillsdale, derived Through His Wife from her Father, John Van Rensselaer, Nov. 12, 1790,* at the Schuyler Mansion, Albany.

POPULATION GROWTH AND LAND PATTERN

out his gun and killed the officer. The outrage stirred the public to great excitement. Four of the conspirators fled to Nova Scotia while twelve others were tried and acquitted in February, 1792, by a special term held at Claverack.

That the killing of the sheriff did not put an end to agitation is clearly evident. On January 7, 1795, 214 tenants petitioned the legislature demanding an investigation of the Livingston title.[66] They charged that the Livingstons had fraudulently enlarged their estate from 2,600 to 175,000 acres. They further charged that the terms of the leases were degrading and incompatible with the natural rights of free men. The Assembly referred the petition to a committee which on March 19, 1795, denied these allegations, stating that the petitioners were probably unaware of the various patents confirming the original grants.[67] Four days later the Assembly dismissed the petition, saying that it would be most improper to resume title to lands which had been held by the Livingstons for more than a hundred years.[68]

Their appeal for legislative relief rather summarily dismissed, the tenants continued to obstruct the collection of rents. Armed mobs attended the auctions at which the goods of evicted tenants were put on sale, and intimidated potential purchasers. Apparently they enjoyed considerable success, for in 1798 Governor John Jay sent a special message to the State Senate declaring that "combinations of disorderly people have been formed" in the town of Livingston and that the "sheriff and deputies . . . have been opposed in a manner, and to a degree offensive to justice and subversive of good order." [69] The state legislature, by a concurrent resolution of February 24, 1798, requested the Governor to enforce

---

[66] Petrus Pulver et al., in Doc. Hist. of N.Y., III, 834–839.
[67] *Journal of the Assembly of the State of New York* (1795), p. 126.
[68] *Ibid.*, pp. 134–135.
[69] *Messages from the Governors, Comprising Executive Communications to the Legislature and Other Papers . . . , 1683–1906*, ed. by Charles Z. Lincoln (Albany, 1909), II, 411.

the laws by all means, including the militia, if he considered drastic steps necessary.[70]

It is no small wonder that insecurity of tenure, widely advertised by these turbulent tenant uprisings, not only discouraged New Englanders from settling in the county but also caused the bolder spirits to join the stream of emigrants flowing toward the west. Many tenants on Livingston Manor surrendered their leases between 1800 and 1810 and undoubtedly some of them set out for the West.[71] Columbia County paid a heavy price in agrarian discontent for the doubtful privilege of supporting a landed aristocracy. The leasing of farms also had a disastrous effect on husbandry, resulting in exhausted soil, dilapidated buildings, and wretched cultivation.

The greatest manor of all was Rensselaerswyck, with over three thousand tenants.[72] Embracing hundreds of thousands of acres on both sides of the Hudson River, this manor was indeed a princely domain. But it was not until Stephen Van Rensselaer came with his bride, Margaret Schuyler, to live at the manor house at Watervliet in 1785 that large areas of the manor were surveyed and peopled. The weight of family tradition and the sense of *noblesse oblige,* so characteristic of his later life, gave him a paternal attitude toward the lower classes. Young Stephen Van Rensselaer felt a responsibility to God for his extensive estate. With great energy he pushed the settlement of his lands, offering "durable leases" to his new tenants.

---

[70] *Ibid.,* footnote. James Fenimore Cooper in his novel *The Redskins* on page 41 has a character praise John Jay for putting down this antirent conspiracy.

[71] See "Livingston Manor Memoranda," no. 10, 489, New York State Library.

[72] *People* v. *Van Rensselaer,* 9 N.Y. 301. The attorneys for the Van Rensselaers estimated that there were 3,163 farms under lease. The family leased 233,000 acres in Albany County and 202,100 acres in Rensselaer County (*ibid.*). The number of leases in Albany County numbered 1,397.

POPULATION GROWTH AND LAND PATTERN

The term "lease" requires further examination. Actually the "durable lease" was a freehold estate in perpetuity to which were attached certain restraints on alienation and a reservation of perpetual rent.[73] The Rensselaerswyck leases provided that when a tenant disposed of his farm, he should pay one fourth of the money to the patroon or, in some leases, he should pay an extra year's rent.[74] The quarter sales not only permitted the landlord to keep out undesirable tenants but also provided a considerable revenue. Thus it was estimated in 1850 that eight farms in West Sandlake, Rensselaer County, totaling only 1,190 acres, had paid in quarter sales and extra rents, including simple interest, the amount of $5,237.49.[75] This restriction aroused great resentment, especially since it was considered by many as an invalid restraint on alienation, a view which the courts finally took.[76]

The Van Rensselaer tenants enjoyed a freehold estate in perpetuity, which was far superior to the freehold for two lives held by the Livingston tenants. Nevertheless, obligations to the landlord were burdensome and somewhat degrading. In the lowland townships of Guilderland, Watervliet, Bethlehem, and New Scotland, which had been settled largely before the Revolution, the leases called for an annual payment of ten bushels of winter wheat per hundred acres, four fat hens, and a day's work with a team of horses or oxen. In the four western mountain towns, settled for the most part in the late 1780's, the leases provided for an annual rent of 14 bushels of wheat per hundred acres. In addition, the landlord reserved all rights to mines, milling, and water sites. The

---

[73] Mark, *op. cit.*, pp. 62–68. Dr. Mark gives a clear discussion of the legal aspects of leases in the eighteenth century. Nissenson (*op. cit.*, pp. 56 ff.) discusses the origin and legal precedents of the perpetual lease. Spaulding, *op. cit.*, pp. 60–61, has a brief summary.

[74] Van Rensselaer Leases, N.Y. State Library.

[75] M. W. Carmichael to Hon. Thomas Carroll in *Freeholder*, April 10, 1850; Cheyney, *op. cit.*, p. 15.

[76] *De Peyster* v. *Michael*, 6 N.Y. 467.

LANDLORDS AND FARMERS

tenant had to pay all taxes and permit the landlord to have ingress and egress and cut timber on his lands. In case of default, the landlord could distrain the property of the tenant.

The spirit of expansion and improvement caught the imagination of the young patroon, who promptly began to develop the ancestral estates.[77] New surveys divided the mountain townships of Albany County into farms of approximately 160 acres each. Hundreds of immigrants, some from the old Dutch and German settlements and some from the hills of New England, found the farms to their liking and began to clear the land. The patroon required no down payment and offered free rent for seven years. In 1789 Stephen Van Rensselaer openly challenged the people to see if "any hired lands" in this or any state "are let on as favorable terms to tenants as my lands are."[78] He was apparently justified in this boast, for settlers took up farms rapidly. Between 1786 and 1800 most of the leases on the east manor were signed,[79] and 1793 was the year when most of the rents on the west manor first came in.[80]

Antirent orators later charged that the agents of the patroon had tricked the settlers into signing the leases.[81] After the seven years of free rent had passed, the tenants were invited to come to the manor office and sign a lease. According to the antirenters, the settlers found the terms in the leases much stiffer than the original verbal agreements. Faced with the loss of their improvements, the

---

[77] Some idea of the sparse population on his domain can be had from the map made in 1767 by J. R. Bleeker (*Doc. Hist. of N.Y.*, III, 967). Bleeker drew the map for the Van Rensselaers and it shows only 148 families on the west side and 133 families on the east side of the river. The great majority of these holdings were concentrated within a few miles of the Hudson. By 1800 the less than 300 families had expanded to more than 3,000 tenants.

[78] Broadside, April 27, 1789, N.Y. State Library.

[79] *People v. Van Rensselaer*, 9 N.Y. 301. In 1911 the original leases for the west manor were destroyed in the capitol fire.

[80] *N.Y. Senate Documents*, no. 92 (1846), v. 3. In the town of Rensselaerville the leases were granted from 1787 on, mainly to New Englanders (*Rensselaerville Reminiscences and Rhymes* [Albany, 1896]).

[81] For an example, see the *Freeholder*, June 25, Dec. 24, 1845.

POPULATION GROWTH AND LAND PATTERN

objectors usually signed, as did the illiterate Dutch farmers who did not understand what they were signing.[82] It would be difficult at this time to affirm or deny these charges.

The Van Rensselaer leases of 1790 were substantially the same as those contracted during the early part of the eighteenth century.[83] Maria Van Rensselaer in the 1680's and 1690's had vigorously applied the policy of nonalienation of land, a policy which had already been advocated by the earlier patroons. As a result, tenth sales and quarter sales had long been included in the lease, along with the day's service with horse or oxen, and reservations of mines and water rights. The charge of the antirenters that these conditions had been introduced only after Stephen Van Rensselaer inherited the property are unfounded. Of course it is quite possible, and perhaps highly probable, that his agents failed to mention such provisions to the settlers when they first encouraged them to take up a lot. A Yankee might very well have looked with surprise as well as dismay at the long list of restrictions in the lease when it was presented to him for his signature.

That the patroon should exert considerable political influence in the manor was only natural considering his wealth, prestige, and sense of public duty. That he should be accused of improperly influencing the votes of his tenants was also inevitable. In 1789 he emphatically denied that he was threatening his tenants with lawsuits unless they voted for his candidates.[84] When Stephen Van Rensselaer ran for governor in 1801, a flurry of letters appeared in the *Albany Register* denouncing his attempts to secure the votes of his tenants.[85] It was charged that in 1794 he had offered to remit quarter sales to "all real friends" in the east manor.[86] During the campaign of 1801 he denied that he would hold the political

---

[82] Statement by Mr. Hayner in speech to the Assembly, Jan. 17, 1846, quoted in *Freeholder*, Feb. 25, 1846.
[83] Mark, *op. cit.*, p. 67; Nissenson, *op. cit.*, pp. 52–53.
[84] Broadside, April 27, 1789, N.Y. State Library.
[85] March 5, 20, April 3, 10, 21, 24, 28, June 19, 1801.
[86] *Albany Register*, March 20, 1801.

opinions of his tenants against them.[87] It is indicative of either the gratitude or fear of the tenants that in 1801 the patroon ran three to one ahead of Governor Clinton in Albany County, while in several townships bordering on the manor he failed to receive a majority.[88] Perhaps both motives combined to shape the political opinion of the tenant. At any rate, we can safely agree with the confidential statement of William North to his friend, Benjamin Walker, that "the people of the Manor have been influenced by the Patroon." [89]

The fine sandy loam soil covered with scrubby pitch pine which lies between Albany and Schenectady remained practically uninhabited. The early settlers avoided this barren waste, which also extended into Saratoga and Schenectady counties. We may also note in passing that in the towns of Coeymans, Albany County, and Pittstown and Schaghticoke, Rensselaer County, all three of which lay outside the manor, the lands were chiefly held in fee.[90]

Washington and Saratoga counties on the upper Hudson grew at a moderate pace between 1790 and 1810, with both counties almost doubling their inhabitants during the twenty-year span. From the east Yankees were filtering into the frontier communities, while up the Hudson other Yankees and foreign immigrants were making their way to the flourishing Champlain region. Unfortunately, rugged mountainous areas, cold soils, and sandy barrens made large portions of both counties unattractive for agricultural settlement.

Washington County contained many small patents. In general, the proprietors were willing to sell the land in fee. Perhaps the success of the Green Mountain Yankees in fighting land jobbers from New York warned the proprietors that any attempt to keep

---

[87] Jabez Hammond, *History of Political Parties in the State of New York* (Cooperstown, 1846), I, 161–162.

[88] *Ibid.*; letter to *Albany Register*, March 5, 1801.

[89] Sept. 4, W. North Papers, N.Y. State Library.

[90] Spafford, *op. cit.*, pp. 166, 273, 293.

POPULATION GROWTH AND LAND PATTERN

control of their lands might be challenged by the aggressive "levelers" of Vermont. At any rate, the owners of the Cambridge Patent totaling 31,500 acres gradually sold the land.[91] The Banyar estate, however, held some 5,435 acres under lease which rented at the annual rate of $15 per hundred acres.[92] The prominent Federalist politician, General John Williams, held a large amount of land.[93]

Turning to Saratoga County, we find the large Kayeraderosseras Patent of 400,000 acres covering the northern two thirds of the county. In 1771 commissioners had divided it into twenty-five allotments to satisfy the claims of the thirteen patentees.[94] Indian quarrels and Revolutionary warfare checked any large settlements until the peace of 1783 removed these dangers. From fragmentary evidence offered by the correspondents of Spafford's *Gazetteer* of 1813, we are probably justified in assuming that the proprietors were selling the land in fee.[95]

Settlements had long been established on the intervals bordering the upper Hudson and lower Mohawk. The famous Schuyler family, connected by marriage with the Van Rensselaers, the Livingstons, and Alexander Hamilton, owned thousands of acres in the Saratoga Patent which contained much of the rich bottom land along the Hudson. True to the aristocratic tradition of his class, General Philip Schuyler favored the leasehold. In 1776 he told Charles Carroll that the custom of the great proprietors was to lease their farms for three lives, reserving sometimes a fourth

---

[91] French, *op. cit.*, p. 680.

[92] *John Wigram's Proceedings on Goldsbrow Banyar Business, 1812*, Box 1, G. Banyar Papers, N.Y. State Library. See also "Schedule of All Lands Belonging to Banyar and Mr. White," Box 6, Folder 8.

[93] *History and Biography of Washington County and the Town of Queensbury* (Richmond, Indiana, 1894), p. 400.

[94] Nathaniel B. Sylvester, *History of Saratoga County, New York* (Philadelphia, 1878), p. 76.

[95] See reports on Ballston, p. 129; Milton, p. 237; Providence, p. 277; and Charlton, p. 157. In all these towns leases are also mentioned.

but more often a tenth of all the produce.[96] He considered the quarter sale as an excellent source of revenue. An examination of his own rent ledger shows that he followed this policy.[97] The annual rent amounted to about $12.50 for each hundred acres. More than 120 tenants were listed for Saratoga County and 80 more on other tracts. General Schuyler had extensive landed interests besides his family holdings, for in 1787 he joined with twelve associates to purchase over half a million acres of confiscated Tory estates at the rate of 14 cents an acre.[98]

The narrow ribbon of alluvial land near Schenectady was famous during the colonial period for its high yield of wheat. The small population of almost six thousand was chiefly scattered along the Mohawk flats. In the two decades before the Revolution, James Duane acquired more than 30,000 acres of upland southwest of Schenectady.[99] By 1775 he had granted twenty-one farms in fee and twenty-three farms for three lives. Those who bought in fee were normally granted seven to ten years' credit at 7 per cent, but were also required to serve one day's riding with horses or oxen, pay two pairs of fat hens, and renounce to the landlord water, falls, and half the mineral rights. The farms leased for three lives usually were rent-free for five or ten years, after which the tenants were to pay either 20 or 25 bushels of winter wheat at Albany or 12½ cents an acre. Like many landlords with an eye on the unearned increment, Duane refused to lease six of the best farms except on an annual basis.

After the Revolution Duane found it much easier to attract

---

[96] *Journal of Charles Carroll of Carrollton During His Visit to Canada in 1776* (Baltimore, 1845), p. 45.

[97] Schuyler Papers, *Ledger of Rents at Saratoga, 1760–1805*, N.Y. Public Library. See also *Schuyler Account Book*.

[98] Schuyler Papers, no. 2046, cited by Spaulding, *op. cit.*, p. 55.

[99] Edward Porter Alexander, *A Revolutionary Conservative, James Duane of New York* (New York, 1938), p. 54. Dr. Alexander has two excellent chapters on the early history of Duanesburg (pp. 52–67; 215–236).

POPULATION GROWTH AND LAND PATTERN

settlers. Between 1785 and 1792 he signed 229 agreements.[100] Duane now leased most of his farms on perpetual leases which called for a rent of $15 a year after the first five years. Mines and water rights were also reserved, although quarter sales were not included. Other farms were leased for three lives with five years of free rent and one shilling an acre annual rent.[101] After 1790 the competition of western lands prevented Duane from stiffening his terms.

That the life of a landed gentleman was not untroubled by worries and losses can be seen in Alexander's account of Duane's activities. Unruly and impoverished tenants, poor crops, the erection of saw- and gristmills, and the task of road building were problems which absorbed much of his time and ate away his revenues.

Colonel William North, Duane's son-in-law, has left us several interesting reflections on the leasehold system. His comments were made in personal letters to his close friend, Benjamin Walker, and are applicable to the institution of leasehold tenure as it developed in eastern New York. He warned Walker:

> This letting farms on shares and indeed for rent in money is a miserable business. . . . Sell—money enough down to pay a years rent and credit for the rest— They will then work for the farm as for themselves and make it better—and after all, if they can not fulfill the contract, you are the gainer. Farms here which will sell for 800 + will not rent for 20—what a lot of interest.[102]

A narrow tongue of settlement had pushed up the Mohawk Valley as far as German Flats in the first half of the eighteenth

---

[100] *Ibid.*, p. 218. Dr. Alexander has drawn up a table giving the number of agreements made between 1777 and 1795.

[101] See leases to John Campbell and Levi Griffiths, Sept. 2, 1795, in *Extracts from Journals of Hon. James Duane,* James Duane MSS, N.Y. Historical Society.

[102] May 16, [18—]. See also letters of May 12, 1799, and Dec. 3, 1801, in W. North Papers.

43

LANDLORDS AND FARMERS

century. Palatine Germans had found the Mohawk intervals highly productive, but the destructive Indian and Tory raids had seriously cut down the frontier population. With the coming of peace German and Dutch farmers returned to their devastated homes and quickly repaired the damage. Hard on their heels came the New Englanders, who filled up the vacant lands along the river and pushed into the hill towns on both sides of the valley. Within fifteen years some ten thousand immigrants from New England and the eastern counties settled in present-day Herkimer County.[103] Every township in Herkimer, Montgomery, and Fulton counties made rapid gains between 1800 and 1810 (see map).

The tide of settlement soon found a natural barrier to the north in the rugged Adirondack Mountains.[104] Thin sandy soil, forbidding climate, steep slopes, and impassable swamp areas conspired to prevent the northern portions of Saratoga, Fulton, and Herkimer counties from being developed on an agricultural basis. Several attempts, such as those by John Brown, the Providence merchant, and Mr. Noble, to make settlements in northern Herkimer County ended in dismal failures despite the outlay of considerable sums of money.[105] Except for the inroads of lumbermen, the Adirondacks remained a wilderness until well after the Civil War.[106]

Colonial land speculation had engrossed most of the land in Montgomery, Fulton, and Herkimer counties. The most notable landowner was Sir William Johnson, who used his official position and close friendships among the Indians to acquire large tracts. Perhaps his largest holding was the royal grant containing 90,000 acres between the East and West Canada Creeks. Goldsbrow Banyar, who had served as a colonial official for many years, had

---

[103] Nathaniel S. Benton, *A History of Herkimer County, Including the Upper Mohawk Valley* (Albany, 1856), p. 111.

[104] In 1802 the Rev. John Miller stated that the northernmost settlements were about thirty miles north of the river (*Doc. Hist. of N.Y.*, III, 1109).

[105] Benton, *op. cit.*, pp. 469-470.

[106] *N.Y. Assembly Documents*, no. 68 (1850). This report recommended state aid to open up the "wilderness."

POPULATION GROWTH AND LAND PATTERN

likewise acquired over 25,000 acres scattered about in several patents within these counties.[107] That the Livingstons owned a large tract in Montgomery County should come as no surprise when we recall the many opportunities they had of persuading colonial governors to distribute more land patents.[108] George Clarke, Jr., scion of another colonial family, one member of which had held the office of lieutenant governor, possessed 13,000 acres in the Corry Patent south of the Mohawk River.[109]

The confiscation of Tory estates in central and northern New York gave a great impetus to a more democratic land system in this area. The holdings of Henry White, Edward Jessup, Guy Johnson, James De Lancey, Robert Leake, Sir John Johnson, and others, whose lands were located in the western part of the state, were sold for $1,250,000.[110] The process by which these lands passed from the Commissioners of Forfeitures into the hands of speculators and farmers would undoubtedly repay careful study.[111] The names of Peter Smith, John Taylor, and Jeremiah Van Rensselaer as owners of land conveyed by the Commissioners of Forfeitures suggest that a considerable amount of these lands passed through the hands of speculators before they reached the small landowner.[112] However devious the process, it often happened that New Englanders bought these lots which were

---

[107] G. Banyar Papers, "Schedule of All Lands Belonging to Banyar and Mr. White," Box 6, Folder 8.
[108] In 1798 Elizabeth Livingston transferred to her husband, Henry A. Livingston, title to 20,000 acres in Montgomery County (G. Livingston Papers, N.Y. Public Library).
[109] George Clarke, Jr., Leases, N.Y. State Library.
[110] Flick, *Loyalism in N.Y.*, p. 151. Between 1784 and 1788 the commissioners of forfeitures for the western district sold 451 lots in Sir John Johnson's Royal Grant as well as parts of other patents (Benton, *op. cit.*, pp. 203–204).
[111] Yoshpe, *op. cit.*, has already made such a study for the counties of the southern district. Unfortunately the capitol fire of 1911 destroyed many of the records of the commissioners (p. 210).
[112] Deeds, Libri I, II, IV, V, VIII, Oneida County Clerk's Office.

coming on the market at the beginning of the great westward migration.

The Clarke family owned much land in Oneida, Otsego, Delaware, Montgomery, and Saratoga counties. In 1812 one estimate placed the value of these tracts at more than one million dollars.[113] Almost invariably the Clarkes adopted three-life leases, a form of land tenure which led to continual discontent. In the town of Charleston, Montgomery County, George Clarke, Jr., signed at least twenty-eight leases between 1792 and 1794.[114] The annual rent starting in the sixth year was $12.50 for each hundred acres. Tenants were granted possession during the lifetimes of the three persons named in the lease with a minimum of thirty-one years guaranteed. Several leases specifically required the tenants to keep one sixth of the farm in woods.

Before 1810 the Banyar estate showed little interest in its holdings in Montgomery County. Squatters were permitted to make improvements, after which perpetual leases yielding 20 bushels of wheat a year were signed.[115]

The spurt in the population of Oneida County from 1,891 in 1790 to 20,839 in 1800 was little short of phenomenal. In 1784 Hugh White of Middletown, Connecticut, moved with his four sons to the fertile flats west of the present city of Utica. Within a few years a thriving New England settlement grew up which almost every traveler praised for its prosperity. Elkanah Watson in 1788 marveled at the influx:

Settlers are continually pouring in from the Connecticut hive, which throws off its annual swarms of intelligent, industrious, and enterprising settlers, the best qualified of any men in the world, to subdue and civilize the wilderness. . . . They already estimate three hundred brother Yankees on their muster list.[116]

---

[113] *N.Y. Senate Journal* (1812), p. 56.

[114] George Clarke, Jr., Leases.

[115] *John Wigram's Proceedings on Goldsbrow Banyar Business, 1812,* Box 1, G. Banyar Papers.

[116] *History of the Western Canals,* p. 13. With equal rapidity Yankees

POPULATION GROWTH AND LAND PATTERN

Settlers were moving into the northern towns of Steuben, Floyd, and Lee before 1790 as well as to the south. Oneida County was growing fast and the sound of the ax was heard on all sides. An inland commonwealth was being established reproducing in the wilderness the church, the school, and the "sprightliness, thrift, and beauty" of New England.[117]

Many of the great landed proprietors of Oneida County, and particularly those whose holdings lay to the north of the valley, preferred to lease their farms. George Clarke, Jr., held some 10,000 acres in the Oriskany Patent which straddled the Mohawk River just below Fort Stanwix.[118] The lease for three lives in being was the common form of tenure on his lands. The 22,000 acres of Cosby Manor embracing lands in the valley near Utica had passed into the hands of the Schuyler and Bleeker families. In December, 1786, Philip Schuyler arranged a partition with Rutger Bleeker, heir of one of Albany's aristocratic mercantile families, whereby Philip Schuyler received three fourths of the tract which had been surveyed into 400-acre and 1,200-acre lots.[119] Schuyler set to work to develop his portion and leased over sixty farms, principally in 1790 and 1792.[120] The Bleeker family also refused to sell the title in fee, thus retarding the growth of Utica.[121] Philip Schuyler again displayed his preference for the three-life lease which would bring in an annual rent of 20 bushels of wheat for each hundred acres after the tenant had settled on his lot for five free years. No mention was made of such services as a day's riding or the payment of four fat fowls, provisions which were probably omitted as im-

---

took up the land in Kirkland and Paris townships, buying the land on Coxe's Patent for one dollar an acre (A. D. Gridley, *History of the Town of Kirkland, New York* [New York, 1874], pp. 19 ff.; Jones, *op. cit.*, pp. 165–172; Henry C. Rogers, *History of the Town of Paris* [Utica, 1881]).

[117] Dwight, *op. cit.*, III, 179.
[118] *Freeholder*, Jan. 16, June 19, 1850.
[119] Deeds, Liber II, Oneida County Clerk's Office.
[120] P. Schuyler Papers, *Schuyler Account Book*.
[121] Horton, *op. cit.*, p. 131.

LANDLORDS AND FARMERS

practicable considering the long journey to the home estate of the General. A few leases specified a twenty-one-year tenure while still others included quarter sales or no alienation without the permission of the owner. The will of Philip Schuyler divided his holdings in Cosby Manor into eight equal parts and thus prevented the perpetuation of a large estate operated on the leasehold system.[122] In 1805 the forty-seven leases, in addition to several unsold lots, were partitioned among his heirs according to ballot. In February, 1812, Philip Schuyler, Jr., gave power of attorney to James Cochran of Montgomery County to sell his holdings in Cosby Manor in fee.[123] We find that the heirs of Rutger Bleeker were making similar sales in fee. In 1809 over fifteen transactions providing for sale of the land were made by his heirs.

Six proprietors, including Governor Clinton, General Floyd, and John Taylor, owned the 40,000 acres of Fonda Patent.[124] General Floyd, a patriot from Long Island who had been a signer of the Declaration of Independence, plunged heavily in back-country land speculation and finally moved in 1803 to his tract where he planned to establish a permanent estate. Like his neighbor, Baron Steuben, Floyd gave out perpetual leases. After five free years the tenant was to pay 18 bushels of wheat for each hundred acres.[125] In the deed books several leases by William Floyd can be seen.[126] George Clinton on May 1, 1791, leased to Moses Coffin a 100 acre farm for 18 bushels of wheat a year, the payment to begin in 1795. It is interesting to note that this lease, as well as several of those given out by Floyd, was sold several times. In 1794 Coffin's lease sold for 100 pounds; in 1795 it sold for 180 pounds. Although William Floyd made some sales in fee, over half of the town of

---

[122] Deeds, Liber XIX, 519 ff., Oneida County Clerk's Office.
[123] *Ibid.*, Liber XX.
[124] Lincklaen, *op. cit.*, p. 98.
[125] *Ibid.*, Colonel William North to Benjamin Walker, Aug. 8, 1802, W. North Papers.
[126] Deeds, Libri II, VIII, XI, XIII, Oneida County Clerk's Office.

POPULATION GROWTH AND LAND PATTERN

Western as late as the year 1850 was still held under lease.[127]

George Washington acquired a small tract of land in Coxe Patent for which George Clinton served as joint owner and attorney.[128] On January 23, 1796, Henry Lord Viscount Gage of Great Britain paid Robert Kemble of New York City $2,500 for 5,000 acres of land bordering on Cosby Manor.[129]

The history of the Holland Patent, which originally contained 20,000 acres, is probably typical of the process whereby many large tracts were divided up and sold to smaller landholders. On November 17, 1796, Horace Johnson and Seth Johnson, both New York merchants, and their wives, and Andrew Craigie, speculator, of Cambridge, Massachusetts, bought the tract from Henry Richard Lord Holland, son of Lord Holland, the patentee. Within a few years the new proprietors had disposed of many lots to various individuals. Although the following table is incomplete, it illustrates the division of this patent among several small landholders.[130]

On May 5, 1786, the state legislature passed a law providing for

1. Paul De Angelis	12 lots	$5,598.75	July 30, '98
2. Bozabel Fisk	8 lots	4,002.50	July 30, '98
3. Isaac Hubbard	12 lots	6,186.25	July 30, '98
4. Hezekiah Hurlbert	12 lots	6,031.00	July 30, '98
5. Jonathan Barratt	7 lots	3,250.00	Aug. 30, '98
6. John Witchie	3 lots	1,800.00	April 1, '99
7. Wm. Johnson	6 lots	3,993.00	May 3, '99
8. Wm. Johnson	2 lots	1,339.50	Mar. 29, '99
9. Phoebe and George Fish	1 lot	909.00	June 26, '99
10. Rowland Briggs	1 lot	792.00	Jan. 26, '99
11. Elephalet Cortes	1 lot	1,075.50	Jan. 26, '99
	65 lots	$34,977.50	

---

[127] Jones, op. cit., p. 700.

[128] Deeds, Liber XV, pp. 483–484, Oneida County Clerk's Office.

[129] Ibid., Liber XII. Note that the term *manor* is used as part of the title and did not convey special legal rights.

[130] Compiled from Libri VI, VII, XV, XVIII, Oneida County Clerk's Office.

LANDLORDS AND FARMERS

the sale of lands belonging to the state.[131] One section authorized the land commissioners to grant to Baron Steuben 16,000 acres in any township laid out in accordance with the act. The Baron quickly made his selection, believing that his lands would be near the portage at Fort Stanwix. Unfortunately his tract lay some five miles to the north of the Mohawk River. In the spring of 1787 James Cockburn surveyed the tract, laying out 160 lots of approximately 100 acres each.[132]

Baron Steuben was an intimate friend of Colonel William North and Alexander Hamilton, both of whom had married into the old aristocratic oligarchy. The Baron had spent many happy days at Livingston Manor and Duanesburg. It was quite natural for him to adopt the leasehold policy which probably fitted in well with his experiences in the German states. At any rate the Baron, like so many of the prominent men of the day, resolved to carve out an estate in the wilderness.[133]

The Baron had great plans for the future. In 1787 he employed Samuel Sizer, of Springfield, Massachusetts, to build a house, fence 60 acres, and erect a small sawmill.[134] Work proceeded slowly, and when Steuben visited his lands in 1790 he was greatly annoyed at the lack of progress.[135]

Baron Steuben found considerable difficulty in attracting reli-

---

[131] *Laws of the State of New York,* chap. LXVII, 129-137.

[132] John M. Palmer, *General Von Steuben* (New York, 1939), p. 347; Augustus Richards, *Steuben the Pioneer* (1936), p. 5. Both accounts contain valuable information on Steuben's activities on the frontier.

[133] D. R. Fox, *Decline of Aristocracy,* pp. 130 ff. Fox cites numerous cases of landowners moving to their lands in the upstate regions. James Duane, David Ogden, Hamilton's law partner, the Clarksons, Henry Van Rensselaer, the Parishes, Laws, Kents, Jacob Morris, and William Cooper were only a few of these proprietors.

[134] See agreement in Baron Steuben Papers, Oneida Historical Society. The old general, now over sixty years of age, planned to reserve an 800-acre farm which would be surrounded by the farms of his tenants. See his map of the estate.

[135] Richards, *op. cit.,* p. 10.

POPULATION GROWTH AND LAND PATTERN

able tenants. When Yankees learned that his lands were not on the Mohawk, they naturally turned to the more fertile lands in the valley and to the first tier of towns south of the river.[136] As a result the Baron was forced to offer more attractive terms. In fact, he wrote in a "Prospectus and Evaluation" that he "disposed of about 20 farms gratis . . . to accelerate the settlement."[137]

Originally his leases were for perpetuity with an annual rent of $15 a year. Soon he was forced to lower the rent to $10.[138] A rather unusual provision was the nominal payments of 37½ cents a year during the first five years. All mines, minerals, streams, and falls were reserved. Also, the tenants were to set up an apple orchard.

In 1791 Steuben decided to sell lots (1–96) containing over 9,000 acres. In his instructions to his agent, Colonel Colbrath, he suggested the following terms. Lots would be sold for cash at the rate of $1.00 an acre. Otherwise, the lots were priced at $1.25 an acre with three years' credit. An initial payment of one fourth was required, and the balance was to be retired in three annual installments. The buyer was to sign a mortgage and a bond for his lot until he had paid his debt. Colonel Colbrath received the customary commission of 5 per cent for handling the estate.

On the remaining part (lots 96–160) Steuben intended to preserve the leasehold system. In 1791 he estimated that he had 3,446 acres under perpetual lease, each hundred acres bringing in either $10 or $15 a year. The Baron, however, ran into the usual difficulties and he died in 1794 before he had derived any substantial returns.

The old soldier left the bulk of his estate in equal shares to his Revolutionary aides, Benjamin Walker and William North.[139] In

---

[136] Palmer, *op. cit.*, p. 360. Palmer cites a letter from an agent to Steuben, April 17, 1788, which complains that Hugh White was telling prospective settlers that Steuben's lands were cold and that Governor Clinton's lands were the "Holy Land" (*ibid.*, p. 360).
[137] Steuben Papers.
[138] See lease to John Platt, Sept. 14, 1791, Steuben Papers.
[139] Will in Steuben Papers.

LANDLORDS AND FARMERS

the following year Walker paid $5,000 to North for the latter's interest.[140] Walker was a prominent land agent and speculator in central New York and was a close business ally of Charles Williamson.[141] We know very little of Walker's management of his holdings, but his will in 1818 reveals 2,800 acres under lease and yielding $350 a year.[142] Walker, however, showed a willingness to sell in fee.[143]

The mania for speculation in wild lands not only absorbed many Americans but also intrigued cautious Dutch and English capitalists.[144] In 1792 Dutch banking houses in Amsterdam and Rotterdam generously financed a project whereby maple sugar was to be produced on a large scale. Gerrit Boon was dispatched to America to find a suitable location. Accompanied by a young Hollander, Jan Lincklaen, Boon explored the back country in search of lands. In 1792 he bought at the average price of $1.10 an acre the Servis Patent, which contained some 30,000 acres stretching northward from Utica.[145] At the same time Cazenove, representing the same financiers, was purchasing the smaller of the Adgate patents (45,000 acres) for about 60 cents an acre.

Boon immediately attempted to bring his sugar maples into production but with no success. The sun and rain warped the wooden troughs down which the sap was to flow from the trees. After he had spent over $15,000, Boon gave up the venture and devoted his energies to selling land.

The Adgate tract was surveyed in 1794 and divided into lots of 150 acres, whereas the surveys in the Servis tract during the fol-

---

[140] Deed, Correspondence of Benjamin Walker, Oneida Historical Society.
[141] See letters of Walker to Williamson, July 12, 1793, and June 10, 1795.
[142] Correspondence of B. Walker.
[143] Evan Thomas bought full title for $3.00 an acre on Oct. 5, 1805 (see Deeds, Liber XIII, 128, Oneida County Clerk's Office).
[144] Evans, *The Holland Land Company* (Buffalo, 1924). Professor Evans has carefully described the activities of the Amsterdam promoters. See also Helen Cowan, *Charles Williamson* (Rochester, 1942), XIX, 1–56.
[145] Evans, *The Holland Land Company*, pp. 17–18.

POPULATION GROWTH AND LAND PATTERN

lowing year laid out farms averaging 120 acres.[146] Immigrants quickly selected forty-eight lots on the Adgate Patent, one third paying $2.00 an acre, the rest $1.50. In 1795 fifteen more lots brought in $3.00 an acre. But between 1795 and 1801 sales suddenly stopped and were only slowly resumed in subsequent years. The price of $4.00 an acre, coupled with a cold soil and the lure of western lands, discouraged further settlement.

In 1795 Boon announced that sales would begin on the Servis-Steuben tract. Over thirty lots were sold on July 18, 1795, at the rate of $4.50 an acre. So rapidly did immigrants come in that by the end of the year over 6,000 acres had been taken up. From 1800 to 1815 Boon and his successors sold about 700 acres a year, with the price leveling off at $10 an acre in 1806. The settlers received only five to six years' credit, unlike the generous credit of ten years on the less desirable Adgate tract. Before any deeds were issued, the settler had to clear six acres of land and construct a frame house.

Boon experienced the same problem confronting all landholders, namely: how were the settlers to secure enough money to meet their obligations? The usual answer was easy credit terms with numerous extensions. Acceptance of payments in kind was another solution. To a certain degree the perpetual lease was a convenient device to shift some of the burden to future generations.

Gerrit Boon had caught some of Cazenove's enthusiasm for lavish expenditures as a means of developing his lands. He built sawmills and gristmills, and cut makeshift roads through the forest. Mechanics and storekeepers were the recipients of generous subsidies until over $15,000 had been advanced to mechanics alone. Settlers received small loans to buy horses and implements. Alarmed by the continuous drain for these outlays, the Dutch capitalists in 1798 ordered the new agent, Mr. Mappa, to follow a policy of strict economy.[147]

---
[146] *Ibid.*, pp. 66–68.
[147] *Ibid.*, p. 75.

LANDLORDS AND FARMERS

Large numbers of settlers fell into arrears. To encourage payment, Mappa agreed to take corn in exchange. This policy was fairly successful and in 1816 Abraham Varick and Mappa, who had just bought out the interests of the Dutch, extended the system. By paying more than the market price, the partners encouraged payments on debts, although this policy inevitably resulted in a paper loss as well as the cost of handling the stock and products received from the settlers. Mappa rarely evicted delinquents, largely because it was difficult to resell the lots.

In 1816 Varick and Mappa bought the residuary interests of the Dutch investors for $20,000. Forty-three thousand acres of the original 76,000 acres were still unsold. Most of this land was in the "cold" Adgate Patent. Professor Evans estimates that the Dutch had invested about $260,000 in this venture, out of which they received a total of $250,000.[148] In brief, the Dutch bankers had sustained a slight loss on their speculations in Oneida County land.

That the practice of leasing lands had certain injurious effects on the development of Oneida County is confirmed by the testimony of contemporary observers. In 1802 the Reverend John Miller passed through the frontier settlements and confided to his journal that leases "necessarily operate to debase the minds and destroy the enterprise of the settlers."[149] Even allowing for his Yankee bias for the freehold, a bias which is significant in itself, his observation must be seriously considered. In 1799 Timothy Dwight noted that the refusal of the proprietors to sell lands in Utica was retarding the growth of the village.[150] Rome also felt the blight of leasehold tenure.[151]

Speculators from Pennsylvania and New Jersey had acquired in the early 1760's large tracts along the upper reaches of the Dela-

---
[148] Evans, *The Holland Land Company*, p. 85.
[149] *Doc. Hist. of N.Y.*, III, 1136.
[150] Dwight, *op. cit.*, III, 179.
[151] Spafford, *op. cit.*, p. 284. See leases of Dominick Lynch of Nov. 2, 1797, and Nov. 23, 1806, in Libri XII and XVIII, Deeds, Oneida County Clerk's Office.

POPULATION GROWTH AND LAND PATTERN

ware and Susquehanna rivers.[152] Among the most prominent of those participating in these ventures were George Croghan, Benjamin Franklin, Samuel Wharton, Philadelphia merchant, and, somewhat later, William Cooper. George Croghan, the deputy agent to Sir William Johnson, engrossed about 250,000 acres of land in the area now contained within Otsego County. Croghan's plan to divide his holdings and sell them in small lots to settlers died abortive. Eventually a portion of his lands near Otsego Lake passed into the possession of William Cooper and Andrew Craig of Burlington, New Jersey.

The removal of William Cooper to Otsego County ushered in a period of rapid growth. Within twenty-five years the population grew from practically nothing to 39,000, the last figure within striking distance of the present population.[153] There were actually more people on the farms of Otsego County in 1810 than there are today. Otsego County possessed no advantages in soil or location over many other counties, but it did have a land agent of unusual ability who could attract thousands of settlers.

William Cooper, father of the famous novelist, made a fortune in land speculation. At one time he held over 750,000 acres of land valued at $700,000.[154] The irascible old Federalist built on Otsego Lake the finest home west of the Hudson Valley. His proud boast was: "I have settled more acres than any other man in America. There are forty thousand souls holding directly or indirectly under me."[155] In 1785 he sold over 40,000 acres within sixteen days.[156]

[152] Albert T. Volwiler, "George Croghan and the Development of Central New York, 1763–1800," *Quarterly Journal of the New York State Historical Association*, XXI (Jan., 1923), 21 ff.

[153] In 1940 the population was 46,082 (*Sixteenth Census of United States: 1940, Population*, II [Washington, 1943], p. 5).

[154] J. F. Cooper, *The Legends and Traditions of a Northern County* (New York, 1921), p. 234.

[155] William Cooper, *A Guide in the Wilderness; or the History of the First Settlements in the Western Counties of New York, with Useful Instructions to Future Settlers* (New York, 1910), p. 7.

[156] J. F. Cooper in his introduction to *A Guide in the Wilderness*, p. i, states that this land was sold chiefly in small holdings.

LANDLORDS AND FARMERS

The secret of Cooper's success was his policy of selling rather than leasing land. In a letter to Charles Evans in 1790 he wrote:

> My mode of selling Lands . . . is to allow the Purchaser a credit of ten years for the Purchase Money giving him a Warrantee Deed and taking a Mortgage with Bond and Warrant carrying Legal Interest. This I have found by experience to be the only way to raise our back lands from a nominal to a lively Estate—as the Purchaser when he holds the Soil in fee sees a probability of making it his own, he therefore builds better Houses Barns and other Buildings clears his Lands in a better and more effectual manner attends to planting Orchards, and in fact looks up as a Man on record with more ambition than he that is settled on any other plan ever yet practiced.[157]

Cooper in the same letter stated that he had just sold 300,000 acres.

In his *Guide in the Wilderness*, Cooper offered excellent advice to land speculators. He considered a tract of 50,000 acres as a convenient unit of purchase. He strongly advised public sale of the land with no reserved lots, since vacant tracts discouraged the settler and retarded the erection of bridges, churches, and other improvements.[158] Most important of all, the lands must be sold in fee with credit extensions of from seven to ten years. Cooper laid great stress on granting the settler ample time for making his payments. During the first few years the settler was too busy clearing his lands and making improvements to acquire cash resources. Despite his preference for land held in fee simple, Cooper looked favorably upon the perpetual lease as a solution for the poverty-stricken settler.[159] It saved him from being driven off his farm and it gave to the landlord the assurance that the farm would be improved.

The Goldsbrow Banyar estate held several small tracts in Otsego

---

[157] Quoted by J. F. Cooper in *Legends and Traditions*, pp. 141–142.
[158] Interestingly enough, Jan [John] Lincklaen observed in 1791 that Cooper carefully reserved squares of 1,000 acres in various settlements (*op. cit.*, pp. 73–74).
[159] W. Cooper, *op. cit.*, p. 10.

POPULATION GROWTH AND LAND PATTERN

County.[160] Five farms in the Belvidere Patent yielded $20 annually. Five farms on the Hartwick Patent were under three-life leases. In the Wallace Patent it held twenty-five farms which in 1850 were under both life and five-year leases. Other landholders included General Jacob Morris, prominent Federalist politician who owned 5,000 acres,[161] and a Mr. Edmeston who owned about 10,000 acres of poor land in western Otsego County.[162]

Small bands of Palatine Germans migrated to the Schoharie Valley as early as 1713.[163] Despite a bitter dispute with Governor Hunter and the owners of the land patents in the area, a few Germans remained and made the valley a famous wheat-growing center. The number of inhabitants, however, was exceedingly small. How few there were can be seen in the census of 1790 which lists only 2,073.[164] The wave of Yankee immigration advanced the zone of settlement into the uplands and helped to bring about an eightfold increase in population by 1810.

Schoharie County was to figure quite prominently in the anti-rent controversy. The two centers of discontent were the John Morin Scott Patent and the Blenheim Patent, both in the southern part of the county. John Livingston had acquired the Scott Patent which included 40,000 acres. His terms were severe in that the farms were to revert to him after the two individuals named in the lease had died.[165] John Livingston also owned one fifth of the patent of Cobus Kill.[166] On the Blenheim Patent the tenants were

---

[160] "Schedule of All Lands Belonging to Banyar and Mrs. White, 1850," Box 6, Folder 8, C. Banyar Papers.
[161] D. R. Fox, *Decline of Aristocracy*, p. 135.
[162] Spafford, *op. cit.*, p. 182.
[163] Higgins, *op. cit.*, pp. 47–55.
[164] *N.Y. Census for 1855*, XXXIII.
[165] *N.Y. Assembly Documents*, no. 156 (1846), pp. 3–4. A highly prejudiced letter by Juno, Jr., to the *Anti-Renter*, Sept. 13, 1845, declared that Livingston had bribed the lawyer representing the tenants in 1789 to advise his clients that the Livingston title was valid.
[166] Patent of Cobus Kill, P. Livingston Papers.

LANDLORDS AND FARMERS

given a perpetual lease which yielded an annual income of $14 per hundred acres to the landowner.[167]

Apparently the speculators who owned other patents in Schoharie gradually disposed of their land, for in 1846 we have no evidence that the leasehold system was widely used except on the Scott and Blenheim patents. We do know that Peter Smith and John Jacob Astor followed the policy of selling their lands in the Byrnes Patent.

Kenneth Porter has carefully analyzed the joint venture in land speculation embarked upon by John Jacob Astor, William Laight, a New York merchant, and Peter Smith, father of Gerrit Smith.[168] The partners bought 37,000 acres formerly belonging to Sir William Johnson. Unfortunately, other claimants appeared and frightened away potential buyers. The partners sought evidence in Canada and England to safeguard their title and openly warned settlers not to take titles from other parties.[169] A compromise was finally arranged in 1802 whereby the settlers who had cleared at least five acres could have their farms for a sum ranging from $2.50 to $7.50 an acre with ten years' credit. Other settlers were to become tenants at will.

Peter Smith, who owned a half interest, supervised the tract. His chief object was to sell the land as rapidly as possible. He usually granted three free years before the settler had to pay his first installment. Despite generous credit extensions, the purchasers were frequently in arrears. In 1827, 23,000 acres still remained unsold, although many of them were under lease. In 1829 Peter Smith acquired full control by paying Astor and Laight $29,000 for their interests. Porter estimates that on an investment of $10,000,

---

[167] *N. Y. Assembly Documents*, no. 156 (1846), p. 4. In 1846 John A. King, a prominent Whig politician who was elected governor in 1856, owned about 17,000 acres in this patent.

[168] *Op. cit.*, I, 85–102.

[169] See notice to the public, *ibid.*, I, 377–378.

POPULATION GROWTH AND LAND PATTERN

Astor had received $36,771.73 over a period of twenty-five to thirty years.[170]

The great Hardenburgh Patent covered about one half of the present counties of Ulster, Greene, Delaware, and Sullivan. In 1749 the proprietors divided the patent into forty-two tracts and apportioned them among themselves. Robert Livingston received five sixteenths; Gulian Verplanck, three sixteenths; Johannes Hardenbergh, Abraham Hardenbergh, and Charles Brodhead together received two sixteenths; John Wenham, two sixteenths; the heirs of Leonard Lewis, two sixteenths; and the heirs of Peter Faneuil, famous merchant, two sixteenths.[171] Little effort was made to settle the patent before the Revolution. Even after 1790 settlement proceeded slowly and in 1810 the total number of people living on the great patent could not have reached 20,000. Size alone could not compensate for the hundreds of square miles of mountain slopes, the stony soils, and remoteness from markets and lines of travel. Particularly slow was the growth of Sullivan County, where there were only 6,108 inhabitants in 1810. In that year the real estate of nonresident proprietors was assessed at $848,748, while the total amount of taxable property was only $1,260,457.[172]

The Livingston family owned several tracts in Sullivan, Delaware, Greene, and Ulster counties. The original holdings of Robert Livingston had been divided among his numerous relatives, each of whom followed slightly different policies in disposing of the land. In one instance Robert R. Livingston, who subsequently became chancellor of the state, donated 5,000 acres to the inhabitants of Kingston whose homes had been burned by the British.[173]

---

[170] *Ibid.*, I, 99. This estimate does not include the expenses of Peter Smith, who did all the supervision of the land at no charge to the partners.
[171] Quinlan, *op. cit.*, pp. 10–11.
[172] Spafford, *op. cit.*, p. 107.
[173] Schoonmaker, *op. cit.*, p. 324. The trustees of the town selected a tract between the Delaware and Packataten rivers in eastern Delaware County. Lots of fifty acres were given to the "sufferers."

LANDLORDS AND FARMERS

In the 1790's Robert R. Livingston leased several farms in Neversink, Sullivan County.[174] A typical lease was that to Abel Rose on September 23, 1792, which called for a perpetual rent of 16 bushels of wheat per hundred acres, four fowls, and one day's riding after the five free years of rent. In 1808 John R. Livingston, his brother, offered fifty farms in Rockland, Sullivan County.[175] These farms were to be leased for three lives. After three free years, the tenants were to pay 5 bushels of wheat per hundred acres during the fourth year, 10 bushels in the fifth year, and 15 bushels thereafter.

An examination of the rent roll for Livingston's great patent in Middletown, Delaware County, between 1792 and 1805 shows the extreme mobility of the early settlers.[176] A large proportion of the 138 tenants who signed leases abandoned their improvements. General Morgan Lewis, who became governor in 1804 and who married Gertrude Livingston, acquired a 20,000 acre tract in Delaware County.[177] In 1796 he laid out lots varying from 100 to 150 acres which he leased for a perpetual rent of 20 bushels of winter wheat per hundred acres. His leases reserved water and minerals and gave the landlord the right of pre-emption in case of sale. The lease also required the tenant to keep 30 per cent of the farm in wood lot. Robert L. Livingston owned several tracts in the western part of Ulster County and collected his first rents in 1812.[178]

The Verplanck family owned upwards of 50,000 acres but by

---

[174] "Great Patent Memorandum," *R. R. Livingston's Account Book, Clermont, New York*, N.Y. Historical Society.

[175] Advertisement in *Ulster Plebian*, quoted by Quinlan, *op. cit.*, p. 497.

[176] *Livingston's Great Patent Account Book, Middletown, New York*, N.Y. Historical Society.

[177] *Argus*, Sept. 4, 1845; *N.Y. Assembly Documents*, no. 156 (1846), p. 5.

[178] "Robert L. Livingston's Account with Tenants, 1812–'13," no. 6906, N.Y. State Library. The judge in a famous case involving the western boundaries of the town of Rochester declared that the evidence was conclusive that Robert L. Livingston had given upwards of ninety leases between 1807 and 1829 on various parts of Great Lot 4 of the Hardenburgh Patent (*Hunt v. Johnson et al.*, 19 N.Y. 277).

POPULATION GROWTH AND LAND PATTERN

1846 they had disposed of all but 20,000 acres.[179] In 1813 D. C. Verplanck, who was a judge and congressman, wrote to James Cockburn, an eminent surveyor of the time, that he had sold to a Mr. Johnson 23,000 acres, but that he still owned several thousand acres which were under lease.[180]

The Hardenberghs retained large tracts which were leased on a variety of terms, although chiefly for life and perpetuity.[181] Upon the death of Isaac Hardenbergh in 1821, his holdings were widely scattered among his numerous children.[182] Isaac Hardenbergh served as land agent for James Desbrosses, prominent in the import trade, who owned 60,000 acres in lots 5, 25, and 41 of the Hardenburgh Patent.[183] In 1807 Hardenbergh listed two hundred tenants on the Desbrosses tracts, most of whom were delinquent in their rent payments.[184]

John Hunter, scion of an aristocratic colonial family, and Henry Overing were two of the largest landholders in the patent. Their leases were usually in perpetuity with a yearly rent of from 12 to 18 cents an acre.[185] In some cases rents were waived for five years, in others for seven years. In 1811 John Hunter employed John Kiersted, a Catskill lawyer, to act as agent for $500 a year.[186] In the same year Kiersted became agent for Henry Overing and Charles McEvers, who was president of the New York Insurance Company.[187]

The tenants on the Hardenburgh Patent had no special cause

---

[179] N.Y. Assembly Documents, no. 156 (1846).
[180] Verplanck Papers, Box 10, N.Y. Historical Society. See also Box 7, J. Cockburn Papers, N.Y. State Library, for leases by Samuel Verplanck in Great Lot 38.
[181] Hardenbergh Papers, Box I, Folder 3, N.Y. State Library.
[182] Will of April 27, 1821, Box 2, Folder 4, Hardenbergh Papers.
[183] N.Y. Assembly Documents, no. 156 (1846).
[184] Box 2, Folder 2, Hardenbergh Papers.
[185] N.Y. Assembly Documents, no. 156 (1846).
[186] John Kiersted Account Book, p. 76, Kingston Papers, N.Y. State Library.
[187] Ibid., pp. 19, 27.

LANDLORDS AND FARMERS

for complaint against the landlords. With land abundant and tenants few, the landlords had to offer many inducements such as free rent to attract settlers. Taming the wilderness, transporting goods to market, and securing specie were the major problems of the tenant.

A conflict over land titles did lead to the killing of Gerard Hardenbergh in 1808.[188] Hardenbergh was a stubborn and intemperate old man who discovered that settlers in the Neversink Valley were actually on his tract. At first, he offered to give them an equivalent of wild land in exchange for their improved farms. When the tenants refused, he ejected several families and seized their goods. In 1808, a rifle shot ended his life and his heirs quickly made satisfactory compromises with the settlers.

The wide variety of duties imposed on the land agent is well revealed in the letters and papers of Samuel A. Law.[189] A native of Connecticut and a Yale graduate, Law engaged in several land speculations before he became the land agent for the large Franklin Patent in Delaware County. The Philadelphia proprietors had divided the tract and in 1798 Law made an agreement with Samuel Meredith and George Clymer whereby Law was to move to Delaware County and supervise the settlement of about 5,000 acres.[190] In 1806 he bought out their half share in the venture for $5,000. Law also became the agent for the Whartons, Fishers, and Drinkers, who owned other portions of the Franklin Patent. Except in the case of the Fishers, from whom he received a 10 per cent commission, Law agreed to handle the management on the condition that he would receive one half of the price over $3.00 an acre.[191]

---

[188] Quinlan, *op. cit.*, pp. 230 ff.

[189] Professor Samuel Rezneck has a good account of Law's activities ("Samuel A. Law: Delaware County Entrepreneur, 1798–1845," *New York History*, XXXI [Oct., 1933], pp. 382–401).

[190] "S. A. Law's Improved Estate at Meredith, Correspondence, 1796–1817," Box 1, S. A. Law Papers.

[191] S. A. Law to Charles Wharton, Feb. 25, 1825, Correspondence, 1824–1828, Box 4.

POPULATION GROWTH AND LAND PATTERN

In all cases, excepting again the Fisher lands, the owners were to bear half the cost of making the surveys and opening roads. In 1816 Law bitterly complained that by his exertions in establishing a farm and making improvements he had added $2.00 an acre to 20,000 acres of land in the patent.[192]

Law adopted the policy of selling his lands from the start. In a broadside of 1798 he appealed to Connecticut people to inspect the lands and secure titles that were "clear, absolute, and unembarrassed."[193] He offered forty-four farms on the tract belonging to James Fisher for $4.00 to $5.00 an acre. The purchaser had to pay one fourth down and secure the debt by a mortgage.[194] Again in December, 1803, Law placed 140 lots on the market at prices ranging from $3.50 to $6.00, the standard price being $5.00 an acre. Of these, twenty-seven farms belonging to James C. Fisher, thirty-one to the Meredith and Clymer estate, forty to Henry Drinker, and forty-two to Charles and J. Wharton.

Sales proceeded rather slowly, although the years 1806 and 1807 saw a noticeable increase.

FARMS SOLD ON TRACTS BELONGING TO:[195]

	JAMES FISHER	MESSRS. WHARTON	MEREDITH & CLYMER
1798	1		
1799	3		4
1800	3		5
1801	5	3	7
1802	5	1	2
1803	4	6	5
1804	4	5	5
1805	5	1	3
1806	2	1	3
1807	0	8	7
1808	7	2	
1809	4	2	
1810	1		
1811	4		

[192] "S. A. Law's Improved Estate at Meredith, Correspondence, 1796–1817," Box 1.
[193] Box 34.
[194] "Statement of Accounts, Land, 1771–1816," Box 8.
[195] *Ibid.*

LANDLORDS AND FARMERS

The collection of payments soon became a great problem to Law.[196] Nevertheless, he was able to transmit substantial sums to the absentee proprietors. For example, James Fisher received $394 in 1812, $870 in 1813, and $1,360 in 1814.[197] Law estimated in 1816 that since the year 1798 Fisher had received $13,321.14 above costs, while there still remained $30,000 outstanding in debts and unsold lands.[198]

The heirs of Goldsbrow Banyar owned 24,000 acres in northwestern Delaware County.[199] This tract was brought into large-scale development somewhat later than the period under discussion but the comments of the agent, John Wigram, have contemporary significance. In 1812 he stated in his report that he had given out thirty or forty leases and "they are coming in fast to take more, altho' I expect to have to eject some of them before they will comply with our terms—you know the settlers have for these several years been turbulent and much averse to taking up three life leases—however, they are complying fast." [200]

The Kortright Patent of 24,000 acres in northern Delaware County was also developed by leases. In 1785 the proprietor offered 150 farms free of rent for five years and thereafter subject to an annual charge of six pence sterling per acre.[201] In 1846 most of the farms were still under lease.[202]

This completes our survey of the population changes, the land pattern, and the extent of tenancy in eastern New York. Little attempt has been made to keep within the precise chronological

---

[196] In a letter to his friend Isaac Burr on April 10, 1812, Law wrote of his troubles, observing "how crabbed, and contrary and even Knavish some of the settlers prove" (Correspondence, 1796–1812, Box 1).

[197] Land, 1771–1816, Box 8.

[198] *Ibid.*

[199] "Schedule of Lands," Box 6, Folder 8, G. Banyar Papers.

[200] *John Wigram's Proceedings on Goldsbrow Banyar Business, 1812,* Box 1. The estate also owned almost 8,000 acres in the Rapelye Patent farther south. "Schedule of Lands," Box 6, Folder 8.

[201] French, *op. cit.*, p. 263 n.

[202] *N.Y. Assembly Documents,* no. 156 (1846), p. 5.

POPULATION GROWTH AND LAND PATTERN

limits of the period from 1790 to 1808. In fact, the land pattern described above remained essentially the same until the antirent wars of the 1840's. It is hoped that the detailed analysis of the land pattern and the various forms of land tenure will serve as a useful background for our understanding of agrarian life in eastern New York.

CHAPTER III

THE GOOD YEARS

1790 - 1808

CLEARING away the forest was the big task facing eastern New York farmers between 1790 and 1808. From dawn to dusk and in winter and summer the average farmer spent most of his time chopping down trees, burning piles of brush, manufacturing potash from wood ashes, and building fences, sheds, cabins, and houses. Only a few farmers living on the bottom land fringing the Schoharie, Mohawk, and Hudson were able to subordinate the ax to the plow.

Historians, novelists, and patriotic orators have long celebrated the hardships of the frontier. The pioneer has become a legendary figure, the symbol of self-reliance, courage, and resourcefulness. The New York frontier has been singularly fortunate in its historians. Crèvecoeur, with a charm seldom equaled, has described not only Dutch cellars, one-horse carts, and back-country frolics, but has also analyzed shrewdly the influence of the frontier in molding American characteristics. James Fenimore Cooper saw the forests surrounding his beloved Otsego Lake yield to clearings and finally to prosperous farms. He created characters patterned after the people of eastern New York—Natty Bumppo, the frontiersman; Thousandacres, the hard-bitten timber thief; and Cornelius Littlepage, the aristocratic landholder. In western New York Orsamus Turner wrote down the reminiscences of old settlers

THE GOOD YEARS

who relived the trials of the "heroic age of farming." Of course, the pioneer pushing west from the Hudson faced almost the identical problems of all frontier settlers, whether in New England or Tennessee. For some, frontier life was an adventure, a release from conventional restraints, and an opportunity to direct their own futures. For most, it was an arduous but necessary step toward a happier, or at least a more prosperous future.

Making a farm was a slow process requiring unremitting toil over a long period of years. New York farmers were still clearing fresh land after 1850.[1] The frontier farmer was actually devoting a disproportionate share of his time and energy to creating capital goods such as improved lands, fences, barns, and buildings. Eventually he hoped to secure a greater income, if not for himself, at least for his children. It was this unshakable faith in the future that helped the farmer and his family to endure the "starving time," the fevers, and the rags of the first lean years.[2] Moreover, in his own small way the settler benefited from the rising land values. His was not the opportunity to make huge profits through paper transactions. Nevertheless, he was a speculator at heart. The knowledge that his farm was becoming more valuable gave him considerable satisfaction.

Most pioneer farmers had virtually no financial resources.[3] Yankee immigrants who had supplied almost all their own wants from their rough acres had little chance to acquire specie. By the time the settler had bought a few tools and had paid the cost of

---

[1] In 1830 large areas of eastern New York were still unimproved (Macauley, *op. cit.*, I, 379). Not until 1880 did this state reach its highest total of improved land (*Report of the Commission of Housing and Regional Planning to Governor Alfred E. Smith, May 17, 1926* [Albany, 1926], p. 24).

[2] *American Husbandry*, I, 122; *Doc. Hist. of N.Y.*, III, 1138; Beardsley, *op. cit.*, pp. 19–24.

[3] On June 10, 1795, Colonel Walker wrote to Charles Williamson that "indeed, there is no getting cash for land" (Walker Correspondence). W. Cooper (*op. cit.*, p. 8) notes that farmers did not have the means to clear more than a small spot in the woods.

67

LANDLORDS AND FARMERS

transporting his family to the wilderness clearing, he had exhausted his slender resources. Both the land agents who extended liberal credit and the landlords who offered their lands rent-free for three to seven years realized that the average settler had no money and that he could make payments only after he had cleared some land and raised winter wheat for the market. Barter and payment in wheat and services were devices used to get around the lack of currency.

Foreign visitors often noted the versatility of the American farmer, who was a combination of plowman, carpenter, wheelwright, and butcher.[4] The scarcity of skilled labor combined with the lack of money to hire artisans forced the farmer to do as much of his own work as he could. No less versatile were the womenfolk, who put down meat for the winter and clad each member of the large households in rough homespun.

The frontier usually acted as a leveler. Nevertheless, the various stages of pioneering called for people of different abilities and temperaments. Three rather well-defined groups emerged on every frontier: the hunter, the hunter-farmer, and the farmer. Sometimes all three would be found in the same community. Frequently individuals began as hunters and ended up as substantial farmers.[5]

The hunters and trappers naturally were in the vanguard. Self-reliant and unruly, these rugged individualists had shed almost all the habiliments of civilization. "Both in manners and appearances" the pioneer resembled the savages among whom he mingled. His rifle and nets brought in plenty of game and fish. Next to his rude cabin he sometimes planted a patch of vegetables. Peas and beans supplemented the monotonous diet of corn, which grew up between the girdled trees. The advance of settlement bringing neighbors uncomfortably near, the thinning out of wild life, and the

---

[4] William Cobbett, *A Year's Residence, in the United States of America* (3d ed.; London, 1828), p. 191; *American Husbandry*, I, 123.

[5] Dwight (*op. cit.*, II, 459–469) has an excellent account of pioneering. Orsamus Turner is equally good (see his *History of the Pioneer Settlement of Phelps and Gorham's Purchase, and Morris' Reserve* [Rochester, 1852]).

THE GOOD YEARS

pressure of landowners insisting on written contracts and leases irked the hunters and drove them to seek other homes farther to the west. Elkanah Watson aptly described them as a "useful race of citizens calculated to subdue the wilderness and make way for more civilized settlers rising by gradations." [6]

The farmers, who took over the shadowy claims of the hunters,[7] were more interested in farming than in hunting. Clearings became fields; the forest became wood lots. The settler built a larger cabin and more sheds for the livestock. Barns, roads, and schoolhouses gradually appeared, concrete evidence that community feeling and co-operation were making their first beginnings. A fairly large proportion of this group remained on the farms and became members of the permanent rural population. Others jumped at the chance of selling their improvements and moving to another frontier.

The third group may be described as the solid respectable farmers who possessed the necessary capital, ambition, and industry to transform the rough clearings, log cabins, and open sheds into well-cultivated fields, frame houses, and substantial barns. This task often took a lifetime. These farmers produced more and more wheat, which they sold at the Hudson River landings. Out of this class came the church deacons, the school trustees, and the promoters of roads and canals.

An interesting side light on frontier farming was the experience of capitalists and large landholders. A few capitalists moved to the frontier in order to supervise land sales and to establish large estates. Thus Samuel Law settled in the hill town of Meredith in Delaware County, Judge James Duane supervised the develop-

---

[6] Watson, *History of the Western Canals*, p. 48.

[7] Cooper describes how squatters sold "betterments" to successors (*The Chainbearer*, pp. 103 ff.). John Wigram in 1812 told the widow of Israel Harlen in Magin's Patent that the Banyar estate did not want her improvements and advised her "to sell them to some person who would allow her something for them and pay us the arrearages of rent" (*John Wigram's Proceedings on Goldsbrow Banyar Business, 1812*, G. Banyar Papers).

ment of Duanesburg, near Schenectady, Baron Steuben spent his last years on the frontier in Oneida County, and William Cooper built a fine house at Cooperstown. No matter what resources he might muster, the capitalist found it wise to adopt those methods of pioneering which generations of settlers had learned by experience. Of course, certain gentlemen had to learn the hard way. One attempt to clear the land by block and tackle and the introduction of hounds, tenants, and claret into the wilderness greatly amused William Cooper.[8]

Frequently these gentlemen-pioneers found that squatters had preceded them. Thus Samuel A. Law wrote in 1800:

> A number of possession-men or squatters have got on, and more will be getting on—a very desirable circumstance indeed— I consider them a nuisance. . . . Let them be ever so long without titles and just so long will it be their interest to beat down the price, run down the character and ruin the reputation of the land.[9]

James Fenimore Cooper devotes a large portion of his novel, *The Chainbearer*, to this conflict between landowners and squatters. Sometimes squatters used threats and extralegal means to prevent the landlord from taking away their clearings.[10]

To attract settlers and to clear his lands, the large landholder had to offer substantial rewards. Sometimes he would offer free farms to the first families on the tract. Frequently he would waive rent payment for a few years. This device, realistic as it was in recognizing the fact that few settlers could pay cash, did not always work well. The comments of William North to his friend, Benjamin Walker, show some of the exasperation he felt toward settlers.

---

[8] *Op. cit.*, pp. 39–40. Cooper noted that he was forced to adopt local methods for making fences and using tools, wagons, and implements.

[9] S. A. Law to George Fox, May 9, 1800, cited by Samuel Rezneck, *op. cit.*, p. 382. In a letter to Samuel Meredith and George Clymer, August 30, 1799, Law notes that 200 squatters on the tract "damn the country" (Law Papers).

[10] Harriott, *op. cit.*, II, 114, 127.

THE GOOD YEARS

They may take farms and stipulate so and so, and you and I may think the free years will be a sufficient compensation but they will not, and at the end of the free years, the farm will not be better than it was at first. I would rather tempt them with 50 dollars cash to clear 10 acres, and have thereon 100 apple trees growing at the end of three years than any other way. I should then, at least have the worth of my money in improvements and they would owe me 3 years rent which if they remained and paid in . . . [not decipherable] You may stipulate to make improvements but if they are not tempted with a bait they will not. I know it.[11]

Little is known of the agricultural experience of large landowners who moved to the frontier. The plans of Baron Steuben take on added importance when we remember that he was a frequent visitor at Duanesburg, Clermont, and other estates of the aristocracy. Always impetuous and overly sanguine in his personal life, the Baron embarked with characteristic enthusiasm on his new role as landlord in the wilderness. He drew up an elborate plan for developing his holdings and managing his home estate.[12] Of the 792 acres in the home farm, 616 acres were to be kept in wood. This land would supply his sawmill and also serve as a makeshift pasture. He planned to clear 174 acres and by 1791 60 had been cleared. Fifty acres were set aside for wheat and grass, 50 for meadow, and a like amount for an enclosed pasture. Four acres for garden and orchard, 10 acres for Indian corn, and 10 acres for potatoes, flax, hemp, and peas took up the remaining acreage. The Baron carefully calculated that he could raise 16 bushels of wheat on each acre, which would bring in an income of $675 a year. Steuben's plans reveal most clearly the agricultural pattern of eastern New York. The main emphasis was on all-round agriculture and self-sufficiency. Wheat was virtually the only cash crop. Difficulties in attracting settlers and his early death prevented the Baron from carrying out his original plans.

Picking out his lot, clearing the forest, keeping his family alive, and exchanging his wheat and potash for cash were a few of the

---

[11] May 12, 1799, W. North Papers.
[12] Baron Steuben Papers.

more pressing tasks of the frontier farmer. Shrewdness and good judgment were necessary, as well as industry and courage, if the farmer were to succeed. It was literally a struggle for existence, enlivened only at infrequent intervals by the liquor flowing freely at logging bees and by the sermons of itinerant preachers describing the delights and torments of the life to come.

Migration to the frontier was not an impulsive, unplanned move undertaken on the spur of the moment. Of course, the hunter paid scant attention to agricultural possibilities and land titles, but the more serious settler carefully weighed such factors as climate, location, soil, and future land values.[13] He eagerly scanned advertisements and broadsides. No doubt he accepted the rosy predictions of landholders with healthy skepticism. Frequently he set out on horseback to see for himself. When a lot satisfied him, he usually called on the land agent and reached an agreement before returning home. The able-bodied men often returned to the lot the following winter to prepare the way for the family which usually followed a season or two later.

Partly because the river bottoms had already been settled by Dutch and German farmers, and partly because they had become accustomed to hill farming, the Yankee immigrants headed for the uplands.[14] Hill land was dry. It did not need draining, as was often the case with valley land. The higher land was more free from the dreaded "swamp fevers." In general, it was easier to clear since the level lands were more heavily timbered and were covered with underbrush and fallen trees. The scythe and the sickle were fully as effective on hilly as on level ground. Finally, the rich

---

[13] Michel Guillaume Jean de Crèvecoeur, *Sketches of Eighteenth Century America* (New Haven, 1925), p. 67; Beardsley, *op. cit.*, p. 19; Jones, *op. cit.*, pp. 783–785.

[14] Hasbrouck, *op. cit.*, p. 394. Stillwell (*op. cit.*, pp. 101–102) and Harold Wilson (*The Hill Country of Northern New England* [New York, 1936], pp. 124–131) point out the same tendency in Vermont to settle the hill land first.

THE GOOD YEARS

vegetable mold covered the highlands as well as the bottom land. Pioneers could not foresee that much of the land they were clearing would not be able to compete with more fertile lands under conditions of commercial agriculture. The settler judged the quality of the soil from the forest cover. Hardwoods indicated a good soil.[15] Of course, the rich humus which yielded lavish crops concealed the infertility of the poorer soils.[16] Once the forest-made soil ran out or washed away, hill farmers often encountered hardpan or stony silt loams. The native rock exposures in the Hudson Valley and the broken surfaces of the Catskill region, as well as the presence of less fertile glacial till soils, limited agriculture severely in these regions. On the other hand, the deep accumulation of glacial and glacial lake deposits in the Mohawk Valley furnished a good foundation for grain, hay, and pasturage. The river valleys had a thin ribbon of alluvial soils upon which Dutch and German farmers had settled.[17]

Sweat, skill, and strength were needed to clear the forest. First the pioneer cut away the underbrush and grubbed up the small trees. He gathered up the brush in great piles. Next he chopped down the trees. To fell the trees in such a way that the oxen could easily drag the logs away was both an art and a science in which the skilled axman took great pride. After the sun and wind had dried out the brush piles, the pioneer applied the torch. Fire swept through the clearing, leaving only blackened stumps and charred logs. These stumps were left to decay. Their rotted remains caused many plowmen to curse and amused foreign travelers. Other pioneers, either through necessity or laziness, merely cleared the underbrush and girdled the trees. Among the deadened trees they

---

[15] W. Cooper, op. cit., p. 22.
[16] Spafford (op. cit. [1824 edition], p. 38) noted that settlers often picked poor lands. See also Argus, August 15, 1817.
[17] For information on soils, see Frank B. Howe, Classification and Agricultural Value of New York Soils (Ithaca, 1934).

planted their corn. Falling limbs and trunks made this expedient dangerous.[18]

The cost of clearing the land ran high, often exceeding the original cost of the land. The cost of clearing, however, was the easier to bear. The pioneer could gradually pay for it with his own strong arm. For land he eventually had to pay cash except in a few rare instances. Sometimes logging bees lightened and enlivened the drudgery. Neighbors for miles around brought their oxen and chains. They chopped down trees, dragged away the logs, and burned the brush. Generous portions of rum made the work seem lighter; foot racing and wrestling matches supplied entertainment. In general, it took a skilled woodsman seven to ten days to clear an acre.[19] Undoubtedly a pioneer could clear and sow ten acres the first year, provided he did little else.[20] But he also had to erect a small house, fences, and perhaps a barn, as well as to hunt and fish for himself and his family. In addition, he had to aid his neighbors in cutting through roads, and perform sundry other duties, all of which seriously interfered with the task of clearing. Furthermore, unless he had a market for his produce, there was little point in clearing more land than was necessary to raise foodstuffs for his own use.

Hiring the work done was costly. William Cooper estimated the

---

[18] Information on clearing forests is plentiful. See Beardsley, *op. cit.*, pp. 35 ff.; *Transactions of the New York State Agricultural Society* (1851), pp. 678–685 (hereafter to be referred to as *Trans.*); Orsamus Turner, *Pioneer History of the Holland Purchase of Western New York* (Buffalo, 1849), pp. 562–566.

[19] Beardsley, *op. cit.*, p. 36.

[20] J. F. Cooper, *The Chainbearer*, p. 205. This figure seems rather high but has been accepted by Ulysses P. Hedrick (*A History of Agriculture in the State of New York* [Albany, 1933], pp. 109–110). In 1812 John Wigram noted that George Smith had occupied a lot in Lott and Low Patent and had put three acres under grain and chopped four more acres in one year (*John Wigram's Proceedings on Goldsbrow Banyar Business, 1812*, G. Banyar Papers). O. Turner (*Holland Purchase*, p. 565) has his successful farmer clearing 30 to 40 acres in ten years.

THE GOOD YEARS

cost at $7.50 an acre.[21] Ten dollars an acre seemed to be the minimum in 1830 and again in 1850.[22] Naturally, the cost varied with each locality and the thickness of the forest growth. Fencing the land in addition raised the cost to $25.[23] In 1791 Baron Steuben advertised that he would pay $6.00 an acre in cash plus all the ashes and four bushels of wheat if the trees were cut and the land properly fenced.[24] In 1811 Samuel Law in Delaware County calculated that girdling would cost 50 cents, but that clearing and fencing would amount to $10 an acre.[25] All these estimates, varying from place to place, show quite clearly the heavy cost of clearing, a cost which the farmer had to absorb before his farm could operate at the highest level of productivity.

Fortunately, the felled trees provided not only fuel and logs but also brought in a welcome cash income. The anonymous author of *American Husbandry*, an excellent source for this period, stated that along the Hudson the lumber would almost pay for clearing the land.[26] Those farmers unable to float timber to market could get ready cash for potash and pearlash. Land promoters no doubt exaggerated this income,[27] but early settlers sleighed tons of potash to the Hudson River landings.

Keeping his family from starving was the most pressing task facing the pioneer. Of course, he hunted deer and trapped wild fowl, but sometimes he was unlucky. During the first year or two pioneer settlements often reached the brink of starvation.[28] The

---

[21] *Op. cit.*, p. 32.
[22] John Fowler, *Journal of a Tour in the State of New York in 1830* (London, 1831), p. 79; N.Y. *Assembly Documents*, no. 68 (1850).
[23] W. Cooper, *op. cit.*, p. 32.
[24] Steuben Papers.
[25] Box XIII, Law Papers. See also "Acct. Book, Centre Farm," Box XXIX, Law Papers.
[26] *American Husbandry*, I, 113.
[27] Thomas Cooper, *Some Information Respecting America* (London, 1794), p. 119; W. Cooper, *op. cit.*, p. 32.
[28] W. Cooper describes how he imported grain in 1789 to relieve a threatened famine. The situation in Cooperstown was worsened by the in-

LANDLORDS AND FARMERS

settler hastened to put in corn. It required little preparation, yielded well, and supplied food for both family and livestock.[29] The next crop was wheat, which the farmer frequently began to plant during the first season.[30] After the pioneer had enlarged his clearing into a farm, and especially after he was producing wheat for the market, he became a part of the older rural economy.

Appropriately enough, we have discussed the problems of pioneering first. The period between 1790 and 1807 was, however, more than a period of pioneering for most of eastern New York. Many towns which in 1790 were only clearings had become by 1807 well-established communities boasting a schoolhouse, church, tavern, and perhaps the county courthouse. We now propose to describe the growth of commercial agriculture, stressing the influence of the market and the development of the transportation network. Subsequently we shall examine in some detail the husbandry of eastern New York.

Economic conditions in the United States were definitely on the upturn by 1787. New York participated fully in this recovery. Land values soared, wheat prices rose, England and Europe demanded more wheat and meat, and the tide of Yankee migration to New York rose to new levels. The more land that was cleared, the more wheat reached the wharves at Albany. New York faced the future with great expectations.

The agriculture of eastern New York was quite similar to that of New England, New Jersey, and Pennsylvania. The use of fertilizers and the rotation of crops, so essential to sound husbandry, were practically unknown. Self-sufficiency, extensive cultivation, and primitive methods were the prevailing features. In one particular the agriculture of eastern New York was unique. Tenancy

---

rush of settlers who ate up the scanty surplus (*ibid.,* p. 8; Munsell, *Annals of Albany,* II, 209; *American Husbandry,* I, 123).

[29] *Doc. Hist. of N.Y.,* III, 1148; James Stuart, *Three Years in North America* (Edinburgh, 1833), I, 260.

[30] *Trans.* (1851), p. 685; Strickland, *op. cit.,* p. 38.

THE GOOD YEARS

was deeply entrenched in the Hudson Valley counties. In two other respects eastern New York differed slightly from most sections of northeastern United States. The shift to commercial agriculture came at an earlier date. No section except southeastern Pennsylvania devoted more energy to the raising of wheat.

Wasteful and primitive as the husbandry of New England was at this time, that of New York lagged still further behind.[81] The system of tenancy was incompatible with good husbandry. The tenant's farm was invariably the worst cultivated. In fact, landlords took it for granted that land tilled by tenants would be quickly exhausted.[82] In a period when almost all farmers were mining the soil by constant cropping, observers singled out tenants as particularly guilty. The complaint of William North echoed the sentiments of most landlords.

> Steuben . . . is like all farms which are leased for a short period—leased, is at best but bad property, but for years, it is nothing but a plague. A part of the farm on which I live is leased to a fellow whose time expires next February a year. This fall he puts in a crop of wheat on *every foot* of the land, and next fall he will the whole with rye! I made no reservations and he takes the advantage.[83]

Between 1790 and 1807 our foreign trade made startling gains. One historian has written that in no other period in our history has foreign trade "so completely absorbed the attention of a large portion of the people." [84] The warring nations of Europe demanded more and more food. In response, American farmers put more land into wheat; American skippers made our country the greatest neutral carrier. In 1791 the value of our exports totaled

---

[81] Jedidiah Morse, *op. cit.*, I, 489; Dwight, *op. cit.*, IV, 11; Harriott, *op. cit.*, II, 59.

[82] Thomas Strong to Benjamin Strong, Nov. 25, 1805, *Papers of the Lloyd Family of the Manor of Queens Village, Lloyd's Neck, Long Island, New York, 1654–1826*, in *Collections of the New York Historical Society* (New York, 1926–1927), II, 360.

[83] Letter to Benjamin Walker, Dec. 3, 1801, W. North Papers.

[84] Emory Johnson *et al.*, *History of the Domestic and Foreign Commerce of the United States* (Washington, 1915), II, 14.

LANDLORDS AND FARMERS

$19,012,141. Ten years later it had reached $94,115,925, only to slump during the next two years when Napoleon arranged a temporary peace. By 1807 it had soared to $108,343,150. In the latter year over half of the total represented exports of foreign goods. Purely domestic exports, however, rose substantially by 1807.[35]

The merchants of New York made that city the entrepôt for much of the re-export trade. Exports from the state rose from $2,505,465 in 1791 to $19,851,136 in 1801. The next peak came in 1807 when exports reached the $26,357,963 mark.[36] Of course, transshipments accounted for a large share of this tenfold increase. To handle this trade boom more teamsters, clerks, and merchants were needed. The growing urban population in turn furnished a market for the farmers in eastern New York, New Jersey, and Long Island.

During the Napoleonic Wars the United States was England's breadbasket as in 1940 it became her arsenal. New York, Pennsylvania, and Virginia were the great wheat-producing states. In Virginia wheat rapidly replaced tobacco on many plantations. Statistics do not show New York's wheat production or exports. That they were considerable was often confirmed by contemporary observers.[37] So great was the demand for wheat that "runners" traveled from New York City to Albany where they outbid the local merchants.[38]

The figures cited above, important as they are in revealing the main trends of the national economic life, are doubly significant in explaining the rural economy of eastern New York. Nowhere,

---

[35] Trade statistics are taken from Timothy Pitkin's *A Statistical View of the Commerce of the United States of America* . . . (2d ed.; New York, 1817), p. 36.

[36] *Ibid.*, pp. 51–52.

[37] Morse, *op. cit.*, I, 491; Dwight, *op. cit.*, III, 466–467; Strickland, *op. cit.*, p. 42; François Alexandre Frédéric de la Rochefoucauld-Liancourt, *Voyage Dans Les Etats-Unis D'Amerique, Fait en 1795, 1796, et 1797* (Paris, 1799), II, 290.

[38] Munsell, *Annals of Albany*, III, 155.

THE GOOD YEARS

except perhaps in southeastern Pennsylvania, did such a large number of farmers enjoy comparable transportation facilities. The farmers of eastern New York lay in the hinterland of the port of New York. The Hudson, fed by its network of turnpikes, offered unrivaled facilities for getting goods to the wharves of New York. Potash, wheat, flour, corn, lumber, and salted provisions descended the Hudson in vast quantities. The hundreds of heavily laden sloops and the occasional trim schooner beginning the long voyage to the West Indies, the Mediterranean ports, and even the Orient were the visible signs of dependence upon the outside world. For better or for worse, most eastern New York farmers were gradually entering the phase of commercial agriculture.

The growth of towns along the Hudson is perhaps our most accurate index of the trend toward commercial agriculture, as well as of the development of upstate New York. Before the Revolution only Albany and perhaps Schenectady can rightfully be dignified as commercial centers. After the Revolution new towns such as Hudson, Troy, and Lansingsburg and older settlements such as Albany and Catskill enjoyed a mushroom growth. At the foot of "every considerable road" there grew up a cluster of houses and stores. The inhabitants aped the customs of the cities and exuded a "bold spirit of commercial adventure." [39] Enterprising Yankees by the thousands found working behind the store counter as fascinating and as profitable as frontier farming.

New York was the foremost city on the Hudson. Its population grew from 33,131 in 1790 to 96,373 in 1810. To only a minor degree, however, can we attribute this amazing growth to the development of eastern New York. The metropolis not only served adjacent areas of New Jersey and Connecticut, but also became the great transshipment port of the nation. On the other hand cities such as Albany, Kingston, Troy, Poughkeepsie, Newburgh, and Catskill owed their rapid growth almost exclusively to upstate development. Hudson owed a good deal to the whaling industry. Each

---
[39] Dwight, *op. cit.*, IV, 12–13.

LANDLORDS AND FARMERS

river market built up a hinterland, the size of which was fairly definitely circumscribed by the crucial factor of transportation. Ten to twenty miles was the limit beyond which it did not pay to transport goods overland.[40] Cheese, butter, potash, and maple sugar could be carried farther. They were valuable in relation to their weight. Livestock, of course, transported itself to market.

After 1800 the river towns vigorously promoted turnpikes in order to tap the isolated rural areas into which the pioneers had penetrated. The flow of wheat to the wharves grew ever larger. Along the Mohawk several towns served as marshaling points for the produce which later reached Albany. Schenectady grew rather slowly. It did become the transshipment point for the produce coming down the Mohawk.[41] After 1800 Utica grew with great rapidity. By 1804 a careful observer estimated that its trade was exceeded only by New York, Albany, and Troy.[42] The flourishing settlements of central and western New York bought many supplies through Utica merchants and sent their goods to that city in exchange.

Albany had monopolized the import and export trade of upstate New York during the colonial period. Her ships carried furs, flaxseed, lumber, livestock, and salted provisions down the Hudson to New York and brought back rum, sugar, cloth, furniture, gunpowder, linen, and merchandise of all kinds. After the Revolution the grain trade completely overshadowed the fur trade.[43] The inrush of thousands of immigrants into the mountain towns behind the Helderbergs and into the upland regions both south and north of the Mohawk River created a large new hinterland for the

---

[40] Bidwell, *Rural Economy*, p. 317.

[41] A traveler noted in 1792 that the Indian trade had almost vanished and that Schenectady served as forwarding point for Albany (*Doc. Hist. of N.Y.*, II, 1105).

[42] Dwight, *op. cit.*, IV, 131.

[43] Spaulding, *op. cit.*, p. 9. As late as 1796 a newspaper reported the arrival of twenty to thirty wagonloads of furs. One shipment totaled $40,000 (Munsell, *Annals of Albany*, III, 178).

THE GOOD YEARS

city. Yankee merchants infused new spirit into Albany. Between 1790 and 1810 the city's population tripled. To its storehouses the farmers brought more and more wheat on their sleighs and carts. When the ice broke up in the spring, fleets of sloops departed laden with foodstuffs of all kind. In 1795 Duke de la Rochefoucauld-Liancourt heard that ninety vessels, half of them locally owned, served the city.[44] Albany butchers slaughtered hundreds of cattle and sheep which were driven from the interior counties.[45]

Six miles to the north of the capital New England adventurers laid out the new town of Troy in 1787. The citizens of this town soon acquired a reputation for bold enterprise and civic pride. They elbowed Lansingsburg, their nearest rival, from its claims to the county seat and grabbed the major part of the lucrative trade with the upper Hudson and Vermont.[46] For the next sixty years the Trojans, as they were called, made repeated attempts to supplant Albany as the major entrepôt for the western trade. What the merchants lacked in capital, they made up in boldness and industry. They built storehouses close to the river so that wheat hoisted into the lofts by tackle might be conveyed by spout to the sloops below. In 1798 nearly three thousand cattle were butchered during the early part of the season.[47] In two short decades the family farm of the Van Der Heydens, a notable Dutch family in colonial New York, had become a bustling city of three thousand persons.[48]

---

[44] *Voyage*, II, 290.

[45] Captain John Maude in 1800 noted in South Albany the largest slaughterhouse he had ever seen. Twelve butchers were at work (*op. cit.*, pp. 21–22).

[46] Elkanah Watson, *Men and Times of the Revolution; or, Memoirs of Elkanah Watson . . . 1777–1842* (New York, 1856), p. 276; John Woodworth, *Reminiscences of Troy from Its Settlement in 1790 to 1807* (2d ed.; Albany, 1860), pp. 21, 36.

[47] A. J. Weise, *Troy's One Hundred Years, 1789–1889* (Troy, 1891), pp. 8–11.

[48] Spafford (*op. cit.*, p. 314) estimated that in 1806 Troy had almost 3,000 inhabitants.

LANDLORDS AND FARMERS

Other cities along the Hudson grew at the same pace. In 1783 Nantucket whalers banded together in an association to found Hudson. The city became a port of entry and its ships sailed directly to foreign countries.[49] Its energetic citizens built turnpikes eastward over which the agricultural products of western Massachusetts and Connecticut passed to market. Across the river Catskill showed a similar growth. In 1792 it had only ten dwellings and one sloop of sixty tons. In 1800 it boasted 156 houses, two ships, a schooner, and eight sloops. Between the same dates the amount of wheat brought to the Catskill market rose from 624 to 46,164 bushels.[50]

About 1800 the nation-wide clamor for roads and canals became overwhelming. Frontier counties in New York demanded an outlet to the Hudson. Merchants in each river port hoped to attract the freight and passenger traffic from the growing west. The inspection tours of George Washington to Lake George and to the headwaters of the Mohawk and Susquehanna rivers in 1784 were typical of the intensified interest in opening up the "new empire" of the west.[51]

The Mohawk Valley was to become after the Revolution an important gateway to the interior. Unfortunately, the great falls at Cohoes completely sealed the mouth of the river, forcing both merchandise and produce to be transported across the sandy plain lying between Schenectady and Albany. At Little Falls rapids and cascades formed another barrier to navigation. In 1756 the Germans living in the neighborhood pulled the boats on sleds for one mile over the marsh land. By 1790 they were using wheeled

---

[49] Dwight (*op. cit.*, IV, 135) lists customs duties received between 1801 and 1810.

[50] *Hampshire Gazette*, April 1, 1801, cited by John Bach McMaster, *History of the People of the United States from the Revolution to the Civil War* (New York, 1883–1913), II, 572.

[51] See letter of George Washington to Marquis Chastellux in *The Writings of George Washington*, ed. by John Fitzpatrick (Washington, 1931–), XXVII, 189.

THE GOOD YEARS

vehicles.[52] This portage, the shifting sandbars, and several dangerous rapids, coupled with the low water in the upper Mohawk and Wood Creek, severely restricted the size of the boats and made navigation on the river hazardous, uncertain, and costly.

During colonial days officials had urged improvements of the Mohawk waterway. After the Revolution such ardent advocates of canals as Elkanah Watson revived public interest. In 1792 the legislature responded favorably to Governor George Clinton's recommendations and incorporated the Western Inland Lock Navigation Company and the Northern Inland Lock Navigation Company. The former was to open navigation to Lake Ontario and Seneca Lake; the latter was to build a waterway to Lake Champlain.[53]

The Northern Company, after wasting about $100,000, was dissolved. The Western Company was more successful, although lack of experience and mismanagement resulted in the expenditure of an excessive amount of money.[54] The company built a canal nearly one mile long at Little Falls. It also cleared the upper Mohawk and Wood Creek of fallen timber and minor obstructions. The canal permitted boats of 10 to 11 tons to pass, whereas formerly the largest boats had displaced a mere 1½ tons. After 1797 shippers turned to the Durham boat which had proved so useful on the Delaware River. These broad scows, often 60 feet in length, were pushed upstream by long poles while the captain steered with a long sweep-oar.[55] The number of boats on the Mohawk rose steadily. Nevertheless, the waterway did not guar-

---

[52] Archer B. Hulbert, *The Great American Canals* (Cleveland, 1904), II, 18–19.

[53] Caroline MacGill et al., *History of Transportation in the United States before 1860* (Washington, 1917), pp. 170–180.

[54] *Ibid.*, p. 174.

[55] Mary Diefendorf, *The Historic Mohawk* (New York, 1910), p. 307. For a good description of the Durham boat, see Wheaton J. Lane, *From Indian Trail to Iron Horse, Travel and Transportation in New Jersey, 1620–1860* (Princeton, 1939), pp. 68–69.

LANDLORDS AND FARMERS

antee the cheap and safe carriage required by the farmers. Delays, accidents, heavy tolls, and low water so complicated river transportation that many immigrants and merchants preferred to go by land.[56]

The farmers in the Mohawk Valley had always transported the bulk of their produce by land. During the winter hundreds of sleighs carried wheat, potash, and other products to storehouses at Albany. During the summer oxen and horses pulled heavily laden wagons over the "infamous" and "disgraceful" roads. According to Christian Schultz in 1807, the farmers

> still continue to transport their produce by land in preference to water, as each has his team, which will carry one hundred bushels. They generally go to town once or twice a year, to dispose of their crops, see their friends, and look for great bargains at auction; and when ready to return, can take back a load as cheap as the boatman who passes the locks. Besides they have not only saved in this respect, but also a charge of one or two shillings a bushel on all they bring.[57]

"The present road system is disgraceful to this fine state, and calls loudly for a radical change." So Elkanah Watson noted in 1791.[58] The roads were little more than traces through the forests, with stumps and roots still remaining. Corduroy causeways and primitive bridges across low places and streams were dangerous for horse and wagon. Heavy spring rains turned the deeply rutted earth into an impassable quagmire. Unfortunately, the towns upon which the entire burden of road building rested prior to 1789, had neither the financial resources nor the experienced overseers necessary to construct adequate roads.[59] Frontier commu-

---

[56] We find Charles Williamson advising prospective settlers to come by land and not by river (*Doc. Hist. of N.Y.*, II, 1155). In 1804 Dwight noted that merchants preferred wagons (*op. cit.*, IV, 124). Watson estimated that the cost of transport per ton from Schenectady to Seneca Falls had fallen from a minimum of $75 to $32 (*History of the Western Canals*, pp. 98–99).

[57] Quoted in Munsell, *Annals of Albany*, V, 249.

[58] *History of the Western Canals*, p. 26.

[59] See Historical Records Survey, *Records of the Road Commissioners of Ulster County, 1722–1795* (Albany, 1940). The Introduction has a good summary of colonial practice in regard to roads.

THE GOOD YEARS

nities also lacked population. Older communities could not or would not keep roads in repair, especially when through traffic was heavy. In 1792 a committee of the state legislature stated that the Albany to Schenectady portage represented a "very heavy charge on the produce of the upper country." [60] This statement was true for the entire road system.

To meet the pressing need for better roads, the legislature made liberal grants of money raised by lotteries and other means. But the frontiersmen, the large landowners, and the ambitious river towns were still not satisfied.[61] They looked around for something better than the inland navigation companies and state grants. The success of the Philadelphia and Lancaster Turnpike aroused intense interest. Soon the "spirit of turnpiking" spread throughout the state.[62] Petitions flooded the legislature. So great was the enthusiasm that by 1807 eighty-eight turnpike and bridge companies, with an authorized capital of $5,556,750, had received charters. Benjamin De Witt in 1807 estimated that nine hundred miles of turnpikes had already been constructed.[63]

A glance at the accompanying map shows that the Hudson River was the terminus for all turnpikes completed before 1807. In 1797 the legislature chartered the first turnpike company, the

---

[60] *Doc. Hist. of N.Y.*, III, 1098–1099.

[61] Benjamin De Witt, "Sketch of the Turnpike Roads in the State of New York," *Transactions of the Society for the Promotion of Useful Arts in the State of New York*, II (1807), 192. (This periodical and its predecessor, *Transactions of the Society for the Promotion of Agriculture, Arts, and Manufactures*, will hereafter be referred to as *Trans. for Promotion of Arts*.)

[62] *Ibid.;* Joseph Austin Durrenberger, *Turnpikes; A Study of the Toll Road Movement in the Middle Atlantic States and Maryland* (Valdosta, Georgia, 1931), p. 47. A letter in the *Albany Register,* June 13, 1796, endorsed turnpikes. "Republican" in the *Albany Register,* March 9, 1802, ably defended turnpikes against the charge that they were hostile to republican institutions and the pawns of speculators. "Civis" replied in the *Register* of March 23, 1802, that competition by companies for labor had been so great that it had injured the "agricultural interest."

[63] De Witt, *op. cit.,* p. 198.

LANDLORDS AND FARMERS

Turnpikes of Eastern New York.

THE GOOD YEARS

Albany and Schenectady Turnpike Company, which completed a hard-surfaced road by 1805. From Schenectady the Mohawk Turnpike and Bridge Company constructed a toll road to Utica, from which place the Seneca Road Company struck westward to Canandaigua. The Mohawk route soon had a strong competitor in the Cherry Valley system of turnpikes, which in 1807 had reached Sherburne. Several turnpikes from Massachusetts permitted travelers to approach Albany from the east, thus creating a through road from Lebanon Springs to Canandaigua.

Rivaling the Mohawk and Cherry Valley turnpikes in importance were those pushing westward from Newburgh and Catskill. Both the Newburgh and Cochecton Turnpike and the Susquehanna Turnpike, the latter terminating in Wattles Ferry, had western extensions which permitted immigrants to reach Ithaca and Bath. Kingston made desperate attempts to secure a route to the west but was unable to finance the road through the mountainous and sparsely settled Hardenburgh Patent.[64] On the eastern bank of the Hudson the advancing prongs of the turnpike network of New England met roads leading eastward from Albany, Hudson, and Poughkeepsie. In less than a decade the private toll companies had provided New York with several trunk routes connecting the Hudson cities not only with the eastern states but also with the flourishing settlements of the West.

Most stockholders in turnpike companies were farmers, land speculators, merchants, and individuals interested in trade. City governments such as those of Kingston and Albany helped finance certain companies. Albany owned one hundred shares of the First Great Western Turnpike Road Company and thus became the largest stockholder.[65] Judge William Cooper built six miles of the Second Great Western Turnpike and received payment in stock.[66] Few stockholders made money from turnpike stock. Farmers,

---

[64] Schoonmaker, *op. cit.*, pp. 405–407.
[65] Durrenberger, *op. cit.*, p. 102 n.
[66] J. F. Cooper, *Legends and Traditions*, p. 115.

however, did benefit from the reduced cost of transportation. Actually, tolls remained high.[67] For each 10 miles the average toll was 8 cents for each score of sheep and hogs, but 20 cents for each score of horses, cattle, or mules. A horse and rider paid 5 cents; a wagon with two horses or oxen paid 12½ cents. Unfortunately, many companies failed to keep their roads in repair. As a penalty the county superintendents ordered the gates to be thrown open.[68]

During the eighties the currency used within the state was "confused, depreciated in value, and scarce." [69] The rural element tried to force the legislature to issue paper money. The Federalists vigorously opposed cheap money as destructive to the creditor and trading interests. It likewise endangered rents paid in cash. Stephen Van Rensselaer and other landlords favored payment in wheat not only because their tenants had little money but also because such payments avoided the danger of depreciated currency. After 1790 the danger had passed. James Duane, George Clarke, Jr., and Baron Steuben leased their farms after that date for an annual cash rent. The adoption of the Constitution reassured landowners that they had little to fear from inflation.

Scarcity of currency forced farmers to resort to barter. Landowners accepted cattle or wheat in lieu of cash.[70] Merchants exchanged merchandise for grain, butter, ashes, furs, and other products.[71] Pioneers exchanged labor in logging bees. Citizens paid road taxes by their own labor. The schoolmaster was "boarded round." The preacher was paid by "donation parties." Millers reserved a certain proportion of the grind. In short, barter

---

[67] For tolls charged on Mohawk Turnpike, see MacGill, *op. cit.*, p. 69. For tolls on Catskill Turnpike, see Halsey, *op. cit.*, p. 383.

[68] In 1810 De Witt Clinton found two gates on Mohawk Turnpike opened for this reason (William W. Campbell, *The Life and Writings of De Witt Clinton* [New York, 1849], p. 197).

[69] Spaulding, *op. cit.*, p. 139.

[70] Horatio Seymour's address in *Trans.*, XII (1852), 217.

[71] Dwight, *op. cit.*, IV, 14.

THE GOOD YEARS

often took the place of money. Certain millers, corporations, and towns issued their own paper scrip which earned the name of shinplaster.[72]

Credit was equally scarce and limited. Merchants, who handled the bulk of farm products, furnished short-term credit to their customers.[73] Farmers brought in their wheat to be balanced against the wet goods and other merchandise purchased for the farm family. The local merchant bought on credit from the large houses in New York. Once or twice a year he visited the city to secure supplies. Country stores often boasted a wide variety of merchandise, with dry goods and liquors in particular abundance.[74]

Already a number of specialized middlemen had arisen. At Troy, Albany, Catskill, and other centers there were merchants handling large amounts of wheat, potash, and salted provisions. James Kent observed in 1791 that Kane's store at Whitestown was mainly interested in supplying the petty traders in the Genesee country.[75] New York merchants were sending agents to Columbia County by 1797 to purchase salt meat, wheat, Indian corn, cider, butter, potash, flaxseed, and other produce.[76] Sometimes skeptical farmers, hoping for a better price, took their produce to Kinderhook, where it was either sold or sent on the farmer's own account to New York. Henry L. Livingston complained to Gilbert Livingston in July, 1794, that he was dissatisfied with the latter's handling of his produce at his store at Poughkeepsie.[77] He charged that

---

[72] Woodworth, *op. cit.*, p. 75 n.

[73] Jones, *op. cit.*, p. 735; Dwight, *op. cit.*, IV, 14. See "Old Fort Schuyler," Peter Smith Papers, in Gerrit Smith Collection, Syracuse University Library.

[74] *Ibid.*; advertisement by Robert McClellan of Albany in 1790, cited by Munsell, *Annals of Albany*, I, 322; "Store inventory of Oneida Company at Rotterdam on Oneida Lake, Oct., 1797" (Scriba Papers, vol. XXIII, New York State Library).

[75] John T. Horton, "The Mohawk Valley in 1791," *New York History* (April, 1941), XXXIX, 211.

[76] La Rochefoucault Liancourt, *Travels*, II, 426–427.

[77] Letter in Gilbert Livingston Correspondence, 1794.

LANDLORDS AND FARMERS

Gilbert Livingston failed to give him the market price. Henry Livingston estimated that in 1794 he would have 3,000 bushels of wheat, 1,000 bushels of corn, 500 barrels of beef and pork, and considerable amounts of rye, oats, and butter.

The extension of credit by country storekeepers necessarily involved a large amount of bookkeeping and usually forced the farmer to pay higher prices. On the other hand, competition between merchants tended to keep the price level within reasonable bounds. Some merchants attracted trade by offering cash. Others sold merchandise at low prices. In 1807 Christian Schultz was surprised to find that he could buy goods almost as cheaply in Utica as he could in New York City.[78]

The growth of our export trade, creating a demand for the foodstuffs of eastern New York, and the spread of the turnpike network, permitting the interior towns to market their products at the Hudson River wharves, had done much by 1807 to promote and develop commercial agriculture. We must hasten to add that the farmer still supplied most of his own needs. Nevertheless, he was becoming more dependent on imported merchandise and more sensitive to the fluctuations of world prices.

The agriculture of eastern New York was basically predatory. Naturally, the farmer exploited the only factors of which he had an abundance—timber and soil. That he was in effect exporting the future fertility of his farm did not trouble him. Were there not millions of fresh cheap acres beyond the horizon? His need for cash was too urgent to be delayed. Furthermore, labor shortages and the lack of capital prevented him from adopting many methods of efficient husbandry. The anonymous author of *American Husbandry* succinctly observed: "The rural management in most parts of this province is miserable; seduced by the fertility of the soil on first settling, the farmers think only of exhausting it

---

[78] Munsell, *Annals of Albany*, V, 250.

THE GOOD YEARS

as soon as possible, without attending to their own interest in a future day." [79]

Wheat and potash were the main cash crops. The farmer planted six to eight crops of maize, wheat, barley, rye, or oats in succession.[80] Even in areas under cultivation for decades, the practice of cropping, once justified by frontier necessity, was now solidified by habit and buttressed by ignorance. The average farmer did not try to prevent exhaustion by adding manures and fertilizers or by introducing root and leguminous crops. When no more crops would grow, he turned to fresh lands. He left the old fields fallow for several years. The rank growth of "rubbish," weeds, and briars that sprang up was unfit for cattle. After a few years of rest, the land would be planted to grain crops as long as it would yield.

William Strickland, the eminent English agricultural leader, noted at the turn of the century that the usual course was as follows: [81] Maize was succeeded by rye or wheat in the second year. Immediately buckwheat was planted to stand for seed. In the third year flax or oats or a mixed crop was grown. This course would be repeated until the land would yield no more, whereupon it became an old field without being seeded. Another system which he observed called for wheat, rye, and thereafter corn four or five years. In another instance wheat was planted four or five years, followed by corn for one or two years. The field was then laid aside as fallow for four or five years. A Dutchman on the Mohawk planted successive crops of wheat, peas, wheat, oats or flax, and corn.

That such practices could lead only to exhaustion was soon evident. In 1774 Governor Tryon reported that in the extreme southern parts of the colony the soil had been badly exhausted since it had been "longer under Culture and subject to bad Hus-

---
[79] I, 126–127.
[80] *Ibid.*, p. 107.
[81] *Op. cit.*, p. 38.

LANDLORDS AND FARMERS

bandry." [82] In 1792 Dr. Samuel Latham Mitchell, the eminent scientist who held the chair of natural history, chemistry, and agriculture at Columbia College, warned the Society for the Promotion of Agriculture, Arts, and Manufactures that in many places the land had been so depleted that it would not yield crops.[83] President Samuel Bard of the Dutchess County Agricultural Society pointed out in 1806 the "impoverished state of our farms." [84] Travelers likewise called attention to the poor methods of husbandry which resulted in worn-out fields.[85]

Despite the prevailing practice of cropping, a few attempts were made to improve cultivation. Aristocratic landowners such as John Jay, Robert R. Livingston, and Ezra L'Hommedieu, like their counterparts George Washington and Thomas Jefferson in Virginia, wished to imitate the highly successful reforms in agriculture which leaders had inaugurated in England. Still more influential, however, was the New York market. The farmers in its vicinity found it profitable to use large amounts of manures. In 1795 Ezra L'Hommedieu, vice-president of the state agricultural society, noticed "great emulation" among the farmers of Long Island to secure street refuse, dung, whitefish, ashes, and other fertilizers for their fields.[86] As a result, wheat yields by 1804 had risen from 10 to 40 bushels an acre and land values had increased proportionally.[87]

A most important development was the sowing of fields with some kind of grass seed when they were to be used as pasture. The introduction of artificial grasses had two beneficial results. First, grasses furnished a good pasture for livestock, thus increasing the supply of animal manure on the farm. Secondly, the legumes

---

[82] *Doc. Hist. of N.Y.*, I, 739.

[83] *Trans. for Promotion of Arts*, I (1792), pt. 1, 10–20.

[84] *Poughkeepsie Political Barometer*, April 1, 1806, quoted by Martha C. Bayne, *County at Large* (Poughkeepsie, 1937), p. 54.

[85] Dwight, *op. cit.*, IV, 14; La Rochefoucault Liancourt, *Travels*, II, 425.

[86] *Trans. for Promotion of Arts*, I (1798), pt. 3, 25–33.

[87] Dwight, *op. cit.*, III, 303–304.

THE GOOD YEARS

helped to store up nitrogen in the soil. In 1793 Chancellor Robert R. Livingston, president of the New York Society for the Promotion of Agriculture, Arts, and Manufactures, strongly urged its members to sow grass seed, and particularly clover, and to put in "wheat on a clover clay instead of an expensive fallow." [88] The farmers were slow to change their traditional methods. In 1794 William Strickland observed that clover was just beginning to be cultivated.[89] Within twenty years the marvelous effects of clover on worn-out fields had convinced all but the most skeptical farmers.[90]

Farmers invariably neglected manures except in the vicinity of New York City. German farmers in Herkimer County dragged the barnyard manure on the ice so that the spring floods would carry it away.[91] Farmers permitted their cattle to roam during most of the year. This practice cut down the available supply of manure. Some farmers, however, found wood ashes valuable.[92]

But the greatest single factor improving husbandry before 1807 was the introduction of gypsum. Gypsum is by no means a complete fertilizer, but it does supply the essential elements of calcium and sulphur. In addition, it indirectly increases the nitrogen content of the soil because it is commonly used with clover and leguminous crops. Most land in eastern New York does not contain sufficient lime except along the rivers and in the limestone region of central New York.[93] The counties along the lower and middle

---

[88] *Trans. for Promotion of Arts*, I (1798), pt. 2, 63.

[89] *Op. cit.*, p. 39.

[90] "American Agriculture," an article by Chancellor Robert Livingston in the *Edinburgh Encyclopaedia* (1st Amer. ed.; ed. by David Brewster; Philadelphia, 1832), I, 335. People came for miles to see fields of clover (Ralph Le Fevre, *History of New Paltz, New York, and Its Old Families* [2d ed.; Albany, 1909], p. 194).

[91] *Trans.*, XI (1851), 516.

[92] Strickland, *op. cit.*, p. 39; Dwight, *op. cit.*, III, 303; *Albany Register*, June 28, 1805.

[93] See Lime Requirement Map in New York State Planning Board, *op. cit.*, p. 29.

LANDLORDS AND FARMERS

Hudson and the entire Catskill area are particularly deficient in lime. Frequently gypsum had "wonderful" and almost "miraculous" effects on depleted soils.

Gypsum first came into widespread use in Pennsylvania. In 1770 Judge Richard Peters, Revolutionary patriot and long an outstanding agricultural leader, found that gypsum rejuvenated exhausted soil.[94] Agricultural societies and leaders in other states began to experiment with calcareous materials. The Society for the Promotion of Agriculture, Arts, and Manufactures sent out a circular asking, among other things, what the experience of its members had been in regard to marl, gypsum, and limestone.[95] Chancellor Robert R. Livingston wrote an article summarizing the results of several tests conducted on or near his estate.[96] The Chancellor was so enthusiastic about the tests that he supplied gypsum to several tenants for purposes of experiment. We find in his account book for 1793 the item of 137 pounds, 18 shillings spent for gypsum.[97]

Agricultural leaders such as the Chancellor and John Jay helped to popularize the use of gypsum. Even more persuasive, however, than their writings was the renewed vigor of exhausted land. The proof was convincing. Horatio Spafford wrote in 1813:

> The introduction of gypsum as a manure, has marked a new era in the agricultural and rural economy of this region. By this means, and consequent attention and improvements, the products of the 2d or 3d quality of land have been nearly doubled within the last 10 years; and land of this description has risen in value 20 to 30 and 40 per cent.[98]

The transit of civilization is a problem which has intrigued and baffled historians not only in the sphere of intellectual and political history but also in the field of economic and social develop-

---

[94] Lyman Carrier, *op. cit.*, p. 270.
[95] *Trans. for Promotion of Arts*, I (1801), pt. 1, ix.
[96] *Ibid.*, pp. 25–54.
[97] *Robert R. Livingston's Account Book, Clermont, 1780–1807*, New York Historical Society.
[98] *Op. cit.*, p. 18.

THE GOOD YEARS

ment. It is a problem particularly susceptible to snap judgments and unwarranted inferences. In the field of agrarian life this problem presents several basic questions. What patterns of habit and what congeries of knowledge did the immigrant bring with him? How much of this tradition was jettisoned under the impact of new environmental conditions? Conversely, what irreducible core of the cultural heritage persisted? Finally, what effect did new discoveries and practices in outside communities have on the various racial and class groups in an agrarian society?

It is generally recognized that the Germans in southeastern Pennsylvania introduced and maintained superior methods of husbandry.[99] T. J. Wertenbecker points out, however, that their husbandry was also "profoundly altered" under the influence of cheap land and a scarcity of labor.[100] The frontier was a leveling force shaping and molding most habits and institutions that were exposed to its influence. Nevertheless, it would be a mistake to assume that the frontier had the identical effect on the deeply ingrained habits and customs of various racial groups. The very isolation of the frontier helped to perpetuate distinctive practices. Language barriers, religious prejudices, and widespread ignorance tended to protect racial enclaves from rapid assimilation.

In 1811 Reverend Timothy Dwight observed that there were various kinds of agriculture in New York. "The Dutch farmers extensively follow that of their ancestors. The New-England Colonists, and their descendents pursue that of New-England; German, Scotch, and Irish settlers, vary from both, and from each other." [101]

Again in 1841 the local correspondent of the state agricultural society wrote that in Herkimer County there had been until recent

---

[99] Richard Shryock, "The Pennsylvania Germans in American History," *Pennsylvania Magazine of History*, LXIII (July, 1939), p. 263.
[100] *The Founding of American Civilization, The Middle Colonies* (New York, 1938), p. 279.
[101] *Op. cit.*, III, 528.

years a "marked difference" between Yankee and German methods of farming.[102]

What constituted this difference is not entirely clear. There is no indication that the German and Dutch settlers failed to succumb to the frontier habit of exploiting the soil resources. The German farmers on the upper Mohawk were guilty of a blind disregard for the principles of rotation and the value of manures. As early as 1765 Sir William Johnson reported that the Germans had adopted most of the habits of the other settlers, although they were usually the most industrious farmers.[103] The Dutch farmers of Kinderhook in Columbia County, which Duke de la Rochefoucauld-Liancourt visited in 1799, were likewise guilty of exhausting the soil by continuous grain crops.[104] In short, such factors as abundance of land, scarcity of labor, and the demands of the market operated with similar effect on Dutch and German as well as the Yankee farmers.

Yet differences persisted. One of the most noticeable differences between Yankees and Germans, which was observed both in 1791 and fifty years later, was the German preference for horses instead of oxen.[105] Elkanah Watson denounced the few backsliding Yankees in Herkimer County who had adopted the "lazy and unprofitable custom of using horses." This issue may seem of small consequence to modern readers, but during the period from 1790 to 1850 it aroused considerable controversy. Samuel L. Mitchell in 1791 deplored the trend away from oxen.[106] Ex-President James Madison, in an address to the Albemarle (Virginia) Agricultural Society, strongly urged the use of oxen.[107] The horse was considered a "voracious and expensive animal," whereas the ox was

---

[102] *Trans.*, I (1841), p. 136.
[103] *Doc. Hist. of N.Y.*, IV, 348–349.
[104] *Travels*, II, 425.
[105] Elkanah Watson, *History of the Western Canals*, pp. 27–28; *Trans.*, I (1841), 136.
[106] *Trans. for Promotion of Arts*, I (1792), pt. 1, 23.
[107] Speech quoted in *Plough Boy* (June 26, 1819), p. 23.

THE GOOD YEARS

stronger, could eat coarser foods, and furnished beef and hide when his working days were over.

The farmers at German Flats paid less attention to cattle and sheep than their Yankee neighbors. They concentrated on raising large numbers of horses.[108] Another German custom which shocked Reverend Timothy Dwight was that of women working in the fields.[109] Womenfolk back in New England did not perform field labor.

The size of the barn was perhaps the most striking difference between Yankee and Dutch farmer. To the Dutchman the barn was the only criterion by which his prosperity could be judged.[110] The Dutch farmer spent large sums for his barn, whereas the Yankee laid out his money on a house.[111] The Dutch built large barns "almost equal to a small church." The average barn was 50 by 30 feet. That of Philip Schuyler in Albany County was more than 100 feet long and 60 feet wide.[112] The Swedish traveler Per Kalm has described such barns in the Albany area:

The roof was pretty high, covered with wooden shingles, declining on both sides, but not steep. . . . In the middle was the threshing floor, and above it or in the loft or garret they put the corn which was not yet threshed, the straw, or anything else according to the season; on one side were the stables for the horses, on the other for the cows. . . . On both ends of the building were great doors, so that one could come in with a cart and horses through one of them and go out at the other. Here, therefore, under one roof were the threshing floor, the barn, the stables, the hay loft, the coach house, etc.[113]

The two-horse wagon, capable of carrying a ton of hay, barrels of flour, rails, wheat, and dung, became on Sunday the family coach. The Dutch also contributed harrows, plows, and various

---

[108] *Trans.*, I (1841), 136; La Rochefoucauld-Liancourt, *Voyage*, II, 277.
[109] *Op. cit.*, III, 205–206.
[110] Crèvecoeur, *Sketches*, p. 141.
[111] Campbell, *De Witt Clinton*, p. 166.
[112] Grant, *op. cit.*, pt. 2, 116–117.
[113] *Travels into North America*, tr. by John Forster (2d ed.; London, 1772), I, 111.

other items such as "Dutch cellars" to the agricultural life of the state.[114]

The aristocracy, as well as the Dutch and German farmers, practiced a husbandry slightly different from that followed by the vast majority. If the agricultural practices of the average farmer were almost entirely patterned after those of his parents, those of the landlord aristocracy were being slowly modified by the momentous changes taking place in European agriculture. The findings of Tull, Bakewell, Townshend, and Arthur Young could not long escape the attention of the New York aristocrats who had always had close personal and commercial connections with England. Furthermore, it was definitely good form for members of the closely-knit and self-regarding upper class to take an interest in the new scientific agriculture. This interest was underscored by the realization that only by restoring the lost fertility of their fields could the large landowners take advantage of the opportunities presented by the expanding foreign and metropolitan markets.

The significant contributions made by such individuals as Robert Livingston to the agricultural advance of the state deserve recognition. Actually, the extent of their influence was rather limited. The Society for the Promotion of Agriculture, Arts, and Manufactures, organized in 1791 and reorganized in 1804 as the Society for the Promotion of Useful Arts, had a membership composed almost exclusively of professional men and gentlemen-farmers. No person could become a member unless elected by the majority. In 1807 the society boasted only thirty-eight members, including Robert R. Livingston, Simeon De Witt, surveyor-general of New York, Stephen Van Rensselaer, Samuel L. Mitchell, Elkanah Wat-

---

[114] Crèvecoeur, *Sketches*, pp. 138–145. Henry Coleman, outstanding agricultural writer, noted in 1835 the difference between New England and Rensselaer County. The Dutch used barracks for hay, preferred horses to oxen, built big barns, and employed wagons of different construction. See his account reprinted in the *Genesee Farmer*, V (July 4, 1835), 214.

THE GOOD YEARS

son, Peter Smith, De Witt Clinton, and Morgan Lewis, the last two occupying the governor's chair at one time.[115]

The ties between New York agricultural leaders and their English compeers were fairly intimate. Robert R. Livingston wrote to Arthur Young in 1794 and praised the idea of exchanging information.[116] In 1798 Dr. Samuel Mitchell acknowledged the kindness of Sir John Sinclair in sending to the New York society some of the original county reports which the British society had made.[117] Again in 1800 John Jay thanked Sir John Sinclair for the gift of a case of gypsum.[118] In similar fashion agricultural leaders along the Atlantic seaboard passed along information. For example, Jay was grateful to Judge Peters of Pennsylvania for sending several volumes to him.[119]

The writings and in particular the example of the aristocracy helped spread the principles of sound husbandry. But progress was slow except in the adoption of clover and gypsum by many ordinary farmers. They looked on book farming with suspicion. Some information, however, did reach them through almanacs and newspapers which began to pay more attention to scientific agriculture.[120]

Economic historians are now speculating over the question of whether American agriculture was ever profitable. The question

---

[115] See list of members on page following title page of *Trans. for Promotion of Arts*, II (1807).

[116] *Trans. for Promotion of Arts*, I (1798), pt. 2, 142–148. The correspondence of the Lloyd family in Queens Village, Long Island, reveals the transmission of information from England to New York. For pertinent references, see the *Papers of Lloyd Family*, II, 790–791, 830–831, 836.

[117] *Trans. for Promotion of Arts*, I (1798), pt. 3, p. xxx.

[118] *The Correspondence and Public Letters of John Jay, 1763–1826*, ed. by H. P. Johnston (New York, 1890–1893), IV, 282.

[119] *Ibid.*, p. 342.

[120] Carl R. Woodward (*The Development of Agriculture in New Jersey, 1640–1880, A Monographic Study in Agricultural History* [New Brunswick, 1927], pp. 64–71) has some interesting comments on the early almanacs. In 1805 the *Albany Register* began its agricultural column (June 28, 1805).

LANDLORDS AND FARMERS

is exceedingly complex. Nearness to market,[121] fertility of soil, capital investment, and labor by members of the family vary with each locality and each individual farm. Many farmers have made or hope to make more money from rising land values than from their crops. Did not the farmers of eastern New York raise wheat because it brought in cash rather than because it was economically profitable? To cite the rapid expansion of wheat production as proof that it was profitable is much too simple. For one thing it fails to consider soil depletion. It likewise fails to evaluate family labor. It does not consider whether self-sufficiency absorbed some of the cost of raising wheat.

Two eminent authorities have left us their estimates of farm profits in eastern New York. William Strickland was a close associate of Sir John Sinclair and Arthur Young. In 1793 he estimated that the cost of acquiring one acre of land in New York and bringing it into wheat production totaled one pound and three pence. This land would yield twelve bushels of wheat valued at four shillings and six pence each. The net profit would be approximately one pound, thirteen shillings, and nine pence.[122]

In 1796 Chancellor Livingston drew up an interesting balance sheet of that part of a New York farm which followed the usual methods of cultivation.[123]

		Profits per acre		
		£	s.	d.
1.	20 acres of Indian corn, 35 b. at 4s.	7	0	0
2.	20 acres of oats on corn ground of the preceding year, 20 b. at 2s.	2	0	0
3.	20 acres of summer fallow			

---

[121] Transportation costs definitely limited area of production for market. In 1807 James Wadsworth noted that it was unprofitable to ship flour to Albany from any point west of Utica. See O. Turner, *History of the Pioneer Settlement*, p. 581.

[122] *Op. cit.*, p. 40.

[123] *Trans. for Promotion of Arts*, I (1799), pt. 4, 25–26.

THE GOOD YEARS

		£	s.	d.
4.	20 acres of wheat, 10 b. at 8s.	4	0	0
5.	20 acres of wheat stubble in pasture	0	2	0
	100 acres in five years would yield per acre	13	2	0

EXPENSES PER ACRE FOR FIVE YEARS

		£	s.	d.
1.	Indian corn, plowing, etc.	2	0	0
2.	Oats, twice plowed	1	0	0
3.	Harrowing, seed, sowing, and harvesting		14	0
4.	Summer fallow	1	10	0
5.	Wheat seed and harvesting	1	0	0
6.	Rent on five acres at 4s. a year	1	0	0
		7	4	0

The balance of profit on one acre in five years, or on five acres in one year £5 18s. Profit per acre is £1 3s. 5d. a year.

If we accept these estimates as approximately correct, we can hazard a few conclusions as to the cash income of the average farmer. Rarely did he have more than 10 to 12 acres under tillage unless he lived close to important markets.[124] Chancellor Livingston's figures would give this farmer a cash income of from $30 to $36. Potash, butter, cheese, salted provisions, and maple sugar would bring in more money. Of course, his real income was much greater. He raised almost all of his food, produced almost all of his clothing, and supplied most of his tools as well as fuel.

The frontier farmer needed cash urgently. He had to pay for his farm, stock, utensils such as potash kettles, and various other items. Certainly his cash income was not the princely sum mentioned by James Fenimore Cooper in *The Chainbearer*.[125] Cooper wrote that the pioneer could clear 10 acres the first season and plant it to wheat. The yield of 150 bushels would bring $300 at Albany. In addition, he could collect a ton of potash worth $200.

---

[124] Bidwell, "Rural Economy," p. 321.

[125] Page 205. Cooper is trying to disprove the claims of the antirenters. Thus he exaggerates the income of the pioneers.

LANDLORDS AND FARMERS

Closer examination reveals that the prices of both products were usually much lower. It is also doubtful that a farmer could clear 10 acres in one year and even more doubtful that he could raise 10 acres of wheat in addition to his other labors. Furthermore, Cooper ignores the cost of transporting the produce to Albany. His father's observation as to the "poverty of the people" contradicts Cooper's optimistic estimates.[126] That frontier farmers were desperately in need of cash is sufficient refutation of this rosy picture.

Scarcity of capital as well as of labor forced New York farmers to exploit the land of which there was an abundance. We have already noted that constant cropping led to serious soil depletion. The complaints of foreigners that American farms "look more like wild heaths" than cultivated farms were all too true.[127] Their criticism, however, did not take account of the peculiar conditions of American agriculture. Robert R. Livingston aggressively maintained that American agriculture should not be judged by European standards. He stated that "agriculture is good, or bad, in proportion to the return it makes for the capital employed." [128] Americans would be foolish not to take advantage of their greatest asset, cheap land. The only true test, he asserted, was output per worker and the standard of living. Measured by that standard, our agriculture was at least the equal of that of England, the acknowledged leader in agricultural improvements.

Farmers who today complain that they cannot hire responsible farm labor at "reasonable" wages are echoing the complaints of their forefathers. Labor was hard to get and hard to keep. When landlords were enticing settlers to their tracts by offering free lots to the first families and by granting liberal credit terms, few able-bodied men were content to work for some other farmer.[129]

---

[126] Cooper, *op. cit.*, p. 8.

[127] Harriott, *op. cit.*, II, 59.

[128] *Op. cit.*, p. 333.

[129] La Rochefoucault Liancourt (*Travels*, II, 459) noted that farm laborers at New Paltz were moving west.

THE GOOD YEARS

Furthermore, the egalitarian ideas of the frontier and the Revolutionary period created a popular prejudice against any work in which a status of social inferiority was implied. The observations of St. John de Crèvecoeur illustrate the importance of treating farm help with extreme care:

> As to labour and labourers,—what difference! When we hire any of these people we rather pray and entreat them. You must give them what they ask: three shillings per day in common wages and five or six shillings in harvest. They must be at your table and feed, as you saw it at my house, on the best you have.[130]

Data as to wage levels are fragmentary. In 1797 one observer noted that laborers were receiving from $10 to $15 a month in addition to board.[131] Another farmer experienced great difficulty in securing labor for his estate on Long Island, although he was offering $10 a month besides board and lodging.[132] Advertisements and handbills were of no avail. The few he did hire insisted on being boarded, with the result that his wife was overworked. In disgust, he wrote that the "tax" of servants outweighed all other taxes in England. In 1807 Chancellor Livingston paid $100 a year to John Lasher, a farm laborer.[133]

The Negro slave as farm laborer deserves a special note. In 1790 over eleven thousand Negroes lived in the rural areas of eastern New York.[134] Of course, many of these were personal and household servants. Others worked in the fields. The census lists Negroes for each county, but the largest number lived in the older settled areas where the farmers had more wealth and where the danger of escape was less. There seems to have been a high correlation between Dutch farmers and the number of slaves. Ulster County, almost entirely rural and strongly Dutch in blood,

---

[130] *Sketches*, pp. 82–83.
[131] La Rochefoucault Liancourt, *Travels*, II, 425, 445, 459.
[132] Harriott, *op. cit.*, II, 193–198.
[133] *Robert R. Livingston's Account Book, Clermont, 1780–1807*.
[134] *Heads of Families at the First Census of the United States Taken in the Year 1790, New York* (Washington, 1908).

LANDLORDS AND FARMERS

listed over 10 per cent of its inhabitants as Negro slaves.[135] In the Albany area practically every Dutch farmer purchased one or more slaves if he were financially able.[136] The newspapers carried advertisements of Negroes offered for sale. A boy of twenty years, described as "well-acquainted with farm work" was offered in 1809 for $250.[137] Ownership of slaves was a source of personal gratification and prestige to those individuals wealthy enough to purchase them, but it is doubtful that they proved profitable. Dr. John Beekman, president of the New York Agricultural Society in 1844, concluded that slaves had proved inefficient and unprofitable as farm help. As the saying went, the "hogs ate the corn and the Negroes ate the hogs." [138]

Family labor was of course the mainstay of eastern New York farmers. Most youngsters in the large families had chores assigned to them. The housewife took care of the dairy, the poultry, the kitchen, and the garden. The menfolk tilled the fields, brought in the firewood, and performed the heavy tasks. Family labor supplied almost all the food and clothing that was used.

Let us now consider the various crops raised on a typical farm in eastern New York. The average farm contained 100 to 200 acres.[139] Landlords frequently had their tracts surveyed in 100-acre lots.[140] That seemed to be the optimum size. In one instance

---

[135] La Rochefoucault Liancourt (*Travels,* II, 458) observed in New Paltz that each Huguenot family had one or two Negroes.

[136] La Rochefoucauld-Liancourt, *Voyage,* II, 305; Beardsley, *op. cit.,* p. 20.

[137] *Albany Balance,* Nov. 28, 1809. See also Albany Gazette, Nov. 9, 1798.

[138] *Trans.,* IV (1844), 36. Scharf (*op. cit.,* I, 477) noted that upon emancipation farmers had to adopt more intelligent tillage.

[139] R. R. Livingston, "American Agriculture," p. 333.

[140] Most leases of George Clarke, Jr., are for farms of approximately 100 acres (Clarke Leases). James Cockburn divided the Steuben tract into 160 farms averaging 100 acres each (Palmer, *op. cit.,* p. 347). W. Cooper noted that a poor man wanted about 100 acres (*op. cit.,* p. 8). Morgan Lewis, who became governor, divided his tracts into lots varying from 100 to 150 acres (*Albany Argus,* Sept. 4, 1845).

THE GOOD YEARS

a land agent found that only two lots of 200 acres each had been sold in his tract of 10,000 acres. To meet the demand for smaller farms, he divided each lot in two.[141]

Winter wheat was the main crop. The Van Rensselaer leases, in common with most of the leases calling for payment in wheat, specifically mentioned "good merchantable winter wheat." Yields varied with the freshness and richness of the soil. The good lands near Albany brought forth 20 to 40 bushels an acre.[142] Similar yields were noted on the fresh lands along the upper Hudson and Mohawk valleys.[143] In fact, the newly cleared uplands temporarily gave as high yields as the lowlands since the rich humus overlaid the poorer soils. The ordinary farm averaged 12 to 13 bushels an acre.[144] But constant cropping soon had its effect on the uplands. Soon the frost heaved out the wheat. To avoid winter-killing, many upland farmers turned to spring wheat. Eventually they turned to barley and oats and concentrated their energies on grazing. The ability of the valley land to keep on producing wheat year after year made it exceptionally desirable in the eyes of New York husbandmen.[145]

During the Revolution the Hessian fly had ravaged the fields of Long Island. Gradually the pest spread to the upstate region. By 1811 the fly had become so destructive that John Jay, who had his estate in Westchester County, could write, "To sow wheat here is like taking a ticket in a lottery; more blanks than prizes. The fly destroys more than we reap." [146] Except for the southern part

---

[141] *John Wigram's Proceedings on Goldsbrow Banyar Business, 1812,* G. Banyar Papers.

[142] *American Husbandry,* I, 98.

[143] La Rochefoucauld-Liancourt, *Voyage,* II, 273, 274, 309; Maude, *op. cit.,* p. 34.

[144] R. R. Livingston, "American Agriculture," p. 335; Strickland, *op. cit.,* p. 40. In Dutchess County the average was 16 bushels an acre (*ibid.*).

[145] Spafford (*op. cit.,* p. 293) states that lands in the Schoharie Valley were still producing 20 bushels an acre after eighty years of cultivation.

[146] Letter to Judge Peters, January, 1811, *op. cit.,* IV, 341.

LANDLORDS AND FARMERS

of the state the Hessian fly made only minor inroads on wheat crops in this period.

The reputation of New York wheat and flour declined rapidly in our period. The result was lower prices. Farmers often included smut, rye, and cockle in their wheat.[147] Farmers, smarting under the charge of fraud, accused the millers of grinding too close and of mixing spoiled flour with new.[148] In 1821 the appointment of John Brown as state flour inspector led to the careful branding of all flour barrels.[149] In a short time New York flour again sold at premium prices.

Indian corn or maize was a staple grain extensively grown in eastern New York. Resistant to drought and insect pests, dependable in its yield, and useful as food both for man and beast, maize probably deserved the description of the "most valuable [plant] in the whole circle of American husbandry." [150] It was particularly valuable in fattening cattle, pigs, and poultry. Furthermore, maize required less hard labor and care than most crops. In heavy soils the ground was prepared by harrowing and cross-plowing. At the intersection of the furrows four or five grains were put in with the hoe. In loose soils the field was plowed twice. Hoeing and cross-plowing kept the field clean. Travelers often noted that farmers failed to cultivate their corn and other crops properly.[151]

Before gypsum became widely accepted as a fertilizer barnyard manure was sometimes applied to Indian corn. With the introduction of gypsum the seeds of corn were steeped in water and gypsum sifted over them. Farmers also put gypsum in each hill of corn. Pumpkins grew between the hills of corn. In the fall the hogs and cows ate them. Sowing pumpkins among the corn did

---

[147] *Trans. for Promotion of Arts,* I (1792), pt. 1, 13; Spafford, *op. cit.,* p. 85.
[148] *Orange County Patriot,* Aug. 1, 1815; *Trans. for Promotion of Arts,* III (1814), 178.
[149] Robert Albion, *The Rise of New York Port* (New York, 1939), p. 82.
[150] R. R. Livingston, "American Agriculture," p. 334.
[151] *Doc. Hist. of N.Y.,* III, 1130–1131; Belknap, *op. cit.,* p. 14.

not diminish the yield per acre. It averaged 35 bushels an acre.

Rye was frequently planted on inferior lands.[152] Some farmers planted rye in September and turned in their cattle to fatten the next month. Invariably rye succeeded buckwheat. The latter was highly regarded because it did not diminish soil fertility. Barley was a fairly important crop in the southern part of the state. It enjoyed a ready sale at the breweries and malthouses. Oats were a favorite crop of those farmers who relied on horses. Potatoes were less highly regarded in that day than at present. Nevertheless, most farmers planted half an acre to four acres, sometimes in rows and sometimes in hills.[153] Even before the Revolution the metropolitan market demanded potatoes, but most farmers raised them to feed to their sheep and hogs. Peas were commonly grown in conjunction with wheat on interval land. Its straw proved valuable as winter fodder.

Hemp and flax were likewise grown. Hemp growing was highly profitable on the bottom land and the muck lands of Orange County.[154] It required intensive cultivation and more capital than the average farmer could spare. In 1807 the state legislature authorized the appointment of commissioners for the drainage of the drowned lands in Orange County. These commissioners laid assessments ranging from 6¼ cents to $1.00 an acre and let contracts for drainage. These lands were advertised for sale as "hemp land."[155]

Flax was an important crop during the colonial period. Large amounts of flaxseed and linseed oil passed down the Hudson to foreign ports. After the Revolution the export of flax began to decline.[156] Almost every farmer had a small patch of flax, often

---

[152] *American Husbandry*, I, 99.
[153] R. R. Livingston, "American Agriculture," p. 334.
[154] *Trans. for Promotion of Arts*, II (1807), 122–123. Profits of $20 an acre were reported.
[155] *Orange County Patriot*, Dec. 5, 1809, July 17, 1810, July 16, 1811.
[156] *Annual Report of the Commissioner of Patents*, 1842, p. 21.

less than an acre in extent. The housewife used flax thread to make homespun linen and tow cloth.

Almost every farm had an orchard containing from one hundred to three hundred trees.[157] Pears, peaches, plums, cherries, and quinces were raised, but the apple was by far the most popular fruit. Practically every farm had a press in order to make cider, which was a universal drink. At times, cider passed for legal tender. Farm families drank up amazing amounts of unfermented apple juice and hard cider. Dried apples festooned the rafters and relieved the monotony of the diet in the winter. Some leases compelled the tenant to plant one apple tree for each acre and to keep the orchard in good condition.[158]

The development of New York as a grazing and dairy state had barely begun by 1800. But the New York frontier was like most frontiers in America. It boasted of its cowboys and cattle drovers. The stunted "native cattle" roamed the forest, browsing on the wild grass and the branches of saplings. Periodically, drovers would take them to the slaughterhouses at Troy and Albany. Sometimes agents would tour the countryside and buy the cattle at the farm. The opportunity for swindling was not overlooked by either party. Most frontier farmers had only a few animals. In 1789 William Cooper noted that Otsego County pioneers were so poor that not one in twenty owned a horse.[159] Closely allied with the cattle business was the raising of horses and mules. In Canada and along the upper Hudson farmers raised these animals for sale to Connecticut, the southern states, and the West Indies.[160]

Chancellor Livingston estimated in 1813 that a farm of 130 acres would have eight or nine horses or four horses and four

---

[157] R. R. Livingston, "American Agriculture," p. 333.

[158] George Clarke, Jr., Leases.

[159] *Op. cit.*, p. 8; Beardsley (*op. cit.*, p. 19) recalls that his father and two uncles drove one or two yoke of oxen, three or four horses, and a few cattle, sheep, and hogs.

[160] La Rochefoucauld-Liancourt, *Voyage*, II, 308–309.

THE GOOD YEARS

oxen.[161] In addition, it would have ten cows and six yearlings. The average farmer would have about twenty-five sheep and swine. Wool from the sheep, beef from the cattle, and labor from the horses were primarily for the farmer's own use. Occasionally he would sell surplus animals to neighbors or to the local drovers. The introduction of clover and gypsum made a startling improvement in meadows and pastures. This permitted the farmer to keep more cattle than he could on the old fields.

Butter and cheese enjoyed a ready sale in New York City. Even before the Revolution Orange County had won a reputation for fine butter.[162] This reputation was maintained and increased during the first half of the nineteenth century. Welsh immigrants, who settled on Baron Steuben's lands in Oneida County, brought with them their skill in butter making. Within a few years they were selling large amounts of butter to New York City.[163] Yankee immigrants likewise brought with them some knowledge of butter and cheese making. The future importance of central New York as one of the nation's primary cheese-producing regions had its first faint beginnings in this period. In the town of Norway, Herkimer County, Jared Thayer kept a dairy of twenty cows. He made cheese through the whole season, despite the ridicule of his neighbors.[164] De Witt Clinton in 1810 was lavish in his praise of an Oneida County dairy farmer whose thirty-six cows produced milk for over four hundred cheeses and gave him an income of more than $1,000 a year.[165]

The early colonists brought to New York considerable numbers of sheep, but they were not successful in developing an important

---

[161] "American Agriculture," p. 335.

[162] W. H. Smith, op. cit., p. 219. In 1797 Duke de la Rochefoucault Liancourt (Travels, II, 461) stated that 6,000 casks of butter were shipped annually from Newburgh and New Windsor to New York.

[163] Spafford, op. cit., p. 306.

[164] George A. Smith, The Cheese Industry of the State of New York (Albany, 1913), p. 52.

[165] Campbell, De Witt Clinton, p. 52.

wool-growing industry.[166] Wolves and later dogs raided the small flocks and made sheep raising highly hazardous. The long severe winters and the universal neglect of scientific breeding and selection left their mark. To these natural obstacles must be added the determined attitude of the British wool manufacturers who jealously guarded their monopoly of the imperial market by laying restrictions on the colonial woolens industry. The colonial legislatures stubbornly encouraged the raising of flax, wool, and hemp and their manufacture into clothing and household textiles.[167] Throughout the colonial period household manufactures remained the main source of clothing for the great majority of the people.

In 1790 few could have foretold that in less than fifty years over two million sheep would graze on the upland pastures of eastern New York. In our period most farmers had only a few sorry-looking specimens whose wool was entirely used up to clothe the household. An examination of several inventories of Ulster County covering the years from 1788 to 1792 clearly reveals the extent of household manufacture.[168] In forty-four itemized inventories, spinning wheels appeared twenty-three times, with a total of forty-four wheels; woolen wheels, twenty-one times; small wheels, nine; sheep, twenty; flax, eleven; weaver's loom, sixteen; sheep's wool, hatchels, shoe leather, and linen yarn, three each; wool cards, reels, and quill wheels, four each; flannel cloth, wool combs, shoemaker's tools, woolen cloth, cotton yarn, tow yarn, homespun cloth, one each. William Cooper has well described the importance of domestic manufacturing.

---

[166] Chester W. Wright, *Wool-Growing and the Tariff* (Boston, 1910), pp. 1–5; L. G. Connor, "A Brief History of the Industry in the United States," *Annual Report of the American Historical Association for the Year 1918*, I, 95.

[167] Rollo Tryon, *Household Manufacture in the United States, 1640–1860* (Chicago, 1917), pp. 28–43.

[168] This information is taken from Gustave Anjou, *Ulster County, N.Y., Probate Records*, "Wills," II, cited in *ibid.*, pp. 136–137.

THE GOOD YEARS

Wife and daughter of the farmer spin and weave their own bed clothing, and common wearing apparel. The cloth they make is about three-quarters of a yard wide, and very stout. They comb part of the wool, and manufacture a worsted cloth for petticoats and gowns. They also make a strong durable checkered cloth for aprons. When the fleeces are shorn, about the twentieth of May, the mistress sets apart the best for stockings, and the next best for the clothing of her husband and sons; the rougher wool is made into blankets.[169]

The production in the household of woolen and linen fabrics required the specialized labor of all members of the family. After the farmer sheared the fleece, he tub-washed and scoured it of its dirt and grease. The next process was carding, during which the tangled fibers were brushed and combed either by hand or by a simple crank and cylinder device that pulled the fibers through the combs.[170] After 1800 small carding mills arose in almost every township where there was a convenient stream of water to turn a wooden overshot water wheel.[171] The spinning of the wool was generally done upon the hand spinning wheel, an operation usually performed by the women and older girls in the family. Sometimes farmers hired girl spinners to aid the family.[172]

The next step was the weaving of the thread upon the hand loom into the desired cloth. But because the "undressed" cloth was stiff and uncomfortable to wear, it was commonly fulled to thicken it and to prevent future shrinkage. Copperas and a number of homemade vegetable dyes as well as imported indigo were used to color the cloth. The fulling mill often dyed the cloth. The cloth was cut and sewed by hand into the desired garments. Closely allied to these operations was the art of knitting hosiery, mittens, and comforters for the family.

---

[169] *Op. cit.*, p. 36.

[170] Jared Van Wagenen (*The Golden Age of Homespun* [Albany, 1927], pp. 55–63) has a good account.

[171] In 1810 there were 413 carding machines in New York State. See Albert Gallatin, "Report on Manufactures," *American State Papers; Finance*, II, 693. In Dutchess County wool-carding machinery was introduced in 1803 (Bayne, *op. cit.*, pp. 7–8).

[172] Beardsley, *op. cit.*, p. 31.

LANDLORDS AND FARMERS

Imports of cloth were beginning to encroach on the home manufacture. This was particularly true of the Hudson Valley, where farmers could buy the latest patterns in the stores at Troy, Albany, and Hudson. Phineas Bond, a British observer, noted that in 1789 woolens and linens fell "infinitely short of their own consumption."[173] But not until the Embargo Act did we have the woolen manufacture firmly established and the boom in Merino sheep.

The farmer was also a lumberman. Each farmer built his home, barns, fences, and tools from wood. Nevertheless, specialization soon emerged. The first small mills supplied the local needs. Subsequently, larger mills supplied the outside market. It was the development of the export trade that differentiated the lumberman from the farmer.

A dense forest growth covered eastern New York. Pine and hemlock were well distributed among the hardwoods. Getting out the pine was the main object of New York lumbermen until well past 1850. Heavy stands of hemlock and spruce grew on the mountain slopes and provided the material for the lusty tanning industry of the nineteenth century. At Whitehall lumber from the shores of Lake Champlain was loaded on sleds and pulled overland to Albany. Sloops carried the boards to the West Indies, Europe, and the southern states. Practically every stream falling into the Hudson had a sawmill cutting out planks, boards, staves, and scantlings.[174] For example, at Newburgh there were nine mills. Each mill had a store which served the small hamlet surrounding the mill.[175]

Landlords and farmers realized the value of their timber lands. Timber brought in cash. Moreover, the farmer could cut and drag out logs during the winter. It was not long before timber thieves

---

[173] "Letters of Phineas Bond," ed. by Franklin J. Jameson, *Annual Report of the American Historical Association for the Year 1896*, I, 652.

[174] Ralph Brown (*The Lumber Industry in the State of New York, 1790–1830* [Thesis, Columbia University Library], pp. 32 ff.) has a good account.

[175] Ruttenber, *op. cit.*, p. 162.

THE GOOD YEARS

were operating with great boldness, especially on the lands of the absentee landholders.[176] The supply of trees seemed limitless, but a few farsighted individuals were beginning to raise their voices in opposition to the ruthless cutting.[177] They declared that the coming generation would not be able to secure cheap lumber. Furthermore, some landlords became alarmed at the rapid destruction of the forest. They required that their tenants keep a certain proportion of the farm in wood.[178]

The manufacture of potash and pearlash was a sustaining industry of cardinal importance. As late as 1822 Governor De Witt Clinton listed ashes along with wheat as the two leading exports of the state.[179] Potash could easily bear the cost of transportation because of its high value in relation to its bulk. In 1791 at Whitestown, which was on the edge of the wilderness, "perlash" formed the chief article of export.[180] In the following year James Kent found that his brother in Cooperstown had set up six kettles and fifty leach tubs with which he hoped to make one hundred and twenty barrels of pearlash during the next year.[181] In 1800 a traveler visited the famous store conducted by the Kane brothers in Canajoharie. During that year the store bought 34,000 bushels of wheat worth $65,875 and 2,500 bushels of potash valued at $62,500.[182] Such estimates and observations, although of a fragmentary nature, show quite definitely that the manufacture of potash played a significant part in rural economy.

---

[176] W. North to B. Walker, Aug. 8, 1802, complained that timber thieves could not be checked (W. North Papers). See also Amos Douglas to S. A. Law, Jan. 4, 1811, Box 1, Correspondence, 1796–1817, Law Papers.

[177] W. Cooper, *op. cit.*, p. 23.

[178] George Clarke, Jr., Leases.

[179] *Messages from Governors*, II, 1093.

[180] Lincklaen, *op. cit.*, p. 71. James Kent noted 12 kettles mounted at Kane's store (J. T. Horton, "The Mohawk Valley in 1791," *New York History*, XXII [April, 1941], 211).

[181] Edward Porter Alexander, "Judge Kent's 'Jaunt' to Cooperstown in 1792," *New York History*, XXII (Oct., 1941), 454.

[182] Maude, *op. cit.*, p. 30.

LANDLORDS AND FARMERS

The New York farmer has usually resisted new ideas on farming most stubbornly. Only something practical such as the remarkable effects of gypsum could persuade him to change his methods. Occasionally, however, fads have swept through the countryside overcoming the natural opposition to change. Between 1790 and 1850 maple sugar, Merino sheep, silk, and Rohan potatoes aroused much enthusiasm and discussion.

Making sugar from the sap of the maple tree was a routine procedure among the farmers of New England and New York. Collecting and boiling the sap provided work during the months of March and April when there were few opportunities for the farmer to perform outside work. Each maple tree produced about five pounds of sugar. Practically all members of the family could take part in the simple tasks which required no costly and complicated apparatus.

During the 1790's a strong movement got under way to develop the maple sugar industry on a large scale. Prominent agricultural leaders, politicians, land speculators, and financiers endorsed the movement and urged public support.[183] The destruction of the sugar plantations in Hispaniola by rebellious slaves gave added impetus. William Cooper persuaded Tench Coxe, close associate of Hamilton, that the entire domestic supply could be raised from this source.[184] He stated that in 1793 Otsego township produced 150,000 pounds, worth $15,000. During the same year Gerrit Boon carried on his ill-fated experiment in Oneida County. His chief reason for buying the Servis and Adgate patents was to secure a fine stand of maple. Unfortunately wind, rain, and sun warped the wooden troughs down which the sap was to run. Before he

---

[183] Robert Livingston to Elkanah Watson, Feb. 16, 1793, quoted by Watson in *Men and Times of the Revolution*, p. 340. Livingston called the matter to the attention of the Agricultural Society, which urged support. Governor George Clinton urged the legislature to investigate the need of public aid (Lincoln, *op. cit.*, II, 313).

[184] Tench Coxe, *A View of the United States of America* (Philadelphia, 1794), pp. 78 ff.

THE GOOD YEARS

had finished he had lost $15,000 for his Dutch sponsors. Individual farmers, however, were more successful. In 1792 more than 2,000 sugar kettles were sold in Albany during the winter. It was estimated that 8,000 kettles were in use within a radius of 80 miles of Albany.[185]

The self-sufficiency of farm families did not prevent the growth of village industries which served the needs of the locality. Within a few years of the original settlement, every town had its share of small mills. Thus in 1792 the town of Amsterdam had four gristmills, three sawmills, two oil mills, and one iron forge.[186] Small custom mills ground grain for the neighboring farmers; merchant mills in Troy, Albany, Catskill, and other centers sold the flour to exporters.[187] In many towns were tanneries, which turned the raw hides into leather, saddles, harnesses, and other goods. The proprietors of these enterprises usually operated them in conjunction with their own farms. Generally they kept a certain percentage of the product as compensation for their services.[188]

A surprisingly large number of taverns fringed the main roads.[189] Farmers, then as now, could not resist the temptation to earn extra cash by supplying food and lodging to transients. Newcomers to the frontier naturally sought shelter at the homes of old settlers until they had erected their own cabins.[190] Both the promptings

---

[185] Munsell, *Annals of Albany*, III, 151.

[186] *Doc. Hist. of N.Y.*, III, 1108.

[187] Charles B. Kuhlmann, *The Development of the Flour-Milling Industry in the United States* (Boston, 1929), p. 33.

[188] In 1800 Samuel Law made a contract with John Bristol whereby the latter could cut timber on J. C. Fisher's land and operate a mill erected by Law. Bristol was to retain one fourth of all the timber cut ("Statement of Acc'ts, Saw Mill Lumber 1800–1858," S. A. Law Papers).

[189] Dwight (*op. cit.*, IV, 24) stated that the number was "enormous" and denounced the poor service. Harriott (*op. cit.*, II, 118) estimated that every third or fourth farmhouse along the Mohawk Valley road was a tavern.

[190] Beardsley (*op. cit.*, p. 27) pointed out that people seeking land in Otsego County filled his father's house.

LANDLORDS AND FARMERS

of hospitality and the chance of profit caused many farmers to aid the traveler.

The innkeeper likewise served his local community. Social and political activities which could not very well be transacted at church and meetinghouse naturally gravitated to the tavern. The proprietor was a man of importance. Many were former captains, colonels, and judges. In fact, one observer noted that to become a lawyer or a tavern keeper was the "surest road to public honours and riches." [191] Not infrequently the local tavern became the rendezvous for hard-drinking ruffians.

Clearing the forest and feeding his family absorbed almost all the effort of the New York farmer between 1790 and 1808. His husbandry was predatory and inefficient. All the praise for his versatility and resourcefulness cannot disguise the fact that the farmer could not be an efficient farmer, carpenter, mason, lumberman, toolmaker, cobbler, and handy man at one and the same time. Self-sufficiency meant a low standard of living. No matter how skilled the farmer was at lifting himself by his own bootstraps, he was limited by such obvious factors as lack of time, primitive tools, declining soil fertility, and shortage of labor. Our modern age treasures the spinning wheel as the symbol of the independence of its ancestors. Viewed from another angle, the spinning wheel is also the symbol of an inescapable and unrelenting servitude to time-consuming and arduous drudgery.

If toil and poverty were the constant companions of a great many families of eastern New York, a buoyant optimism was the mark of their spirit. Pioneers were creating farms for themselves and their children. The merchants in the river ports were calling for more and more wheat and potash. The network of turnpikes penetrated farther and farther inland. An ever-increasing number of farmers could cart their wheat to market. Those farmers who lived within easy reach of the Hudson increased the tempo of their wheat production. They began to grow clover and to use

---

[191] Harriott, *op. cit.*, II, 116.

THE GOOD YEARS

gypsum. In short, eastern New York was growing and, in general, was prospering.

By 1808 eastern New York taken as a whole had left behind its pioneering days. The abundant harvests of wheat, the fields of corn, and the barrels of cider had all but obliterated the bitter memories of the starving time. Social classes were emerging. Of course, the old aristocracy retained its political and social hegemony. But a new aristocracy based on hard work, shrewd trading, and rising land values was rising in the inland counties and in the commercial towns. Enterprising Yankees behind the plow and the counter were beginning to challenge the political and economic power of the older families along the Hudson.

The farmers of the Hudson-Mohawk region met the challenge of pioneering and the demands of the market with great success. Looming in the future, however, were a host of pressing problems: the war embargoes, the competition of cheap western produce, unprofitable wheat production, and the shift to grazing and dairying. In the next chapter we shall examine how well the farmers adjusted themselves to the new conditions.

CHAPTER IV

YEARS OF UNCERTAINTY

1808 - 1825

THE EMBARGO ACT gave a sudden wrench to our economy. The collapse of farm prices in 1808 began the procession of shocks which made the lot of the farmer highly precarious for the next seventeen years. Soaring prices during the War of 1812 encouraged speculation; rock-bottom prices following the panic of 1819 spelled disaster. Both made it difficult for the farmer to lay sound plans and to meet his obligations. Much more alarming, however, was the fact that the exhausted fields of the Hudson-Mohawk region could no longer raise wheat in competition with the fresh fertile lands of the west. The suspicion would not down that eastern New York had passed its heyday. The overweening optimism of the earlier years gave way to a feeling of uncertainty.

This uncertainty tended to obscure the very real gains accomplished in this period. The more enterprising farmers of eastern New York did not give up in despair. They turned to sheep raising; they greatly increased the production of cheese and butter. Agricultural societies sprang up and for the first time reached the average farmer with their information. New turnpikes and canals stimulated trade and travel. Factories began to challenge the spinster in the home. This was indeed an awkward but challenging period. Not without much distress and hardship were the farmers able to make the shift from wheat raising to dairying.

YEARS OF UNCERTAINTY

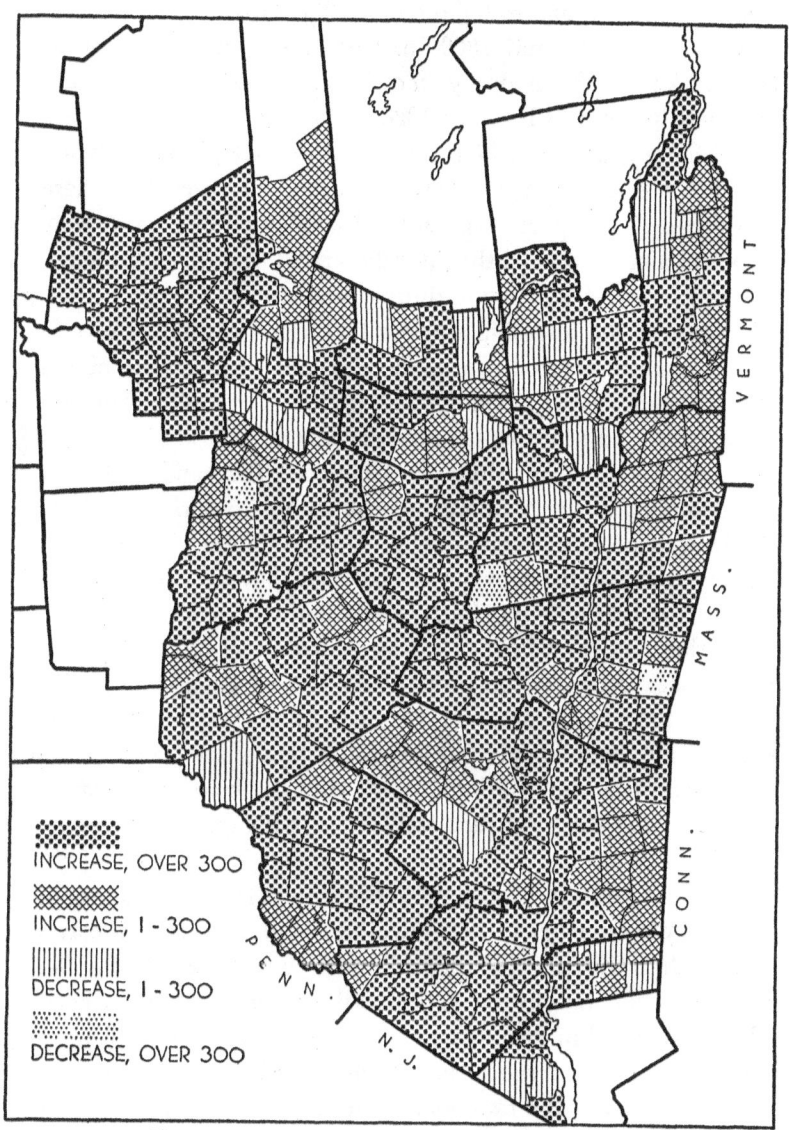

Changes in Population by Townships, 1810–1820.

LANDLORDS AND FARMERS

The population figures tell the story. The rapid increases of the decades 1790–1800 and 1800–1810 became a memory. Instead there took place the modest gain of 17 per cent between 1810 and 1820 and 18 per cent between 1820 and 1830.[1] Eastern New York was definitely lagging behind the rest of the state, the population of which was increasing at the rate of 43 and 39 per cent for these two decades. The purely agricultural population of eastern New York had almost reached the saturation point. In fact, over a score of townships lost population during each decade.

A study of the township map for the period 1810–1820 reveals many interesting facts. The pioneer regions to the west of the Hudson were growing rapidly. The ribbon of townships fringing the Hudson and Mohawk rivers were likewise growing at a vigorous rate. The map for the period between 1820 and 1830 tells much the same story. Many hill townships bordering on New England were losing population. Upland towns in Herkimer County which in the previous decade had showed a strong tendency to decline now regained population as the farmers substituted dairying for wheat. The townships in the upper Hudson region suffered from the same trend toward emigration which affected the nearby areas of Vermont so severely. Surprisingly enough, the mountainous and infertile region of the Catskills was attracting many new settlers. As we shall see below, population was following the westward trek of the tanning and lumbering industries.

President Jefferson's embargo in December, 1807, dealt a serious blow to the commerce and agriculture of the Hudson-Mohawk region. Until the spring of 1809 all foreign trade except that under special presidential license was formally prohibited. In the Champlain Valley and in the Oswego area smugglers boldly challenged the government and succeeded in minimizing the effectiveness of the embargo. But the farmers of eastern New York were too far

---

[1] Computed from tables in Introduction to the *N.Y. Census for 1855*, p. xxxiv.

YEARS OF UNCERTAINTY

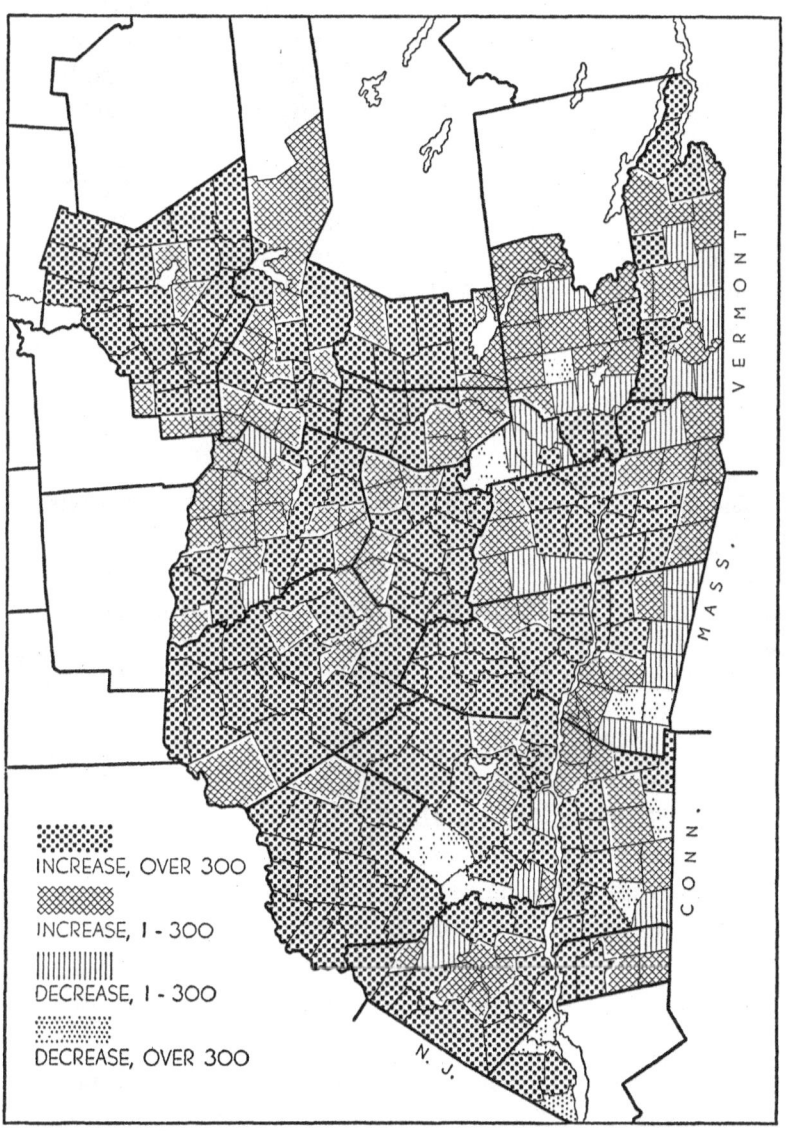

Changes in Population by Townships, 1820–1830.

away from Canada to make smuggling feasible. One unforeseen result of the embargo was that a good share of Vermont's trade, which had formerly flowed to Troy, now was diverted to the north. According to one account, Troy's property values declined at least 25 per cent in the next three years.[2]

The immediate effect of the embargo was to send farm prices tumbling and to paralyze the shipping industry of the port of New York. The Federalist party, desperately in need of a popular slogan, seized the opportunity to denounce the Jefferson administration:

> When federal men did stand at helm,
> We shipped off many a cargo—
> When Wheat and all produce was high,
> 'Cause there was no embargo.[3]

The farmers of eastern New York were singularly dependent upon the export market. The cessation of foreign trade affected them almost as seriously, if not as spectacularly, as it did the seamen and merchants. Farmers in Oneida County, led by Thomas Gold and Jonas Platt, both ardent Federalists, declared that it was the foreign market that gave value to their land.[4] The frontier counties would go bankrupt unless they could sell their potash and flour. The downward spiral of prices caused intense suffering.[5] Obviously a drop in the value of American wheat and flour from $10,753,000 in 1807 to $1,936,000 in 1808 could only spell disaster for many farmers.[6]

More agreeable but no less disturbing to the farmer were the booming war prices. The reopening of trade in 1809 ushered in a

---

[2] Dwight, *op. cit.*, III, 422.

[3] *Albany Gazette*, Feb. 29, 1808, cited by D. R. Fox, *Decline of Aristocracy*, p. 100.

[4] *New-York Spectator*, Sept. 13, 1808.

[5] Walter W. Jennings, *The American Embargo, 1807–1809, with Particular Reference to Its Effect on Industry* (Iowa City, 1921), pp. 189, 194.

[6] Pitkin, *op. cit.*, p. 116.

YEARS OF UNCERTAINTY

period of rising prices. Peace brought the inevitable postwar collapse in prices. The drop was temporary. Renewed demand for American products bolstered up the price level until late in 1818. Thereupon prices plummeted to new lows and surpluses glutted the markets. One writer stated that if all the personal or movable property in Herkimer County could have been sold at a fair appraisal in 1820, it would not have brought enough money to pay the domestic debt of the county and probably "not more than half of it." [7] Debts incurred during the war years hung like a millstone around the neck of the farmer.

Perhaps as good an index as can be found of the condition of the rural population of eastern New York between the years 1807 and 1825 is the list of wheat prices taken at Albany on the first day of January.[8] It might be pointed out that eight shillings equaled one dollar.

	Sh.	p.		Sh.	p.
1807	11	0	1816	14	0
1808	9	0	1817	18	0
1809	8	0	1818	15	0
1810	12	6	1819	14	0
1811	14	0	1820	8	0
1812	15	0	1821	6	0
1813	18	0	1822	9	0
1814	15	0	1823	10	0
1815	13	0	1824	10	0
			1825	8	0

In 1813 and in 1817 wheat prices reached $2.25 a bushel. After 1819 prices fell sharply and leveled off at the average price of slightly better than $1.00 a bushel.

We must now examine more closely how these price changes affected the New York farmers. During the War of 1812 the farmers became the supply base, so to speak, of the armies sta-

---

[7] N. Benton, op. cit., p. 209.
[8] N.Y. Assembly Documents, no. 156 (1846), pp. 51–53.

tioned on the Niagara frontier and in the neighborhood of Plattsburg. The demand for foodstuffs caused farm prices to soar. One editor in 1813 admitted that farm produce commanded "extravagant" prices, but that the prices of articles which the farmers puchased had reached "exorbitant" levels.[9] Thus tea, formerly selling at from 4 to 9 shillings a pound, had jumped to an average price of from 16 to 24 shillings a pound. Broadcloth had jumped from $5.00 to $8.00 a yard in 1810 to $12 to $18 a yard in 1813. Farmers, then as now, were eager to sell at high prices but were reluctant to pay more for merchandise.

The combination of good harvests and high prices made the cold seasons and postwar deflation still more difficult to endure. In 1816, famous as the year without a summer, it was so cold that the Indian corn did not ripen in the Mohawk Valley.[10] Farmers in the hill towns were finding throughout this period that winter-killing was making the raising of winter wheat more and more hazardous. Furthermore, the mushroom growth of the textile industry ended abruptly in 1815. English manufacturers dumped shiploads of woolen goods on the New York market. In addition, smut, the Hessian fly, worn-out fields, and cheap western wheat made the cultivation of winter wheat not only unprofitable but sometimes impossible. Stephen Van Rensselaer observed in 1820 that the price of wheat would no longer "repay the labor" that the farmer had "expended on its production."[11]

The correspondence of Samuel A. Law describes graphically the hard times overwhelming a Delaware County farmer in the decade following 1815. Of course, Law as a land agent had an obvious interest in explaining his ill success in collecting payments and in selling land. Nevertheless, the fact that he was

---

[9] Editorial in *Herkimer American*, reprinted in *Orange County Patriot* and *Lansingsburgh Gazette* on Dec. 28, 1813.

[10] Macauley, *op. cit.*, I, 385.

[11] *Memoirs of the Board of Agriculture of the State of New York*, I (1821), xxiii.

YEARS OF UNCERTAINTY

forced to throw himself on the mercy of his creditors in 1824 lends credence to his complaints.[12]

In 1824 Law wrote that prices had slumped disastrously since 1817. A yoke of oxen worth from $65 to $100 in 1817 brought only $30 to $60. Cows formerly worth from $20 to $40 a head brought $12 to $17. Butter prices had fallen from a range of 20 to 30 cents a pound to a range of 8 to 12 cents. Law made the melancholy observation, "In this state of things, the settlers, who had got and paid for their lands, have mainly, barely held their own. . . . Those in debt for their lands have become extensively disheartened and discouraged."[13] Law, who often indulged in self-pity, declared that he needed the "patience of Job, the discretion and the address of Chesterfield" to allay the dissatisfaction which threatened to depopulate the patent.

Law urged the proprietors of the land not to press for payments. As long as the farmers were not disturbed, they would remain and keep the land from reverting to commons.[14] Law found that the neighbors used such land to feed sheep and he wisely observed, "It is to their interest to stop a sale or lease."[15]

Typical of Law's lamentations is the following excerpt from his letter to Charles Wharton, member of the famous Philadelphia family:

The Michigan fever and other Western fevers, infect them far and wide. They sigh, not single or solitary; but in bands and cohorts, for fairy, far-famed lubber lands where "roast pigs ready baked, run thro the streets, crying who'll come eat me." . . . Many hundreds of improvements in this county lie to commons—abandoned—their makers fled, as oft by night as by day, to seek beyond the setting sun the rest and riches they'll never reach; and improved farms and places all around, in abundance, can be bought in some cases for less than the improv'ts made on them, have cost.[16]

---

[12] S. A. Law to Thomas Stewardson, Feb. 16, 1824, Box 4, Correspondence (1824–1828), S. A. Law Papers.
[13] Letter to James Fisher, March 15, 1824, *ibid.*
[14] S. A. Law to Charles Wharton, Nov. 27, 1826, *ibid.*
[15] S. A. Law to Charles Wharton, March 5, 1825, *ibid.*
[16] Feb. 25, 1825, *ibid.*

LANDLORDS AND FARMERS

In order to encourage the settlers to pay their debts, Law was forced to make many abatements and to accept payment in cattle and produce.[17] But the farmers realized that their equity was gone and often refused to pay. As Law remarked, "Yet so ticklish is their tenure, that if pressed, they'll all fly, and the land fall back."[18]

The collapse in farm prices led to a fall in land values. The landowners had set their prices so high by 1815, according to Timothy Dwight, that settlers avoided New York and took up farms in the old Northwest.[19] In 1819 land values fell sharply. Law kept complaining for the next few years that land values in Delaware County were so low that agents had to beg riffraff to go upon the land. In western New York real-estate values underwent a similar shrinkage. Settlers on the Holland Purchase, as the area once owned by the Holland Land Company was called, were so hard pressed that they protested against further payments on their lots.[20] James Wadsworth, one of the largest landholders in the state and a resident of Ontario County, wrote in 1819:

> Real estate has fallen in this county, or it would be more correct to say improved farms have fallen 33 per cent in the last three years. Such is the scarcity of money that improved farms from Boston to Lake Erie will not sell. The consequence is we have none of that class of settlers who used to come among us, with money in their pockets from the sale of improved farms.[21]

The husbandry of eastern New York as described in the previous chapter remained much the same in 1825 as in 1808. Despite the strenuous efforts of Elkanah Watson and his little band of agricultural reformers, farmers carried on the same exploitation of the soil and showed the same disregard for the principles of crop

---

[17] *Ibid.*
[18] S. A. Law to Thomas Stewardson, Feb. 26, 1824, *ibid.*
[19] *Op. cit.*, III, 266.
[20] Evans, *Holland Land Company*, p. 332.
[21] Letter to J. Keating, Feb. 25, 1819. I am indebted to Dr. Neil Adams McNall of New York State College for Teachers (Albany) for this reference.

YEARS OF UNCERTAINTY

rotation, drainage, and fertilizing the soil. To be sure, changes of great significance were taking place. Wheat cultivation was yielding first rank to grazing. By 1825 the raising of sheep had become an industry of importance. The production of dairy products became as important in certain counties as wheat raising had been in the earlier period.

The year 1825 saw the completion of the Erie Canal. No longer could farmers in the Hudson-Mohawk region hope to compete with western wheat producers. No longer could these farmers afford to ignore the expanding urban markets. In short, the period between 1808 and 1825 forced the farmers to restudy their basic assumptions and to make the necessary readjustments.

The growth of industry and the expansion of the transportation network affected both directly and indirectly the rural economy of eastern New York. Unfortunately, the federal and the state censuses fail to supply complete or accurate information as to the manufacturing establishments in the state.[22] The 1820 census lists only 6,409 men, 927 women, and 2,423 children as employed in manufacturing. This number seems trifling when compared with the total population of 1,372,812. It emphasizes once more the statement of a Senate committee in 1826 that "agriculture is the great business of the state."[23] The decade following 1825 was to see manufacturing boom in the state.[24]

To dismiss the industrial development as inconsequential would be a mistake. The wave of nationalism accompanying the War of 1812 made encouragement of domestic manufactures a patriotic duty. After the war the state legislature heeded the appeals of the textile operators, who were overwhelmed by a flood of English imports. They urged the congressmen from the state to vote for a protective tariff.[25] At the same time they exempted

---

[22] Introduction to *N.Y. Census for 1855*, 1v.
[23] *N.Y. Senate Journal*, 1826, pp. 438–442.
[24] D. R. Fox, *Decline of Aristocracy*, p. 323.
[25] See report of the joint committee of Senate and Assembly on the governor's message (*N.Y. Senate Journal*, 1816, pp. 52–54).

127

textile mills from taxation and the workers from jury and militia service. Gradually the Democrats withdrew special favors from industry. In 1818 an Assembly committee highly praised household manufactures. They offered no aid to the prostrate companies, some of which, the committee hinted, had been managed with a certain "want of economy." [26] The movement for protection, however, continued to make many influential converts among the rural population. Especially was this true of the wool producers, who naturally blamed all their troubles on foreign competition. Landed aristocrats, who in the constitutional convention of 1821 had viewed the manufacturer with considerable suspicion, were beginning to show a friendly interest in manufacturing. Perhaps the most enthusiastic statement in favor of protection came from George Tibbits, a prominent farmer and politician of Rensselaer County, who read an able article in behalf of protection before the Board of Agriculture.[27] His arguments were the familiar pleas for protection, but his analysis of the causes of the backwardness of New York agriculture was penetrating. Tibbits declared, "A ready demand for agricultural productions, at remunerating prices, it is presumed, is the only adequate inducement which can be relied upon, for insuring a careful cultivation of the land, or for increasing the quantity of its produce." [28]

In Oneida County the infant textile industry won a firm foothold. Dr. Seth Capron and Benjamin S. Walcott, both familiar with the cotton manufacture in Rhode Island, organized in association with local and Albany capitalists the Oneida Manufacturing Company in Whitestown in 1809. It is interesting to note that Stephen Van Rensselaer, De Witt Clinton, and John Taylor, prominent Albany speculator, were financially interested in this

---

[26] *N.Y. Assembly Journal*, 1818, pp. 616–617.

[27] "A Memoir on the expediency and practicability of improving or creating Home Markets for the sale of Agricultural Productions and Raw Materials, by the introduction or growth of Artizans and Manufacturers" (*Memoirs of Board of Agr.*, III, 289–325).

[28] *Ibid.*, p. 289.

YEARS OF UNCERTAINTY

company.[29] Encouraged by handsome profits, the stockholders in 1811 established a woolen factory at Oriskany which was among the few to survive the postwar collapse. By 1813 textile factories to the number of forty-three had been incorporated in the state.[30] Most of these factories were concentrated in Oneida, Columbia, and Dutchess counties. In Fishkill, Dutchess County, Peter Schenck, John Jacob Astor, Philip Hone, and other New York capitalists built the important Mattewan Manufacturing Company.[31] Small and weak as these mills were, they did provide a home market for the foodstuffs and wool of many farmers. Again it must be stressed that the development of manufacturing had hardly passed from infancy. To take but one example, the textile mills of Oneida County, which boasted the largest concentration of this industry in the state, employed fewer than eight hundred workers in 1827.[32] Of these well over five hundred were listed as children. The textile workers thus formed less than 2 per cent of the population of the county.

Cities acting as commercial centers still absorbed the great bulk of farm surpluses. The merchants either sold the produce to their fellow townsmen or shipped it onward to the larger markets. If we lump together the centers with populations of more than three thousand, we find that in 1825 this total was less than 15 per cent of the total population of the state.[33] Significant shifts were taking place in the location of important urban centers. Cities on the route of the Erie Canal were already entering a boom period. But the old river ports below Albany had definitely

---

[29] W. R. Bagnall, *The Textile Industries of the United States, 1600–1810* (Cambridge, 1893), pp. 503–505.

[30] Harry Carman, "The Beginnings of the Industrial Revolution," in Flick, *History of N.Y.*, V, 347.

[31] *Ibid.*; Hasbrouck, *op. cit.*, p. 341.

[32] *Utica Intelligencer*, July 3, 1827, quoting from *Utica Sentinel and Gazette*. See table in Appendix.

[33] Computed from the Census of 1825. Figures are conveniently arranged in the introduction to the *N.Y. Census for 1855*, xvi–xxxii.

LANDLORDS AND FARMERS

slackened their growth. For example, Hudson increased from 4,048 to 5,004 in the period between 1810 and 1825. Poughkeepsie, Catskill, Kingston, and Newburgh made more or less moderate gains. They showed none of that exuberant upswing and activity which characterized their earlier history. This failure to grow was particularly marked in the years toward the end of the period. Thus both Kingston and Hudson suffered slight losses between 1820 and 1825. Albany and Troy, both of which were already enjoying by 1825 the first benefits of the Erie Canal, grew steadily. The population of Albany climbed from 10,762 in 1810 to 15,971 in 1825. Troy's population went up from 3,895 to 7,859. Utica and cities to the west were on the threshold of their future importance as commercial and industrial centers.

Prior to 1808 the economy of eastern New York rested on the cheap transportation facilities provided by the Hudson River. The turnpikes branching into the back country on both sides of the river and the lock navigation canals along the Mohawk River served as feeders for the Hudson. But neither the turnpikes nor the Mohawk waterway had solved the crucial problem of cheap transportation. With the spread of population into the western counties, the agitation for improved roads and waterways became increasingly vocal and politically powerful. A similar problem was disturbing most of the states on the Atlantic seaboard. Jefferson's vague suggestions in 1805 and Gallatin's detailed recommendations in 1810 reflected this widespread demand and at the same time stimulated the movement for internal improvements.

Among the most enthusiastic promoters of a canal linking the Hudson and Lake Erie were the Federalists in New York City and the Hudson counties.[34] Not only did they own large tracts of land, the value of which would appreciate if a canal were built, but they also realized that a canal would open up the natural resources of the state and promote the development of

---

[34] D. R. Fox in *Decline of Aristocracy* (pp. 148–159) has a detailed discussion of the economic interests of the Federalists backing the Erie Canal.

YEARS OF UNCERTAINTY

manufacturing. The farmers in central and western New York naturally joined the chorus for a state canal. The Western Inland Lock Navigation Company had failed to provide them with cheap transportation.

The story of the steps by which the state of New York was induced to undertake what was at the time the colossal task of building a canal for more than 300 miles across the state is fairly well known and certainly needs no repetition.[35] De Witt Clinton and his associates were able to persuade the legislature to authorize construction in the spring of 1817. With a vigor and a speed commonly not associated with public enterprise, the construction was pushed forward. Most of the contractors were well-to-do farmers who built short sections of the canal. As early as 1820 the middle section, running for almost a hundred miles west of Little Falls, was in operation. By 1823 the canal stretched from Rochester to the Hudson River. Tolls at Rome in 1821 show that over 44,000 barrels of flour, 17,000 barrels of salt, 1,061,000 feet of lumber and 2,500 tons of merchandise passed through the locks.[36] Such amounts represent only a trickle when compared with the torrent of goods which the canalboats were to carry within the next decade.

The Champlain Canal was also constructed in the same period. A channel 4 feet deep and 40 feet wide connected Whitehall on Lake Champlain with the upper Hudson at Fort Edward. Subsequently the canal was extended to reach Waterford. In the early 1820's large quantities of lumber floated down the canal. The new outlet gave a direct stimulus to the lumbering industry in the Champlain region.[37]

---

[35] See Noble Whitford, *History of the Canal System of the State of New York* (Albany, 1906), I, 48–131; MacGill, *op. cit.*, pp. 160 ff. David Hosack's *Memoir of De Witt Clinton* (New York, 1829) contains many valuable documents.

[36] Hulbert, *op. cit.*, II, 187.

[37] Elsie Potter, *The Influence of the Champlain Canal on Eastern New York and Western Vermont, 1823–1860* (Thesis, Cornell University Library, Ithaca, 1939).

LANDLORDS AND FARMERS

The years from 1800 to 1825 might be called the "turnpike era." [38] Public enthusiasm for toll roads, already a matter of intense interest prior to 1807, mounted even higher during the War of 1812 when the difficulties of supplying the armies stationed at Plattsburg, Sacket Harbor, and Fort Niagara underscored the demands of the farmers for cheap transportation. The legislature turned to the turnpike company as a convenient device by which the government could transfer the burden of road construction to private hands. Laws fostering turnpike construction were usually of a liberal nature. The companies were assured of monopolies of certain routes for long periods of time. They could often take over and repair existing roads, thus eliminating the competition of public thoroughfares. The companies received ample time to build the turnpikes, and the tolls were quite high. In order to secure a wide distribution of the stock, the law sometimes placed a limit on the amount of stock any one individual could buy. That the turnpike companies were often mere speculative ventures has already been seen. One observer, writing in 1813, remarked, "The rage for speculation that blew up the turnpike bubble, and *burst it*, is now transferred to manufactures." [39]

The political leaders of the state quickly responded to the appeals and petitions pouring in on them from every section of the state. The number of companies incorporated by the legislature will give us a rough idea of the expanding turnpike network. Between 1807 and 1811 the number of turnpike companies had increased from 67 to 135, and bridge companies from 21 to 36.[40] Ten years later the figures had reached 278 and 58, respectively.[41]

---

[38] The historian of turnpikes declares they reached the "zenith of importance" in the years immediately preceding the completion of the Erie Canal (Durrenberger, *op. cit.*, p. 61).

[39] Spafford, *op. cit.* (1813), p. 17.

[40] Sterling Goodenow, *A Brief Topographical and Statistical Manual of the State of New York* (2d ed.; New York, 1822), p. 17.

[41] Goodenow, *op. cit.*, p. 17. In passing we may note that the legislature appropriated liberal sums for state roads. See *N.Y. Assembly Documents*, no. 94 (1860), III, 16–17.

YEARS OF UNCERTAINTY

Even more significant are the figures for turnpike mileage actually completed. In 1811 it was estimated that approximately 1,500 miles had been turnpiked; in ten years the state possessed 4,000 miles of turnpiked road. Not all of this mileage was located in eastern New York. Important trunk roads were tapping the rich valley of the Genesee. Nevertheless, the major roads terminated at the Hudson River ports which handled the great bulk of farm produce and merchandise.

Albany became the foremost turnpike center in the state. Eight turnpikes thrust outward from the city like spokes in a wheel. The main highway from the east approached the city from New Lebanon. To the west were two trunk roads, one passing up the Mohawk Valley, the other following the present route of the Cherry Valley Turnpike. In 1827 the *National Advertizer* commented, "Probably there is no point in the United States where so many public stages meet and find employment as at Albany." [42] Utica was second only to Albany in importance within the state. Stage lines ran coaches to Rome, Oswego, Ogdensburg, Cooperstown, Binghamton, and Ithaca in addition to the cities along the main route from Albany to Buffalo. In 1826 a local paper boasted that over forty thousand passengers had passed through Utica on stages during the year.[43] Despite the provision that the companies must keep their roads in good condition, all too frequently the roads became little better than tracks filled with ruts and mudholes. Travelers were continually deploring the roughness and poor condition of the turnpikes.

Fully as important as the staging business was the freighting of heavy goods along the turnpike. Heavily built wagons, drawn by three or four spans of Pennsylvania horses, carried to market beneath their canvas tops wheat, flour, cheese, potash, and

---

[42] Quoted by Oliver Holmes, "The Stage-Coach Business in the Hudson Valley," *Proceedings of the New York Historical Association,* XXIX (July, 1931), 243.

[43] Cited in *ibid.,* p. 246.

whisky. Shortly before 1819 one reporter estimated that on the turnpike above Little Falls there passed annually 290 wagons drawn by two or three horses and carrying 2½ tons of produce.[44] These wagons averaged twelve trips a year. The same reporter estimated that forty wagons drawn by five to seven horses and carrying an average of 6 tons both ways made at least six trips a year. Progress was, of course, slow. Drivers were unable to average more than 15 to 20 miles a day with heavy loads. The tolls and the cost of maintaining the horses and drivers made land transportation expensive as compared with water transport. In 1814 Robert Fulton declared that it cost $2.00 to cart a barrel of flour 130 miles overland.[45] In the same year it cost but slightly more than 25 cents to ship a barrel of flour from Albany to New York, a distance of more than 160 miles.

The Hudson River increasingly demonstrated its importance as an artery of inland commerce. Upon its waters four hundred vessels of every description and averaging 60-ton burden carried foodstuffs, merchandise, and passengers.[46] Sloops operating from Albany made eleven trips to and from New York during the season, while those serving Newburgh, Poughkeepsie, and other landings made many more trips. At Malden on Hudson John Bigelow's father ran a store and operated several sloops for his own use and to serve his customers.[47] His captains often sold goods for his customers, charging only freight. Among the produce taken to the metropolis were bark, lumber, leather, butter, hay, and sometimes grain. The captains brought back merchandise and hides which were sent to the tanneries in the Catskills. If we

---

[44] William Darby, *A Tour from the City of New York, to Detroit, in the Michigan Territory* (New York, 1819), p. xl.

[45] Robert Fulton to Gouverneur Morris, Feb. 22, 1814, in *Niles' Weekly Register*, VI (May 14, 1814), 169–171.

[46] *Ibid.*

[47] John Bigelow, *Retrospections of an Active Life* (New York, 1909–1913), I, 11.

YEARS OF UNCERTAINTY

multiply the business of this merchant a thousand times, we shall find the sources of the estimated 400,000 tons of goods carried annually on the Hudson.[48]

We shall not undertake to describe in detail the agricultural pattern. The broad outlines are much the same as those described in the previous chapter. Rather we shall be content to point out new departures from the old pattern. The rise of the sheep and dairy industries needs to be told. The short-lived but significant county fair movement needs to be explained. The problem of agrarian unrest needs to be examined. Forces outside the control of the New York farmer were forcing him to change his methods and to embark upon new enterprises.

Perhaps as good a description of New York agriculture as can be found are the comments of George W. Featherstonhaugh. This English-born and English-educated gentleman-farmer was the son-in-law of James Duane. For several years he served as corresponding secretary of the state Board of Agriculture.

> Until very recently the farming operations which have come under my notice in this state, may be generally described as follows. Indifferent grass made into hay at unseasonable times, and abounding in the worst weeds that can infest the ground. . . . Dung of several years standing, making the cold barnyard a perfect mud hole. Fat sheep weighing eight pounds a quarter; other meat in proportion. Wheat from ten to twenty bushels an acre; corn fifteen to thirty. On the arrival of winter, the sheep, the cows, the lambs, the calves, the oxen, finding their way to a bad shed, or no shed, in a bleak barn-yard, and remaining in that situation all winter; having a little hay flung to them two or three times a day; the cows giving a quart or a pint at a milking. I have often seen the emaciated cows, after passing the night in a drizzling rain, freezing as it fell, incapable of rising in the morning; and the sheep frozen fast to the ground. On the arrival of spring, the scanty hay being almost exhausted, the whole stock finding nothing more to be had at the barn, again sneaks off to the meadows, through the well-known gaps, poach and tear what had not been quite destroyed in November; to prepare for another scanty crop of hay, and thus to commence another season of hopeless and profitless toil to their unfortunate owner.[49]

---

[48] R. Fulton to G. Morris, *op. cit.*, p. 170.
[49] *Memoirs of Board of Agr.*, I (1821), 35.

LANDLORDS AND FARMERS

The supremacy of wheat as the principal cash crop of eastern New York continued but it did not go unchallenged. Constant cropping was exhausting not only the thin stratum of vegetable mold covering the newly cleared forest lands but was also undermining the fertility of the river flats. The bumper crops which the pioneer farmer grew on his fresh soils soon vanished. Thus the Board of Agriculture in 1823 declared: "The secret of the general poverty prevailing in some elevated districts of country, is, the erroneous practice of forcing a natural grass country into the grain system." [50] Even the bottom lands, so dearly prized for their ability to produce crop after crop, were declining in fertility. Thus the famed Schoharie Flats were described as "totally inert" due to the exhaustion of the surface soil "by one hundred and one years successive wheat crops." [51] The farmers of eastern New York were reaping the harvest of long years of mining the fertility of their soil. If they were to compete successfully with western farmers, they would have to adopt advanced agricultural methods and new crops.

Wheat grown on the upland farms was particularly subject to winterkilling. In desperation many farmers turned to spring wheat as a substitute.[52] Unfortunately, spring wheat did not command as high a price or yield as well as winter wheat. In addition, the Hessian fly often caused even more destruction in the fields of spring wheat than in those of winter wheat.[53] Smut, rust, and mildew blighted many fields of wheat, while swarms of grasshoppers, like those of 1820, seriously injured the plants. Another foe of the farmer was the Canada thistle, a persistent weed which crowded out the wheat plants.[54] To add to his troubles, the fall

---

[50] *Ibid.*, II (1823), Preface.

[51] *Ibid.*, III (1826), p. 525; *Plough Boy*, I (Dec. 11, 1819), p. 221.

[52] *Ibid.*, I (June 12, 1819), 10; II (Sept. 16, 1820), 121; *Argus*, Dec. 25, 1818.

[53] For destruction caused by Hessian fly, see *Argus*, June 16, 1818, and June 14, 1822.

[54] *Plough Boy*, I (June 26, 1819), 26.

YEARS OF UNCERTAINTY

in wheat prices after the war made the lot of the wheat farmer almost unendurable. It is small wonder that the farmers of eastern New York were willing to turn to other crops as the basis of their economy.

The progressive decline in the quality of New York wheat and flour was reflected in the low prices which they brought in the market. Governor De Witt Clinton in 1819 complained that New York flour sold for $1.50 to $2.00 less a barrel than flour made in Philadelphia and Baltimore.[55] Newspaper editors, farm leaders, and legislative committees viewed with alarm the poor reputation of New York flour and wheat.[56] The farmers were blamed for sowing poor seed and for bringing dirty wheat to market. The buyers were accused of mixing grains of various qualities indiscriminately. The millers were charged with grinding too fine and of mixing spoiled flour with the new. The state inspectors were attacked as the incompetent minions of the manufacturers. The mounting tide of criticism forced the state to put into operation in 1821 a more rigorous inspection system which carefully graded wheat and flour. In a relatively short time breadstuffs of New York had regained their original reputation for high quality.

We have already seen that farmers of eastern New York had adopted the use of gypsum and the sowing of clover. They could see with their own eyes how effective these new methods were in rejuvenating exhausted fields. But the ordinary farmer was not interested in the literary discussions about scientific agriculture in which the wealthy landlords in the aristocratic agricultural societies had engaged. Suspicious of book farming and distrustful of all change, the average farmer had to be won to the cause of agricultural reform more through the heart than the head.

The first successful attempt to stimulate the ordinary farmer to improve his techniques was the county fair movement founded by

---

[55] *Messages from Governors*, II, 970.
[56] *Argus*, Dec. 25, 1818; *Plough Boy*, 1 (May 27, 1820), 412; *N.Y. Assembly Journal*, 1819, pp. 387–388.

LANDLORDS AND FARMERS

Elkanah Watson.[57] Watson, than whom there was no more ardent friend of agriculture, had lived an adventuresome life. A native of Plymouth, Massachusetts, he had worked his way up from an apprenticeship to a position of responsibility in the firm of John Brown in Providence. After spending several years in the salons and countinghouses of France and England, he returned to this country where he promoted projects for canals, banks, and schools. Having acquired a modest fortune, Elkanah Watson retired to an estate near Pittsfield where he devoted himself to agriculture. It was not long before he saw the value of Merino sheep. In 1807 he exhibited two sheep in the public square at Pittsfield in order that his neighbors might inspect them. Three years later he had persuaded his neighbors to exhibit their livestock before the public. The success of the showing led to the organization of the Berkshire Agricultural Society, the purpose of which was to stimulate the interest of the farmer by means of prizes awarded at the annual fair. Capitalizing on the nationalism of the war years and shrewdly inviting the farm women to participate in the movement, Watson made the county fair a civic ceremony.

To arouse public interest he devised an elaborate pageantry, strangely reminiscent of the fetes to nature, to reason, and to liberty which had taken place in the early years of the French Revolution. The fair in Schoharie County in 1819 is a good example of the patriotic character of the movement.[58] At dawn the populace was awakened by bells and cannon. Then came the parade, headed by the president of the Society and the guest speaker. Directly behind the officials of the society and the clergy, who occupied second place, came a member carrying a file of the Albany *Plough Boy* and his comrade carrying an agricultural

---

[57] The best sources for Watson's activities are his own writings. See especially his *Rise, Progress, and Existing State of Modern Agricultural Societies on the Berkshire System* (Albany, 1820).

[58] *Plough Boy*, I (Oct. 30, 1819), 174.

YEARS OF UNCERTAINTY

flag. In the procession were horses pulling harrows and plows. The band played spirited music and martial airs. Members of the society and the citizenry brought up the end of the parade. On this particular occasion the procession marched to the church, where the service began with the reading of an ode and a prayer. The high spot of the ceremony came after the president's address. The proud winners of awards marched to the rostrum to receive their prizes. When the service was over the members repaired to the courthouse for dinner. An agricultural ball climaxed the day's festivities.

Such a ceremony made a deep impression upon the rural population whose bleak meetinghouses and churches had failed to satisfy the deep-seated love of ritual and pageantry. Furthermore, it skillfully invested the cause of agricultural reform with religious and patriotic trappings. Unfortunately, although the county fair could pique the curiosity of the farmer, it could not overcome his indifference to such an extent that he would cheerfully finance the annual showing.

Agricultural leaders in New York soon recognized the value of the Berkshire plan. The Society for the Promotion of Useful Arts recommended to the legislature in 1815 a program of county fairs and a list of suitable premiums.[59] In the same year Elkanah Watson moved to Albany. Despite his reluctance to re-enter public life Watson threw himself into the work of organizing county societies. Within a few years fifty-two out of fifty-eight counties had formed societies.[60] In 1817 Watson gave the opening address at the Otsego County fair. Watson's observation that it caused great excitement was more than justified. Jesse Buel, the proprietor of the *Albany Argus* at this time, showed great interest. Buel urged the farmers of Albany County to organize an agricultural society so that they could improve the "wretched husbandry"

---
[59] *Trans. for Promotion of Arts*, IV, pt. 1 (1816), Appendix, 6–13.
[60] Watson, *Modern Agricultural Societies*, pp. 137–165.

LANDLORDS AND FARMERS

of the countryside.[61] Governor De Witt Clinton in January, 1818, gave further impetus to the popular interest in the fairs by recommending to the legislature that it create a board of agriculture which could direct and help finance the activities of the county societies.[62] A joint committee of the Senate and Assembly responded favorably to his suggestion and urged that $30,000 be granted to county societies for premiums.[63] The legislature, however, took no action and, if we are to believe Watson, resolved by a "thundering majority": "Be it further enacted that the farmers of this state be permitted to manage their own farms in their own way." [64]

In 1819 Clinton again recommended public aid for agriculture. But this time the legislature, under the prodding of Watson, overrode the opposition of many members and appropriated $10,000 a year for the next two years.[65] The money was to be distributed among the counties on condition that the local societies raise a certain amount which the state would match. The presidents or delegates of the county societies were to form a state Board of Agriculture. The board would receive annual reports from which the most important items would be selected for publication.

In 1820 the board met for the first time, with twenty-six counties represented. The members elected Stephen Van Rensselaer their president and George Featherstonhaugh their corresponding secretary.[66] In its first address to the local societies the general committee of the board pointed out such evils as ruinous cropping,

---

[61] See the *Argus*, Oct. 7, Dec. 2, 30, 1817, June 9, Oct. 30, Nov. 10, 17, 1818.

[62] *Messages from Governors*, II, 898.

[63] *N.Y. Assembly Journal*, 1818, pp. 407–411.

[64] *Modern Agricultural Societies*, p. 153. I can find no such resolution in the journals of the Assembly and the Senate.

[65] Alfred Charles True, *A History of Agricultural Education in the United States, 1785–1925* (Washington, 1929), p. 24.

[66] *Memoirs of Board of Agr.*, I, x.

YEARS OF UNCERTAINTY

excessive drinking, the desire for speculative gains, and the disregard for improved agricultural methods. The county societies were particularly urged to send in reports to the board.

To aid the officials Elkanah Watson published a pamphlet describing the history of the Berkshire Society. It gave directions for the establishment of new societies. He sent a copy of the pamphlet to each president and to the supervisors in those counties which had not organized agricultural societies. By 1820 almost all the counties in the state were holding fairs.

In 1819 the *Plough Boy* was founded at Albany by Solomon Southwick, formerly editor of the *Albany Register*. The pages of this periodical carry much information about the agricultural societies and the fairs. In 1820 the state Board of Agriculture designated it as the official journal. Southwick did not exert a powerful influence, largely because he did not possess the necessary practical background in agriculture.[67] In 1823 he discontinued publication because of inadequate support.

In 1825 the legislature permitted the law authorizing the state to finance county societies to expire, despite the recommendation of De Witt Clinton and the Board of Agriculture that it be continued.[68] The original opposition to public aid had been reinforced by the unjudicious way in which many of the local societies had managed their exhibitions. Prizes had been awarded only to members of the society, and nonmembers resented this discrimination. The policy of awarding premiums to those who produced the most, regardless of production costs, aroused the ire of practical farmers.[69] The most compelling argument was the failure of the societies to stem the fall in prices and to provide new markets.

---

[67] Albert Demaree, *The American Agricultural Press, 1819–1860* (New York, 1941), p. 336.

[68] *Messages from Governors*, III, 64; *N.Y. Senate Journal*, 1825, pp. 332–335.

[69] See letter of Dutchess County farmer in the *Memoirs of Board of Agr.*, II (1823), 185–189. See letter by "Country Farmer" in *New-York Farmer*, IV (Nov., 1831), 301.

LANDLORDS AND FARMERS

A legislative committee in 1821 pointedly questioned the value of subsidizing methods designed to increase the production of livestock and foodstuffs when there was no market for them.[70] No amount of pageantry and exhortation could persuade the farmer to improve his techniques unless he found it profitable.

The short life of the county fair movement does not mean that its influence on the agricultural life of eastern New York was without permanent value. Certain concrete benefits emerged. More attention was paid to manuring the fields, selecting seeds, and planting fallow crops. The county fair was a good channel to disseminate knowledge about English livestock, Merino sheep, and new implements. The plowing matches demonstrated quite clearly to the onlookers that the cast-iron plow was a vast improvement over the wooden plow. The German farmers in the Schoharie Valley discovered that deep plowing enabled them to produce the high yields of their ancestors.[71] Probably the most lasting benefit was the spirit of enterprise. It inspired many farmers to adopt new agricultural methods. In a few short years Jesse Buel and his associates were to revive interest in agricultural improvement to such an extent that the rural population was willing to support a strong state society and to make possible the success of the *Cultivator*.

The county fair, with its emphasis on sheep and cattle, speeded up the shift toward a more diversified agriculture. As the raising of wheat became more hazardous and less profitable, farmers turned to the many branches of the grazing industry. The most spectacular development was the enthusiasm for Merino sheep. More significant for the future was the gradual growth of the dairy industry.

The introduction of the Merino sheep laid the foundations for fine-wooled sheep breeding and woolgrowing. In 1802 Robert Livingston, who was minister to France at the time, shipped two

---

[70] *N.Y. Assembly Journal*, 44 sess., 1820–1821, p. 842.
[71] *Memoirs of Board of Agr.*, III (1826), 525.

YEARS OF UNCERTAINTY

pairs of merinos to his Hudson River estate.[72] Contemporary observers had already made it clear that the manufacture of woolens could not get a foothold in America unless the local supply of wool was improved. The New York Society for the Promotion of Useful Arts asked its members for suggestions as to how to improve wool.[73] In 1800 mechanics and manufacturers in New York City asked the legislature for aid in improving the breed of sheep.[74]

But before 1808 the Merino sheep created scarcely a stir in the placid ways of the farmers. Livingston upon his return from Europe in 1805 was astonished that the sheep had attracted so little attention.[75] The following year he tried to arouse interest by writing two essays on sheep for the Society of Useful Arts. His arguments apparently made little impression on the farming community. It was not until the economic crisis created by the Embargo and Nonintercourse Acts had vividly dramatized the necessity and desirability of producing fine wool for a home industry that the farmer saw the Merino sheep as a source of profit. The editor of the *Hudson Balance* on December 8, 1807, noted that John R. Livingston had sold all the wool of his Spanish sheep for $1.50 a pound. Such prices, he declared, would arouse farmers to their true interests.

The demand of the new woolen factories for fine wool caused the price of pure Merino wool to rise from 75 cents a pound to $2.00, whereas common wool remained at 37½ cents.[76] Corresponding with this rise was the spectacular advance in the value

---

[72] A full account of these early importations is given in *Special Report on the History and the Present Condition of the Sheep Industry of the United States,* ed. by D. E. Salmon (Washington, 1892), pp. 131–169. See also *Trans.,* XXI (1861), 681–689.

[73] See its *Transactions,* I (1807), xiii.

[74] *N.Y. Assembly Journal,* 24 sess., 1800, p. 24.

[75] *Essay on Sheep* (New York, 1809), p. 7.

[76] J. L. Bishop, *A History of American Manufactures from 1608 to 1860* (Philadelphia, 1861–1868), II, 135; *Special Report on the Sheep Industry,* p. 142.

of Merino sheep. Full-blooded rams in 1810 sold for as high as $1,000 and $1,500, while common sheep were selling for $2.00 each.[77] In his *Essay on Sheep,* Robert Livingston methodically worked out the profits from his various kinds of sheep. Ten common sheep produced wool to the value of $15; ten merino sheep yielded wool to the value of $70. Since the wool of a half blood was worth twice that of a common sheep, there arose a great demand for Merino rams.

In 1810 Chancellor Livingston's estate on the Hudson was the scene of a famous sheepshearing.[78] Colonel Humphreys, eminent promoter of sheep in Connecticut, Dr. Samuel Mitchell, and Elkanah Watson were a few of the notables present. Several wore elegant suits of Merino wool. One hundred and ninety-six ewes went under the shears. The fleeces were immediately sold to manufacturers. The event took on something of the character of a public ceremony. At one end of the table was a large sign, "Success to Agriculture"; at the other end was the sign, "Success to Manufactures."

Chancellor Livingston stated in a letter to the Honorable Colonel Barclay, prominent English agricultural leader, that his flock was improving each year both in quantity and quality of wool.[79] Included in this letter was a table of his sales:

4 full-bred ram lambs	$4,000
14 fifteen-sixteenth ram lambs	3,500
20 seven-eighths ram lambs	2,000
30 three-fourths ram lambs	900
	$10,400

Obviously these extremely high prices for fine wool and sheep could not last. The inevitable collapse took place in 1810–1811. One cause was the importation of over twenty-five thousand Merino sheep from Spain, where William Jarvis, American consul to Portugal, took advantage of the chaotic conditions caused by

---
[77] *Trans.,* XXI (1861), 690.
[78] *Albany Register,* June 26, 1810.
[79] A copy of this letter is in *Trans.,* XXII (1862), 65–66.

YEARS OF UNCERTAINTY

the Napoleonic invasion to buy and export thousands of valuable animals.[80] Such importations naturally depressed the price of Merino sheep to a level sufficiently low so that many farmers could afford to buy a Merino buck and perhaps a few ewes. More important still, it provided a firm basis for a substantial production of fine stapled wool. The new agricultural societies as well as subsidies offered by the government facilitated the dispersion of these sheep throughout the countryside.[81]

Washington County was to become famous for its sheep industry. As early as 1809 Merino sheep appeared in the county. Mr. Wilson of Salem acquired a full-blooded buck in 1809, for which he received the bounty of $50 from the state.[82] Other merinos from Colonel Humphreys' flock were introduced. An interesting partnership in sheep raising shows quite clearly the speculative nature of the Merino "mania." The merchant, Robert Prince of New York, made an agreement with Alexander McNish of Salem, Washington County, by which Mr. Prince was to furnish three full-blooded Merino sheep consisting of one ram and two ewes. Mr. McNish was to furnish one hundred common ewes. On the first day of each June one half of the wool was to belong to Mr. Prince. At the end of the first year, the hundred common ewes were to be sold and one half of the proceeds given to Mr. Prince. Furthermore, on the first day of each September the buck lambs were to be divided. At the end of seven years the flock was to be evenly divided.[83]

The history of this agreement shows some of the hazards to which the sheep industry was exposed. Not realizing that the merinos could not endure the cold and snow to which the hardy

---

[80] See *Special Report on the Sheep Industry*, pp. 193–197.

[81] Wright, *op. cit.*, pp. 25–30. Washington County had its first merino in 1809, which earned the $50 premium given by the state (*Trans.*, IX [1849], p. 760). Samuel Law had a full-blooded ram in 1810 (see "Statement of Acc'ts, Sheep and Wool," Box 14, S. A. Law Papers).

[82] *Special Report on the Sheep Industry*, p. 351.

[83] *Trans.*, IX (1849), 760–770.

LANDLORDS AND FARMERS

native breed had become accustomed, Mr. McNish found that nearly all his lambs perished. Despite the utmost care McNish failed to raise any substantial number of lambs and his contract was annulled, in part because the disastrous slump in wool prices following 1815 had made the whole operation unprofitable.

There was often a close connection between the distribution of Merino sheep and the location of early factories.[84] In Oneida County the local capitalists who were setting up woolen mills along the banks of Sauquoit Creek also organized the Mount Merino Association in 1808, with a capitalization of $40,000.[85] Imported Merino bucks were crossed with a hundred selected common ewes. Subsequently the flock was divided into groups of one hundred on the farm of Dr. Seth Capron, who was also active in the early textile mills. The wool was worth 9 to 10 shillings a pound. This price does not seem high when we remember that broadcloth was selling for $10 to $15 a yard. With the coming of peace the Oneida Manufacturing Company closed its doors. The company killed two thousand sheep for their pelts.

Even the ordinary farmer was quick to see the profits in wool, especially since the embargo and the war drastically cut his grain exports. Farmers in a neighborhood would buy four or five sheep with some Merino blood and a full-blooded Merino ram.[86] Soon their flocks were largely Merino in blood. The flood of imported sheep precipitated a sharp decline in the value of merinos. By 1815 merinos were selling for $1.00 each, a price which brought them within the reach of all farmers. The low price so disgusted many farmers that they killed their flocks for the tallow and the skin.

The average farmer kept on his farm from twenty to fifty mongrel animals for his own use.[87] Farmers living close by the market-

---

[84] Arthur Cole, *The American Wool Manufacture* (Cambridge, 1926), I, 77.

[85] *Special Report on the Sheep Industry*, pp. 357–358.

[86] *Ibid.*

[87] *Memoirs of Board of Agr.*, I, 305.

YEARS OF UNCERTAINTY

ing centers turned to heavier breeds which would produce more mutton than the light merino.[88] So widespread was the reaction against growing wool for the market that the Board of Agriculture in 1823 pointed with alarm to the fact that woolen factories could only be kept going by importing cheap foreign wools.[89]

In 1826 Samuel A. Law wrote to Charles Fisher, one of the landholders in Delaware County, that his flock of twelve hundred to thirteen hundred fine-wooled sheep was "by much my most productive income."[90] Law had come to this conclusion after raising sheep for eighteen years. In 1810 he had forty-eight sheep. By 1824 he had twelve hundred.[91] The quality of the fleeces improved over the years.

Law kept detailed accounts of all his operations. His balance sheet for 1818 has some interesting estimates:

INCOME (from 443 fleeces)		COSTS	
1. 1,295 pds. of wool	$888.88	1. 75 tons of hay (3)	$225
2. Lambs	250.00	2. 1 shepherd and bd.	200
3. Manure	110.00	3. Salt	20
		4. Tar	5
		5. Use of 150 acres	450
	$1,250.00		$900

[Note actual total came to $1,248.88]. Estimated profit $350

Raising sheep was a hazardous business. Wolves and dogs were a constant menace.[92] In 1814 Law reported that he had lost fifty-seven sheep from wolves and wintering. In 1821 a "dreadful spell of weather" and a shortage of hay led to a loss of fifty sheep.

---

[88] Ibid., p. 311. George W. Featherstonhaugh, active member of the Board of Agriculture, used mixed Bakewell and Teeswater rams to increase the weight of his Merino flock (ibid., II, 141).

[89] Ibid., Preface.

[90] March 11, 1826, Box 14, "Statement of Acc'ts," S. A. Law Papers.

[91] Information concerning Law's sheep activities can be found in "Statement of Acc'ts, Sheep and Wool," Box 14, Law Papers.

[92] R. R. Livingston urged in 1806 a state law against sheep-killing dogs (Trans. for Promotion of Arts, II [1807], 102).

LANDLORDS AND FARMERS

Equally troublesome was the problem of disposing of the wool. In 1811 Law employed Mary Hill to spin his Merino wool. Three hundred pounds of wool produced 372 yards of unfulled cloth and blanketing. In 1821 William Gunn made for Law 30 yards of fulled woolen cloth and 114 yards of satinette out of 193 pounds of scoured wool. Law made the notation that he lost $11.09 on the transaction.

Law dispatched most of his wool between 1815 and 1819 to Archibald Crosswell, who operated a small factory at Gilboa. He sold 6,466 pounds for $3,893.68. Some wool was turned over to Crosswell on shares, each retaining one half of the product. This arrangement caused Law much trouble. First of all, he had difficulty in selling the broadcloth at what he deemed satisfactory prices. Secondly, Crosswell was unable to pay for all the wool. As a result Law looked elsewhere for a buyer. In 1823 he sold 4,700 pounds of wool for $2,723.58 to the Oriskany Manufacturing Company in central New York. Later he sold wool to a factory near Goshen, Orange County.

The great advance in woolen manufacture was not made at the expense of the household industry.[93] The farm family was still producing the bulk of the woolen cloth. New inventions such as the carding machine, spinning jenny, and loom with flying shuttles helped speed up the home output. The state legislature early felt the need of encouraging the industry. Thus an act of April 8, 1808, offered premiums of $80 to the person in each county who manufactured the best specimen of woolen cloth of uniform texture and quality.[94] County judges were to designate the winners. In 1810 and 1812 the law was renewed but slightly changed.[95] Under these

---

[93] Wright, *ibid.*, p. 21. Wright estimates that woolen factories produced about 200,000 yards of cloth in 1809, whereas home manufacture turned out 9,500,000 yards. See also J. L. Donovan, *Textile Manufacture in New York before 1840* (Thesis, Columbia University Library, 1932), p. 52.

[94] *Laws of N.Y.*, 31 sess., c. 360.

[95] *Ibid.*, 33 sess., c. 108 and 35 sess., c. 230.

YEARS OF UNCERTAINTY

acts a total of $21,000 was awarded, going to individuals in almost every county.[96]

The household manufacture did not fall off rapidly until the period after 1825.[97] There was a growing tendency, however, for many of the operations to be carried on outside the family. Thus the farmers often took their wool to small establishments to be carded.[98] Sometimes the same establishment would spin and weave the wool.[99] Usually the women of the family, aided by the semi-professional spinsters in the neighborhood, performed this task. The agricultural societies laid great emphasis on the household manufacture and awarded handsome premiums.[100] The failure of many textile factories after 1815 and the disastrous decline in prices forced the rural population to rely on their own efforts. Nevertheless, the flood of cheap English goods was a threat to the home industry, which naturally could not produce as efficiently as the factory. Calicoes and bright prints did reach many country store counters. Already in 1822 a farmer in Orange County publicly complained that his wife and children preferred imported cloth to the rough homespun.[101]

Eastern New York emerges in this period as an important producer of butter and cheese. The uplands which were no longer able to grow wheat provided good pasture for cattle. The butchers and merchants of New York, Albany, and other cities were demanding more and more beef, mutton, and particularly dairy products. Farmers living in the immediate vicinity of cities grew

---

[96] See *Transactions of the Albany Institute* (Albany, 1864), IV, 117 ff.

[97] Tryon, *op. cit.*, pp. 304–307.

[98] See advertisement of G. N. Phillips of Phillipsburgh in *Orange County Patriot*, June 4, 1811. Phillips would accept cash, wool, wheat, rye, boards, and siding for payment.

[99] See advertisement of John Jenkins in Hudson *Northern Whig*, Jan. 3, 1815.

[100] For typical comments, see *Utica Patriot*, Oct. 24, 1820. See also *N.Y. Assembly Journal*, 41 sess. (1818), p. 617.

[101] See letter in *Orange County Patriot*, April 1, 1822.

vegetables and supplied milk. Farmers farther away fattened stock and sold cheese and butter. Slowly but surely the home market was supplanting the foreign market. Prior to 1808 much of the wheat, flour, potash, and lumber was exported. After 1808 most of the wool, cheese, butter, and milk was sold within the state.

Orange County is the most conspicuous example of the influence of the home market on agriculture.[102] Farmers grew rich making butter. So eager were the merchants to buy this butter that in November, 1813, a group of speculators in Newburgh and other Orange County towns cornered the butter market and forced up the price. Grocers and editors in New York City protested against the monopoly.[103] They urged the people to delay their winter purchases for a month. Most Orange County butter bore the name "Goshen butter." Its reputation was unequaled. The farmers of Orange County were incensed when other regions pirated the name.[104]

A few other localities produced considerable amounts of butter for sale. The town of Steuben, Oneida County was reported to have sold butter valued at over $20,000 in 1819.[105] The agent of the Banyar estate made in 1816 some interesting comments about the farmers in Delaware County:

The proprietors of the purchased farms and many of the tenants who have leased are turning their attention to stock and very large quantities of butter was sent to New York market last year so much as to net upwards of $100,000 from 3 towns in Delaware (Kortright, Stamford, Roxbury)—as I was told.[106]

---

[102] Orange County, western Long Island, and northern New Jersey supplied most of the butter reaching New York markets (*Plough Boy*, II [July 15, 1820]), 53.

[103] *New York Gazette,* Nov. 1, 1813, quoted by Thomas F. De Voe, *The Market Book* (New York, 1862), I, 408.

[104] *Orange County Patriot,* Dec. 10, 1821 and Jan. 21, 1822.

[105] *Plough Boy,* II (Sept. 9, 1820), 117.

[106] "Wm. H. Jephson's Memorandums, May 16, 1816 to Dec. 1823 Banyar Estate," Box 1, v. 11, G. Banyar Papers.

YEARS OF UNCERTAINTY

The manufacture of cheese had become by 1825 the major occupation of many farmers in Herkimer and Oneida counties.[107] The Yankees settling in the upland towns had brought with them a skill in cheese making which had made famous the products of the Berkshire area. According to one account, cheese speculators from Berkshire came to Herkimer County in 1815 and made contracts with the farmers.[108] Unfortunately, most cheese and butter made in this period was of a distinctly inferior quality.[109] One very persuasive factor causing farmers to improve the quality of their product was the premium prices which superior Goshen butter enjoyed.

The old antagonism between landlord and tenant flared up once again. In 1811 the legislature received several memorials from farmers in Montgomery, Delaware, Dutchess, Otsego, and Saratoga counties denouncing the title of George Clarke, Jr., the English-born heir of Lieutenant Governor Clarke in the colonial administration. The tenants insisted that the lands belonged to the state since Clarke had been an enemy alien at the time he inherited his property. The committee which the Senate appointed to investigate the matter endorsed the views of the tenants. They urged the governor to begin a judicial investigation of the title which was tentatively valued at $1,000,000.[110] The truculent attitude of Clarke, who refused to testify before the committee, and his "high English notions of strict right," [111] in his relations with tenants made him a conspicuous target. The Senate passed a bill authorizing the governor to start legal proceedings against Clarke's title, but the bill did not get any further.[112]

In the same year a concurrent resolution of the Senate and Assembly requested Ambrose Spencer, one of the judges of the

---

[107] N. Benton, *op. cit.,* p. 209.
[108] *Cultivator,* I (Aug., 1834), 84.
[109] *Memoirs of the N.Y. Board of Agriculture,* III, 128.
[110] *N.Y. Senate Journal,* 1812, p. 56; *New-York Spectator,* March 4, 1812.
[111] Beardsley, *op. cit.,* p. 446.
[112] *New-York Spectator,* June 3, 1812.

Supreme Court, John Woodworth, and William P. Van Ness, who had been recently appointed members of a commission to revise the laws of the state, to examine the existing laws regulating tenures and to suggest possible remedies.

The commissioners declared that "restraints in the nature of fines or quarter-sale against alienation are exceedingly objectionable and constitute rigid and unreasonable burdens upon the tenants." [113] They held that it was the duty of the state to protect individuals from oppressive conditions even though the tenants had voluntarily entered into the agreements. Specifically they recommended the withdrawal of the right to forfeit leases, although the landlords were to be permitted to sue for damages in a court of equity. In order to avoid similar troubles in the future, they urged that a ban be placed on the granting of leasehold tenures.

A bill designed to carry out these reforms was drawn up, but it died in the Senate after passing the second reading. Popular opinion was not sufficiently aroused to force through such a drastic overhauling of the deeply entrenched institution of tenancy. The aristocratic landlords were still powerful politically. In the constitutional convention of 1821 the landlords strenuously opposed the adoption of manhood suffrage, which they claimed would permit the rabble to despoil the rich. Jacob R. Van Rensselaer from Columbia County, predicted that the landless would pass agrarian laws and topple over the pillars of society.[114]

General Van Rensselaer, the leading member of a collateral line of the Van Rensselaer family, was speaking from bitter experience. Only ten years earlier he had been forced to defend his title from attacks by both his tenants and the attorney general of the state. In 1811 Martin Van Buren, a new arrival in Hudson, is supposed to have written a series of letters appearing in the Hud-

---

[113] *N.Y. Assembly Journal*, 35 sess., 1812, pp. 110–111.
[114] D. R. Fox, *Decline of Aristocracy*, p. 256.

YEARS OF UNCERTAINTY

son *Advocate*.[115] These letters resurrected the old story that the Van Rensselaers and the Livingstons had acquired their lands in a fraudulent manner. His enemies insisted that Van Buren was trying to round up more legal business by probing the old sores which had not entirely healed over from the agrarian uprisings of the 1760's and the 1790's.[116] They also accused him of using his position as counsel for the tenants as a springboard from which he hoped to reach the state Senate, a rather lofty ambition for a youth under thirty living in the rock-ribbed, landlord-ridden Federalist county of Columbia.

Whatever his motives may have been, Martin Van Buren stirred up the old controversy between landlord and tenants. In his successful campaign for the Senate in the spring of 1812 he denounced the Federalist patroons as tyrants and oppressors of the poor. In his autobiography Van Buren side-steps some of these charges but he does give many interesting details of his relations with General Van Rensselaer.[117] According to Van Buren, the General felt concerned about a rumor which was hurting his chances for re-election to the Assembly. It had been reported that he had declared on the floor of the Assembly that the "tenants were not fit to govern themselves, and deserved to have a master." [118] Van Rensselaer proposed to Van Buren that the latter publicly brand the rumor as false. Van Buren made a counter-proposal that the Federalist press stop its attacks on him. No agreement could be reached. The General thereupon called a meeting on the manor at which he told

---

[115] Holmes Moss Alexander, *The American Talleyrand; the Career and Contemporaries of Martin Van Buren, Eighth President* (New York, 1935), p. 76.

[116] See pamphlet by "Corrector," *Letters Addressed to Martin Van Buren, Esq.* (New York, 1830), pp. 3–4.

[117] "The Autobiography of Martin Van Buren," ed. by John Fitzpatrick, *Annual Report of the American Historical Association for the Year 1918*, II, 22–26.

[118] *Ibid.*

the tenants that Van Buren was delaying action on the tenants' petition until after the spring elections of 1812.

Martin Van Buren immediately sent out handbills advertising a public meeting at the same place. He formally denied that he had written a letter to Mr. Whallon of Albany urging delay on the petition. Jacob Van Rensselaer, who was present at the meeting together with the Livingstons and their agents, came forward and declared that he would deposit $500 as a forfeit if he could not prove the truth of his allegations. According to Van Buren, the General refused to go through with his pledge after the election.

In the meantime, the legislature had directed the attorney general, Thomas A. Emmet, to commence suits on behalf of the state against the land titles then in dispute. Emmet, the famous leader of the United Irishmen, proceeded to carry out an investigation with the same vigor that he had demonstrated in his agitation for Irish home rule. But in a short time he was replaced in office by Abraham Van Vechten, a staunch conservative and widely known as a "landlord's lawyer." The antirenters of another generation darkly intimated that the landlords had ousted Emmet from office.[119] Van Vechten arrived in Hudson to bring to trial the suit against the title of Van Rensselaer. According to Van Buren, he and the defense attorneys, who now included Thomas Emmet, attempted to secure a postponement.[120] The attorney-general refused to grant the extension. As a result the trial ended in a verdict for the defendants.

The incendiary speeches of Van Buren in the courts and on the platform fanned to flame the smoldering discontent among the tenants.[121] The usual disorders took place. Tenants refused to

---

[119] *Freeholder,* Nov. 24, 1847. See letter by "B" in *Freeholder,* Jan. 5, 1848.

[120] *Autobiography,* p. 24.

[121] H. Alexander, *op. cit.,* p. 77. Martin Van Buren was counsel for the tenants in many ejectment suits. See Jackson, *ex dem.* Livingston and Wilsey, against Wilsey and Another, N.Y. Supreme Court, *Reports of Cases Argued and Determined in the Supreme Court of Judicature,* ed. by R.

YEARS OF UNCERTAINTY

pay the rent. Mobs prevented the officials from collecting the rent. In 1813 the sheriff of Columbia County was killed.[122] One report states that Jacob Van Rensselaer led a force of nearly three hundred men to the town of Hillsdale in order to oust his recalcitrant tenants.[123] That particular township was the only one in Columbia County to suffer a decline in population between 1810 and 1820.

In addition to the recurrent outbreaks of the tenants, the landlords experienced other difficulties in operating their estates. We have already mentioned the difficulties of Samuel A. Law in collecting payments on the land that he had sold to the settlers. Moreover, the fall in commodity prices necessarily meant a decline in income for those landlords who received their rent in kind. The trenchant observations of Paul Busti, agent of the Holland Land Company, confirm our earlier criticisms of the leasehold system as it was usually operated in the state. Busti wrote in 1816 that it was impossible for a gentleman-farmer to work to advantage a farm in America.

Whether he leases it out, or gives it on shares or keeps it in his own hands the Gentleman farmer will always find that the possession of farms affords no revenue. A Tenant on lease in few years—exhausts and impoverishes the lands, neglects the keeping in due repair the buildings, houses—, brings no manure on the fields, suffers his cattle to run at large, but too often even permoved by a criminal avarice sells the dung to others—.[124]

Busti continued in similar vein castigating the wastefulness of tenants and the downright dishonesty of overseers and tenants in dividing the produce with the owner. Undoubtedly his experience found many parallels among the landowners of the period.

Another glance at the population maps will confirm our earlier

---

Johnstone (Albany, 1859–1860), IX, 268. For a similar case, see *ibid.*, X, 335.

[122] Governor John Young's Proclamation of Jan. 27, 1847, in the *Argus*, Jan. 28, 1847.

[123] *Freeholder*, May 31, 1848.

[124] *Extracts from Blockley Farm Journal Commencing 1816*, by Paul Busti, Fairchild Collection, New York Public Library.

155

observation that the purely agricultural areas of the Hudson-Mohawk region were approaching population stability. In some sections rural decline had already begun. Eastern New York, with the exception of the commercial towns, was no longer the goal of the emigrants who were still pouring out of New England. With its best lands occupied and its poorer soils showing the effects of exhaustion, eastern New York had little to offer the newcomer. In fact, eastern New York was contributing its own sons to the westward-flowing stream.[125] It was easier to clear a new farm and to continue the one-crop husbandry of their ancestors than to manure an old farm and to adopt improved methods. To the farmer whose wheat fields had been ruined by the Hessian fly, winterkilling, or the rust, the name Ohio or Michigan was a symbol of the prosperity which he had failed to reach. The publicity in the papers,[126] the departure of neighbors, and the stories of fertile and cheap lands stirred the restless spirits of the population. Once the movement began it tended to gain momentum. Furthermore, lack of capital prevented many farmers from making the necessary improvements and acquiring cows and sheep which successful farming required.

Almost as seductive as the west was the lure of the city. Ambitious young men were drifting to the cities to enter mercantile and professional life.[127] The construction of the Erie Canal and the new centers growing up along its route attracted thousands of new inhabitants. To the consternation and dismay of some farmers, their daughters as well as their sons often found city life more attractive than the simple life of the countryside. The editor of the *Plough Boy* felt so strongly about this trend that he wrote a

---

[125] *N.Y. Senate Journal*, 1826, pp. 438–442.

[126] Advertisements in the papers offered to exchange lands in Ohio, Illinois, and Michigan for improved lands in Albany, Rensselaer, Columbia, and Saratoga counties (see *Argus*, Feb. 26, 1829, and *Utica Intelligencer*, Oct. 9, 1827).

[127] *Memoirs of Board of Agr.*, I, xxvii.

YEARS OF UNCERTAINTY

poem urging the farm girls to remain in the country. The opening verse ran as follows:

> Sweet Mary, sigh not for the town,
> Where vice and folly reign;
> Spurn not the humble homespun gown
> That suits the rural plain.[128]

When the country was new, there was a great demand for labor to clear and fence the land, erect buildings, build roads, and construct churches. Once these improvements had been made there was less need for labor except among those actually employed in cultivation.[129] Furthermore, the sheep industry getting under way required a larger farm unit which in turn tended to displace population.[130]

It would be uncharitable as well as untrue to leave the impression that farm life was one unbroken succession of misfortunes and a hopeless struggle against unkind nature. Serious evils did exist, evils which contemporary observers were quite frank in admitting. These evils, whether the excessive drinking prevailing among the people [131] or the lack of interest in agricultural improvements, complicated the general problem of readjusting agriculture to meet new conditions. On the credit side, many farmers displayed a willingness to support innovations such as Merino sheep and the county fair. The fact that their high hopes from such new ventures were disappointed did not cause the death of agricultural reform. Energetic individuals such as Jesse Buel kept up the agitation for improved methods and demonstrated that book farming was profitable. Between 1812 and 1820 Earl Stimson, a progressive farmer of Galway, Saratoga County, averaged over

---

[128] *Plough Boy*, II (Aug. 19, 1820), 89.

[129] *Trans.*, XIX (1859), 320.

[130] S. A. Law to Charles Wharton, March 5, 1825, Box 4, Correspondence, 1824–1828, S. A. Law Papers.

[131] *Memoirs of Board of Agr.*, I, 223. George Featherstonhaugh condemned the practice of giving coarse rum and whisky to children (*ibid.*).

LANDLORDS AND FARMERS

$16 an acre annually on an eight-acre lot.[132] Other farmers, favorably located to take advantage of the growing home markets, were likewise able to make farming a profitable occupation. William Cobbett, reflecting on his experience on Long Island, could say in 1819, "A farmer here depends on nobody but himself and on his own proper means; and, if he be not at his ease, and even rich, it must be his own fault." [133]

To generalize too broadly about agricultural life in eastern New York would do violence to its increasing diversity. In their efforts to readjust themselves to the new conditions caused by the growth of the home market, the decline in wheat culture, and the competition of the west, the farmers often followed divergent paths leading toward specialized activities. Thus the farmer in Orange County concentrated on butter, the farmer in the upland towns of Herkimer County devoted his energies to cheese making, and the farmer of Washington County turned to sheep raising. Of course, some individuals lacked the ability, willingness to work, capital resources, and opportunities to make successful readjustments.

In general, the mass of farmers found it difficult to endure the price fluctuations and especially the deflation which took place during this period. They also found it difficult to give up their old dependence on wheat. Nevertheless, certain basic forces were compelling farmers to look to grazing for their salvation. By 1825 the movement was distinctly under way and the Hudson-Mohawk Valley region was soon to emerge as the outstanding butter and cheese region in the country.

---

[132] *Ibid.*, II (1823), 69–73; Stuart, *op. cit.*, I, 256.
[133] *A Year's Residence, in the United States of America* (3d ed.; London, 1828), p. vi.

CHAPTER V

THE TRANSPORTATION NETWORK

1825 - 1850

THE GROWTH of the transportation network exerted a profound influence upon our economic development. The effects on our agrarian life were revolutionary. By 1850 all but the most isolated farmers in the hill country were raising foodstuffs for sale. Conversely, the old life of self-sufficiency was rapidly vanishing. Turnpike, canal, and railroad were linking market and farm closer and closer together. Not without reason, therefore, do historians sometimes refer to this period as the agricultural revolution.[1]

Perhaps in no other section of the country was the impact of western competition and the home market more keenly felt than in the Hudson-Mohawk Valley. Certainly no other region was more exposed to the flood of western produce which poured in by way of the Erie Canal. Few other sections possessed as fine markets as New York City and the upstate centers. But eastern New York farmers did not react to these economic forces in a uniform manner. Some turned to sheep raising, others to specialized crops, and the great majority to the production of butter, cheese, and milk. In order to understand the full significance of

---

[1] For an interesting article covering the period in New England, see Percy W. Bidwell, "The Agricultural Revolution in New England," *American Historical Review*, XXVI (July, 1921), 683-702.

LANDLORDS AND FARMERS

these agricultural changes we must describe and analyze the extension of the canal and railroad network.

Population maps for the period reflect in part transportation changes as well as the general trend of rural economy. The most obvious conclusion is that the rural population had reached a state of stability, if not of saturation. Between 1830 and 1840 eastern New York showed a population gain of 14 per cent.[2] During the following decade the rate of gain was 15 per cent. Most of this modest increase took place in the cities. For example, the four cities of Albany, Schenectady, Troy, and Utica gained a total of almost twenty-five thousand inhabitants during each decade. But over one hundred rural townships suffered losses in the decade following 1830. Some eighty-odd towns lost population between 1840 and 1850.

Dutchess, Washington, and Otsego counties are conspicuous for large numbers of declining towns between 1830 and 1840. If this map is compared with the map showing the number of sheep in 1836, a high correlation between the two can be seen. Significantly, thirty-eight of the towns showing a high concentration of sheep lost population. There is no need to elaborate the close connection between the sheep industry with its large units and small amount of labor and the decline in population.[3] The most noticeable gains in this period were in the townships surrounding Albany, Troy, Schenectady, and Utica. Another region of marked growth was the Catskill area. The tanning and dairy industries were invading the mountain townships.

The changes between 1840 and 1850 follow much the same pattern. The Catskill region stretching clear across to the Delaware

---

[2] These estimates are computed from the table in the Introduction to the *N.Y. Census for 1855*, p. xxxiii. Between 1850 and 1860 the area of eastern New York increased its population approximately 13 per cent. Over half of the total gain was made in the two counties of Albany and Westchester.

[3] Lewis Stillwell (*op. cit.*, pp. 172 ff.) finds a similar parallelism between Vermont towns containing a large number of sheep and those declining in population.

THE TRANSPORTATION NETWORK

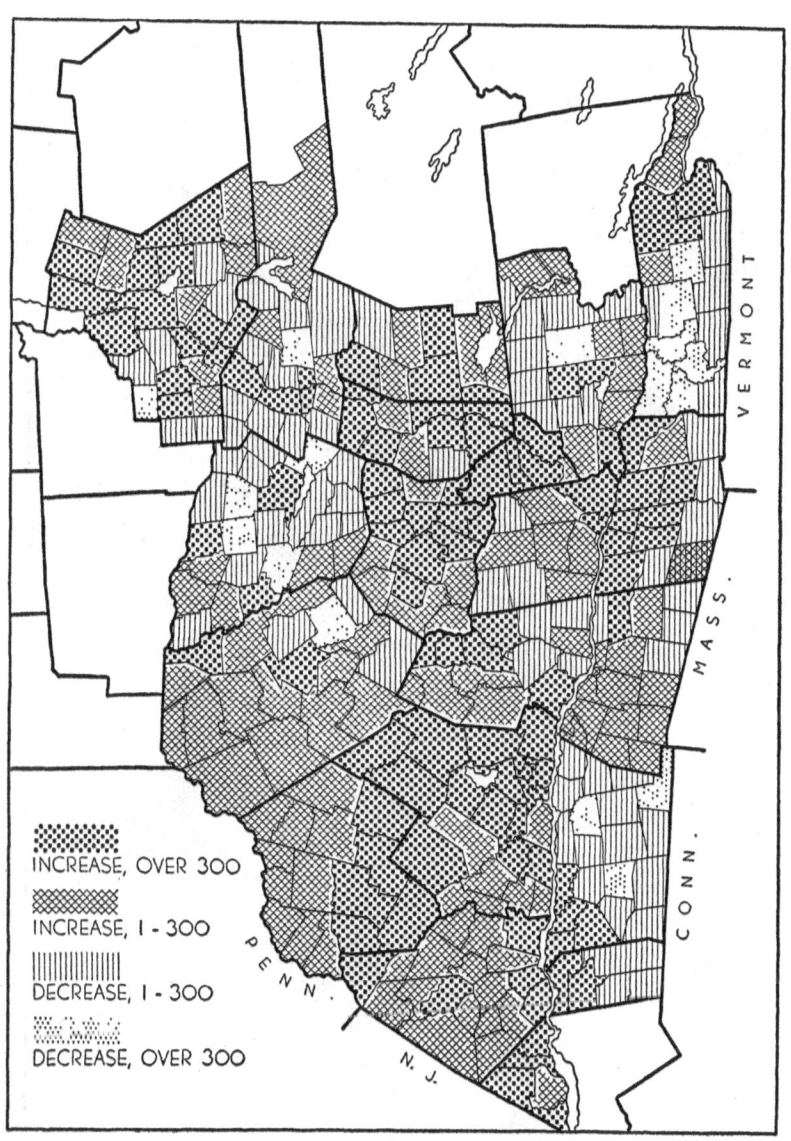

Changes in Population, 1830–1840.

LANDLORDS AND FARMERS

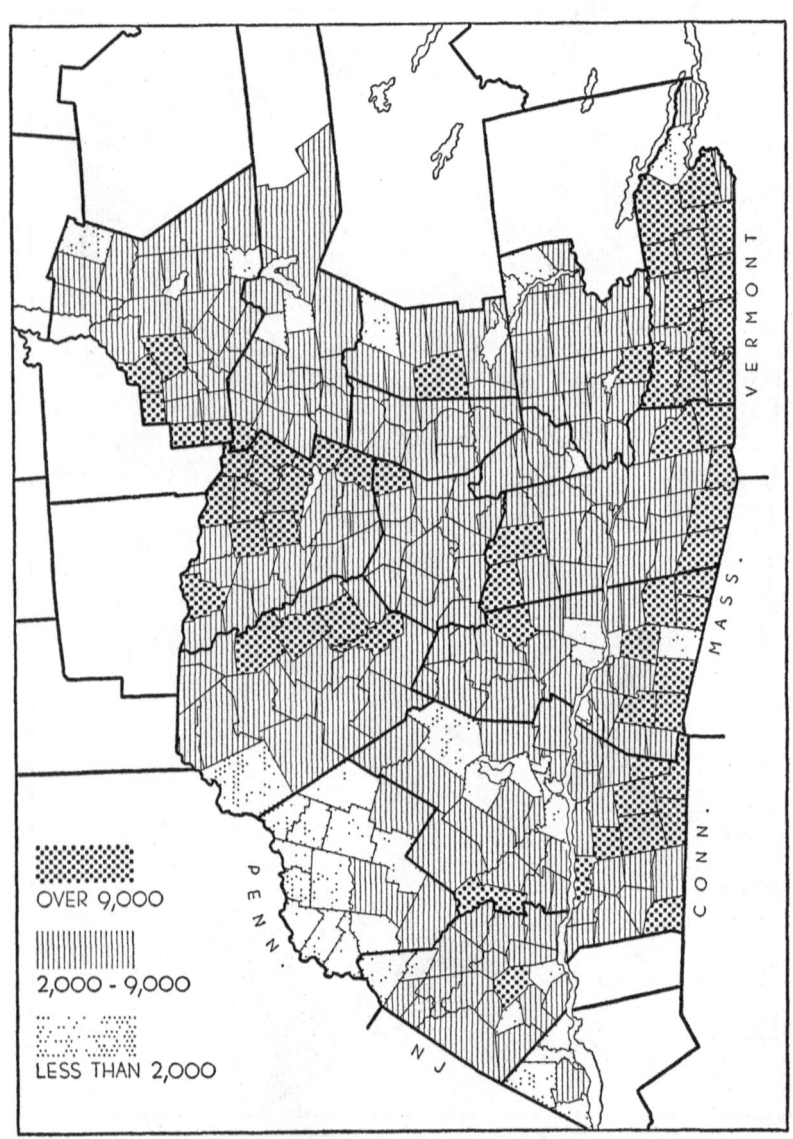

Sheep in Each Town in 1836. (Based on Benton and Barry)

THE TRANSPORTATION NETWORK

River was gaining population at a rapid rate. Townships containing cities gained rapidly. Dutchess County, which was abandoning its allegiance to sheep raising, recovered some of the losses of the previous decade. Columbia County, on the other hand, actually lost population. The explanation lies in the violent antirent disturbances which led to the exodus of discontented tenants. Otsego County, which had enjoyed a remarkable growth under William Cooper's direction, lost population for the second decade in succession. Not only were the thin hill soils wearing out, but the construction of the Erie Canal and the railroad diverted freight shipments away from the Cherry Valley Turnpike to the Mohawk Valley.

For purposes of comparison, a map of the period between 1850 and 1860 has been included. The triangular area comprising northern Delaware, southern Schoharie, and western Albany and Greene counties was losing population. Antirent troubles which flared up sporadically throughout this decade were responsible for part of this decline. The exhaustion of hemlock resources by the tanning industry helps to explain the decline in Greene and Delaware counties. One of the most startling losses took place in the Mohawk Valley, which had already shown a tendency to decline during the previous decade. Long years of close cropping had exhausted the fertility of the soil so severely that farming was becoming unprofitable.[4] Important gains took place in the towns fringing the Hudson. These townships found a ready market for their hay, butter, and milk in New York City.

Transportation is indeed the central theme, the key to an understanding of the political and social as well as the economic history of New York in this period. Well might the editor of the *Argus* declare in 1825 that every section of the state was "alive with the

---

[4] Evidence on soil exhaustion in the Mohawk Valley is abundant. See especially the *Cultivator*, II (Sept., 1835), 107; the *Central New-York Farmer*, II (March, 1843); *Trans.*, I (1841), 136; Jones, *op. cit.*, p. 144.

LANDLORDS AND FARMERS

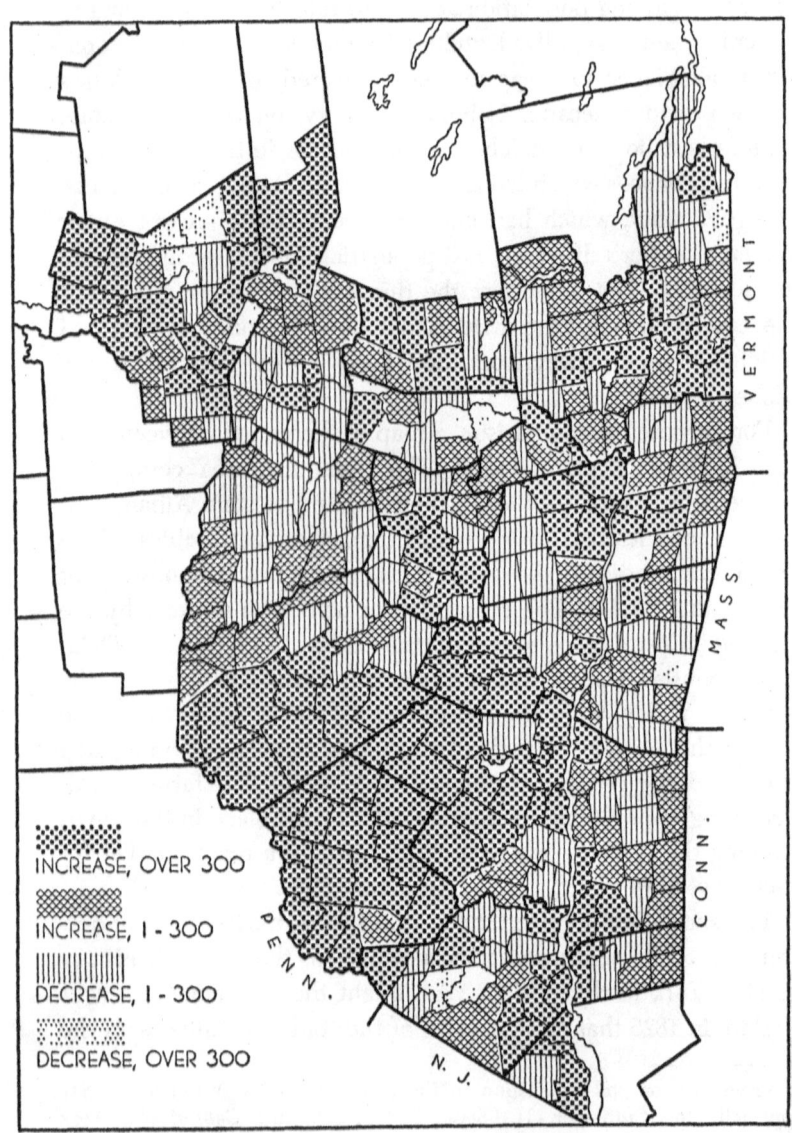

Changes in Population, 1840–1850.

THE TRANSPORTATION NETWORK

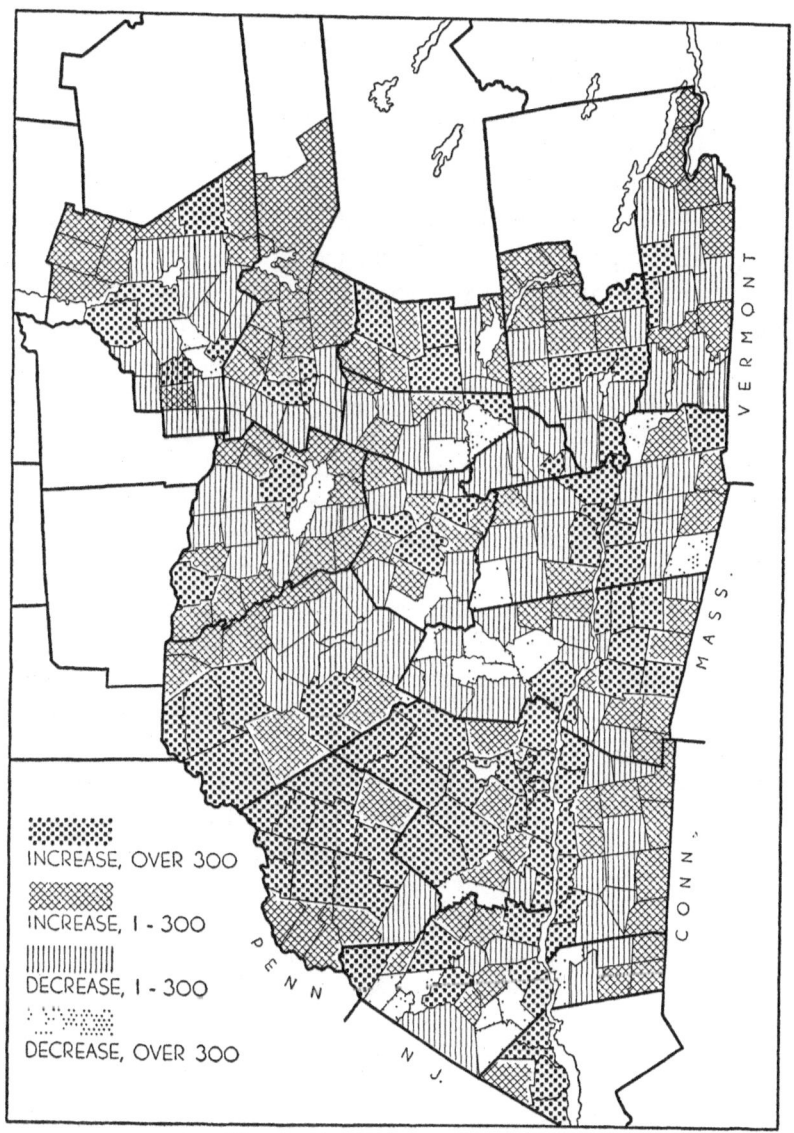

Changes in Population, 1850–1860.

spirit of internal improvements." [5] The success of the Erie Canal in raising land values, stimulating the growth of new cities, and providing easy access to market converted all but the most skeptical. Throughout the entire period agitation for canals, railroads, and plank roads filled the newspapers and dominated the controversies between Democrats and Whigs. Party organs would berate their foes for opposing specific projects or wasting the people's money.[6] Whether or not the state should grant aid for canals and railroads became a hot political issue in various sections of the state. It sometimes divided members of the same political party.[7]

The success of the Erie Canal was so outstanding that it stimulated the drive for similar projects throughout both the state and the nation. Pennsylvania at once embarked upon an elaborate system of canals. The Lake states likewise caught the canal fever. Within New York itself the "sequestered counties" joined the chorus for internal improvements. The citizens living in the southern tier demanded that the state construct a road from the Hudson to Lake Erie.[8] Governor Clinton urged the legislature to investigate the problem and to appropriate funds for the road. During the next two years a bitter struggle took place between the proponents and the foes of the measure. The latter came for the most part from counties through which the canal was built.[9] Members from Delaware and other counties in the southern tier declared that the construction of the Erie Canal had led to a

---

[5] *Argus*, Dec. 28, 1825.

[6] For example, the *Argus*, Feb. 5, 1838, defended the record of Democrats in supporting various projects. See also the *Argus*, March 7 and May 7, 1839.

[7] The canal question was a main source of division among the Democrats during the decade following 1840 (Herbert Donovan, *The Barnburners* [New York, 1925], p. 25; Beardsley, *op. cit.*, p. 295).

[8] *Argus*, March 4, June 10, Dec. 25, 1825; March 14, April 19, 1826.

[9] Beardsley, *op. cit.*, p. 218; Jabez Hammond, *Political History of the State of New York* (Syracuse, 1852), II, 201, 219–225, 245.

THE TRANSPORTATION NETWORK

disastrous fall in land values.[10] They insisted that the legislature mete out justice to all parts of the state. Finally in April, 1827, the legislature turned down the proposal.[11] In a short time, however, the people of the southern tier were back in the capital seeking state aid for the Erie Railroad.

Citizens in the Chenango Valley redoubled their agitation for a canal linking the Erie Canal with the Susquehanna River. Such a canal would permit coal from Pennsylvania to reach central New York. Public meetings, editorials, and conventions demanded state aid.[12] They petitioned the legislature to build the canal. In 1833 the legislators followed Governor Marcy's recommendation and authorized the project. Within three years workers had dug a shallow ditch from Utica to Binghamton.

People living in the watershed of the Black River, which flows into Lake Ontario, were petitioning the legislature for a canal which would enable them to ship their products to the Erie Canal at Rome.[13] The sponsors advanced the usual arguments. Tolls on immense quantities of lumber, agricultural produce, and iron ore, they declared, would more than pay the cost of the venture. The canal would also open up the public lands of the state by making them more valuable. Governor Clinton's benediction on the project encouraged its proponents, who persuaded the legislature to authorize a survey. Unfortunately, certain technical difficulties and especially the rivalry between Camden and Boonville [14] as to the location of the canal caused many delays. It was not until 1850 that the canal was completed.

The Delaware and Hudson Canal, extending from the Hudson

---

[10] The *Argus*, March 14, 1826, carries a speech by Erastus Root of Delaware County stating that property values in his county had declined from $5,000,000 to $3,000,000. See also *ibid.*, Jan. 30, 1827.

[11] *Ibid.*, April 7, 8, 1827.

[12] *Utica Sentinel and Gazette*, Dec. 27, 1825; *Utica Intelligencer*, Jan. 2, 1827, Aug. 26, 1828, Jan. 20, April 14, 1829.

[13] Whitford, *op. cit.*, I, 506-563.

[14] For an account of this rivalry, see *Utica Intelligencer*, Jan. 30, 1827.

near Kingston to the Pennsylvania coal districts, became an important link uniting the commercial and industrial areas of New York with the vast fuel resources of Pennsylvania.[15] The enthusiasm for canals had become so universal in the 1820's that individuals were willing to risk their own capital in this venture. Maurice Wurtz and his brothers, who had recently begun to exploit the Lackawanna coal district, sought a convenient water route to New York City. In 1822 the Pennsylvania legislature granted a charter for the canal. In the following year the New York legislature granted similar rights. The company enjoyed the financial backing of prominent New York capitalists such as Philip Hone and the political support of De Witt Clinton.

In 1825 the first board of managers ordered the work to begin. The company exhausted its funds and in 1827 received a loan of $500,000 from the state, offering in exchange a first mortgage on its lands.[16] In 1829 the state legislature granted another loan of $300,000 to the company, which permitted it to complete its 106 miles of canal bed and 16 miles of railroad. With the gradual adoption of coal by steamships and homeowners the amount of coal shipped over the canal increased rapidly. After 1840 the company made handsome profits and succeeded in paying off its debt to the state. One observer reported in 1843 that five hundred boats carrying 35 tons of coal each were in use.[17] Supplying the boatmen and their horses food and shelter provided a good income for farmers in the vicinity.

The Erie Canal remained by all odds the most important waterway. Increasing traffic soon made urgent its enlargement. Merchants, shippers, contractors, and inhabitants of the canal counties pointed out that the income from tolls would justify increased expenditures for making the canal wider and deeper. The Whigs

---

[15] Whitford, *op. cit.*, I, 728–751.

[16] *Ibid.*, p. 741.

[17] *Argus*, April 1, 1843. A letter by "A. M." in the *New-York Weekly Tribune*, Sept. 1, 1847, reported 800 boats on the canal.

THE TRANSPORTATION NETWORK

gave unstinted support to the cause of internal improvements. Their smashing victory in 1838 enabled Samuel Ruggles, chairman of the Assembly canal committee, to issue his famous report. Ruggles urged the state to subsidize a large number of canal and railroad projects to the extent of $40,000,000.[18] So overwhelming was the demand for internal improvements that the state government lent money to the Erie, the Catskill and Canajoharie, the New York and Harlem, the New York and Albany, the Hudson and Berkshire, and the Troy and Schenectady Railroads. The legislators also voted funds to enlarge the Erie Canal and to subsidize several other railroad companies.[19] Practically every section of the state received state aid for its favorite project. Farmers were fully as enthusiastic as town dwellers. President Nott of Union College, in his address to the state agricultural society in 1841, noted that the subject which would "pre-eminently claim their attention" was that of internal improvements.[20]

The increase of the state debt at a time when the country was feeling the full effects of the panic of 1837 seriously impaired the credit of the state. In 1842 the legislature yielded to the public demand for retrenchment and ordered all work on public works to come to a halt.[21] The "stop" order aroused great resentment in many localities but it did restore the credit of the state. Perhaps its most permanent effect was to widen the breach between the Hunker faction and the Barnburners in the Democratic party.[22] Such a hurried survey does not begin to unravel the tangled skein of state politics in which the canal issue remained a major thread until late in the nineteenth century.

---

[18] D. R. Fox, *Decline of Aristocracy*, p. 404; *Argus*, March 23, 1838.
[19] *Argus*, May 3, 1839, May 15, 1840.
[20] *Trans.*, I (1841), 36.
[21] Whitford, *op. cit.*, I, 166. The Whig papers tried to place all the blame for financial troubles on the Democrats who had started many projects during Governor Marcy's administration. For typical comments, see the *Oneida Whig*, Sept. 5, 1843; the *New-York Weekly Tribune*, Nov. 13, 1841.
[22] H. Donovan, *op. cit.*, p. 25.

LANDLORDS AND FARMERS

The influence of the Erie Canal on the nation and the state has been rather thoroughly examined. Obviously the reduction of 90 per cent in freight rates between Buffalo and Albany had a revolutionary effect on western New York and opened up the world market to farmers living in the Lake states. At the same time eastern working people secured cheaper foodstuffs. For a time most of the canal traffic originated within the boundaries of the state. In 1836 New York State provided 364,906 tons of freight arriving at tidewater, while western states furnished only 54,219 tons.[23] By 1847 freight originating in the western states had passed that of this state and by 1851 it was more than double the internal traffic. Well might an eastern New York paper deplore the expenditure of money to enlarge the canal which helped western farmers to undersell eastern farmers.[24]

The commercial supremacy of New York City has usually been attributed to the fact that the Erie Canal gave it a marked advantage over other seaports in the struggle for control of the western trade. More recent investigations have stressed the importance of the cotton export trade and the easy credit policies of New York merchants in building up the city.[25] It cannot be denied, however, that the Erie Canal brought thousands of little country stores from central New York to eastern Michigan into dependence on the New York wholesalers. At the same time it built up along its route a large number of auxiliary centers where merchants exchanged merchandise for foodstuffs.

The Albany area naturally became the entrepôt for goods coming to tidewater. Between 1825 and 1850 the capital and its neighboring cities of Troy and Watervliet increased their combined population from 27,404 to 91,994. Especially interesting

---

[23] For a table covering the period following 1835, see *N.Y. Assembly Documents*, no. 31 (1877), Table 28.

[24] *Ulster Republican*, Sept. 23, 1846, quoting from the *New York Democrat*.

[25] Robert Albion (*op. cit.*) emphasizes other factors such as the triangular cotton trade in explaining the primacy of New York.

THE TRANSPORTATION NETWORK

are the figures outlining the expansion of trade in Albany in the five years after 1824.[26] In 1824 the collector's books recorded 5,374 boats paying $67,231 in tolls. In 1828 14,478 boats paid $164,248. The number of vessels plying between Albany and New York and stopping at intermediate points was estimated in 1827 as 218. In addition there were 87 vessels sailing to ports south of New York. A thriving trade grew up between Albany and Boston. From a total of 41 vessels in 1821 the number rose to 163 in 1828. Flour, pork, lard, butter, cheese, ashes, whisky, staves, and wool were major items in this trade. Statistics on travel show comparable increases. In 1828 twelve steamboats docked each day at Albany, bringing an average of 365 passengers a day. In the course of the previous year over 165,000 passengers passed through Albany. Except for temporary interruptions Albany's trade grew steadily throughout the period. By 1850 Albany had become a leading lumber center.[27] Immense amounts of staves, boards, scantlings, and shingles came in on barges from the Champlain, Genesee, and Chemung valleys.

The effect of the Erie Canal upon the population and property valuations of different sections of New York State has attracted the attention of several historians.[28] Winden divided the state into three sections. The first included the counties between New York City and the headwaters of the Hudson; the second, the counties both north and south of the Mohawk Valley; the third, the region between the headwaters of the Mohawk River and Lake Erie. In the first section he found little evidence of popu-

---

[26] The *Argus*, April 4, 1829, carried a detailed account of the city's trade during the previous decade.

[27] U.S. Patent Office, *Annual Report*, 1850–1851, pp. 566–567. Hereafter this will be cited as *Patent Office Report*. See also account in *Albany Evening Journal*, Jan., 1851, cited in Munsell, *Annals of Albany*, III, 221–224.

[28] Julius Winden, *The Influence of the Erie Canal upon the Population Along Its Course* (Thesis, University of Wisconsin, Madison, 1901). Noble Whitford has included a similar statistical study (*op. cit.*, I, 839–908).

lation increase except in the townships lying within a six-mile zone bordering the Hudson. Moreover, many old river ports such as Catskill, Poughkeepsie, and Hudson made but slight gains in the twenty-five years following 1825. One notable exception was Kingston, which experienced a growth of more than 300 per cent. The reason is clear. Kingston served as the outlet for the Delaware and Hudson Canal. This canal opened up a new hinterland, whereas the lateral canals branching off southward from the Erie Canal and the railroad lines extending in the same direction diverted most of the trade of the southern tier from Catskill to the cities along the Erie Canal. Furthermore, the hill towns in the Hudson Valley counties had largely reached their maximum growth. They could not increase very much the amount of foodstuffs which they brought to the Hudson River ports.

The second section, stretching from the Hudson to the headwaters of the Mohawk River, naturally reflected the building of the Erie Canal. Towns bordering the river grew rapidly. Towns six or more miles away, however, showed little effect. On the other hand, the section stretching from the Mohawk Valley to Lake Erie showed rapid growth not only within the immediate vicinity of the canal but also in the remote areas twelve or more miles from the canal.

Along the route of the canal property valuations rose rapidly, although the most striking gains were made in the western section. Figures on property valuations are highly subject to error and consequently must be used with caution. Boards of supervisors have often underestimated the actual values in order to evade state taxation. If these reservations are kept in mind, it is possible to find certain trends which show that the interior counties were losing ground in comparison with the counties bordering on the canal.[29]

---

[29] These figures are taken from the *N.Y. Assembly Journal*, 1820, pp. 402–405; 1825, pp. 184–198; *N.Y. Assembly Documents*, no. 5 (1836), Table K.

THE TRANSPORTATION NETWORK

	1819	1824	1835
Albany	$ 6,886,430	$6,748,072	$ 9,050,370
Dutchess	14,147,231	8,670,967	13,787,484
Herkimer	4,880,197	4,137,446	4,301,801
Otsego	5,771,082	4,799,753	4,788,285
Delaware	3,642,661	2,358,747	2,858,990

Both Otsego and Delaware counties showed a decline in values. During the same period Dutchess on the Hudson River and Herkimer on the Mohawk River underwent similar, if smaller, declines. Albany, Oneida, and Ulster counties, where the commercial cities of Albany, Utica, and Kingston were growing, showed an increase in real property valuation.

The Hudson River remained the main artery of trade and travel throughout this period. Sloops, steamboats, barges, rafts, and vessels of every description crowded the river. Steamboats made Albany their main upstate terminal despite the strenuous efforts of Troy to cut into Albany's control of the passenger traffic. The Troy Steamboat Company was organized and in 1824 built the palatial boat appropriately named the "Chief Justice Marshall" after the great jurist whose decision in the Gibbons case had freed the river from the steamboat monopoly.[30] The canal kept bringing an increasing quantity of goods to tidewater throughout the period before the Civil War. The 750,000 tons of 1835 increased to 2,223,743 tons by 1854.[31] In contrast, the railroad in 1854 brought only 328,186 tons to Albany. Despite this disparity the ultimate victory of the steam railway over canalboat and river boat was becoming apparent by 1850.

The success of the canal system and the continuing usefulness of the Hudson River tended to retard the construction of the railroads. The state jealously guarded its investment in its canals, the handsome revenues of which greatly simplified the problem of raising taxes. In addition to the politicians, who nat-

---

[30] Troy *Sentinel*, March 8, 15, April 26, July 8, 1825.
[31] Figures are cited in the *Argus*, March 14, 1856.

LANDLORDS AND FARMERS

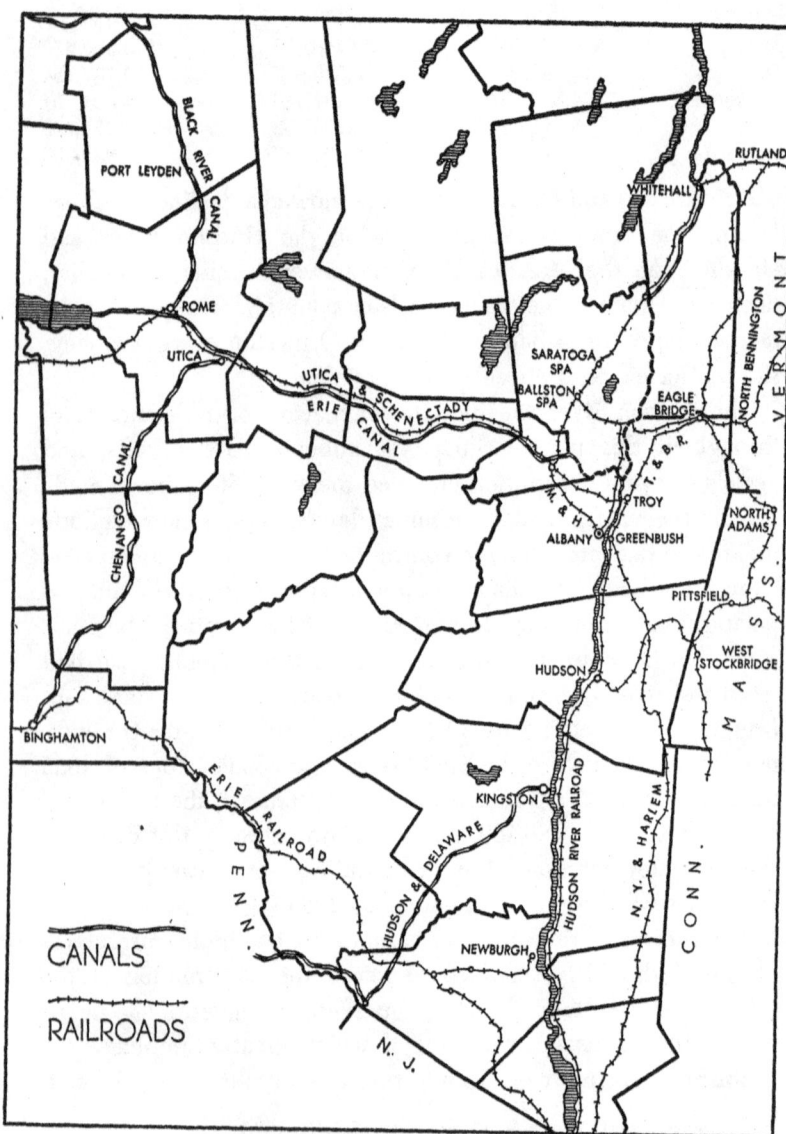

Railroads and Canals of 1855.

THE TRANSPORTATION NETWORK

urally did not want to disturb this source of income, a large body of private interests including shippers, canalboat operators, contractors, and employees opposed any threat to the canal or river traffic. Nevertheless, the peculiar advantages of the railroad, especially in regard to the speedy transportation of passengers, became more and more obvious. By 1851 the state legislators had to recognize that the railroad must be aided and not hindered. The state legislature repealed the provision that all railroads parallel to the canal and within a distance of 30 miles should pay canal tolls on the freight they carried. This action paved the way for a tremendous expansion in the business of the railroads crossing the state. By 1853 the main trunk lines connecting Albany with New York, Boston, and Buffalo had been constructed. The organization of the New York Central in that year is a symbol of the growing importance of the railroad in our state and national life.

Throughout the first half of the nineteenth century Albany and Troy were bitter rivals for the honor of becoming the entrepôt of the western and northern trade.[32] Soon after the Revolution Troy was founded by a group of Yankees whose enterprise and aggressiveness became the taunt and the despair of Albany merchants. Before the Erie Canal was built Albany had no difficulty in retaining her virtual monopoly of the western trade. The canal, however, diverted the flow of freight to the artificial waterway paralleling the course of the Mohawk. As a result Troy merchants were able to challenge their rivals on equal terms. The efforts of Albany and Troy promoters to gain mastery over the rail connections to the west, north, east, and south provide a story fully as interesting, if less spectacular, as the struggles between the railroads of the west for strategic positions.

The first railroad in New York, the famous Mohawk and Hud-

---

[32] For a detailed account of this rivalry, see David Maldwyn Ellis, "Albany and Troy—Commercial Rivals," *New York History*, XXIV (Oct., 1943), pp. 484–511.

son, paralleled the route of the first turnpike. George Featherstonhaugh of Duanesburg, Schenectady County, had observed the value of railroads in England and in 1825 he secured the support of Stephen Van Rensselaer, the leading citizen of Albany, for a line btween Albany and Schenectady. Although the main financial support came from capitalists in the New York City area, the enterprise naturally attracted much local support. Schenectady merchants, whose profitable forwarding and transshipment business had been destroyed by the construction of the Erie Canal,[33] were particularly eager to build a railroad to Albany.

After considerable delay the Mohawk and Hudson began operations in August, 1831. Even before its completion the legislature granted a charter to the Saratoga and Schenectady Railroad Company, which rapidly built its line to the famous watering center. The success of these railroads set off a wave of similar ventures. It is estimated that in 1831 the applications for charters for new companies called for capital amounting to $22,000,000.[34]

Troy citizens were not ones to let any business opportunity pass them by. In 1831 they organized the Rensselaer and Saratoga Railroad, which constructed its roadbed to Ballston Spa. The management of the Saratoga and Schenectady refused to accept through freight or through passenger tickets from the other road. The Troy promoters complained bitterly of discrimination. Suddenly their opportunity came. To Albany's disgust Troy merchants managed to secure a controlling interest in the Saratoga and Schenectady Company. As a result Troy interests could and did dictate railroad service to the Springs.[35]

---

[33] Frank Stevens, *The Beginnings of the New York Central Railroad* (New York, 1926), pp. 1–3.

[34] MacGill, *op. cit.*, p. 357.

[35] See Delaware and Hudson Company, *A Century of Progress, A History of the Delaware and Hudson Company* (Albany, 1929), p. 95. For denunciations by Albany people of Troy's efforts to divert passenger traffic through

THE TRANSPORTATION NETWORK

Gratifying as this maneuver was to their pride, the "Trojans" cherished still more ambitious plans. In 1836 promoters organized the Schenectady and Troy Railroad with a capital of $500,000. This railroad was to enjoy the distinction of being one of the few steam railroads financed, constructed, and operated by a municipal government.[36] The city council bonded the city for $600,000, and the state granted the railroad a loan of $100,000. By late 1842 trains were using the road from Troy to Schenectady. Albany citizens looked with alarm upon this new route that threatened to supplant the Mohawk and Hudson. The equipment and roadbed of the latter were in poor condition. Furthermore, the company was particularly handicapped by the fact that it had to use inclined planes to pull trains out of both Albany and Schenectady.[37] The removal of the inclined planes and a relocation of the Albany terminal near the docks were not accomplished until 1843.[38]

On the east bank of the Hudson as well Troy and Albany were waging a bitter struggle to become the terminus for the railroads striking across from New England and up from New York. Rivalry reached a high point in the years following 1841 when the Western Railway of Massachusetts made connections with Greenbush (now Rensselaer) across the river from Albany. Albany had very largely financed the Albany and West Stockbridge Company which met the Western Railway near the state border, and its citizens were determined not to permit Troy to reap the benefits of the trade from New England.

Troy, see *Argus*, July 24, 1840, Aug. 11, 1841; *New-York Weekly Tribune*, Oct. 23, 1841.

[36] Fred Powell, "Two Experiments in Public Ownership of Steam Railroads," *Quarterly Journal of Economics*, XXIII (Nov., 1908), 137–150.

[37] Philip Hone noted the advantage that the Troy route had over the "dangerous" inclined planes on the Mohawk and Hudson (*Diary of Philip Hone, 1828–1851*, I, 215). See also *Troy Daily Budget*, Nov. 5, 1842.

[38] *Niles' Weekly Register*, LXIII (Nov. 26, 1842), 208; LXIV (July 22, 1843), 325.

LANDLORDS AND FARMERS

A major factor in spurring on the Albany and West Stockbridge Railroad was the completion in 1838 of the line from Hudson, New York, to connect with the Western Railway.[39] Albany viewed this road with deep suspicion. Her citizens were particularly disturbed at the prospect that the New England and western trade would pass through Hudson, cross the river to Catskill, and then follow the Catskill and Canajoharie route to the west. This last railroad was a speculative venture which soon went bankrupt despite a state loan of $300,000.[40] To answer this threat, Albany promoters determined to build their own road to meet the Western Railway at West Stockbridge, Massachusetts. At first, plans included the construction of a tunnel under the Hudson near Castleton. In fact, the Albany city council agreed in 1834 to subscribe $1,000,000 for the tunnel, but the project soon died.[41] In 1836 the Albany and West Stockbridge Company received a charter, and immediately there got under way a movement to have the city subscribe to the stock. In October of that year the corporation of Albany lent $250,000 for this purpose.[42] Again in 1839 the citizens in a special election voted another $400,000.[43] Speakers at the public meetings held in every ward and letters written to editors urged the necessity of bringing to the capital this vital railroad line.[44] In 1840 the Western Railway took over the venture and constructed the line to Greenbush in 1841.

The completion of this railroad awakened the businessmen of New York to the danger that Boston merchants might seize the major part of the western trade. To counter this move, promoters in the metropolis redoubled their efforts to construct a line up the east bank to Albany. Since its incorporation in 1831 the New York and Harlem had made little progress beyond the Harlem

---
[39] F. Ellis, *op. cit.*, p. 130.
[40] MacGill, *op. cit.*, pp. 360–361.
[41] *Ibid.*, pp. 361–362.
[42] *Argus*, Oct. 7, 1836.
[43] *Ibid.*, May 20, 1839.
[44] *Ibid.*, Feb. 22, 1839. See also Jan. 14, 29, Feb. 14, May 17, 1839.

THE TRANSPORTATION NETWORK

River. The New York and Albany, chartered in 1832 and intended to parallel the river, likewise failed to attract much support until the decade of the 1840's when several attempts to whip up enthusiasm were made.[45] The success of the Harlem Company in securing a recharter in 1845 which permitted it to extend its road to Albany stirred the river towns to action. In 1851 and 1852 both the Harlem and the Hudson River Railroads reached Greenbush.

The leaders of Troy realized that if their city could get rail connections with New York and Boston they would have their rivals at a disadvantage, since passengers coming to Albany had to undergo the inconvenience, expense, and danger of crossing the Hudson by ferryboat. In 1840-1841 Troy built a spur to Greenbush in order to make connections with the trains coming over the Western Railway. This action outraged Albany citizens. It seemed unfair for Albany to pour over $1,000,000 into the Boston railroad only to have their hated rival profit thereby. The common council issued a remonstrance to the legislature protesting this action, and five thousand citizens signed the appeal.[46]

This controversy over the Troy-Greenbush line was only part of a greater issue, namely, control of the through railroad traffic between the west and Boston. In 1841 the legislators faced an important decision. If Albany secured the right to build a bridge, railroad traffic would definitely flow through the city. If Troy succeeded in making connections at Greenbush, railroad traffic from the west would cross the bridge at Troy and thus by-pass Albany. The legislators showed considerable skill in postponing the question without unduly antagonizing either city. They refused to charter the Albany bridge, but they likewise refused to permit Troy to take advantage of the newly constructed line to Greenbush. Troy leaders vigorously fought the Albany bridge proposal again in 1845, 1854, and 1856, with the same energy

---

[45] *Ibid.*, Jan. 10, 1839, May 8, June 4, 18, 1840, Mar. 9, 15, 17, 18, Apr. 8, 12, 1842.
[46] *Ibid.*, Mar. 4, 5, 1841.

and vehemence that they had always displayed in promoting their own ventures.[47] Not until 1866 was a span thrown across the river at Albany.

Other railroad lines in eastern New York should be mentioned. Both Troy and Albany were interested in roads running to the north and to Vermont. Much more important, however, were the series of short lines which later combined to form the New York Central. In 1833 the legislature chartered the Utica and Schenectady Railroad, but it specifically prohibited the company from transporting any freight.[48] In addition, the company had to buy out the interests of the Mohawk Turnpike and Bridge Company. Despite these handicaps the stock sold rapidly and in 1836 trains were running over the line. Three years later the Utica and Syracuse provided a westward extension.

The ban on freight carriage by the Utica and Schenectady created a serious bottleneck. It effectively barred through freight shipments from Buffalo and points east. The canal interests fought hard to keep this restriction, but in 1844 the legislature relaxed it somewhat by permitting the company to carry freight during the suspension of canal navigation. The company had to pay tolls equivalent to those on the Erie Canal.[49] Some farmers in central and western New York disliked the restriction. In 1846 the state agricultural society passed a resolution urging its repeal.[50] The opposition, coming very largely from eastern New York, insisted that the canal debt must first be paid. Finally in 1851 the railroads won freedom from the payment of tolls. Immediately the amount of freight carried by rail rose.

The ceremonies in April, 1851, celebrating the completion of the Erie Railroad were indeed a fitting tribute to the persistence and enterprise of the citizens living in the southern tier.[51] From

---
[47] D. M. Ellis, *op. cit.*, pp. 501–511.
[48] Stevens, *op. cit.*, p. 115.
[49] *Ibid.*, p. 268.
[50] *Trans.*, VI (1846), 13–18.
[51] *New-York Weekly Tribune*, May 15, 22, 1851.

THE TRANSPORTATION NETWORK

its charter in 1832 to its completion in 1851, the history of this railroad is one long series of financial difficulties, mismanagement, and political setbacks. Its later history under Drew, Gould, and Fiske was merely an elaboration of its earlier vicissitudes. We shall not describe its general history because this railroad was primarily concerned with serving the area beyond eastern New York. One significant fact, however, deserves attention. The Erie Railroad helped to expand the New York milk market. To cite but one example,[52] in 1843 one report noted that New York City had saved $200,000 annually on milk after the Erie had pushed its line to Goshen, Orange County. The same report declared that the railroad had brought about a 25 per cent reduction in the price of meat.

Not without interest is the fact that the railroads aroused resentment among the farmers. In fact, the charges are strangely similar to those which the Granger movement was to use in the 1870's. Poor service, financial corruption, high rates, discrimination in rates, monopolistic tendencies, watered stock, and free passes were grievances.[53] Other economic groups joined the foes of the railroads. First and foremost were the canal interests. Tavern keepers, wagoners, and farmers living along the Cherry Valley Turnpike blamed the railroad for taking away what passenger traffic the canal had left them.[54]

The canals and railroads solved the problem of transporting farm produce from local depots to distant markets. But they did not help the farmer in his short hauls. As always he had to rely on the ordinary road. Almost invariably the public highway was in a wretched condition. The unskilled officials had neither funds nor knowledge to construct all-weather roads.[55]

---

[52] *Niles' Weekly Register*, LXIV (May 13, 1843), p. 165.

[53] *Utica Daily News*, Jan. 4, 1842; *Oneida Whig*, Jan. 11, May 31, June 26, 1842, Jan. 31, Feb. 7, 1843; *New-York Weekly Tribune*, July 9, 1842.

[54] John Sawyer, *History of Cherry Valley from 1740 to 1898* (Cherry Valley, 1898), p. 112.

[55] *Trans.*, XXVI (1866), p. 157; *Cultivator*, III (March, 1836), 5.

LANDLORDS AND FARMERS

Shortly before the mid-century mark the plank road movement swept the country. It revived for a decade the toll road movement which had built many turnpikes forty years earlier. The first plank road which ran between Syracuse and Oneida Lake proved so popular that in 1848 the legislature passed a general plank road act. Within two years over 182 companies received their charters.[56] Cheap and easy to build, plank roads seemed ideally suited to serving local needs. Within a short time a network of plank roads grew up around every commercial center.[57] To the farmer, who had found public roads impassable except for a few weeks in the fall, the plank road was indeed a boon. He could haul heavier loads to market in any kind of weather.

Unfortunately the roads quickly deteriorated. Soon they became dangerous for horses to use since there were many holes between the planks. Heavy traffic wore out the planking, while decay made necessary a new surfacing in five years. Few roads had sufficient traffic to justify this cost. The panic of 1857 dealt a deathblow to most hopes of raising more money to replace the roads.

Plank roads, railroads, canals—all had revolutionary effects on the economy of the Hudson-Mohawk Valley. Commercial agriculture virtually displaced all but a few vestiges of the predominantly self-sufficient economy of the past. The same canals, railroads, and roads which permitted the farmer to sell his produce brought in a flood of cheap factory-made goods. One inevitable result was the virtual abandonment of household manufacture.[58] Another result was the increasing specialization in farming. Farmers in different parts of eastern New York found it profitable to produce wool, butter, cheese, milk, and vegetable

---

[56] Oliver Holmes, "The Turnpike Era," in Flick, *History of N.Y.*, V, 271.

[57] For typical articles urging the public to support plank roads, see *Freeholder*, Feb. 14, March 21, 28, May 23, July 18, 1849; *Schoharie Republican*, Dec. 19, 1848, Feb. 13, Aug. 7, 1849.

[58] Tryon, *op. cit.*, p. 307.

THE TRANSPORTATION NETWORK

crops. The extension of the transportation network also made it easier to desert the hill farm for richer fields in Illinois or for a clerk's desk in New York.

The farmers of New York were fully aware of the importance of transportation. They hailed the construction of new facilities as the open door to prosperity. They grumbled when the Erie Canal flooded the eastern markets with cheap wool, wheat, and meat products. Throughout the period under consideration the struggle to finance and build canals, railroads, and plank roads preoccupied the mind of the average farmer. He was only slightly less conscious of the necessity of readjusting his husbandry to meet the new conditions created by the expansion of the transportation network.

CHAPTER VI

THE RISE OF THE DAIRY STATE

1825 - 1850

TO DISCOVER all the interacting forces let loose by the expansion of the transportation network, to weigh the relative importance of each, and to explore their ramifications would be an impossible task. Needless to say, a bewildering variety of individual and local readjustments accompanied the shift to commercial farming.[1] Some farmers turned to the raising of cattle and sheep; others began to produce cheese, butter, or milk; a small number concentrated on the raising of hops, broomcorn, and barley. With the expansion of railroads came an extension of the area of profitable specialization in market gardening and fruit raising. That some farmers, and in particular those who lived on thin soils far from canals or railroads, should find it hard to make a living is not surprising. The specter of rural decline was already stalking the countryside long before the hooded "Indians" were roaming the fields shouting, "Down with the rent."

With the increase of commercial agriculture price fluctuations

---

[1] A careful student of the Quaker Hill section of Dutchess County noted the effects caused by the extension of transportation. In 1800 wheat, rye, flax, and potatoes were the main crops. As more roads were built dairying gradually became dominant: first, the making of butter and cheese; second, the raising of beef cattle; and third, the production of milk (Warren H. Wilson, *Quaker Hill, A Sociological Study* [New York, 1907], p. 69).

THE RISE OF THE DAIRY STATE

affected the farmer more and more. Inasmuch as we have previously used the price of wheat as an index of farm prosperity, we shall continue the quotations of wheat prices which the Van Rensselaer family used to determine the rent of their tenants.[2] To be sure, wheat no longer represented the dominant crop in eastern New York. On the other hand, the rise and fall in its price followed closely the changes in the general price level.[3]

	Sh.		Sh.	P.		Sh.	P.
1830	8	1838	13		1846	9	6
1831	10	1839	14		1847	9	
1832	10	1840	9		1848	10	6
1833	10	1841	8		1849	9	6
1834	8	1842	10		1850	9	6
1835	8	1843	7				
1836	12	1844	8		1855	18	
1837	18	1845	7	6	1856	16	

During the middle thirties agricultural regions as well as the country at large enjoyed a speculative boom. Prices of farm products and real-estate values shot upward. The building of new factories and railroads created a larger market for raw materials and foodstuffs. The speculative fever infected practically all aspects of American life until Jackson issued his famous Specie Circular. Prices dropped precipitously in 1837. The farmers of eastern New York could not escape the severe deflation which lasted for several years. In 1842 the president of the state agricultural society deplored the "pecuniary difficulties" which accompanied the fall of prices.[4] In the late 1840's prices strengthened. The repeal of the corn laws and the recovery of business

---

[2] Munsell, *Annals of Albany*, VIII, 177. Eight shillings equal one dollar.

[3] Compare with chart of farm prices, Bidwell and Falconer, *op. cit.*, p. 191; George Warren and Frank Pearson, *Prices* (New York, 1933), pp. 25–27.

[4] Mr. James Wadsworth's speech appears in *Utica Observer*, Feb. 14, 1843. See also *Trans.*, II (1842), 48. The agent of the Banyar estate found it almost impossible to collect rents from tenants in 1842 ("Agents, Reports, Lott and Low Patent and Magin Patent, 1838–1847," Box 0, Folder 1, G. Banyar Papers).

pushed farm prices upward. The price level remained favorable to the agricultural interests at least until 1857.

Soil depletion constituted a serious problem for New York farmers. For a variety of reasons, some excusable on the ground that land was cheap and labor was dear, some understandable because of the ignorance and poverty of the people, the average farmer followed a policy of exhaustion. In 1852 one well-informed source estimated that one twelfth of the farmers in New York improved their lands, one fourth cultivated their lands in such a way as to prevent deterioration, and the rest "skinned" the land, damaging it to the extent of $3.00 an acre each year.[5] Contemporary evidence of various kinds tends to buttress these conclusions. Not without reason, therefore, did Solon Robinson, an eminent agricultural writer, have one of his characters say that the best thing the legislature could do would be to paint a great sign over each church and schoolhouse door in America with the following words on it: "The Best Land in America, By Constant Cropping, Without Manure, Will Run Out." [6]

By 1850 almost every county in eastern New York reported serious soil exhaustion. From Oneida County in the northwest to Orange County in the south came the same complaint: the yield of crops was falling. A geological and agricultural survey published by the state in 1846 bluntly stated that the Mohawk and Hudson valleys, once acclaimed as the granary of the East, were more exhausted than most areas.[7] Constant cropping had so impaired the interval lands as well as the thinner and weaker soils in the hill towns that farming was becoming progressively more unprofitable.[8] The statement of a Wisconsin correspondent no doubt expressed the thoughts of many farmers who remained in

---

[5] *Patent Office Report*, 1852–1853, pp. 5–6.

[6] *Cultivator*, V (Dec., 1838), 174–175.

[7] Ebenezer Emmons, *Agriculture of New-York* . . . (Albany, 1846–1854), I, 7.

[8] *Central New-York Farmer*, II (Oct., 1843), 152; *Trans.*, I (1841), 136; *Trans.*, V (1845), 447.

THE RISE OF THE DAIRY STATE

eastern New York. The writer congratulated himself that he was no longer "doomed to toil over" the "worn out hills of old Washington." [9]

Tenancy further aggravated the problem of soil depletion. One of the most common and telling arguments advanced by the antirent spokesmen was that tenancy discouraged permanent improvements and virtually precluded "successful husbandry." [10] Dilapidated buildings, half-starved animals, and brush-covered fields made tenant farms eyesores. In 1850 the agent of the Banyar estate made the pertinent observation that a farm in Otsego County "like all expiring leases has been badly used and tenanted." [11] George Clarke, Jr., by 1843 was including provisions that no dung or straw could be taken off the farm.[12] His early leases in Montgomery County did not have any such clause.

Perhaps the best index of the declining productivity of New York lands is the decline in the yield of wheat per acre. In 1845 statistics show that 7½ bushels was the yield in Albany County, 5 in Dutchess, 10 in Montgomery, 7 in Columbia, and 13 bushels in Otsego County.[13] But Monroe County in western New York was raising 19½ bushels per acre. Furthermore, the average yield for eastern New York had declined through the years. In 1813 it was between 12 and 13 bushels; in 1845 it was only 8 to 9 bushels an acre. Gone forever except in a few places were the

---

[9] *Trans.*, V (1845), 460.

[10] *N.Y. Assembly Documents*, no. 156 (1846), p. 8; *Cultivator*, n.s. I (May, 1844), 151; *Freeholder*, Feb. 11, 1846.

[11] "Agents, Reports, Stewart and Schuyler patents, 1859-1875," Box 6, Folder 5, G. Banyar Papers. The same agent noted that tenant farms in Fulton County had "run out" ("Agents, Reports, Lott and Low Patent and Magin Patent, 1838-1847," Box 6, Folder 2, G. Banyar Papers).

[12] *N.Y. Assembly Documents*, no. 261 (1847). Already in 1807 George Clarke, Jr., had provided similar dung and straw clauses for Oneida County lands. See lease for James Simpson, Oneida County, *Deeds*, Liber XIX, Oneida County Clerk's Office.

[13] *Trans.*, V (1845), 388-389, contains the New York State Census figures.

LANDLORDS AND FARMERS

lavish yields of over 20 bushels which the original humus covering produced. Of course, the shift to dairying helped to restore fertility. All too often, however, pastures were overgrazed. Farmers who sold hay off their farms were likewise removing valuable elements in the soil.[14]

Soil depletion and the invasion of the rust and insects made it almost impossible for eastern New York wheat farmers to compete with their rivals in the west. As late as 1831 Jesse Buel could still call wheat the staple of Albany County,[15] but shortly after 1830 the wheat midge and weevil began to destroy the wheat crops. A succession of ruined crops caused most farmers to turn to coarse grains and livestock. By 1834 one report stated that the Mohawk Valley, once well known for its wheat, did not furnish one half of the local needs.[16] Year after year the agricultural press carried reports of the destruction of wheat crops by the midge, the rust, or the fly.[17] Consequently its cultivation became definitely unprofitable. In the early 1850's wheat staged a comeback, but few farmers found it profitable to raise wheat for sale.

The census of 1845 reveals clearly the decline in wheat production in eastern New York.[18] For purposes of comparison an equal number of counties have been selected from eastern and western parts of the state.

	Bushels	Acres Sown		Bushels	Acres Sown
Albany	44,000	5,000	Genesee	695,000	43,000
Herkimer	61,000	5,000	Niagara	713,000	44,000
Schenectady	20,000	1,800	Monroe	1,339,000	73,000
Schoharie	79,000	7,900	Ontario	919,000	58,000

[14] *Trans.*, XIV (1854), pp. 420–421.
[15] *New-York Farmer*, IV (Dec., 1831), 325.
[16] *Cultivator*, I (Oct., 1834), 114.
[17] *Central New-York Farmer*, I (Sept., 1842), 134; *Cultivator*, I (Feb., 1835), 178; II (Jan., 1836), 162; III (Jan., 1837), 170; IV (Jan., 1838), 173–174; *Patent Office Report*, 1843, p. 43; 1844, p. 27.
[18] *Trans.*, V (1845), 388–389.

THE RISE OF THE DAIRY STATE

The wheat grown in eastern New York was not sufficient to supply the needs of that district. But the fertile soils of western New York were still producing wheat for export in 1845.

Corn, oats, barley, rye, and livestock filled the gap left by wheat. Indian corn continued to maintain its position as the most useful crop.[19] After 1840 its production increased. Farmers applied more manure, cultivated it with more care, and often substituted it for fallow. Furthermore, the soils of eastern New York seemed well-suited to corn and oats. Western competition was no problem.[20] Canal tolls precluded its importation. With the growth of the livestock industry corn became more and more valuable as fodder for cattle and for hogs.

Travelers passing west from Schenectady noted large fields of broomcorn.[21] The fertile intervales raised large crops. The farmers cut off and dried the heads of the stalk. They sold the brooms throughout the country.

Oats were a leading crop. Their rise accompanied the decline in wheat. The growing livestock industry needed oats as fodder and bedding. Farmers also sold oats in large quantities to supply the horses used on stage routes, towpaths, and in railroad construction.[22] Otsego, Columbia, and Dutchess were the only counties in 1844 which reported a crop of over 1,000,000 bushels. In Dutchess County oats became part of a rotation consisting of corn, roots, oats, and grass.[23]

When the fly, the rust, and the midge made wheat unprofitable in eastern New York, many farmers turned to rye. Over 80 per cent of the state crop in 1845 was raised in the counties bordering on the Hudson River.[24] Rye was used to feed stock and particularly to supply distilleries.

---
[19] Stuart, *op. cit.*, I, 257.
[20] *Patent Office Report*, 1845, p. 284.
[21] Johnston, *ibid.*, I, 145; *Cultivator*, n.s. IV (Nov., 1847), 336.
[22] *Trans.*, II (1842), 170.
[23] *Cultivator*, n.s. I (April, 1844), 107.
[24] *Patent Office Report*, 1845, p. 159.

LANDLORDS AND FARMERS

Another minor grain of considerable importance was barley, of which New York State raised over half of the national crop.[25] Farmers in the Mohawk Valley often selected barley after wheat failed to yield well. Barley was a good cash crop.[26] Its cultivation gradually spread westward along the line of the Erie Canal. During the 1840's Albany was the barley market of the United States.[27] The extensive brewing industry furnished a good and certain market. The temperance movement which attracted widespread support after 1840 caused a temporary decline in barley production. This loss, however, was soon regained.[28]

Buckwheat was another crop to which farmers turned. It had the advantage of being a reliable crop on poor lands. The census for 1845 shows that the principal buckwheat-producing counties were those in eastern New York. After 1845 buckwheat slowly declined—since it was not highly regarded.

After 1820 the cultivation of potatoes became more general, although the farmers paid little attention to raising root crops such as turnips, rutabaga, and carrots for fodder. The main objection was that these crops required a large amount of labor, especially at harvesting. By 1840, however, New York was the leading potato-producing state in the union. The increasing favor in which the potato was held can be seen in the deep interest with which the farmers welcomed the Rohan potato.

Between 1838 and 1842 the agricultural periodicals were filled with articles and letters either praising or denouncing the Rohan potato. J. A. Thomson, a prominent farmer of Catskill, had imported from France in 1835 several bushels of this variety. Soon he was receiving many requests for seed in answer to his adver-

---

[25] *Statistics of the United States of America . . . The Sixth Census; Corrected at the Department of State June 1, 1840* (Washington, 1841), p. 408.
[26] *New-York Farmer*, VII (1834), 144; *Trans.*, I (1841), 135.
[27] Munsell, *Annals of Albany*, I, 361; II, 299–300; VIII, 313.
[28] *Patent Office Report*, 1843, p. 42.

THE RISE OF THE DAIRY STATE

tisements in the *Genesee Farmer* and the *Cultivator*.[29] In 1837 he offered the potatoes at $6.00 a bushel or $1.00 a dozen. The particular merits of the Rohan potato were its great size and productivity.[30] Observers described the Rohan as "big as a Bible." By 1839 speculators had driven the price to $20 a bushel, but in the following year the price collapsed.[31] A chorus of criticism echoed through the farm journals, although many writers continued to praise the new variety.[32] The significant fact about the controversy is that eastern New York farmers had become fully conscious of the value of the potato both as fodder and as a cash crop.

In 1843 the blight, then known as the "rot," struck a heavy blow at the potato industry. From a total of over 30,000,000 bushels in 1840 the state potato crop dropped to some 23,600,000 bushels in 1845 and to only 15,400,000 bushels in 1850.[33] In 1843 the crop was off one fourth. In the next year the Mohawk Valley crop was off three fourths, and there were total failures in Dutchess, Putnam, Westchester, Rockland, and Orange counties.[34] After a succession of crop failures, many farmers tried to raise only enough for home consumption. Some farmers, however, continued to raise potatoes on a large scale in order to take advantage of the marked rise in prices. Thus Oneida County was reported in 1854 to be raising potatoes "successfully and extensively." [35]

---

[29] J. A. Thomson to Rawson Hamon, Dec., 1837, in Box 2, Correspondence, 1837–1839, Thomson Collection, New York State Library. During 1838 and 1839 Thomson carried on an extensive correspondence with potato growers.

[30] *Cultivator*, IV (Oct., 1838), 142.

[31] *Ibid.*, VI (Jan., 1839), 66.

[32] For typical letters, see the *Cultivator*, VI (June, 1839), 66; VII (Jan. and Dec., 1840), 12, 195, 196; VIII (Feb., 1841), 35; *Central New-York Farmer*, I (March, 1842).

[33] See tables in Bidwell and Falconer, *op. cit.*, p. 375 and in *Trans.*, V (1845), 390–391.

[34] *Patent Office Report*, 1844, p. 73.

[35] *Ibid.*, 1854, p. 166.

LANDLORDS AND FARMERS

Soil depletion and the pressure of western competition induced many farmers to experiment with special crops which could be easily marketed. Despite the low price of flax due to the influx of cheap cotton, flax was still needed for seed and for oil. Thus the farmers in the Hoosic Valley in Rensselaer and Washington counties raised over 400,000 pounds of flax which the oil mills bought.[36] Much seed was exported to Ireland as in colonial days. In 1851 the flax mills were reported to be paying an average of $10 an acre for the use of land prepared for seed.[37] Although the amount of land devoted to flax declined precipitously between 1845 and 1855, flax growing remained an important industry in the counties of Rensselaer, Washington, and Montgomery.[38] These three counties contained over half of the state acreage devoted to flax.

In 1860 almost 90 per cent of the nation's production of hops was grown in New York. Otsego County alone produced over one third of the state's crop.[39] Since 1825 the farmers of Otsego County and the nearby sections of Herkimer, Madison, and Oneida had been turning more and more to hop growing. The hop industry required considerable amounts of manure, and could be fitted in profitably with the dairy industry, which was also growing rapidly in the same region.[40] Hop growing was a highly speculative undertaking, with years of prosperity alternating with years of bankrupting prices. Hop growing brought in handsome returns during most of the nineteenth century. It supplied the money to build large farmhouses, some of which can still be seen in the neighborhood of Waterville and Cooperstown.[41]

Another sign showing the instability of eastern agriculture in

---

[36] *Trans.*, IX (1849), 912.
[37] *Ibid.*, XI (1851), 643.
[38] *N.Y. Census for 1855*, p. 320.
[39] *U.S. Census for 1860, Agriculture.*
[40] N. S. Benton, *op. cit.*, p. 467; *Trans.*, XIV (1854), 576.
[41] J. F. Cooper, *Legends and Traditions*, p. 109.

THE RISE OF THE DAIRY STATE

the 1830's was its susceptibility to speculative ventures such as the Rohan potato, the Berkshire hog, Saxon sheep, and particularly the *Morus multicaulis*.[42] Since colonial days various attempts had been made to grow mulberry trees and silkworms, but the rural population did not pay much attention until the 1830's. With the state legislatures dangling premiums for mulberry trees before him and with the agricultural periodicals urging him to utilize the leisure time of his womenfolk, the farmer began to grow mulberry trees.[43] The mulberry mania collapsed in 1839 largely because climate, labor scarcity, and low prices made silk production unprofitable. Despite this collapse public and private individuals continued to urge farmers to engage in silk culture.[44]

One of the best examples of specialization caused by the home market was the production of vegetables, milk, and perishable fruits in the vicinity of New York City.[45] The construction of the Harlem and the Erie Railroads extended the area in which these crops could be raised. Thus in 1847 over 80,000 baskets of strawberries were carried on the milk trains of the Erie Railroad.[46] Farmers in Westchester County were turning to dairying and fruit raising, although large-scale stealing made fruit growing less profitable.[47]

Many farmers not in the vicinity of New York City likewise found it profitable to specialize in apple orchards. Dutchess County in 1830 was famous for its cider production, which had

---

[42] Arthur Cole, "Agricultural Crazes," *American Economic Review*, XVI (Dec., 1926), 628–632.

[43] *Trans.*, I (1841), 148; *Utica Intelligencer*, Dec. 16, 1828.

[44] N.Y. *Assembly Documents*, no. 352 (1840); *Cultivator*, VII (July, 1840), 102.

[45] *Rural New-Yorker*, I (Feb. 21, 1849), 57. Within ten or twelve miles of Albany farmers produced marketable crops such as hay and garden vegetables (Emmons, *op. cit.*, I, 324).

[46] *American Agriculturist*, VI (Aug., 1847), 260.

[47] *Trans.*, VII (1847), 774; *American Agriculturist*, X (Jan., 1851), 31–32.

received a setback from the early temperance movement.[48] There were extensive orchards in the Hudson and Mohawk valleys. Samuel Downing of Newburgh established a nursery business which sold improved varieties of trees throughout the nation.[49] Across the river in Westchester County Robert Pell is reported in 1845 to have sold 3,000 to 4,000 barrels of his Newton pippins in New York and London.[50] Buyers from the seaboard cities sought out the applegrowers of Oneida County. In 1847 some 18,000 barrels were shipped to market.[51]

The expansion of the grazing industry and especially the growth of dairying were developments of major significance. By 1850 the dairy industry was only on the threshold of its future greatness. Already the value of its products surpassed that of wheat by over $1,000,000.[52] Between 1825 and 1850 sheep raising likewise became an important industry for the hill towns. The insistent demands for wool and dairy products, the expansion of canals, railroads, and roads, the excellent pastures, and the resourcefulness of the farm family conspired to make eastern New York more interested in animal husbandry than in staple crops.

Sheep raising was basically a transition industry facilitating the shift from the earlier grain culture to the mixed farming of which dairying formed such an important part. The map shows a heavy concentration of sheep in the inland towns bordering the New England line and also in the upland county of Otsego. Washington County displayed the same devotion to sheep which distinguished its neighbor, Vermont. In 1845 this banner sheep county boasted six sheep per capita, a number almost matched by Otsego. An examination of the statistics shows quite clearly that the high point of the sheep industry in eastern New York came

---

[48] Fowler, *op. cit.*, p. 181.
[49] Eager, *op. cit.*, p. 176.
[50] *Trans.*, V (1845), 435.
[51] *Patent Office Report*, 1847, p. 363.
[52] Russell H. Anderson, "New York Agriculture Meets the West, 1830–1850," *Wisconsin Magazine of History*, XVI (Dec., 1932), 194.

THE RISE OF THE DAIRY STATE

between 1835 and 1845. Subsequently there took place a precipitous decline.[53] This is not to say that sheep raising became unimportant after 1855. Many farmers continued to keep sheep and the demand for wool during the Civil War gave the industry a new lease on life. Nevertheless, sheep raising continued to decline both relatively and absolutely throughout the rest of the century.

A modest revival of interest in sheep took place in the 1820's. The expansion of the textile industry both in New England and New York more than doubled the market for wool. American manufacturers intensified their agitation for a protective tariff, a goal which they achieved in the famous tariff of 1828. The dumping of English woolens on the American market caused much distress and gave added force to this drive for protection. The manufacturers were canny enough to enlist support among the farmers.[54] Those living in the neighborhood of factories and those selling wool naturally tended to favor protection.[55] For example, Samuel A. Law wrote to Erastus Root, prominent Delaware County politician, that he opposed the McLane bill of 1832.[56] Law declared that he would have to get rid of his sheep if the bill passed Congress.

During the middle 1820's the woolen manufacture enjoyed a steady growth. Fabrics requiring fine wools were in particular favor. As a result farmers began to buy the Saxon Merino sheep. Between 1824 and 1827 there took place a speculation in this breed similar to the earlier "Merino mania." [57] But in 1827 the

---

[53] See Appendix C for table of number of sheep in each county in 1845, and 1855.

[54] For typical letters and editorials advocating the tariff, see the *Utica Intelligencer*, Aug. 28, Dec. 25, 1827; Jan. 8, May 27, July 15, 1828; June 30, 1829.

[55] Petition by Oneida County citizens, *Utica Intelligencer*, Feb. 12, 1828.

[56] May 15, 1832, Box 5, S. A. Law Papers.

[57] In 1827 Samuel Law bought two Saxon bucks for $50 (letter from Law to S. and L. Hurlbut of Connecticut, Box 4, Correspondence, 1824–1828, S. A. Law Papers).

market broke. Sheep growers in many cases abandoned the Saxon breed in disgust.

The industry reached its peak of prosperity during the 1830's. The wool manufacture created a steady demand for all the wool which the farmers could produce. Of course, wool never became the most important business for most farmers. It was merely an item in mixed husbandry, with the average farmer keeping from one hundred to two hundred animals.[58] Nevertheless, sheep raising became a major pursuit in certain upland regions. Otsego, Dutchess, and Washington counties had many fine flocks. The average flock on farms specializing in sheep ranged from three hundred to one thousand sheep.[59] Prices remained high until 1837 despite minor fluctuations. After the boom in Saxon Merino sheep had passed, there was a gradual shift to coarser wools which the Spanish Merino could supply. Some farmers charged that manufacturers did not make proper allowances in price between medium and fine wool. Attempts to reorganize the system of marketing failed to save the Saxon sheep from being replaced by other breeds.[60]

During the 1840's the woolgrowers of eastern New York faced a new situation. Prior to 1840 the western grower had offered but slight competition, but after 1840 wool shipments over the Erie Canal rose to ominous levels. Shipments passing through Buffalo jumped from 600,000 pounds in 1842 to 3,440,000 pounds in 1845.[61] Unlike the foreign producer, the western woolgrower could freely throw his wool on the market without surmounting the tariff wall. Furthermore, it cost him less to produce wool than it cost his eastern rivals. The winters in southern Ohio were

---

[58] *Patent Office Report*, 1852–1853, pp. 190–191.

[59] *Trans.*, I (1841), 143; IX (1849), pp. 770 ff. Henry S. Randall noted that grazing lands were cut into small farms of about 130 acres which could therefore support only 400 sheep at the most (*Plough, the Loom, and the Anvil*, II [March, 1850], 578).

[60] *Trans.*, IX (1849), 781–782.

[61] *Patent Office Report*, 1845, pp. 368–369.

THE RISE OF THE DAIRY STATE

milder. Pasture and feeding costs were much lower. Whereas it cost from $1.00 to $2.00 a head to keep sheep in the east, it cost only 25 cents to $1.00 in the west.[62]

The falling price level made it progressively more difficult for marginal producers in eastern New York to keep their flocks. For a time the tariff seemed to offer a solution. At least it would stop foreign wool imports. When in 1846 Congress repealed the tariff on the higher grades of wool, many farmers gave up the struggle.[63] As Henry Randall, dean of eastern flockmasters put it, there was "a panic among the wool-growers of New York."[64] Farmers in Washington County, the stronghold of sheep raising, began to break up their flocks because they were convinced that they could not compete with western shepherds.[65] Most revealing of all are the census figures. Between 1845 and 1855 the number of sheep owned in eastern New York dropped more than 50 per cent. The county of Oneida alone showed a decrease from 195,000 to 51,000.[66]

The wool producer in 1850 found himself in much the same position as the wheatgrower of 1830. He could not meet the competition of western rivals. As a result he had to turn to new products. Dairying was to become the ultimate solution for most farmers of eastern New York. Some sheepmen immediately rushed into the business of making cheese or butter.[67] Others attempted to meet the new conditions by selling mutton to the city. Large-framed, coarse-wooled breeds such as Leicesters, Southdowns, and Cotswolds became common in Dutchess and Columbia

---

[62] Connor, *op. cit.*, p. 113. Asa Fitch estimated that the minimum annual cost for maintaining sheep in Washington County was $1.34 (*Trans.*, IX [1849], 790).

[63] J. B. Nott in the *Argus* (June 21, 26, 30, July 1, 1846) warned farmers not to destroy flocks laboriously built up.

[64] *Journal of Agriculture*, II (April, 1847), 462.

[65] *Trans.*, IX (1849), 756.

[66] See Appendix C.

[67] *Patent Office Report*, 1852–1853, p. 190; 1849, pp. 244 ff.

counties.[68] The Harlem Railroad tapped the grazing areas of these counties and enabled sheepmen to ship their flocks to the slaughterhouses.

The wool produced in New York was disposed of in three main channels. First of all, there was the declining but still important household manufacture. The factories of New England furnished the greatest market, but the woolen mills of New York were able to absorb a good share of the local output. In 1836 a well-informed observer estimated that out of the state's total production of 16,000,000 pounds of wool, about 3,500,000 pounds were used in the home.[69] Rural New York clung tenaciously to domestic manufacturing as late as 1845, but the next decade was to see its virtual abandonment. Another 5,000,000 pounds went to mills within the state, while approximately 7,500,000 pounds went to supply the great New England manufacture.

The line between domestic manufacture and factory production is often hard to draw. Thus we find in Washington County in 1849 several small mills which took in wool from the neighboring farmers to be manufactured into cloth and flannel for home use.[70] Generally these mills, which employed from nine to twelve people of which about half were women, took the coarsest fleeces and charged about 30 cents a yard for the cloth made. The larger of these mills also made coarse cloth which was placed on sale in New York City. In addition, each family had a small batch of wool made into rolls by the carding machine. The women spun the rolls into yarn which was used for knitting, weaving into carpets, and making flannel. The amount of homespun cloth rapidly declined as the proportion of cloth purchased in the stores increased.

Most of the wool produced in central New York found a market

---

[68] *Ibid.; Trans.*, I (1841), 134.
[69] C. Benton and Samuel F. Barry, *A Statistical View of the Number of Sheep* . . . (Cambridge, 1837), p. 119.
[70] *Trans.*, IX (1849), 812–814.

THE RISE OF THE DAIRY STATE

in the woolen mills of Oneida County. The ruinous prices, however, discouraged many raisers in 1842.[71] Farmers did not always receive cash for their wool. Thus in 1840 the Oriskany factory paid for its wool in goods.[72] Two years later a factory in New Hartford advertised for 100,000 pounds of raw wool in exchange for cloth, salt, groceries, dry goods, and a "little sprinkling of money." [73]

The New England wool manufacture was the greatest market. Buyers would often visit farms offering prices which seemed suspiciously low.[74] In Washington County several local markets grew up in the towns of Granville, Salem, and Cambridge.[75] Farmers would send their wool to buyers who often acted under commission for eastern manufacturers. Sometimes wool from Vermont reached these markets.

Low prices and especially the custom of buyers of lumping all wool together regardless of quality gave rise to a demand that farmers set up co-operative wool depots.[76] The proponents argued that such a depot could classify wool according to grade and thus guarantee the manufacturer the exact quality he desired. At the same time the grower of fine fleeces would secure premium prices. These ventures failed to enjoy any marked success and could not check the decline in the New York sheep industry.

Many farmers raised cattle for sale. This industry centered in the counties on the east bank of the lower Hudson, although practically all sections reported considerable activity in this branch of grazing.[77] The usual procedure was to buy two- or

---

[71] *Trans.*, II (1842), 171.
[72] *Oneida Whig*, Aug. 4, 1840.
[73] *Utica Observer*, Sept. 13, 1842.
[74] *Trans.*, VII (1847), 547.
[75] *Ibid.*, IX (1849), 780.
[76] *Ibid.*, VII (1847), 547; VI (1846), 270–279; *Patent Office Report*, 1849, p. 251.
[77] *Trans.*, I (1841), 154; *Central New-York Farmer*, II (Sept., 1843), p. 135; *Patent Office Report*, 1854, p. 18.

three-year-old cattle in the fall from drovers coming from the north or the west, keep them through the winter and the following summer, and then drive them to market. It was more profitable for eastern farmers to buy and fatten western cattle than to raise their own. Herkimer County farmers managed to fit beef production into their dairying operations. In the spring they bought cows from the drovers, milked them through the summer, and in the fall drove the oldest and poorest to the eastern butchers.[78]

The talents which Daniel Drew later displayed in rigging the market and "watering stock" were a carry-over from his earlier activities as a cattle drover.[79] Drew began his operations in Putnam County and later extended his driving to the Mohawk and Cherry valleys. The most important route led across Schoharie County to Catskill, where the cattle were ferried across the river. The drovers then followed the Harlem River southward to New York City. The stock business reached its peak about 1825.[80] It did not die out until the railroads began to flood the east with cheap meat from Chicago.

Albany remained one of the major beef-packing centers in the country.[81] After 1840 competition from western packing centers such as Cincinnati prevented its expansion. To be sure, the New York Central during the 1850's continued to bring in large quantities of livestock for which yards were built in West Albany.[82]

Closely connected with beef production was the raising of hogs for pork. Eastern New York farmers, however, could not hope to compete with western farmers in this field. As early as 1828 Mohawk Valley farmers were complaining that they were being

---

[78] *Trans.*, I (1841), 137.

[79] Bouck White, *The Book of Daniel Drew* (New York, 1910), pp. 33 ff.

[80] W. Wilson, *op. cit.*, p. 71.

[81] Joel Munsell, *Collections on the History of Albany, from its Discovery to the Present Time* (Albany, 1865–1871), II, 479.

[82] *Ibid.*, II, 392–394.

THE RISE OF THE DAIRY STATE

undersold.[83] Most farmers, however, kept a few animals for their own use. Some dairymen found it profitable to keep hogs in order to use the milk wasted in butter making.[84]

By far the most significant development in the Hudson-Mohawk Valley in this period was the rise of the dairy industry. The farmers were to find the cows, and not sheep or wheat, their most permanent and profitable money-maker. The most important reason was the sure and steady profit which the farmer could make in supplying cheese, butter, and milk for the domestic and foreign market.[85] Henry Randall, prominent sheepman, observed with more than a touch of sadness in 1851 that the "extraordinary recent profits in dairying" combined with the fact that the climate was more favorable to cows than to sheep had convinced the average farmer that he must enter the dairy business.[86] Furthermore, the western woolgrower could easily undersell him especially after wool prices declined after 1845.

Dairying offered other attractions besides that of profit. Manure provided a partial remedy for the prevailing soil depletion. Furthermore, the farmer could utilize the labor of women and children which the decline of home manufacturing had released from other cares. Transport costs were less than those of carrying grain to market. The iron horse solved the problem of getting milk to market quickly. Western dairymen were not yet ready to challenge the supremacy of New York.[87]

Of course many farmers, perhaps a majority, in eastern New York had turned to dairying without going through the transition

---

[83] *New-York Farmer*, I (1828), 268.
[84] *Trans.*, I (1841), 138.
[85] *Cultivator*, II (Jan., 1836), 163; *Trans.*, II (1842), 169; IX (1849), 535.
[86] *Patent Office Report*, 1851, p. 139.
[87] The example of New York and the migration of New York farmers greatly stimulated the development of the Wisconsin dairy industry (Joseph Schafer, *A History of Agriculture in Wisconsin* [Madison, 1922], p. 154).

LANDLORDS AND FARMERS

stage of raising sheep on a commercial basis.[88] Thus Orange County had earned a reputation for fine butter before the colonial period was over. Herkimer County had become famous for its cheese before 1825. Many farmers who found wheat cultivation unprofitable in the early 1830's immediately built up a herd of cows.

The premier cheese county in the state and in the nation was Herkimer County. In 1845 and again in 1855 its dairymen and milkmaids made almost one fourth of the state's output.[89] Together with the neighboring counties of Oneida and Oswego, Herkimer shipped four fifths of all the cheese sent on the state canals in 1847.[90] In 1845 the average cow in this county produced 226 pounds of cheese, as compared with a state average of 110 pounds per cow.[91] The one township of Fairfield made 1,356,000 pounds, or an average of nearly 350 pounds per cow.

Between 1834 and 1836 shipments of cheese reaching tidewater over the Erie Canal doubled in volume.[92] Similar increases took place between 1841 and 1843 and between 1845 and 1847 as new regions began to export cheese to Albany. During the 1840's the English importers began to call for American cheese, and exports rose sharply.[93] In 1840 only 723,000 pounds reached foreign ports. Ten years later over 13,000,000 pounds of cheese left our shores.

Several changes and improvements took place as the production of cheese became big business. First of all, more attention was paid to testing cows in order to find their butter output.[94] After 1840 dairymen imported breeds such as Durhams, Ayr-

---

[88] *Farmer and Mechanic*, n.s. IV (Nov. 2, 1848), 529; *Trans.*, I (1841), 138.
[89] *Trans.*, V (1845), 394–395; *N.Y. Census for 1855*, p. 322.
[90] *Trans.*, IX (1849), 429.
[91] *Ibid.*, VI (1846), 130.
[92] *Patent Office Report*, 1845, pp. 326–327; 1847, p. 653.
[93] *Ibid.*, 1842, pp. 106–107; *Trans.*, XI (1851), 90–91.
[94] *Trans.*, XIV (1854), 204–211.

THE RISE OF THE DAIRY STATE

shires, Herefords, and others.[95] These breeds were often crossed with the native cattle. The results were highly satisfactory. Between 1845 and 1850 the actual number of cows declined, but the output of butter, cheese, and milk increased.[96] This increase was partly due to the introduction of English grasses to improve pastures as well as to better shelter and forage during the winter. The widespread dissemination by farm journals and agricultural societies of information concerning the best methods of production likewise stimulated farmers to improve their herds and to buy improved implements such as presses. Instead of a shanty the farmer constructed a building to cure his cheese. After the railroad penetrated the region the cheese house was abandoned, and the cheese was sent to market as quickly as it was manufactured.

In the early years Herkimer County farmers sold their products to agents who visited their farms. Later the farmers sent their cheese to commission houses. By 1854 the farmers usually took their cheese to the railroad depots where local markets were held twice a week.[97]

One development of great significance, although somewhat beyond the period under discussion, was the rise of the associated dairy system. In 1851 Jessie Williams, a farmer near Rome, began to take in the milk of his neighbors which he manufactured into cheese. During the fifties several other farmers established cheese factories, but it was not until the sixties that the movement for cheese factories got under way.[98] The advantages were obvious. Cheese of a superior quality could be produced by skilled managers at a lower cost than in the home. The cheese factories could employ larger presses, thus relieving the family of the drudgery

---

[95] Stephen Van Rensselaer was active in distributing Durham calves (*American Agriculturist*, I [April, 1842], 21–23).

[96] *Trans.*, XIV (1854), 203.

[97] *Trans.*, XXII (1862), 416.

[98] For an incomplete list of cheese factories set up between 1850 and 1865, see *ibid.*, XXVI (1866), 929.

LANDLORDS AND FARMERS

of churning and pressing. The spread of cheese factories facilitated the organization of marketing. In 1858 Herkimer County producers set up a marketing society which eventually led to the establishment in 1871 of the state-wide Dairymen's Board of Trade.[99]

The production of butter formed the backbone of the dairy industry, both in the value of the product and in the number of farmers engaged.[100] Unlike the production of cheese, which was highly concentrated in central New York, butter production was more evenly distributed throughout the state. Orange, Delaware, Oneida, and Otsego counties were the leading butter producers of eastern New York in 1845. During the next decade the amount of butter made in the Hudson River counties declined, largely because the farmers in these counties were shipping increasing quantities of milk to market.

From colonial times until 1845 Orange County led all other counties in the amount of butter produced. Its butter was considered the best. The United States Navy insisted on Orange County butter because it kept well in tropical regions. But in 1848 it was estimated that over two thirds of the butter sold under that name or labeled "Goshen butter" was not made in that county.[101] Much of it came from the hilly regions of Delaware, Sullivan, Ulster, and Greene counties. Another center of butter making was the town of Steuben in Oneida County, where Welsh immigrants had early displayed skill in making fine butter. Butter making became so profitable that in 1846 one newspaper account observed that grazing lands, and especially those in Delaware County, were in great demand.[102]

All members of the family helped to make the butter. The

---

[99] *Trans.*, XXXI (1871), 368 ff.

[100] In 1855 New York farmers produced over 90,000,000 pounds of butter as compared with about 39,000,000 pounds of cheese and almost 21,000,000 gallons of milk (*N.Y. Census for 1855*).

[101] *Trans.*, VII (1847), 44; VIII (1848), 10–11.

[102] *Atlas*, quoted in *Ulster Republican*, Oct. 21, 1846.

THE RISE OF THE DAIRY STATE

actual work fell to the housewife, who skimmed the cream and packed the firkins. All the farm work "revolved around the dairy cow."[103] As in cheese making, certain improvements and techniques received wide publicity in the farm journals. One interesting device was the churning machine propelled by a dog or wether sheep. New milkhouses likewise attracted much attention. The dairyman usually sold his butter to buyers who visited the farm in the fall and tested the quality of the butter. If the buyer made a satisfactory offer, the farmer would load his firkins on the wagon and deliver the butter to such points as Newburgh, Catskill, and depots along the canal or railroad.

The average dairy farm in Orange County did not reach 100 acres.[104] As a rule each cow provided between 100 and 150 pounds of butter a year, although certain farms, such as that of Zadock Pratt of Greene County, produced over 200 pounds per cow.[105] The number of cows varied with each locality and with each individual farmer. In the town of Steuben the census shows about ten cows per farm; in Minisink, Orange County, there were about twenty to thirty cows on each farm.[106]

The influence of the urban market and the railroad shows up most clearly in the growth of the milk industry. Before the coming of the railroad almost all the milk consumed in the City came from the immediate vicinity. In fact, the bulk of the fluid milk supply came from this source as late as 1854.[107] The student must regard early statistics of the milk trade with even more than the

---

[103] John Burroughs (*My Boyhood* [Garden City, New York, 1922], pp. 11–20) has an interesting account of his father's dairy farm in Delaware County.

[104] *Trans.*, XXV (1865), 241. The average farm in Schoharie County contained 100 to 150 acres (*ibid.*, IX [1849], 435).

[105] *Patent Office Report*, 1854, pp. 21–22; 1861, p. 424. Pratt had 50 cows on a 365-acre farm.

[106] *Seventh Census of United States, Original Returns of the Assistant Marshalls; Agricultural Production (N–O)*, New York State Library. Eager, *op. cit.*, p. 406.

[107] *N.Y. Senate Documents*, no. 100 (1854), p. 5.

LANDLORDS AND FARMERS

usual caution shown both official and private estimates of this period. In 1854 a group of private citizens estimated "after careful inquiry" that the City consumed 25,575,000 gallons of milk annually.[108] This figure contrasts with the census of 1855, which lists only 20,965,861 gallons sold throughout the state.[109] We may call the following counties the milkshed of New York City:

Orange	4,553,514
Westchester	2,696,411
Putnam	1,888,910
Dutchess	1,970,368
Columbia	492,203
Kings	3,033,291
Queens	566,321
	15,201,018

Of course, the city of New York bought a considerable amount of milk from New Jersey and Connecticut.[110]

The spread of approximately 10,000,000 gallons between the estimate of the private committee and the total listed above can be partially explained as another illustration of the inaccuracy of statistics. Perhaps a more profitable explanation is the dilution of milk by the addition of water. Contemporary observers estimated that one fourth to one half of the milk reaching consumers was water.[111] A deduction of one third from the estimate of 25,575,000 gallons leaves a figure fairly close to the total production of those counties designated as the milkshed.

Distillery milk, that is to say, milk from cows fed on the reeking swill of distillery mash, provided the greater part of the fluid milk marketed in the city.[112] The conditions in these dairies were incredibly dirty. The owners tied the cows in filthy pens,

---

[108] *N.Y. Senate Documents*, no. 102 (1854).

[109] This figure as well as those for the counties is taken from the *N.Y. Census for 1855*, p. 322.

[110] *Country Gentleman*, I (Feb. 10, 1853), 81.

[111] *Ibid.*; *N.Y. Senate Documents*, no. 102 (1854).

[112] *Ibid.*; *Country Gentleman*, I (Feb. 10, 1853), 81.

THE RISE OF THE DAIRY STATE

deprived them of any exercise in the open air, and forced them to drink from thirty to forty gallons of hot slush a day. The diseased animals produced a "blue, watery, insipid, unhealthy secretion." The milk not only was of little food value, but it also was a hazard to public health. Frequently the dairyman put in chalk, sugar, flour, molasses, starch, and coloring matter in order to conceal the water which was added.

Physicians kept up a sporadic agitation against distillery milk. They blamed much of the alarming infant mortality to this cause.[113] Fully 50 per cent of the children failed to reach the age of five. A committee of fifty doctors condemned distillery milk as early as 1829. Again in 1847 a report warned the public against adulterated, diluted, and drugged milk. The New York Academy of Medicine joined the outcry against the "iniquitous business." Citizens began to petition the legislature.[114] They called for a ban on the sale of adulterated milk. Probably the most vigorous attack came from the pen of John Mullaly in 1852.[115] His charges and especially his statistics offer a striking commentary on the whole business of selling milk in New York. The following estimate emphasizes the seriousness of the problem.

1.	Pure country milk	$1,350,000
2.	Pure swill milk	2,550,000
3.	For water, chalk, etc.	1,250,000
		$5,150,000

In Orange, Westchester, and other counties those farmers whose farms were within a short distance of the Erie Railroad, the Harlem Railroad, and the Hudson River were quick to seize the opportunity of selling milk to the City.[116] Orange County

---

[113] *N.Y. Senate Documents*, no. 102 (1854); *New-York Weekly Tribune*, June 30, 1847.

[114] *N.Y. Senate Documents*, no. 102 (1854).

[115] For a good summary of his pamphlet, *The Milk Trade in New York and Vicinity*, see the *Country Gentleman*, I (Feb. 10, 1853), 81.

[116] Observers noted that milk dairies were "immediately adjacent" to the railroad (*Trans.*, XIV [1854], 544; VII [1847], 738).

farmers began to abandon butter, despite the premium prices which their butter enjoyed. Selling milk was much more profitable. In 1854 they received 2 to 2½ cents a quart in the summer and 3 to 3½ cents a quart in the winter. The shipments of milk over the Erie Railroad rose sharply after the first experimental shipment in 1842.

1842	385,505	Quarts
1846	7,090,430	
1852	12,610,556	
1861	24,414,608 [117]	

A similar increase took place on the east side of the Hudson, where the Hudson River Railroad and especially the Harlem Railroad tapped the grazing areas of Westchester, Putnam, Dutchess, and Columbia counties.

Milk production rose rapidly under the stimulus of handsome profits. Farmers averaged well over $30 a year on each cow.[118] In 1846 Solon Robinson, prominent agricultural writer, described carefully the milk farm of J. R. Colwell near Newburgh.[119] This farm was unusually large. There were 280 acres, of which 60 were in grains. In 1845 Colwell made $890 with sixteen cows, or $55.62 a cow. A farmer of Putnam County reported that his total sales of milk amounted to $3,600 from his dairy of fifty cows.[120]

The hay crop almost inevitably became the chief crop in the grazing areas of the Hudson-Mohawk drainage basin. Along the line of the canal and on the banks of the Hudson, hay became an important cash crop.[121] After a cultivated crop and a grain crop

---

[117] Figures are from several sources: *Country Gentleman*, I (Feb. 10, 1853), 81; *Niles' Weekly Register*, LXXI (Feb. 27, 1847), 403; *Patent Office Report*, 1861, pp. 214–216.

[118] *American Agriculturist*, X (Jan., 1851), 31–32; *Trans.*, VII (1847), 738.

[119] *American Agriculturist*, V (Feb., 1846), 56–57.

[120] *Cultivator*, n.s. VIII (Nov., 1851), 358.

[121] *Trans.*, XXII (1862), 403. Supplying hay to New York proved profitable for Hudson River farmers (*Patent Office Report*, 1852–1853, p. 221).

THE RISE OF THE DAIRY STATE

had been raised, grass and clover seed were sown among the grain. Thereafter the field lay in grass for hay or pasture from two to six years.

Lumbering continued to play a vital role in the rural economy of eastern New York. Not only did the average farmer rely on the forests for his fuel, fencing, and building materials, but farmers on the southern slopes of the Adirondacks and in the Catskill region were fully as interested in lumbering as in agriculture. In fact, there were many complaints that lumbering prevented the development of an orderly agricultural life.[122] Thus Horace Greeley in 1844 declared that Delaware and Sullivan counties had been cursed with a superabundance of pine, oak, and hemlock.

> Hence shiftlessness and a lack of steadiness in industry, except under the spur of immediate necessity. The effects of this policy on a new country . . . need hardly be stated. General poverty, lack of education, irreligion, love of liquor, Loco-Focoism, etc. are the natural results. . . . To live half a century in the hand-to-mouth, shingle-making way, would seem enough to sour "the milk of human kindness" in the breast of any man.[123]

After 1800 there was a great increase in rafting down the Delaware River.[124] Similarly on the Hudson River log driving began about 1813, and great sawmills were erected at Glens Falls, Sandy Hill, and Fort Edward. In 1851 more than 26,000,000 feet piled up at the Glens Falls boom. Twenty years later this amount had increased eightfold. Lumbering became big business. The small farmers and especially those living in the mountainous towns found woodcutting one of their most profitable occupations. The cities kept demanding large quantities of lumber for

---

[122] *Central New-York Farmer*, III (July, 1843), 102; *Freeholder*, Dec. 20, 1848.
[123] *New-York Weekly Tribune*, April 18, 1844.
[124] Brown, *op. cit.*, p. 117. For a good account of rafting on the Delaware, see the article by N. Willis in the *Freeholder*, Dec. 20, 1848; *Ulster Republican*, Aug. 26, 1846.

LANDLORDS AND FARMERS

construction and also for fuel. The steamboats, railroads, and plank roads likewise used up a great deal of lumber.[125]

In passing, it might be noted that timber thieves were constantly raiding the forest land of absentee owners. The timber was more valuable than the land in many cases. Landowners found it difficult to prevent thieves from pealing bark and cutting out trees.

The tanning industry deserves special attention. Approximately three fourths of the articles (principally leather) manufactured in the tanneries of New York, the leading tanning state in the Union, came from establishments in eastern New York. The industry naturally gravitated to the Catskill Mountains area where the stands of hemlock and oak were most extensive.

In 1817 the discovery of improved methods of tanning leather started a rush to the Catskills.[126] Speculators bought up tracts of timber, and boom towns grew up around the tanneries. The industry kept moving westward as the hemlock stands in western Greene and southern Schoharie counties ran out. The construction of the Delaware and Hudson Canal and the Erie Railroad speeded the movement into Delaware and Sullivan counties.

A comparison of the value of the manufactured product in the years 1845 and 1855 reveals most graphically this westward movement: [127]

	1845	1855
Greene	$811,789	$ 126,296
Sullivan	466,751	2,087,986

This shift is further reflected on the population map for 1850 to 1860, which shows heavy losses in the western towns of Greene

---

[125] The *Utica Intelligencer* (May 13, 1828) noted that Hudson River steamboats were contracting for Oneida County pine wood. The *Farmer and Mechanic* (IV [Feb. 17, 1848], 78) estimated that the Utica and Schenectady Railroad used 25,000 cords of 2-foot wood each year.

[126] Charles Rockwell, *The Catskill Mountains and the Region Around* (New York, 1867), p. 30; *Argus*, June 21, 1826.

[127] N.Y. Census for 1845; N.Y. Census for 1855.

THE RISE OF THE DAIRY STATE

County and marked gains in Delaware and Sullivan counties. The most famous tannery was operated by Colonel Zadock Pratt. Pratt had begun life as the son of a tenant holding a farm on the Livingston holdings in Schoharie County. For an unrevealed reason the family was evicted from their home about the year 1802. Pratt moved to Greene County where he set up a store. With the profits he built a tannery in the town which was later named Prattsville in his honor. The tannery was hailed as the most extensive establishment of its kind in the world. It tanned 60,000 sides of sole leather and consumed 6,000 cords of bark annually for twenty-five years.[128]

The typical farmer continued to follow exhaustive and slovenly methods of agriculture.[129] Nevertheless, the period between 1825 and 1850 did witness substantial advances, both in the dissemination of agricultural knowledge and in the application of that knowledge. It is only necessary to mention the contributions of Jesse Buel either as editor of the *Cultivator* or as practical farmer to demonstrate how vigorous the spirit of improvement had become.

The Berkshire county fair movement had hardly collapsed after the withdrawal of state aid in 1825 before agricultural leaders under the leadership of Jesse Buel redoubled their agitation for a new society and an agricultural college.[130] In 1832 the New York State Agricultural Society was founded with Le Ray De Chaumont of Jefferson County as president and Buel as corresponding secretary. Despite the efforts of Buel the society was unable to stimulate enough interest among farmers to re-establish the county

---

[128] William F. Fox, *A History of the Lumber Industry in the State of New York* (Washington, 1902), p. 33.

[129] Horace Greeley often berated farmers for their "half-fenced, unmanured, shallow plowed, late-planted, poorly tilled apologies for farms" (*New-York Weekly Tribune*, May 4, 1843; June 13, 1844).

[130] Harry Carman, "Jesse Buel, Albany County Agriculturist," *New York History*, XXXI (July, 1933), 240. See also *Argus*, Dec. 24, 1831; Feb. 15, 1832.

societies on a firm basis. The state legislature consistently refused to sponsor a program of state aid until 1841, when money was appropriated for a state fair and premiums for county societies. Any project for state aid had to run the gauntlet of attack. Enemies charged that agricultural societies would become political clubs, that they would be controlled by gentlemen-farmers, and that they would waste the taxpayers' money.[131]

Jesse Buel was the most active advocate of agricultural societies.[132] In fact, Buel contributed more to American agricultural progress in the decade of the thirties than any other contemporary figure. This enterprising Connecticut Yankee migrated to New York State, where he founded five newspapers. The *Argus* of Albany was the most famous of these papers. In 1821 Buel decided to devote his entire energies to farming. He did find time in the next two decades to serve in the state Assembly and to run for governor on the Whig ticket in 1836. Buel purchased an eighty-five-acre farm in the Sandy Barrens to the west of Albany. There he transformed a brier-covered, sterile piece of land into a farm famous throughout the state for its productivity and beauty. Not content with his success as a practical farmer, Buel founded the *Cultivator* in 1834 as the official organ of the state agricultural society. In the columns of this periodical he preached with increasing effectiveness the advantages of scientific farming to a rural population suspicious of book farming. The fact that he had made his own farming so profitable gave added weight to his arguments for manuring, draining, deep plowing, crop alternation, and the substitution of fallow crops for naked fallows.

After Buel's death the *Cultivator* and the *Genesee Farmer* combined under the name of *Cultivator*. Willis Gaylord and Luther

---

[131] *N.Y. Senate Documents*, no. 97 (1834), pp. 3–5; speech of Mr. A. Cook in Assembly reported in the *Argus*, June 18, 1839.

[132] Carman, *op. cit.*, pp. 249 ff.; Demaree, *op. cit.*, pp. 340–344; eulogy by Amos Dean in *Cultivator*, VII (March, 1840), 44.

THE RISE OF THE DAIRY STATE

Tucker, formerly editors of the *Genesee Farmer*, took over the task of editing the magazine. Another journal, the *Central New-York Farmer*, founded at Rome in 1842, merged with the *Cultivator* in January, 1845. Important as these and other farm journals were in disseminating agricultural information, they reached only a small fraction of the rural population.[133] Nevertheless, Tucker was sanguine enough to launch in 1853 a weekly called the *Country Gentleman*.

Another objective close to the heart of Jesse Buel was the establishment of a state agricultural school. As early as 1819 Simeon De Witt had urged an agricultural school for the sons of the wealthy, and Elkanah Watson had advocated a pattern farm.[134] Buel soon took up the fight and persuaded the Assembly committee on agriculture in 1823 to endorse an agricultural school. Unfortunately, the state legislature failed to take any action.

One of the first acts of the new state agricultural society was to appoint a committee to report on a plan for an agricultural school. Buel wrote a series of articles for the *Argus* urging the state to finance a school where students could study the theory and practice of scientific agriculture.[135] A committee of the Assembly made a favorable report in 1833 but a committee of the Senate in 1834 bitterly denounced the plan as costly and unnecessary. The temper of the report can be felt in its approval of the slogan, "Let us alone." Jesse Buel sadly observed to a private friend that the "farmers are the principal opponents." [136]

Despairing of state aid, the proponents asked the legislature to incorporate an agricultural school which would raise funds by

---

[133] S. A. Law in a letter dated March 1, 1842, to the editors of the *Cultivator* blamed the stupor and apathy of the people for his failure to secure subscriptions (Correspondence, 1841–1883, Box 7, S. A. Law Papers).

[134] True, *op. cit.*, p. 46; *Argus*, Jan. 15, 1819.

[135] *Ibid.*, Dec. 11, 13, 1832; March 4, 30, 1833.

[136] Letter of March 13, 1833, to John A. Thomas, Box 12, Thomson Collection.

LANDLORDS AND FARMERS

popular subscription. Hardly had the plan got under way before the panic of 1837 frightened away purchasers of the stock. Sporadic attempts were made throughout the 1840's to secure state support for agricultural education. But success did not come until the following decade. This agitation does reveal a growing concern for improved methods and practices.

In 1841 the state granted $8,000 a year for five years to encourage agricultural societies.[137] County societies had to match the state grant if they wished to receive state support. This offer led to the reorganization of many societies which sponsored county fairs. The annual fair held by the state society attracted large crowds. It was an exciting day for the farm family when they visited the fair. The exhibits of fruit, livestock, and tools helped to spread information about new techniques, machinery, and better breeds. The side shows and horse races provided a pleasant diversion from the monotony of farm life.

The state society published at state expense an annual volume of transactions. Local correspondents reported on conditions in their localities. The information is somewhat fragmentary and repetitious, but it gives a good picture of agricultural life. We find articles on such varied subjects as the potato rot, sheep raising, fertilizers, and butter churns. Speeches to the annual meeting of the society are likewise included. Agricultural surveys of several counties contain a wealth of source material. The editors published the lectures of Professor James F. W. Johnston, eminent English agriculturist, before the society in 1849.[138]

Enticed by the profits to be made in supplying the urban markets with cheese, butter, milk, vegetables, and other products, an increasing number of eastern New York farmers put into practice the information about drainage, fertilizers, rotation, and breeding which the farm journals, fairs, and societies were making public. That the efforts of these agencies enjoyed some success

---

[137] *Trans.*, I (1841), 12–13.
[138] *Trans.*, IX (1849), 163–268.

THE RISE OF THE DAIRY STATE

can be assumed from the remarks of Jesse Buel in one of his last speeches. Buel declared that large tracts of land in the valley of the Hudson which bad husbandry had exhausted had been restored to their original fertility by good husbandry during the thirty years preceding 1840.[139]

Partly because soil exhaustion was the greatest evil facing farmers in eastern New York, and partly because fertilizers were effective and relatively cheap, the farmers first turned their attention to soil improvements.[140] Of course many farmers, faced with the old choice of seeking a new farm to exploit or of preserving the fertility of their old farm by manuring and rotating their crops, chose the first alternative. Those who remained continued to rely on gypsum as the most effective fertilizer. A keen observer noted in 1850 that gypsum was almost the only manure that a large portion of the land of central New York received.[141] Mills crushed it into a powder which was sold at the rate of $1.50 a ton. Gypsum benefited corn and oats. It also helped to keep pastures and meadows in good condition.

With the spread of the sheep and dairy industries the supply of natural manure steadily increased. The farm journals were often in dispute as to the best time when manure should be applied to the crops and whether it should be mixed with barnyard muck and scraps to form a compost.[142] Lime was seldom used as a fertilizer. Some mention is made of guano. Of course, farmers in the neighborhood of the cities were the first to see the value of applying fertilizers in order to raise the productivity of their high-cost land.

With the shift from a grain economy to a more diversified agri-

---

[139] *Cultivator*, VI (Nov. 20, 1839), 178.

[140] In 1820 the value and application of fertilizers were the most popular subjects discussed in speeches to agricultural societies (*Plough Boy*, II [Nov. 18, 1820]).

[141] Johnston, *op. cit.*, I, 177.

[142] *Trans.*, II (1842), 65-97; *Schoharie Republican*, Dec. 24, 1844.

culture, rotation of crops became more common. Each farmer usually followed his own inclination, scarcely aware of the value of a regular system and the importance of legumes. Reports from central New York in this period show that the principle of rotation was but little understood by the mass of farmers who trailed in the wake of progressive farmers.[143]

The age-old custom of fallowing was gradually loosening its hold in this period. Chancellor Livingston had urged fallow crops without success. In 1829 Jesse Buel observed that a few farmers were finding fallow crops not only effective in keeping out weeds but also valuable as a source of income.[144] During the forties there is considerable evidence that more and more farmers were planting beans, peas, potatoes, and grasses as fallow crops.

Little progress was made in draining wet lands before 1850. The chief barrier was the high cost as compared with the low cost of land. There was no such pressure on the farmer to utilize every bit of his land as there was in Flanders and parts of England and Scotland. In addition, the scarcity of capital prevented most farmers from making permanent improvements. After the importation of the drain tile machine, which promised to reduce the cost, farmers were more willing to undertake the improvement.[145]

The invention, improvement, and widespread adoption of agricultural machinery has probably been the greatest single contribution of American agriculture.[146] Scarcity of labor combined with extensive cultivation gave a stimulus to the use of farm machinery. Although the greatest advances took place after 1840,

---

[143] *Genesee Farmer*, III (Jan., 1833), 12; *Trans.*, I (1841), 141.

[144] *New-York Farmer*, II (Dec., 1829), 277. James Stuart in 1828 stated that farmers knew the value of fallows and green crops but found labor costs too high (*op. cit.*, pp. 258–259).

[145] *Trans.*, XII (1852), 203–210.

[146] Horace Greeley wrote after his visit to the state fair at Syracuse in 1851 that the "greatest progress in Agriculture" was being made in the field of agricultural machinery (*New-York Weekly Tribune*, Sept. 25, 1851).

THE RISE OF THE DAIRY STATE

Jesse Buel could note about that time that the improved plow and harrow, as well as new rollers, cultivators, drills, and other farm machines, permitted a farmer to work his farm with half the expense of labor required forty years previously.[147]

By 1840 the cast-iron plow had completely replaced the old wooden plow. Farmers in eastern New York reported that with the new plow they could accomplish more work with half the number of oxen or horses.[148] As a rule, most of the plows were of local manufacture, although a few varieties such as the "Livingston County" were widely distributed throughout the state. Similar improvements were made in the harrow, and new soil-working implements such as rollers, corn planters, and cultivators came into use.[149]

The increasing importance of the hay crop was matched by labor-saving improvements in mowing and raking the hay. Mowing machines won acceptance slowly since they proved ineffective except on level ground. The revolving rake began to displace the ordinary horse rake after 1840. Some farmers in Herkimer County were still using hand rakes as late as 1841.[150] Comparable advances speeded up the harvesting of crops. The cradle completely replaced the sickle. Both the Hussey and the McCormick reaper found their exponents in eastern New York, but the reaper did not come into general use.[151] On the other hand, the threshing machine very largely replaced the older and more primitive ways of threshing grain.[152] Dairy equipment likewise underwent constant improvement. All in all, the farmers found their labor greatly lightened by new machinery.

Scarcity of labor was largely responsible for the adoption of

---

[147] *Cultivator*, V (April, 1838), 38.
[148] *Ibid.*, n.s. II (April, 1845), 44; *Ulster Republican*, Oct. 13, 1847.
[149] *Trans.*, I (1841), 141; II (1842), 171.
[150] *Ibid.*, I (1841), 138.
[151] William Hutchinson (*Cyrus H. McCormick* [New York, 1930–1935], I, 154 ff.) traces the history of the early reapers in New York State.
[152] *Trans.*, I (1841), 138; X (1850), 527.

LANDLORDS AND FARMERS

machinery. The call of fresh lands in Michigan and the lure of relatively high wages in the cities made it difficult for farmers to hold their labor. The young people migrated from the old homesteads in large numbers. It is difficult to trace the rise and fall of farm wages because our evidence is so fragmentary. Ten dollars a month exclusive of board is the wage most frequently cited.[153] Day rates rose sharply during the autumn when labor was especially needed to harvest the crops. The farmer's family, as always, provided most of the labor. The housewife shouldered the heavy burden of churning the butter and making the cheese. Sometimes the farmer could hire dairymaids to perform these tasks.

It does not take a Jeremiah to find abundant evidence of rural decline in the period between 1825 and 1850. Of course, the most spectacular demonstration of agrarian unrest was the antirent episode, which tends to overshadow other basic factors determining the course of eastern New York agriculture. But the problem of leasehold tenure affected only a minority of the farmers, while such developments as the expansion of transportation facilities and the growth of commercial farming reached into the lives of every farm family. An examination of the problem of rural decline will help us to understand more fully the background of the movement to eradicate the last vestiges of leasehold tenure in the region of eastern New York.

---

[153] In 1828 help received $10 to $12 a month besides board (Stuart, *op. cit.*, I, 275). In 1830 help in Oneida County received $5 to $12 a month plus board (Fowler, *op. cit.*, p. 78). In 1841 Herman Gansevoort of Saratoga County hired Thomas Labrum for $12 a month (*Day Book, 1837–1846*, Gansevoort-Lansing Collection, New York Public Library). In 1823 S. A. Law hired I. Todd to work from April 1 to December 1 for $9 a month, of which one half to two thirds was to be in cash ("Statement of Accounts, Labor, 1804–1879," S. A. Law Papers). Husbandmen in Columbia, Greene, Rensselaer, Ulster, Oneida, and Albany counties received $10 a month in 1845 (*Patent Office Report, 1845*, pp. 1149–1150). The *Cultivator* (n.s. IV [Sept., 1847], 286) stated that $10 a month was the prevailing wage.

THE RISE OF THE DAIRY STATE

Emigration and a decline in population are usually considered symptoms of rural decline. The pull of social ties is such that relatively few individuals leave a region unless they are forced out by adverse conditions or are attracted elsewhere by greater opportunities. It must be admitted that the farmers of eastern New York, in common with most Americans, came from a migrating stock. It had already torn itself loose from its European background and had acquired the habit of migrating to new frontiers. This very mobility of the American population has made it a more sensitive barometer of changing economic conditions than would be true in the case of rural populations in Europe, where the ties of family, custom, and religion tend to bind the farmer to the ancestral home.

Occasionally a declining population is the sign of increased prosperity for a portion of the population. The sheep and dairy industries naturally tended to crowd out the small farmers. The most efficient size for a farm at this time was larger than the original farms devoted to wheat. Thus the farmers in the town of Fairfield in Herkimer County found that 100 acres were not enough for the most profitable production of cheese.[154] They therefore bought more land. Editors of farm journals deplored the practice of wealthy farmers of "swallowing up all the small farmers in the vicinity and thus reducing them to the situation of vassals, or compelling them to migrate to the far west."[155] Often the small farmer would sell his holding and use the money to buy a larger farm elsewhere. Sometimes heirs found it easier to sell an estate in order to get funds to buy western farms than to parcel out the old farm. The introduction of machinery also encouraged many farmers to cultivate larger units.

Part of the population decline represented the shift in marketing from the small villages, which had grown up around the meeting-

---

[154] N. S. Benton, *op. cit.*, p. 380.
[155] *Genesee Farmer*, quoted in *Oneida Whig*, May 24, 1836. See also the *Rural New-Yorker*, VI (Oct. 13, 1855), 325.

LANDLORDS AND FARMERS

houses or taverns in the early days, to the large towns and cities, which sprang up along canals and railroads. Local merchants complained that farmers would travel 20 to 30 miles over turnpikes, plank roads, and railroads to buy their goods in the city.[156] Undoubtedly the bustle and excitement of the canal towns gave the farmer a thrill. Competition likewise kept prices below those of the country store.

For purposes of convenience, we may classify the causes of rural decline under three headings: western competition, urban attraction, and miscellaneous reasons.

A letter of Samuel Law to his employer, John Wharton, a large landholder in Delaware County, describes graphically the effect of the "western fever" on eastern agriculture:

> Latterly—all the Rage for emigration, has been to the far west—to Michigan, Indiana, Illinois etc. And of the settlers already here abundance of them are in a mind to sell out and push on farther west. The consequence is,—that land,—both improved and wild, instead of rising, keeps depressed and unsalable.[157]

He went on to analyze competition in land values as one of the most important ways in which the West was competing with eastern farmers living in isolated hill towns.

> Formerly, a poor man could buy a wild lot and go on clearing, and, if he could not pay, could sell out, to some one abler and save something to himself. Now it is not so. The enhanced value from improvements unless expensive ones—from used ones with log-buildings and common clearings,—not keeping pace with interest. Hence the lots I sold, of yours, fell back. The buyers, finding they could neither pay, themselves nor sell, to others that could, grew discouraged and let their clearings and fences go to wreck and ruin, and, finally, abandoned.

To the farmers living in the sequestered counties such as Delaware, the failure of their lands to rise in value was all the more bitter to endure because farm values along the course of Hudson River and the line of the Erie Canal and the railroads were in-

---

[156] *Ibid.; Trans.*, XIX (1859), 320.
[157] Dec. 25, 1833, Box 5, S. A. Law Papers.

THE RISE OF THE DAIRY STATE

creasing rapidly. During the same decade that Law was writing, Dutchess County was experiencing a land boom with the best farms selling at as high as $100 an acre.[158] Ten years later, when the Erie Railroad penetrated Delaware County, a similar real-estate boom took place.[159] The expansion of the transportation network and the demand of the city market raised the value of practically all farm lands in the state during the early 1850's.[160]

The desire to migrate was contagious. The departure of neighbors could not fail to make farmers wonder whether it would not be better to try their fortunes elsewhere. The newspapers and the farm journals carried accounts of cheap and fertile lands in Michigan and other western states.[161] The *Cultivator* ran a series of articles by Solon Robinson between 1840 and 1843 advising potential pioneers what equipment they should take and what dangers they would face.[162] Robinson did not hesitate to point out that if the emigrant would spend as little and endure as much on his farm in the east, he would not advance himself by moving west.

So extensive was the emigration that public officials and editors of farm journals became alarmed and warned the farmers not to make such an important decision without carefully considering all the perils and difficulties. Despite these warnings the more restless and ambitious farmers packed their belongings, waved their friends goodby, and headed westward. In the lush intervales of the Genesee Valley, the rolling countryside of Michigan, or the gold fields of California there would be found those who had deserted the hills of eastern New York.

---

[158] *Niles' Weekly Register*, XLVII (Jan., 1835), 370–371; *Cultivator*, III (May, 1836), 41.

[159] *Atlas*, quoted in *Ulster Republican*, Oct. 21, 1846.

[160] *Patent Office Report*, 1852–1853, p. 6.

[161] Typical letters extolling the fertility of Illinois and the Wabash country are in the *Schoharie Republican* for Aug. 20 and Sept. 10, 1839.

[162] VII (Oct., 1840), 162; VII (Dec., 1840), 192; VIII (Jan., 1841), 19–20; VIII (March, 1841), 53; VIII (June, 1841), 97; IX (Dec., 1842), 193–194; X (Jan., 1843), 17–18; X (Feb., 1843), 37–38.

LANDLORDS AND FARMERS

The state census for 1855 reveals some interesting facts about Otsego County, which was a typical upland county. Of its 49,735 inhabitants, 31,861 had been born there. But 19,105 natives of Otsego County were living in other parts of the state. In short, over 37 per cent were living outside its boundaries. Additional thousands of natives had migrated to the western states. No doubt the inclusion of these emigrants would raise the percentage of natives living outside Otsego County to well over 50 per cent. The state of Vermont was also suffering from the same emigration at this time.

The period between 1825 and 1850 witnessed a growing stream of farm youth drifting to the cities. The big city held many attractions. Not only was farm life a monotonous round of field labor and chores, enlivened only by sermons and an occasional bee or party, but it offered little challenge to ambitious young people. The speaker before the State Agricultural Convention in 1837 was echoing the complaint of many farm boys when he said: "It is a matter of notoriety . . . that almost every other occupation is considered more honorable, or more genteel than that of the farmer. The consequence is, a general abandonment of its pursuits, by all the ambitious youth of the country." [163]

Moreover, the educational system tended to encourage young people to leave the countryside. The numerous academies and colleges which grew up where the New England element predominated did not teach agriculture and mechanics. The classical curriculum held full sway. A mastery of languages and natural philosophy did not fit boys for life on the farm. Rather it led directly to the law, ministry, or teaching. Other students found clerical positions in the city. Not without reason did one writer exclaim: "Educate them! Why the moment you educate them they will leave the business." [164]

Other factors as well contributed to rural decline in the Hudson-

---
[163] *Cultivator*, IV (Aug., 1837), 103.
[164] *Ibid.*, n.s. VIII (Nov., 1851), 360.

THE RISE OF THE DAIRY STATE

Mohawk Valley. Many farmers lacked capital. Improved breeds of livestock, farm machinery, and permanent improvements cost more money than many could muster.[165] Some farmers found it possible to borrow money upon their equities. One farm journal noted that mortgages were becoming more common.[166] Another factor of importance was the stupidity and apathy which characterized large sections of the farm population. Frequently it was the farmer class which was the most active in opposition to laws designed to foster agricultural societies and education.[167] This contempt for book farming certainly did not make for rapid advances in the field of scientific agriculture. Of course, some of this distrust toward new ideas was a natural reaction against the failure of the mulberry mania and the Merino sheep speculation. The crooked practices of some buyers and merchants made the farmer still more suspicious of outsiders advocating reform.

The difficulty of tracing and evaluating the endless variety of individual and local readjustments which accompanied the shift to commercial farming is by now apparent. The construction of canals, railroads, and plank roads so speeded up the tempo of change that a veritable agricultural revolution took place. These new arteries of trade not only exposed the eastern farmer to the full brunt of cheap western products, but they also enabled him to supply the growing home market. Eastern New York farmers showed no small skill and resourcefulness in making the shift to grazing. Farmers in Washington County found their solution in sheep; Herkimer County farmers created a famous cheese industry; Delaware County dairymen earned the same reputation for their butter as their neighbors in Orange County; still other farmers were enterprising enough to specialize in hops, flax, broomcorn, milk, and apples.

The increasing specialization was sometimes the cause and

---

[165] *Trans.*, III (1843), 118.
[166] *New-York Farmer*, IV (1831), 154, 181.
[167] *Trans.*, VIII (1848), 150; III (1843), 372.

sometimes the result of improved agricultural practices. Jesse Buel and his friends were making a gallant and not unsuccessful fight for scientific agriculture and agricultural education. Progressive farmers in every county were beginning to rotate their crops, experiment with new fertilizers and drainage, and buy better livestock and machinery. The dairies of New York were becoming the models for the entire country.

But this period of rapid change was also one of unrest. Many could not make the transition from a pioneering society to a more mature society; others would not or could not adjust themselves to the demands of the market. During the 1830's emigration drained off some discontent. During the 1840's antirentism became the channel through which much unrest expressed itself. In the next two chapters we shall examine this significant episode in the agrarian history of eastern New York.

CHAPTER VII

THE ANTIRENT MOVEMENT

1839 - 1845

RURAL NEW YORK has long been noted for its conservatism. Its deep-rooted opposition to political and social innovation makes it doubly difficult to understand the spirit of reform which infected large sections of the rural as well as the urban population in the four decades preceding the Civil War. Strange sects sprang up in the "burned-over" region of central New York. Spokesmen of temperance, education, and slavery reform found upstate New York a fertile field in which to sow their doctrines. Of course, the establishment of the Oneida Community by John Humphrey Noyes and the kaleidoscopic activities of the ebullient Gerrit Smith were not representative of agrarian life in this period, any more than the successive enthusiasms of Horace Greeley and the crusade for land reform by George Henry Evans were typical of the metropolitan population. Nevertheless, the fact that these individuals acquired a following and found a sympathetic audience does give an insight into the mental climate of the age of which they were to a greater or lesser degree the products. They symbolize the crusading fervor and the social ferment so characteristic of this period.

In a certain sense this was an age of faith, an age which passionately believed in the infinite capacity of the individual to

LANDLORDS AND FARMERS

reform himself and remake his universe. Whether it was against the secret Masonic order, "demon rum," or the "feudal land system," reformers marshaled their adherents to do battle with the forces of darkness. Believers in the Second Coming were matched in their zeal, although on a more mundane level, by the devotees of the silk worm and the plank road. Even the various migration movements were known as "fevers." Behind these outbursts of enthusiasm may be detected a spirit of revolt against traditional institutions, and a conviction that the common man should use his recently acquired political power for social betterment. It is in the light of this background that the antirent movement must be studied.

The antirent agitation, flaring up in 1839, reaching its peak in the middle forties, and breaking out intermittently until well after the Civil War, was more than a mere protest against the remnants of a feudal land system.[1] It became the channel whereby reformers of many stripes attempted to bring about constitutional changes within the state and land reforms within the nation. Furthermore, antirentism became the medium through which much of the discontent accompanying the shift to commercial agriculture found

---

[1] The author would like to call the reader's attention to Henry Christman's new book, *Tin Horns and Calico* (New York, 1945). This lively account of the antirent war recaptures much of the drama and color of the uprising. Christman has shown resourcefulness and industry in tracking down information in private as well as public collections. His deft pen has brought to life such little-known characters as Dr. Smith A. Boughton, Thomas Ainge Devyr, and Alvan Bovay. Unfortunately, his unrestrained enthusiasm for the antirent cause and his uncritical reliance upon Devyr's version of the uprising have led him to serious errors of fact and interpretation. His description of the legal obligations and the economic burdens of the leasehold is confusing and inadequate. Historians will not readily recognize or accept his caricature of Governor Silas Wright, who emerges as the villain. Christman has broken new ground in describing the part played by Devyr and other National Reformers in supporting the antirent movement, but his hero worship of Devyr has caused him to overlook the significant role which the antirenters played in state elections between 1846 and 1850.

THE ANTIRENT MOVEMENT

expression. Farmers living on worn-out fields and isolated farms found the landlord a convenient scapegoat for their poverty and uncertainty.

The second chapter examined in some detail the land pattern of eastern New York. The landed aristocracy still held extensive tracts in 1840. This was particularly the case in Columbia, Rensselaer, Albany, and Delaware counties. The aristocracy held smaller but important tracts in Schoharie, Greene, Montgomery, Schenectady, Oneida, Sullivan, Ulster, and Dutchess counties. Between 1790 and 1840 there took place a complete transfer of ownership from landlord to tenant in several tracts. The Philipse Highland Patent in Putnam County, Baron Steuben's holdings in Oneida, and part of the Verplanck lands in Delaware are important examples. Despite these changes the amount of land held under leasehold remained impressive, especially in the counties along the middle Hudson. As late as 1848 Governor John Young estimated that 1,800,000 acres were under lease.[2] By far the most notable survival of the colonial grants was Rensselaerswyck. This manor was indeed a princely domain. It embraced most of Albany and Rensselaer counties and boasted 3,063 farms, covering some 436,000 acres.[3]

The leases under which the tenants held land were by no means uniform.[4] Most leases were in effect freehold estates which were subject to a yearly rent and other limitations. The "durable lease" was the most widely used form. Stephen Van Rensselaer adopted this method of conveyance almost exclusively. His tenants, or more accurately the freeholders on Van Rensselaer Manor, had to pay him a perpetual rent of between 10 and 14 bushels of wheat per hundred acres, four fat fowl, and a day's work with a team of

---

[2] *Messages from Governors*, IV, 408.
[3] 9 N.Y. 301.
[4] For an analysis of the leasehold, see Mark, *op. cit.*, pp. 62–73. For more detailed information, see Chapter II of the present volume.

horses or oxen. On the other hand the tenants on Livingston Manor generally held their freeholds for two lives. Upon the death of the second person named as lessee, the farm reverted to the Livingston family. Other landlords such as General Philip Schuyler leased their farms for three lives.

Landed proprietors frequently retained additional rights to the land. Most leases provided for fines on alienation; that is, the seller had to pay to the landlord one third, one fourth, or one tenth of the sales price when he sold out his interest in the farm. The Rensselaerswyck leases provided that the tenant should pay one fourth of the money to the patroon, or in some cases an extra year's rent. In addition, the landlord sometimes reserved all rights to mines and millsites. Failure to meet any obligations gave the landlord the right to distrain the property of the tenant.

Any answer to the question of how much burden the tenant farmers had to carry must consider several factors. The original tenant usually obtained his land without any down payment. In fact, he enjoyed a free period ranging from four to seven years during which he paid no rent. Thereafter he paid an annual rent either in kind or in money. This rent varied according to the location, fertility, and date of the original lease. Few leases, however, called for less than 10 or more than 20 bushels of wheat per hundred acres.[5]

Wheat rents naturally fluctuated with the changing price of that commodity. For example, a farm in Otsego County leased on July 1, 1831, for the life of the tenant and his sons paid a rent of 23 bushels, 15 pounds of wheat. In terms of cash the rent varied as follows: [6]

---

[5] In 1813 John Wigram reported to Mr. Le Roy that the payment of 25 bushels per 100 acres was too high. He suggested 20 bushels (*John Wigram's Proceedings on Goldsbrow Banyar Business, 1812*, Box 1, G. Banyar Papers).

[6] See *Rent Book. Schuyler Patent and Lot 24 Staley Patent, 1838–1868*, Box 1, vol. 16, G. Banyar Papers.

THE ANTIRENT MOVEMENT

1837	$55.21	1844	$23.25
1838	40.69	1845	23.25
1839	39.23	1847	37.78
1840	23.25	1850	29.07
1841	23.25	1855	52.31
1842	27.11	1860	31.97
1843	23.25	1867	69.75

It may be argued that the wheat rent was more equitable and easier to pay than a fixed money charge because it was adjusted to the price level. No doubt this was true at the outset. Whatever flexibility or convenience the wheat payment may have possessed during the early years was largely nullified by declining yields and the virtual collapse of commercial wheat cultivation throughout eastern New York during the 1830's. Sometimes the wheat payments were commuted at a fixed sum per bushel.[7] Thus the original Livingston leases were commuted so that the tenant paid $18 for each hundred acres of land he held. Where the tenants were given the option of paying either in wheat or in money, agents found it necessary to fix a definite date in order to avoid loss. Thus in 1837 James Dexter, agent for the Banyar estate, wrote to Robert H. Ludlow, "Tenants took advantage of low price of wheat in the summer to bring in and deposit their rent in grain. I shall refuse to receive wheat in the summer and fall—I shall require pay't in cash of the price of wheat on the 1 Feb." [8]

The rent varied from tract to tract and from year to year. Considering 15 bushels of wheat per hundred acres as an average payment, the rent on a 100-acre farm on January 1, 1837, when wheat was 18 shillings a bushel, would have been $33.75. The same farm in 1840, when wheat was worth only 9 shillings, would

---

[7] *N.Y. Assembly Documents*, no. 156 (1846). The agent for the Banyar estate noted in 1841 that wheat rents on his Fulton County farms had been commuted to $1.00 a bushel ("Agents, Reports on Lott and Low Patent and Magin's Patent," Box 6, Folder 1, G. Banyar Papers).

[8] Letter dated Feb. 8, 1837, in *James Dexter Letter Book, 1835–1838*, vol. 20, G. Banyar Papers.

LANDLORDS AND FARMERS

have paid only $16.88. During the decade following 1830 the average price of wheat, according to the Van Rensselaer records, was $1.38. The rent for a farm of 100 acres would thus amount to $20.63; for a 160-acre farm, $32.38. These figures do not include such items as the four fowl and day's service required in the Van Rensselaer leases, and such charges as quarter sales found in many leases.

Using either the estimate of the agent of the Van Rensselaer family that the average rent of the farms in the four western towns of Albany County had been $31.16 during the thirty years prior to 1846, or the figure of $32 used by Horace Greeley in his description of a typical tenant, the amount should not be dismissed as insignificant.[9] Thirty dollars a year represented a considerable fraction of the cash income of a tenant.

The rent burden struck hardest at the hill farmers. Most antirent disturbances took place in isolated hill country such as the Helderberg townships in western Albany County. The hill farmer found the transition to commercial agriculture particularly difficult. The thin and exhausted hill soils refused to yield profitable wheat crops. Sheep raising offered a temporary way out during the 1830's, but declining wool prices and western competition forced out the marginal producers within the next decade. Possessing little capital to buy improved livestock, lacking incentive to make or buy permanent improvements such as dairy barns, spring houses, and other dairy equipment, and usually located away from the main routes of transportation, the tenant farmer found it exceedingly difficult to adjust himself to the conditions of commercial agriculture. Instead he fell prey to the shiftlessness associated with the tenancy system. The tenant farmer would not follow improved techniques or try to restore soil fertility in a period when the great majority of American farmers were mining the soil and ignoring the principles of sound husbandry. As a

---

[9] *N.Y. Assembly Documents*, no. 156 (1846), p. 49; *New-York Weekly Tribune*, Sept. 8, 1845.

THE ANTIRENT MOVEMENT

result, the houses and barns of tenants were "exceedingly dilapidated," their fields were exhausted, and their husbandry was uniformly predatory. The demoralizing effect of tenancy on agricultural practices is too well known to bear further repetition.

Horace Greeley painted in 1845 a graphic picture of the typical tenant. To this farmer the rent ($32) was "no abstraction." [10] The value of his yearly produce did not reach $300, of which two thirds was directly consumed. What little cash he had was "mortgaged to storekeepers" before the harvest arrived. One half of the 160 acres under lease often remained a wilderness because it was not worth clearing. At least one half of the cleared area was "miserable bush pasture." The tenant, even more than the ordinary independent farmer, ignored scientific farming. Frequently he could not read or write. His corn and rye yielded less than 10 bushels an acre. In addition, he raised some potatoes and kept a few poor cattle. He undoubtedly supplemented his income by stealing timber and peeling bark from the lands of nonresidents.[11]

Practically every landlord had trouble when he tried to collect the rent. Sometimes he accepted payment in kind. Not infrequently the tenant had to beg his landlord to grant an extension. The leniency of some landlords, sometimes arising from paternalism as in the case of Stephen Van Rensselaer, and sometimes stemming from the realization that a tenant on the farm protected it from the depredations of neighbors and from being overrun by underbrush, only aggravated the situation by postponing the day of reckoning and encouraging the tendency to shiftlessness.

The tenant could not help wondering why he should support the idle rich when it was he who had carved the farm out of the wilderness. Greeley, who was a keen critic of social change, noted

---

[10] *Ibid.*

[11] One of the most common complaints of land agents was that tenants and neighbors kept stealing the timber. See "Agents, Reports, Lott and Low Patent and Magin's Patent, 1838–1847," *passim,* Box 6, Folder 1, G. Banyar Papers.

LANDLORDS AND FARMERS

"that much of the Political theorizing of our day—our Fourth-of-July gatherings, Orations, etc. have contributed essentially to fan into a flame the long inflammable material at the bottom of the Anti-Rent excitement." [12]

Not much agitation was needed to revive the smoldering embers of agrarian unrest. The tenantry had long nourished a bitter hatred of the aristocracy. During the colonial period the manor lords on the east bank of the Hudson had to beat down several attacks on their titles by disgruntled tenants. Tenants in Columbia County had resisted with force in the 1790's both the landlords and the sheriffs who attempted to collect the rent. One generation later farmers leasing lands from the Livingston and Van Rensselaer families had staged another revolt. The aristocracy won all these engagements, but they could not kill the spirit of resistance. The tenants stubbornly cherished the dream of eliminating all traces of the semifeudal land system.

Antirentism in the years following 1839 followed much the same pattern as earlier revolts. Sheriffs encountered violence and physical assault; armed riders ranged through the country lanes; tenants pledged themselves not to pay the rent; and antirent lawyers challenged the landlord titles in the courts. There was, however, one crucial difference. The antirenters of the 1840's were far better organized and more skillfully led than were their predecessors. The tenant farmers organized town, county, and state committees. They published their own newspapers, held periodic conventions, and elected their own political spokesmen. The antirenters used political power, long the monopoly of the landed aristocracy, to bring about a more democratic land system.

The death of Stephen Van Rensselaer, the "last of the patroons," on January 26, 1839,[13] symbolized the passing of an era. The spectacle of a landed aristocrat living in semifeudal splendor among his three thousand tenant farmers was becoming more and

---

[12] *New-York Weekly Tribune*, Sept. 8, 1845.
[13] *Argus*, Jan. 28, 1839.

THE ANTIRENT MOVEMENT

more of an anachronism in an age in which democratic fervor elevated the frontier hero, Andrew Jackson, to the White House. The prestige of the Van Rensselaer family, the patroon's sense of public service, and his genuine humanitarian feelings had held in abeyance much of the criticism which his power and privileges would have otherwise aroused. His character had won for him the esteem if not the love of the great majority of his tenants and the general public.

Stephen Van Rensselaer's leniency toward his tenants softened the harsher burdens of the leasehold, but it created a dangerous problem for his heirs. His paternalism only whetted the appetite for more concessions. He permitted the tenant farmers to commute the payment of fowls and one day's labor for a load of wood delivered at Watervliet or $2.00 in cash.[14] Quarter sales were sometimes waived or commuted for a much smaller sum.[15] Tenants who for ill health or misfortune found it difficult to pay their rent received extensions or exemptions from payment. In other cases Stephen Van Rensselaer made little effort to collect the rent. By 1839 it was estimated that the arrears had accumulated to the sum of $400,000.[16]

Imagine the dismay of the tenants when they learned that his will provided for the immediate collection of back rents. Money collected from the tenants was to pay the patroon's own debts, which amounted to almost the same figure.[17] The will did make special provision for destitute tenants, who were not to be molested. But this clause would apply to only a relatively few individuals; it offered no relief to the great majority of tenants. The interpretation of these clauses would depend upon the heirs. Stephen Van Rensselaer bequeathed the manor to his two sons in accordance with the state laws forbidding primogeniture. His

---

[14] *N.Y. Senate Documents*, no. 92 (1846), p. 11.
[15] *Ibid.*; *N.Y. Assembly Documents*, no. 156 (1846), p. 49.
[16] *Ibid.*, no. 261 (1841), p. 5.
[17] See statement of Stephen Van Rensselaer in *Argus*, Dec. 6, 1839.

namesake inherited the west manor, that is, the land lying to the west of the Hudson; William P. Van Rensselaer inherited the east manor.

The attempts of the two sons to collect the back rents touched off the Helderberg War, as the conflict between Stephen Van Rensselaer, Jr., and his tenants was called. As a rule the tenant farmers on Rensselaerswyck had been more contented than tenants on Livingston Manor. The durable lease did guarantee to them their farms in perpetuity, unlike the two-life leases on Livingston Manor. Furthermore, the patroon had usually treated his tenants with kindness and sympathy. Nevertheless, discontent was seldom absent from the manor, even though most of it never found public expression. Indeed, if the experience of present-day charitable organizations is any criterion, some of the recipients of the patroon's generosity subconsciously resented the fact that they were indebted to his kindness. What had first been accepted as a bounty later became a vested right. The status of tenant rankled in the minds of many farmers. The leasehold seemed an anachronism in a country of independent farmers. Time and again the tenants insisted that it was incompatible with our republican institutions. The average tenant was, therefore, eager to change his lot. Sullen acquiescence was the most any landlord could expect.

As long as Stephen Van Rensselaer was alive, unrest seldom reached a boiling point. Of course, we have no means of determining how many discontented individuals voluntarily left the manor for the West or for the city. A few scattered bits of information suggest that tenants were restive even under the paternalistic rule of the patroon. In 1832 the tenants of the four western towns of Albany County requested that the burden of the quarter sales be lightened. In response to this petition the patroon agreed to commute the quarter sales for $30.[18] In February, 1835, citizens of Albany and Rensselaer counties petitioned the legislature, com-

---

[18] N.Y. *Assembly Documents*, no. 156 (1846), p. 49.

THE ANTIRENT MOVEMENT

plaining that ground rents, extra rents, income from quarter sales, and interests in unlocated and undefined water-right reservations were exempt from taxes. The Senate finance committee, to which the petitions were referred, reported that assessors could tax this income as personal property.[19] The committee pointed out that a specific tax on ground rents would have to be paid by the tenants, since the leases provided that the tenants had to pay all taxes and charges levied by any legal authority. Water-right reservations, however, were liable to taxation at full value.

In the Senate, Mr. Kemble from Rensselaer County broadened the base of the attack from tax exemption to the charge that the feudal tenures were inconsistent with the spirit of our free institutions.[20] He repeated the statement put forth by the residents of Rensselaer County that $1,200,000 of the landlord's property in that county was exempt from taxes, although the total valuation of real and personal estate in that county was less than $10,000,000. Although the Senate took no action on these petitions, they are significant in what they reveal of agrarian discontent during the lifetime of the patroon.

Shortly after the death of Stephen Van Rensselaer his namesake, heir to the west manor, sent out notices and handbills telling the people to pay their debts to the estate.[21] The news caused great excitement. The manor became "immediately alive."[22] Meetings were held; committees were organized. The farmers in the four western townships lying on the Helderberg Hills were particularly active in organizing resistance. Early in the spring a mass meeting at Berne, the village which became during the next decade the unofficial capital of antirentism, appointed a committee to call at

---

[19] *N.Y. Senate Documents*, no. 83 (1835).

[20] *Argus*, Feb. 19, 1835.

[21] *Ibid.*, Dec. 6, 1839. One source, not entirely reliable, declared that the tenants were forced to pay $3.00 to the attorney for the letter notifying them to pay their arrears (*Albany Evening Journal*, May 31, 1847).

[22] Daniel Dewey Barnard, "The 'Anti-Rent' Movement and Outbreak in New York," *The Whig Review*, II (Dec., 1845), 581.

LANDLORDS AND FARMERS

the manor office. On May 22, 1839, Stephen Van Rensselaer refused rather brusquely to discuss the question with the committee, but agreed to consider a written statement of the tenants' grievances.

The committee thereupon submitted a formal statement which recommended certain definite concessions.[23] First of all, it declared that wheat prices were far higher than they were at the time that the leases had been signed. Furthermore, wheat could no longer be raised due to the "sterility and roughness of the soil and country." It stated that a rent burden of $35 to $50 a year was beyond the ability of the farmers to pay.[24] The reservations were an additional burden. The committee advanced several concrete proposals. New leases with rents stipulated in money were to replace the old forms. Land of first quality was to pay at the rate of $1.00 a bushel; second quality land, 87½ cents; third quality, 75 cents; fourth quality, 62½ cents a bushel. In addition, the day's service was to be commuted for $1.00 and the four fowl for 50 cents. The farmers were to enjoy the right to buy out the landlord's rights at a fair price. The landlord was to surrender his water, mill, and mineral reservations. Finally, Van Rensselaer was to forgive in full the arrearages of any tenant unable to borrow the money to pay.

A week later Stephen Van Rensselaer dispatched his reply to Lawrence Van Deusen, a member of the committee.[25] He made no effort to meet the demands of the tenants. He pointed out that their ancestors had signed the leases with a full understanding of the terms. For him to accept the proposal of the committee would mean a reduction of over 50 per cent in his annual income. Furthermore, he could do nothing about the back rents which the will specifically set aside to meet the obligations of the pa-

---

[23] For a copy of this statement, see *Argus,* Dec. 6, 1839.

[24] The committee naturally tended to exaggerate the burdens by selecting years when wheat prices were high.

[25] *Argus,* Dec. 6, 1839.

THE ANTIRENT MOVEMENT

troon. The letter challenged the committee's estimate of wheat prices, which had naturally stressed the high prices of January 1, 1837, 1838, and 1839. Van Rensselaer showed that during the previous decade wheat prices had averaged $1.38 a bushel and during the last forty-seven years $1.41½ a bushel. Moreover, land values had made comparable advances with the rise in wheat prices.

His counterproposal offered no relief. He agreed to take the average price of wheat for forty-seven years as the basis of commutation to a money rent. But wheat prices were tumbling and threatening to go below the $1.41½ level suggested by Van Rensselaer. Actually, wheat prices at Albany on January 1, 1840, had fallen to $1.13. Before he would permit a change to a money rent, Stephen Van Rensselaer insisted that all arrears should be paid. This compromise applied only in the four hill townships of Berne, Westerlo, Rensselaerville, and Knox. The more valuable farms on the lowlands were not for sale.

This reply infuriated the farmers. On July 4, 1839, a mass meeting at Berne rejected the proposals of Stephen Van Rensselaer as an "outrage upon the laws of humanity." In language appropriate to the patriotic spirit of the day, the meeting declared that the farmers could no longer "tamely surrender that freedom—which we have so freely inherited from our gallant ancestors." This declaration of independence from landlord rule did not prevent them from retreating a good way from their original proposals. The tenants were now willing to have the rent on all qualities of land estimated at $1.00 a bushel. They further agreed to pay all arrears if computed at the rate of $1.00 a bushel. Fowl and services were not to be counted. If Stephen Van Rensselaer should reject this offer, they resolved to discontinue and discourage the payment of rents.[26]

The answer to their latest proposal was soon forthcoming. The executors of the estate secured writs of ejectment and *fieri facias*

---
[26] See resolutions in *ibid*.

in suits against tenants in arrears.[27] On August 28 Amos Adams, undersheriff of Albany County, attempted to serve process upon persons in the towns of Westerlo, Berne, and Rensselaerville. A tenant named Isaac Hungerford warned him that the people of the region were determined at all costs to prevent the serving of process. In the middle of September a crowd of angry tenants at Berne manhandled Daniel Leonard, who was serving declarations in favor of Stephen Van Rensselaer. They forced him to throw all his papers into a blazing tar barrel.

Despite a warning which Hugh Scott, secretary of a standing committee of citizens of the three towns, had sent to him, Sheriff Michael Archer tried in both October and November to serve process in the town of Berne. On both occasions he and his assistants were met by crowds of angry farmers, called together by the blowing of horns. The farmers blocked the roads, seized his horses, and threatened him with sticks.

Sheriff Michael Archer decided to call together a posse to assist him in overcoming any resistance he might meet in the serving of process. On December 2, 1839, a group of five hundred unarmed men set out for the mountain townships. When Sheriff Archer and his posse reached Reidsville they found fifteen to eighteen hundred people, who barred any further advance by waving clubs and surrounding the horsemen. The sheriff, convinced that the mob would overpower his band of unarmed men, turned back to Albany.

Sheriff Archer immediately asked the governor for military assistance. Governor Seward summoned several high officials and prominent citizens of Albany for consultation. He was reluctant to take extreme measures. He advised the sheriff to secure war-

---

[27] In compliance with a Senate resolution asking for information concerning the resistance to legal authority in Albany County, Governor William H. Seward on March 14, 1840, wrote a detailed account of the disturbances and his activities in support of the sheriff (*Messages from Governors*, III, 822–841). For a detailed account of the Helderberg War, see Christman, *op. cit.*, pp. 28–45.

THE ANTIRENT MOVEMENT

rants of arrest against individuals resisting the law from both the Supreme Court and the justice of the peace. On December 7 Seward directed the sheriff to summon a posse including the uniformed military corps of Albany.[28] Other companies in New York City and Montgomery County were ordered to be in readiness.

Early Monday morning, December 9, Sheriff Archer led his little band through the swirling snow to Reidsville. At the village five hundred to six hundred men on horseback and a like number of men on foot were milling around, but they offered no resistance. Their threatening attitude alarmed Sheriff Archer, who immediately appealed for aid. Governor Seward again called together his staff for consultation. He decided to incorporate the posse formally into the military service of the state and to order additional corps to march to Albany. At the same time the Governor issued a proclamation warning the people not to resist the enforcement of the law. He hinted that he would give their complaints a sympathetic hearing.

The array of military power and the proclamation of the Governor overawed the more coolheaded citizens of the affected townships. Through private channels word reached Seward that no further resistance to civil and criminal process would be made. Seward accepted this pledge and informed Sheriff Archer at Rensselaerville. Archer replied that he was meeting no opposition. On December 13 he reported that he no longer needed any troops. Two days later the militia returned to Albany.[29]

Stephen Van Rensselaer with state help had won the battle of

---

[28] From the start, political parties tried to make capital out of antirentism. Thus the *Argus* (Dec. 9, 1839) tried to embarrass the Whig governor by questioning his power to call out the militia of Albany County. The *Evening Journal*, a Whig paper, defended Seward (Dec. 9, 1839).

[29] *Argus*, Dec. 15, 1839. Seward later confided to his close friend Colonel James Bowen that he had asserted "the supremacy of the laws by needed demonstrations of military power." Seward considered his actions as "energetic measures" (William H. Seward to Colonel James Bowen, Jan. 5, 1845, William H. Seward Letters, William L. Clements Library, Ann Arbor, Michigan.

the Helderbergs. The tenants, however, began to organize the war of attrition which would eventually force the namesake of the Good Patroon to sell his patrimony. The tenants refused to pay the rent. Of course the sheriff could evict a few, but he could not dispossess an entire township. In the meantime the antirenters took their case to the public and to the legislature.

On January 7, 1840, Governor Seward in his annual message not only recounted the steps he had taken but also urged the legislature to consider means "to assimilate the tenures in question to those which experience has proved to be more accordant with the principles of republican government and more conducive to the general prosperity and the peace and harmony of society." [30] In later years opponents of antirentism were to criticize Seward most severely for raising hopes in the minds of the tenants that the legislature could relieve them of their burdens. [31]

The controversy now shifted to the legislative arena. There was considerable desultory bickering between the Democrats and Whigs over the payment of the militia. [32] The Democrats were attempting to needle Seward. They did succeed in persuading him to submit all the documents and papers concerning the Helderberg War to the Senate. Seward did not conceal the fact that he disliked the leasehold system. His special message of March 14 again urged the need of remedial legislation. As a result of his appeals and in response to the flood of petitions from disgruntled tenants, the legislature on May 13, 1840, set up a commission to investigate the problem and to arrange a settlement. [33]

---

[30] *Messages from Governors,* III, 776.

[31] The report of the judiciary committee in 1844 condemned Seward and the legislature for misleading the tenants (*N.Y. Assembly Documents,* no. 183 [1844]).

[32] *Argus,* Feb. 28, March 19, 20, 21, 1840.

[33] A committee of the Assembly opposed the bill to take away remedy by distress as violating obligation of contract. It admitted that the legislature could modify tenures upon just compensation to the landlord (*N.Y. Assembly Documents,* no. 271 [1840]).

THE ANTIRENT MOVEMENT

The commissioners were able to arrange a conference between Mr. Van Vechten, the representative of Stephen Van Rensselaer, and delegates from each of seven towns.[34] The commissioners, however, ran up against a stone wall in trying to arrange a compromise. Van Vechten refused to make any substantial concessions, except that he did offer to commute the rent and to sell out the interest of the Van Rensselaers for $4.00 an acre. This offer had strings attached to it. The tenant must pay the back rents before he could take advantage of either proposal. If he paid up his arrears, a tenant holding a farm of 160 acres could commute the payment of 21½ bushels of wheat, four fowl, and one day's service to $32 a year. An additional $2.00 a year would release the quarter sale. The main stumbling block was the insistence of Stephen Van Rensselaer that the back rents must be paid. He made the further threat that if they were not paid before March 1, 1842, he would charge interest on arrears. His proposals were therefore completely unacceptable. Considering the fact that wheat on January 1, 1841, was valued at $1.00 a bushel, this compromise actually called for a higher money rent than the tenant would have had to pay that year under the old system.

The representatives of the tenants stood fast for the commutation of wheat at the rate of $1.00 a bushel. The total rent for a 160-acre farm under their plan came to $24, as compared with the rent of $32 offered by Van Vechten. The tenants offered to buy the fee at the rate of $2.00 an acre.

The negotiations ended in deadlock. On April 28, 1841, the antirenters gathered together at Berne in a mass meeting. They denounced Rensselaerswyck as a blot upon our republican institutions and the spirit of the great Declaration. They passed the solemn resolution "That the anti-rent inhabitants of the county of Albany go into a ten-year contest with the Patroon of the colony of Rensselaerwyck, or until a redress of grievances be obtained." [35]

[34] *N.Y. Assembly Documents*, no. 261 (1841), pp. 1–7.
[35] *Argus*, May 6, 1841. That this pledge was kept can be seen in the

LANDLORDS AND FARMERS

This was no idle threat. Already the newspapers had noted that the Helderberg farmers were preventing the sheriff from selling property under attachment.[36] Bands of tenants, "disguised in skins and other grotesque dresses," quickly assembled whenever the ram's-horn sounded that the sheriff was near. The use of the Indian disguise cloaked the activities of the antirenters in pseudopatriotic trappings. The antirenters, living in a period when flag-waving speeches often began with a reference to the Boston Tea Party, found this disguise admirably suited to their purpose as well as honored by tradition. We may recall that in 1791 rebellious tenants in Columbia County roamed the countryside disguised as Indians.[37] It is impossible to determine when the Van Rensselaer tenants first adopted this disguise. They probably did not use it before the early part of 1841 when the negotiations conducted by the state commissioners broke down.[38]

In September, 1841, the "Indians" of the Helderberg region successfully prevented the sheriff from selling property offered for sale.[39] When Sheriff Adams and his posse of two hundred men, composed of four uniformed companies, arrived at the farm of one Martin, they found that the antirenters had removed most of the property. The following spring a local court found Jacob Martin guilty of assault and battery on an officer and of riot and affray.[40] At the same session the judge fined Palmer Bouton $150 and thirty days in jail for assault and battery on Isaac Van Leuven, who had been forced by Bouton and others to sign a pledge not to pay rent.

Prior to 1842 Albany County, and more particularly the town-

Manor Book, Berne and Knox, Ledger C, in Van Rensselaer Manor Papers. Few tenants made payments during the 1840's.

[36] *Argus*, March 12, 1841.

[37] *Albany Gazette*, Oct. 31, 1791.

[38] Edward Potts Cheyney ("The Antirent Movement and the Constitution of 1846," in Flick, *History of N.Y.*, VI, 302) cites an affray in Columbia County in 1844 as "one of the first times the 'Indians' were mentioned."

[39] *Argus*, Sept. 8, 9, 10, 1841.

[40] *Ibid.*, April 27, 1842.

THE ANTIRENT MOVEMENT

ships of the Helderberg region, was the scene of almost all the disturbances. But the tenants in surrounding counties such as Rensselaer and Schoharie were watching events with keen interest.[41] Seward's proposal for legislative action, vague as it was, reopened the whole issue of leasehold tenure and encouraged the tenants to petition the legislature. The success of the Helderberg rebels in preventing the collection of rents and in persuading Stephen Van Rensselaer to offer his lands for sale convinced many tenants that organized resistance would bring them relief.

Shortly after the judiciary committee of the Assembly in April, 1842, had regretfully declared that the state could not alter lawful contracts such as leases,[42] disguised persons seized the agent of the Livingston estate in Schoharie County and threatened him with violence.[43] Conditions on this estate were particularly bad. The wheat rent was higher than that on Rensselaerswyck. In addition, the tenant lost his farm after the death of the second person named in the lease. In contrast with this provision the perpetuity clause in the Van Rensselaer lease was much more favorable.

During 1843 there was a temporary lull in antirent violence, but the tenants in the Helderberg region were not idle. They were busy building up an elaborate organization to enforce their resistance to rent collection and to bring increased pressure on the landlords.[44] In the former they were markedly successful. As one of the defenders of the landlord cause stated in 1845, "Concerted, Practical Repudiation" of all obligations had taken place during the previous six years.[45]

---

[41] The Assembly Committee reported on petitions from Schoharie County in April, 1842 (*N.Y. Assembly Documents*, no. 177 [1842]).

[42] *Ibid.; Argus*, May 5, 1842.

[43] *Ibid.*

[44] Early in 1844 a court in Rensselaer County found great difficulty in impaneling a jury since nearly all on the list were challenged on the ground of either being members of the Anti-Rent Association or of having expressed opinions against the patroon's title (*Argus*, March 11, 1844).

[45] Barnard, "Anti-Rent Movement," p. 580.

LANDLORDS AND FARMERS

Early in 1844 there was a test of strength in the legislature. Petitions bearing signatures to the total of twenty-five thousand urged relief from the burdens of the leasehold. In March, 1844, a select committee composed of the delegations from Rensselaer and Albany counties handed down a report. Its condemnation of the leases as "onerous" and "repugnant" could only have stimulated the tenants to renewed activity. The committee charged that such restrictions as quarter sales and water and mill reservations had become a serious brake on the agricultural and manufacturing development of the two counties. It also advanced the argument, which was to become one of the stock complaints of the antirenters, that the titles of the landlords were defective. The committee, however, was vague as to specific means to test titles or to force the landlords to sell their rights.[46]

One month later the judiciary committee of the Assembly made its famous report savagely attacking the antirent movement. This committee denounced Governor Seward and members of the legislature for inciting the tenants to false hopes and violence. Their proposal to test the title of the Van Rensselaers and to have the rents appraised by some public authority was roundly condemned as a violation of the obligation of contract. The committee declared that if the title of the Van Rensselaer family based on deeds, possession, and confirmation by the state were not valid, no title was good.[47]

The report did not content itself with a strictly legalistic approach. It threw down the gauntlet to the tenants in language that was bound to infuriate the antirenters. The committee baldly stated, "But your committee are firmly convinced that the degradations and hardships exist but in the imagination." The report further recommended that the tenants accept the generous offers

---

[46] *N.Y. Assembly Documents*, no. 189 (1844). For a colorful description of Dr. Smith A. Boughton's lobbying in favor of the antirent cause, see Christman, *op. cit.*, pp. 62–63.

[47] *N.Y. Assembly Documents*, no. 183 (1844).

THE ANTIRENT MOVEMENT

of the Van Rensselaers if they wanted to secure complete title to the land.

The spokesmen for the antirenters always referred to this report in the most scathing terms. They charged that it had been drawn up in the landlord's office.[48] That William P. Van Rensselaer was exerting pressure on the legislature was to be expected. He wrote in a letter to a group of landowners that he had employed a "professional gentleman" in order to get certain laws passed and to protect his interests.[49] It is interesting to note that the Freeholders Committee of Safety, the pressure group organized by the landlords, financed the printing of one thousand copies of the judiciary committee report by John Syluster, editor of the *Catskill Recorder*.[50] The antirenters were not unaware of these backstage moves by which the landlords were trying to scotch their movement.

During 1844 the antirent movement passed from a somewhat localized struggle against the Van Rensselaer family to a full-fledged, well-organized revolt against leasehold tenure throughout the eastern part of the state. The uncompromising tone of the judiciary report, underscored as it was by renewed attempts to collect rents,[51] convinced the tenants that if they were to protect themselves from the landlords they must marshal all their forces in a well-knit organization. Late in May, 1844, the delegations of Rensselaer and Albany counties "agreed to send agents to every manor in the State."[52] Inspired by these agitators, or aroused by a

---

[48] For example, see Watson's speech in the Assembly on January 29, 1846, reported in the *Freeholder*, Feb. 11, 1846.

[49] Letter to Messrs. G. C. Verplanck and W. S. Johnson, Dec. 6, 1845, vol. XIII, S, 1827–1846, F. De Peyster Collection. See also letter to Sam Johnson, Dec. 5, 1845 (*ibid.*).

[50] See the account of the Freeholders Committee with James Powers, May 20, 1845, in F. De Peyster Collection, X, 100.

[51] See letter by B. A. Thomas, corresponding secretary of the Rensselaer County Anti-Rent Association, in *Working Man's Advocate*, June 1, 1844.

[52] Letter by John Gallup, prominent antirenter of the Helderberg region (*ibid.*). See Christman, *op. cit.*, pp. 73–74.

LANDLORDS AND FARMERS

spontaneous impulse, the tenants in the counties south of Albany began to hold meetings and to form associations. One observer noted in August, 1844, that Delaware County was "beginning to get excited." [53] The venerable Samuel A. Law complained privately of the "racket, all round us, of tenants,—refusing to pay rent." [54] From Columbia and Schoharie counties came reports that the tenants were joining the fight against the landlords.

Before we take up the disturbances which broke out in 1844 and 1845, it might be well to examine in detail the methods by which the tenants organized their campaign.

The antirent associations were the focal point of antirent resistance. Scores of associations sprang up in the leasehold region. Township associations were the basic units. Above them were the county societies. These societies performed a wide variety of functions. They arranged meetings, collected petitions, endorsed candidates for office, instituted and financed legal suits, and in general supervised the resistance against the collection of rent. In fact, the antirent movement took on much of the structure and many of the functions of a political party. The state convention of antirenters co-ordinated the activities of the local societies and determined what candidates the antirenters would support for state office.

Like most Americans (and the antirenters were always ready to call upon American ideals and traditions to justify their activities), the antirenters wrote constitutions and bylaws to govern their associations. For example, the Delaware County Equal Rights Anti-Rent Association adopted a constitution which provided for a president, six vice-presidents, a treasurer, and a recording secretary.[55] The association was to meet twice a year although

---

[53] *Working Man's Advocate,* Aug. 17, 1844. An article in the *New-York Evening Post,* reprinted in the *Argus,* July 31, 1844, tells of the organization of an Anti-Rent League.

[54] See letter to Francis Wharton, July 30, 1844, Box 7, Correspondence, 1841–1883, S. A. Law Papers.

[55] *Freeholder,* March 15, 1848.

THE ANTIRENT MOVEMENT

the executive committee could call a meeting at any time. The organization could not be dissolved as long as there were five dissenting voices. The aims of these associations changed somewhat over the course of years, depending on the immediate goals which the tenants were most eager to attain. In general, they called for legislative action to force the landlords to make genuine concessions to the tenants. A certain amount of agrarian philosophy inevitably crept into their program, but as we shall see later on in this chapter the eastern New York tenant was interested almost exclusively in local and specific benefits and not in national or theoretical reforms.

What connection the associations had with the outrages became a matter of sharp debate. Of course, the antirenters always protested—perhaps a bit too vehemently—that the associations were not responsible for the bands of disguised "Indians" that committed acts of violence.[56] With equal vehemence the conservative press branded all antirenters as supporters of terrorism.[57]

There is little doubt that the associations connived to a certain extent in organizing and financing the Indians. Disguised chieftains bearing such picturesque names as Big Thunder, Little Thunder, Red Jacket, Yellow Jacket, and Bluebeard addressed meetings which the associations had called together. When a prominent Indian died in Rensselaer County an escort of ninety-six savages formed the head of the funeral procession.[58] Leaders of the association likewise joined the procession. In 1844 Governor William Bouck held a conference with a committee from eight towns in Rensselaer County. About one hundred Indians mounted on horseback were shouting and yelling on the outskirts of the crowd.[59] Testimony at the trials held in Delaware County brought

---

[56] Thus the Anti-Rent Association of Schoharie County denied charges of violence (*Anti-Renter*, Sept. 13, 1845).

[57] The *Semi-Weekly Courier and Enquirer*, May 30, 1845, denounced the antirenters as "banditti."

[58] *Working Man's Advocate*, Aug. 17, 1844.

[59] *Argus*, Aug. 12, 1844.

247

out the fact that funds of the antirent associations had bought dresses, sheepskins, and pistols for the Indians.[60]

The activities of the tenants required considerable cash. Collections were taken at meetings and appeals were sent out at various times for specific amounts to defend prisoners. When voluntary contributions failed to bring in enough money, many societies inserted clauses in their constitutions whereby each member had to pay an assessment of 1½ or 2 cents for every acre that he owned.[61] Only a foolhardy or stubborn man would dare to brook the enmity of his neighbors by refusing to join the local association. Occasionally special assessments were levied. In 1848 the Albany County convention urged that each antirenter pay one year's rent into the hands of the treasurers of the township associations. The money was needed to bear the costs of a suit against the Van Rensselaer title.[62] Friends of the aristocracy often hinted at huge "slush funds."[63] Actually the antirent movement had to rely upon the enthusiasm, loyalty, and sacrifice of its members.

The use of disguises, insuring relative freedom from arrest, encouraged the bolder spirits to commit acts of violence. The Indians placed sheepskins over their heads, with holes for the eyes, nose, and mouth. In addition they wore calico dresses reaching down to the knees. Around their waists were colored belts. Individuals embellished their costume by adding horns, beards, or a horse's tail. Mounted on horseback, armed with rifle or shotgun, and not infrequently fortified with alcoholic stimulants, the Indians became a mobile striking force. They not only overawed recalcitrant

---

[60] *Delaware Express*, a clipping in *Newspaper Clippings Relating to Antirent Disturbances*, p. 80, New York State Library.

[61] *Freeholder*, July 7, 1845; *New-York Herald*, Jan. 3, 1845. Wright condemned this exaction (Lincoln, *Messages from Governors*, IV, 144).

[62] *Freeholder*, March 8, 1848.

[63] Seventy to eighty thousand dollars was reported to have been raised (*New-York Evening Post*, reprinted in *Argus*, July 31, 1844; *New-York Herald*, Jan. 3, 1845). At two cents an acre it would have taken 4,000,000 acres of land to raise this amount. Such a sum was obviously exaggerated.

THE ANTIRENT MOVEMENT

neighbors but also made helpless the local law-enforcement agencies.

The tenants employed a variety of techniques to achieve their purposes. Whenever property was put up at auction, a crowd like the 1932 groups of Iowa farmers would prevent anyone from bidding.[64] Sometimes property which had been attached was spirited away under the nose of the sheriff. Persons so bold as to buy or lease farms from which tenants had been evicted found themselves boycotted and their property destroyed.[65] Whenever the sheriff or the agents of the landlords reached an antirent township the blast of a tin dinner horn sounded the alarm. The blowing of the horn was the signal for the farmers and their Indian escort to assemble. In one case Sheriff Batterman, while passing through the western part of Rensselaerville on August 31, 1844, was set upon by a band of Indians.[66] After giving him a coat of tar and feathers the Indians permitted him to return home. To cite but one more incident among scores of similar acts, we find that two disguised persons killed in 1849 an agent of the Van Rensselaers. This foolhardy individual was trying to serve writs in Rensselaerville in the heart of the Helderberg country.[67]

Antirent leaders found the mass meeting an excellent means of whipping up enthusiasm and of impressing the politicians. The Fourth of July was a favorite day for antirenters as well as for all Americans. Orators drew a close analogy between George III and the landlords. Resolutions leaned heavily upon the egalitarian doctrines of the Declaration of Independence. The antirent movement gradually developed and attracted able leaders. Some were ordinary farmers such as John Mayham of Blenheim Hill in Schoharie County. An unusually large number of leaders was

---

[64] *Young America,* Aug. 23, 30, 1845; *Argus,* Sept. 1, 1847.

[65] *Hudson Gazette,* May 20, 1845, reprinted in *Argus,* May 21, 1845; *Argus,* April 3, 1847.

[66] *Argus,* Sept. 2, 1844.

[67] *Freeholder,* Oct. 3, 1849.

LANDLORDS AND FARMERS

recruited from among the country doctors. Dr. Smith A. Boughton of Rensselaer County was very active in organizing antirent associations, lobbying in Albany, and speaking to mass meetings under the disguise of "Big Thunder." [68] Professional reformers such as Thomas Ainge Devyr and Alvan Bovay were delighted to promote a movement which provided such an excellent sounding board for their ideas of land reform.[69] Politicians such as Ira Harris, an Albany lawyer who later became a United States Senator, were quick to detect the possibilities of enlisting the antirent vote behind their candidacies.

The antirent orators were undoubtedly effective in winning new converts among the rural population and in confirming the views of those tenants who had always opposed the leasehold. The speeches were nicely calculated to appeal to their prejudice, cupidity, and idealism. The tenants heard again and again that the landlords had acquired their titles by fraud. The orators delighted in pointing out the semifeudal character of the leasehold. They held out the hope that if the tenants supported friendly candidates and prevented the collection of the rent, they would soon free themselves from the rent burden. Of course, the antirent orators did not have a difficult task in convincing their audiences of the righteousness of their cause. The long tradition of unrest had made the tenant farmers ready and eager to strike another blow at the landlords.

Most newspapers opposed the antirenters and overplayed the outrages of the Indians.[70] Nevertheless, the tenants did have a few

---

[68] For an interesting account of Boughton's early life, see Christman, *op. cit.*, pp. 47–50.

[69] Thus Thomas Devyr and Alvan Bovay, both National Reformers, frequently spoke at antirent meetings (*Young America*, Aug. 9, 16, 1845; Thomas Ainge Devyr, *Odd Book of the 19th Century, or "Chivalry" in Modern Days, a Personal Record of Reform—Chiefly Land Reform, for the Last 50 Years* [New York, 1882], pp. 42–43).

[70] *Freeholder* (April 8, 1846) declared that the local papers of Albany and Troy were controlled by the landlords. See also *ibid.*, Aug. 20, 1845.

THE ANTIRENT MOVEMENT

champions in the press. Horace Greeley's *Tribune* espoused the cause of land reform and defended the antirenters. Perhaps the most vitriolic enemy of antirentism was J. Watson Webb, who filled the editorial columns of the *Semi-weekly Courier and Enquirer* with attacks on Greeley and the antirenters. The great bulk of editorial comment throughout the 1840's deplored the violence, but at the same time cautiously or tacitly admitted that the leasehold was an unfortunate legacy of the past.

Antirentism itself spawned several journals of uncertain influence and circulation. The *Helderberg Advocate,* which came into existence in the winter of 1840, was the first paper published to advance the cause of the Van Rensselaer tenants. William Gallup of Schoharie was the editor. His paper attracted the attention of Thomas Ainge Devyr, who began to send in articles describing the evils of land monopoly in Ireland, England, and the United States. Devyr's articles aroused so much opposition among conservative Democrats that in 1842 William Gallup agreed to discontinue them. It is also reported that a Schoharie County grand jury brought pressure on Gallup by charging the *Helderberg Advocate* with sedition.[71]

In 1843 the *Guardian of the Soil* supplanted the former paper.[72] It continued the fight against the landlords. Two years later Charles Bouton and Ira Harris founded the *Albany Freeholder.* This paper, which became the official organ of the antirent party, enjoyed a wide influence.[73] It did not suspend publication until 1854. Thomas Devyr was the first editor but he soon quarreled with Bouton and Harris. Late in 1845 Devyr founded his own newspaper, the *Anti-Renter.* This venture lasted scarcely one year. Late in 1846 Devyr gave up the struggle and returned to Williams-

---

[71] Christman has apparently had access to a file of this little-known newspaper (*op. cit.,* pp. 55–58).

[72] *Ibid.,* p. 61.

[73] The editors boasted in 1846 that in one year its subscribers had increased from 270 to more than 2,700 (*Freeholder,* April 8, 1846).

burg, Long Island.[74] In Delaware County the antirent association published the *Voice of the People* as its official organ.[75]

The country and state conventions played an important role in concentrating the power and directing the activities of the antirent movement. On January 15, 1845, eleven counties (Albany, Rensselaer, Schoharie, Delaware, Montgomery, Schenectady, Greene, Sullivan, Columbia, Ulster, and Otsego) sent accredited delegates to the first Anti-Rent State Convention, which was held at Berne.[76] Similar conventions met every year until 1851.[77] Bitter factional fights marked the proceedings of the later conventions. Once the antirenters had demonstrated their political power in the elections of 1845 and 1846, the politicians began to intrigue in order to secure their endorsement. As a result, political considerations tended to outweigh the original purpose of the conventions. Somewhat later we shall trace some of this maneuvering. At this time it is only necessary to point out the genuine power which the convention wielded over the legislature when it formulated its demands.

Unexpected and eventually unwelcome support rallied to the cause of the tenants from the little group of National Reformers who were associated with George Henry Evans.[78] The National Reformers believed that land monopoly was the great obstacle preventing mankind from achieving the republican equality envisioned by the Declaration of Independence. They argued that every man has a natural right to such elements as light, air, water, and earth. No individual should be permitted to own more than a limited amount of land. This land he could bequeath but could not alienate in any way. They demanded that Congress preserve the public domain from speculators by forbidding any further

---

[74] Devyr, *op. cit.*, p. 43.
[75] *Freeholder*, March 15, 1848.
[76] *Argus*, Feb. 10, 1845.
[77] *Freeholder*, Feb. 26, 1851.
[78] Helene S. Zahler, *Eastern Workingmen and National Land Policy, 1829–1862* (New York, 1941), pp. 41–56.

THE ANTIRENT MOVEMENT

land sales. The National Reformers greatly alarmed the conservative press by publicizing the slogan, "Vote Yourself A Farm."

The antirent struggle seemed to confirm the main contentions of the National Reformers. Unless Congress should act and act soon, land monopoly would become firmly entrenched throughout the public domain. Evans and his associates were quick to see the possibilities of the antirent movement as a means of publicizing their own theories of land reform.[79]

The antirenters welcomed the support of the National Reformers. Professional agitators such as Thomas Devyr and Alvan Bovay were highly skilled in the art of propaganda. They knew how to dramatize the grievances of the tenants. They gave valuable advice as to the most effective way of organizing the movement. Their speeches invoking the principles of natural rights and exposing the frauds of the landlords' ancestors struck a responsive chord in the hearts of the tenants. The farmers felt flattered to learn that their simple desire to avoid the rent was in reality a righteous crusade to create a society based on the principles of the Declaration of Independence.

Thomas Ainge Devyr was writing letters to the *Helderberg Advocate* as early as 1840.[80] Devyr was a fugitive from England, where he had incurred the wrath of English authorities for his activities in the Chartist movement. According to his own account, he attended the Fourth of July celebration held in Rensselaerville in 1842. The antirenters agreed to back the program to reserve the public domain for actual settlers provided Devyr would write for them and attend conventions.[81] Loose arrangements of this nature provided the link between the National Reformers and the antirenters. In 1844 John Gallup of East Berne wrote that he and his

---

[79] Evans put himself behind the movement, but he did not want to see antirentism identified with National Reform (*Working Man's Advocate*, Dec. 21, 1844).

[80] Devyr, *op. cit.*, p. 42.

[81] *Ibid.*

253

friends were favorable to Devyr's proposal that a "union" between the two organizations should be negotiated.[82]

The National Reformers earned the gratitude of the tenants by defending their activities from the charges of the "blood-thirsty" press.[83] Although his paper praised the antirenters, Evans was always careful to point out that National Reform was a much more comprehensive movement.[84] Early in January, 1845, the National Reformers shocked the conservative press by holding a public meeting to defend the antirenters.[85] After a violent debate the meeting passed resolutions urging the abolition of all feudal leases and the adoption of laws restricting inheritance to one farm. They also agreed to send delegates to the antirent convention at Berne.

Shortly thereafter Thomas Devyr issued an appeal to the farmers to get together and support a powerful paper in Albany.[86] He modestly stated that if asked he would help manage the paper and would move his *National Reformer* to the capital city. Apparently his offer was accepted, for in March it was reported that he had moved to Albany.[87] On April 9, 1845, the *Freeholder* under Devyr's editorship began publication. Scarcely had Devyr been seated in the editorial chair before he was ousted. According to his own highly colored account, Whig and Hunker politicians wormed their way into the movement and took the paper away from the farmers.[88] But C. F. Bouton, editor of the *Freeholder*, denounced Devyr as an "agent of mischief," and a "vain, dictatorial, infallible, tyrannical, hot-tempered" person who was attempting to gain control of the movement in order to promote his own theories of

---

[82] *Working Man's Advocate*, June 1, 1844.
[83] *Ibid.*, Jan. 4, 1845.
[84] *Ibid.*, Dec. 21, 1844; March 1, 1845.
[85] *New-York Herald*, Jan. 3, 1845; *Argus*, Jan. 6, 1845; *Working Man's Advocate*, Jan. 11, 1845.
[86] *Working Man's Advocate*, Feb. 1, 1845.
[87] *Ibid.*, March 22, 1845.
[88] *Op. cit.*, p. 43; Christman, *op. cit.*, pp. 155–157.

THE ANTIRENT MOVEMENT

land reform.[89] Devyr's career as an extremist and his violent language make it quite evident that he was an irascible and opinionated individual.

While he was editor of the *Freeholder*, Devyr stressed the agrarian principles of the National Reformers. His attacks on the proposed land grant to Asa Whitney to build a transcontinental railroad, his denunciations of land speculation in Texas, and his preoccupation with national affairs did not appeal to most tenant farmers.[90] They wanted to concentrate their attacks on the landed aristocracy of New York. After his dismissal Devyr founded the *Anti-Renter*, in which the ideas of the National Reformers were prominently displayed. Between the two papers there was considerable sniping. The *Anti-Renter* managed to keep its head above water until late 1846, when it suspended publication.

Distrust for agitators from the city is a rural characteristic not unknown even in our own generation. We have only to recall the suspicion and alarm with which upstate farmers in the early 1940's greeted the activities of Archie Wright and John L. Lewis. At first the antirenters welcomed their downstate allies. After all, the theory of natural rights and the castigation of landlord monopoly fitted in perfectly with the ideas of the antirenters. Upon second examination, however, the farmers found some of the features of National Reform radical and distasteful. For example, the proposed limitation of land to a bare 160 acres a person flew in the face of the farmers' hopes and ambitions. At the same time tenant farmers began to feel uncomfortable associating with reformers which the press often described as infidels, anarchists, and fanatics.[91] Would this tie discredit their cause? Were not the National Reformers exploiting the plight of the tenants for their own ends? These questions could not fail to convince many antirenters that they must keep their cause inviolate. They likewise

---

[89] *Freeholder*, Aug. 26, 1846.
[90] *Ibid.*, July 16, 23, 30, 1845.
[91] *Semi-Weekly Courier and Enquirer*, Sept. 20, 1845.

LANDLORDS AND FARMERS

felt that they could secure more concessions from the legislature by working through friends in both parties than by setting up a separate party devoted to a utopian goal.

The National Reformers made several attempts to seize control of the state convention of the antirenters. In July, 1846, the *Freeholder* opposed the calling of the convention on the ground that the National Reformers could dominate the meeting and pass extreme resolutions.[92] The editor continued to attack the National Reformers for meddling in the antirent movement. He found their program "visionary" and "weak."[93] The limit on land ownership aroused much ridicule and unfavorable comment.[94] While admitting that Greeley, Evans, and Bovay were able and sincere, the editor of the *Freeholder* insisted that reform of the national land policies was a question scarcely relevant to the simple goals of the tenants.[95]

The contest between the two factions reached its climax at the state convention held at Albany in October, 1847. Thirty National Reformers demanded seats.[96] Control of the convention was at stake since there were only twenty-three antirent delegates present. The antirenters declared that they represented from fifteen to twenty thousand people as against less than one thousand in the National Reform party. After a heated discussion the antirent delegates voted to keep the other faction from taking seats.

The ideas put forward by George Henry Evans reached the tenants through other channels as well. Thus Alvan Bovay, a veteran campaigner for National Reform, reported that he had encountered no dissenting opinion against National Reform principles in seven meetings which he addressed in the Helderberg region.[97] He singled out the president of one society for his ability

---
[92] July 29, 1846.
[93] *Freeholder*, Aug. 12, 1846.
[94] *Ibid.*, Sept. 16, Dec. 30, 1846; Oct. 6, 1847.
[95] *Ibid.*, June 24, 1846.
[96] *Ibid.*, Oct. 20, 1846.
[97] *Young America*, Aug. 16, 1845.

THE ANTIRENT MOVEMENT

to "insinuate" the leading doctrines without arousing antagonism.[98] Readers of the *Tribune* likewise absorbed a diluted form of National Reform. We find traces of Evans' influence cropping up unexpectedly in resolutions of local associations. Thus among the aims of the Delaware County Equal Rights Anti-Rent Association were the eradication of land monopoly and the restriction of the public domain to actual settlers.[99] The ousting of Devyr from the *Freeholder* and the refusal to seat National Reformers in the state convention did not break all connections between the two factions. As late as 1851 Devyr was appealing to the tenants to become allies of National Reform.[100]

Horace Greeley's relations with antirentism are particularly interesting. First of all his paper, in contrast with the rest of the metropolitan press, was sympathetic to the tenants. As a result he earned their gratitude [101] but he also became the target of such conservative papers as the *Courier and Enquirer,* the *Express,* and the *Commercial Advertiser.* Greeley's editorial of April 20, 1846, takes on added significance in the light of his later prominence in the struggle for the Homestead Act and land reform. He wrote: "An earnest consideration of the causes and progress of the 'Anti-Rent' difficulties has led us to regard with favor the 'National Reformer's' idea of stopping the sale and further monopoly of the Public Lands." [102] Whether the antirent struggle dramatized the danger of land monopoly so vividly that it converted Greeley to the cause of land reform is not easy to say. Prior to this time Greeley had been flirting with Fourieristic ideas and expounding the merits of protective tariffs. Land reform had attracted scant attention in the editorials of the *Tribune.*

---

[98] *Ibid.,* Sept. 6, 1851.
[99] *Freeholder,* March 15, 1848.
[100] *Ibid.,* March 5, 1851.
[101] The *Tribune* was universally read in Delaware County (David Murray, *Delaware County, New York, History of the Century, 1797–1897* [Delhi, 1898], p. 300).
[102] *New-York Weekly Tribune,* April 20, 1846.

LANDLORDS AND FARMERS

The plight of the tenants disturbed Greeley deeply and intensified any ideas he may have had on land reform.

Greeley's open letter to the constitutional convention in 1846 repeated virtually every argument and urged practically the same reforms as those advocated by George Henry Evans.[103] For example, he proposed that no one should be allowed to acquire more than 160 or 320 acres of land after July 4, 1847. He proposed that the state government should break up large holdings already in existence. His espousal of National Reform as well as his defense of the antirenters aroused a storm. The conservative press branded him a revolutionary who was preaching the subversive doctrines of "Fourierism, Agrarianism, and Infidelity."[104] The *Tribune* denied the charge of agrarianism,[105] but its editorials proclaimed its sympathy for the antirent cause. In fact, the *Tribune* urged its readers to petition the governor to pardon the antirenters who had been convicted of slaying Deputy Sheriff Steele of Delaware County. This action caused Webb's *Semi-Weekly Courier and Enquirer* to fume: "We admit too, that in the sight of God, the editor of the Tribune and every Anti-Renter in the country, is just as guilty of murder as the parties convicted, or as the individuals whose balls actually took away the life of Steel [sic]."[106]

Our examination of the organization of antirent societies and their relations with the National Reform movement will help to paint in the background for the events of 1845 and 1846. Throughout the region checkered with leaseholds the smoldering discontent was bursting into flame. Tenant farmers by the thousands were joining antirent associations in the summer of 1844. Bands of mounted Indians galloped past crossroad inns on mysterious missions. Antirent spellbinders stumped the countryside, lashing

---

[103] *New-York Weekly Tribune,* June 29, 1846.
[104] *New York Express,* July 30, Aug. 2, 21, 1845.
[105] See *New-York Daily Tribune,* July 27, 28, 29, 30, August 1, 4, 1845, for typical editorials.
[106] Nov. 12, 1845.

THE ANTIRENT MOVEMENT

their hearers to action. Inevitably violence broke out, climaxed by the shooting of the deputy sheriff of Delaware County in August, 1845. Neither the governor nor the legislature dared ignore the problem.

The judiciary report of April, 1844, was the opening gun in a renewed offensive by William P. Van Rensselaer to force his stubborn tenants to pay the rent.[107] The four thousand members of the East Manor Association met the challenge by resisting the sheriff of Rensselaer County and by supporting sympathetic candidates for the legislature. Early in August a committee from eight towns invited Governor William Bouck to a conference at West Sand Lake.[108] The antirenters proposed that the dispute be submitted to the governors of any three New England states except Connecticut. Bouck rejected this suggestion. Nevertheless, the conference was not entirely a failure from the viewpoint of the tenants. Probably the governor intimated that he would not press law enforcement.[109] It does appear that both Governor Bouck and Sheriff Reynolds were trying to avoid an open clash and to evade responsibility. No doubt the impending fall elections influenced their actions. Leaders of the Democratic and Whig parties were assiduously cultivating the antirent vote. After the election, Thurlow Weed's *Evening Journal* accused Bouck of refusing to repress Indian disorders.[110] The *Argus* rushed to the ex-Governor's defense.[111] The editor gleefully cited an editorial of the *Evening Journal* of September 11, 1844, which had called the leases a relic

---

[107] Letter in *Working Man's Advocate*, June 1, 1844.
[108] *Argus*, Aug. 12, 1844.
[109] This account is based on the *Albany Atlas*, reprinted in Albert C. Mayham, *The Anti-Rent War on Blenheim Hill, an Episode of the 40's* (Jefferson, N.Y., 1906), pp. 40–41. McMaster (*op. cit.*, VII, 187) errs when he states that Bouck urged the crowd to resist the collection of the rent. Christman cites the *Troy Whig* as stating that Bouck told the sheriff not to press eviction suits (*op. cit.*, pp. 88–89).
[110] Dec. 21, 1844.
[111] *Argus*, Dec. 21, 23, 24, 30, 1844.

of feudalism and had chided the Van Rensselaers for not offering a genuine compromise.

The mounting number of outrages began to attract the attention of the metropolitan press.[112] In December, 1844, Indians killed Elijah Smith in the town of Grafton in Rensselaer County.[113] Smith was cutting timber on land recently purchased from William Van Rensselaer. Prodded into activity by the newspapers, the sheriff busied himself examining scores of witnesses. His efforts were fruitless. A conspiracy of silence and also threats of violence made it impossible to uncover the guilty parties. But the public outcry did not deter the Indians from destroying the papers of a deputy sheriff a month later.[114] Many antirenters sincerely regretted the use of violence. Others secretly justified it on the ground of expediency. Whatever reason was uppermost, the Rensselaer County Antirent Association early in January, 1845, appealed to the Indians not to ruin the movement by resorting to violence.[115]

During the fall of 1844 Dr. Smith A. Boughton, a popular orator of Rensselaer County, made a lecture tour throughout Columbia County. His intention was to stir up the tenants on Livingston Manor. In this purpose he was eminently successful. Boughton, disguised as Big Thunder, addressed crowds of eager antirenters. He led a band of Indians which seized the sheriff and burned his papers.[116] Shortly thereafter, violence broke out again in Claverack. Unknown persons shot down a Mr. Rizenburgh, who refused to shout, "Down with the Rent."[117] This crime stirred the easy-

---

[112] *New-York Daily Tribune*, Aug. 23, 1844, showed annoyance at the "flippant allusions" of the papers to the trouble on Rensselaer Manor. Its suggestion of some kind of reform led to a flurry of letters attacking and defending the antirenters (*ibid.*, Aug. 27, Sept. 5, 11, Oct. 31, 1844).

[113] *Argus*, Dec. 21, 23, 27, 30, 31, 1844.

[114] *Ibid.*, Jan. 13, 1845.

[115] *Ibid.*, Dec. 17, 1844.

[116] *Ibid.*

[117] *Ibid.*, Dec. 20, 1844.

going sheriff to action. He immediately arrested Dr. Boughton and several associates and held them on the charge of highway robbery.

The arrest of their chief infuriated the Indians. They raced back and forth throughout the leasehold region, which became alive with excitement. Scores of meetings were held at crossroads to discuss what they should do. Orators called the arrest the crowning injustice of a century of landlord tyranny. The more bold began to talk of rushing the jail at Hudson and liberating their champion.[118] The threats and rumors frightened the citizens of Hudson. The mayor and the sheriff appealed to Governor Bouck to send down the Burgesses' Corps. Three more companies fully armed were sent down to Hudson to guard the jail. Their presence helped to calm the excitement. In March Boughton stood trial, but disagreement among the jury members forced the court to release him.

At the September circuit Boughton again faced the charge of robbing the sheriff of his papers. This trial aroused great interest, not only among the antirenters, who threatened to overawe the court, but also among the population at large, who enjoyed the forensic fireworks. Handsome John Van Buren, attorney general for the state, faced Ambrose Jordan, one of the most skillful defense lawyers of the state. The crowds which packed the courtroom were not disappointed. It was in this trial that the two lawyers bandied insults and exchanged blows.[119] With the aid of Judge Edmonds, John Van Buren was able to convince the jury that Dr. Boughton was Big Thunder. On September 28, 1845, the jury found him guilty of robbery. Judge Edmonds, who hoped to put an end to disturbances instigated by a foreign agitator, charged

---

[118] *Ibid.*, Dec. 23, 25, 27, 28, 30, 1844; Jan. 1, 3, 4, 9, 1845. Christman traces the Columbia County disorders in detail (*op. cit.*, pp. 102–104; 107–127).

[119] See article in *New York Evening Post*, reprinted in John W. Edmonds, *Reports of Select Cases Decided in the Courts of New York* (New York, 1868–1883), I, 143; *Argus*, Sept. 8, 1845.

LANDLORDS AND FARMERS

Boughton with "high treason" and sentenced him to life imprisonment. This unusually severe punishment shocked the courtroom, which watched in complete silence as the slender Dr. Boughton was led away to his cell.[120]

Across the Hudson in Greene County similar reports of Indian violence began to appear in 1844.[121] Judge Amasa Parker, who was holding a circuit at Catskill in September, felt impelled to charge the grand jury that resistance to the orderly processes of the law would inevitably lead to anarchy.[122] In March, 1845, the tenants on the Robert L. Livingston estate in western Ulster County seized one of the landlord's employees who was trying to cut timber on the farm of a delinquent tenant. They poured tar on his head and into his boots. When the sheriff attempted to arrest two of the Indians, he and his posse were turned back. The sheriff, supplied with arms by the adjutant general of the state and backed by the law and order meetings in Kingston, was later able to restore order in the disturbed regions.[123] So widespread had the movement become that in early 1845 the sheriffs of both Otsego and faraway Cattaraugus counties met resistance when they attempted to serve legal papers.[124]

That part of the hill country stretching in a southwesterly direction from the Helderberg escarpment across southern Schoharie and into the northern half of Delaware counties was the most active center of antirentism. As we have pointed out in another connection, the farmers in this region were already discontented because they found it difficult to transport their produce to market. The depression which followed the panic of 1837 struck another

---
[120] For a well-written description of this trial, see Isabel Thompson Kelsay, "The Trial of Big Thunder," *New York History*, XXXIII (July, 1935), pp. 266–277. See also Christman, *op. cit.*, pp. 204–219.
[121] *Working Man's Advocate*, Aug. 31, 1844.
[122] *Argus*, Oct. 7, 1844.
[123] *Ibid.*, March 11, 13, 17, Aug. 22, 1845.
[124] *Ibid.*, Jan. 31, Feb. 7, 1845.

THE ANTIRENT MOVEMENT

severe blow, particularly at the marginal producers living on poor soils in isolated townships. It is not strange, therefore, that the tenants found the doctrines of the lecturers singularly attractive. At the same time the antirenters won the sympathy and support of a considerable group of nontenants who opposed in principle the system of large estates and leasehold tenure. Needless to say, politicians also saw in the movement an opportunity to advance their careers. Freeholders, struggling under heavy interest burdens, likewise favored any movement which would relieve them of the necessity of making payments on their debts.[125]

In Schoharie County, where outrages had taken place as early as 1842, the agitation against leasehold tenure flared up into open rebellion in 1844 and 1845. Early in 1844 the antirent associations passed resolutions that their members would refuse to pay rent and would resist any attempts by the authorities to collect the rents. At the same time the antirenters petitioned the legislature to investigate the titles of the proprietors of the John Morin Scott and Blenheim patents. When he learned of this stand taken by his tenants, John A. King of Jamaica, Long Island, who owned over 15,000 acres in the Blenheim Patent, sent an open letter to his lessees urging them to reconsider their decision. He stated that he had always shown them every kindness, as evidenced by his willingness to commute the wheat payments and to sell the fee at any time. King warned them that if they persisted in their course, he would be obliged to enforce the collection of the rents.[126]

Late in November, 1844, a band of Indians chased Mr. Jacob Livingston, who was returning from his mill in Livingstonville. Livingston outdistanced his pursuers and took refuge in the home of Judge Mattice, near Middleburg. The Indians surrounded the

---

[125] S. A. Law to Francis A. Wharton, July 30, 1844, in "Correspondence, 1841–1883," Box 7, S. A. Law Papers, noted that discontent edged along "from tenants to free-holders—from rent payers to interest payers."
[126] A copy of his letter is in Mayhem, *op. cit.*, pp. 77–79.

LANDLORDS AND FARMERS

house and threw stones in the windows. The sheriff, however, arrived and dispersed the Indians.[127]

The following spring Sheriff Brown and Undersheriff Bouck set out on a tour of the towns of Blenheim and Jefferson in order to serve warrants on recalcitrant tenants. The blowing of horns soon heralded their presence. The Indians, led by their chief, Black Hawk, burst into Fink's Tavern and after a brief scuffle overpowered the sheriff and his party. The Indians forced them to march to a glade in the forest where the papers of the sheriff were burned. Upon his release Sheriff Brown reported the outrage to the governor and immediately secured muskets from the state arsenal in order to arm a posse.[128]

The counterattack launched by the sheriff resulted in a miniature civil war in the southern part of Schoharie County. The sheriff made determined efforts to serve papers. As a result, some delinquent tenants began to pay their rents. In August the sheriff's posse raided Blenheim hill, where they searched the homes of leading antirenters, imprisoned several young lads as hostages, fired shots at fleeing Indians, and succeeded in terrorizing the population. Overawed by the power of the sheriff and sobered somewhat by the news of the murder of Steele in the neighboring county, the leaders of the antirent associations of the towns of Blenheim, Broome, Conesville, Jefferson, and Summit called a conference. They decided to dissolve their organizations, turn over the disguises, and keep the peace. In exchange, the sheriff agreed to free the prisoners taken by his posse.[129] Antirentism in Schoharie County did not die out immediately thereafter, but the

---

[127] *Schoharie Republican,* reprinted in *Argus,* Nov. 28, 1844; *Argus,* Dec. 3, 1844.

[128] *Argus,* March 27, May 29, 1845; *Schoharie Republican,* March 25, May 27, 1845. Mayham has erroneously placed this event in the spring of 1844 (*op. cit.,* p. 34). Such an error confuses the sequence of his narrative.

[129] *Argus,* June 6, Aug. 23, 27, 29, 1845; *Schoharie Republican,* Aug. 26, 1845. See also Mayham, *op. cit.,* pp. 52–63.

THE ANTIRENT MOVEMENT

willingness of the landholders to sell their farms gradually eliminated the source of trouble.

Meanwhile, events in Delaware County were moving to a crisis.[130] By the summer of 1844 the tenantry on the Hardenburgh Patent had joined the crusade against the payment of rent. Antirent societies sprang up overnight. Tenants fashioned crude disguises out of sheepskins. Chieftains such as Red Cloud and Bluebeard rode in full regalia at the head of their motley corps of Indians. Tenants refused to pay rent and defied the landlords' agents. Indians pounced upon the sheriff and seized his papers. The attempt of the sheriff in September, 1844, to serve papers upon Daniel Squires of Roxbury ended disastrously.

Undersheriff Steele of Delaware County was an officer of great personal courage. The antirenters hated him because he hounded their leaders and dared to invade their strongholds. On February 11, 1845, Steele set out to capture Daniel Squires, who had stolen the sheriff's papers the previous year.[181] Near Andes a hundred Indians trapped him in a tavern, but speedy action by a posse rescued Steele. Undeterred by their threats, Steele led a raid on Roxbury. The intrepid Steele grappled with a husky savage and unmasked him. His prisoner was the constable of Roxbury.[182] Twelve Indians soon found themselves in jail awaiting trial. As the spring passed by, tension between officers and antirenters became more pronounced. The sheriff led raids on the Indian strongholds; the antirenters kept the countryside in a state of constant alarm by blowing their horns and firing their guns.

On August 7, 1845, Sheriff Moore, Undersheriff Steele, and two companions arrived at the farm of Moses Earle in the town of

---

[130] Good accounts of the Delaware County troubles can be found in Edward P. Cheyney, *Anti-Rent Agitation*, pp. 42–47, and in David Murray, "The Anti-Rent Episode in the State of New York," in *Annual Report of the American Historical Association for the Year 1896*, I, 156–163.

[181] *Argus*, Feb. 15, March 18, 1845; *Albany Evening Journal*, Feb. 13, 1845.

[182] *Argus*, March 20, April 1, 1845.

Andes. Their purpose was to sell property to the value of $64 in order to compensate Charlotte Verplanck for the two years of back rent which Earle owed her. When the sheriff tried to round up the cattle for a public sale, two hundred Indians who had been skulking in the neighborhood surrounded him and Steele. The leader of the Indians shouted "Shoot the horses! Shoot the horses!" At the second volley Steele fell to the ground. In a few hours he was dead.[133]

The murder of Steele caused a chorus of denunciation both in Delaware County and throughout the state. The general public was naturally shocked at the news. Even the sympathizers of the tenants could do nothing but echo the general demand for severe and stern measures to put down the uprising. The opponents of the antirenters naturally played up the tragedy in an effort to discredit the antirent movement. At the same time many of the moderate antirenters, who had been pushed aside by their more reckless brethren, saw in the death of Steele a fine opportunity to regain control of the movement. Throughout Delaware County meetings were held at which the citizens deplored the murder of Steele, demanded the dissolution of the secret societies, and denounced politicians courting the antirent vote.[134]

The sheriff, with a posse of hundreds of volunteers, raided the antirent strongholds. He arrested scores of tenants who were suspected of having been present at the shooting of Steele. On August 27, 1845, Governor Silas Wright proclaimed Delaware County to be in a state of insurrection and he dispatched the adjutant general to take command of the military forces in the county.[135]

Judge Amasa Parker presided over the trials which began in September. Great excitement prevailed, especially when a prowler fired a shot at one of the guards who was outside the jail. Some

[133] *Argus*, Aug. 11, 1845.
[134] *Ibid.*, Aug. 13, 19, Sept. 1, 1845. Christman accepts without reservation the assertion made by the antirenters that Steele fired the first shot (*op. cit.*, p. 179).
[135] *Messages from Governors*, IV, 297–308.

THE ANTIRENT MOVEMENT

sixty men were convicted for offenses ranging from murder to manslaughter in the fourth degree, as well as for appearing disguised and armed.[136] Judge Parker sentenced two young men, Edward O'Connor and John Van Steenburg, to be hanged on November 29, but Governor Silas Wright commuted these sentences to life imprisonment.[137] Despite the activities of the sheriff many of the Indian chiefs, including Warren Scudder, who was supposed to have issued the fatal command, managed to evade arrest by fleeing from the county. The vigorous policy of the local and state authorities in suppressing the antirenters gradually restored peace and order to Delaware County. In recognition of this changed state of affairs, Governor Wright on December 18 revoked his proclamation declaring the county in a state of insurrection.[138]

Although opposition to rent collection did not cease after 1845, organized resistance on a large scale and the use of disguises largely vanished. Sporadic outrages took place for many years thereafter, but they never assumed the proportions of full-fledged uprisings such as occurred in Columbia, Schoharie, and Delaware counties in 1845. Antirent agitation, however, did not diminish. The tenants were as determined as ever to rid themselves of the burden of the leasehold. The antirenters now began to concentrate their energies in the political sphere. Their successes in the local elections of 1845 paved the way for remedial legislation and laid the groundwork for their signal success in the gubernatorial election of 1846. In our next chapter we shall attempt to describe the skillful tactics by which the antirenters made their influence feared and respected in the corridors of the capitol.

---

[136] *Argus*, Sept. 5, 9, 12, 16, 19, 23, 24, 26, 29, Oct. 2, 4, 6, 7, 11, 14, 1845, for information as to the trial. Christman has an interesting account (*op. cit.*, pp. 185–190; 220–241).

[137] *Messages from Governors*, IV, 309–325. *Young America* (Oct. 18, 1845) called these sentences a "disgrace," the worst "since the hanging of witches in New England."

[138] *Messages from Governors*, IV, pp. 326–327.

CHAPTER VIII

ANTIRENTISM IN POLITICS

THE LABYRINTHINE WINDINGS and turnings of New York politics were at no time more in evidence than in the decade following 1840. New parties emerged and the old parties split into warring factions. Enthusiasm for humanitarian reform led to the creation of the Liberty, the Prohibition, and the Free-Soil parties. Resentment against the leasehold and alarm at the flood of Irish immigrants spawned the Antirenters and Native Americans. The issue of more state funds for canals, the Wilmot Proviso, and the spoils of office sorely vexed the Democrats. The Whig party was already showing signs of the fatal split over the question of slavery.

Factionalism seriously undermined the supremacy of the Democratic party which the skillful politicians of the Albany Regency had established during the 1830's. The more radical Democrats, popularly known as the Barnburners, carried on a bitter feud with the Hunkers, as the followers of William Marcy were called. The Barnburners stood for retrenchment in state finance, a cautious attitude toward public works, and, after 1846, opposition to the extension of slavery into the territories. The Hunkers were eager to secure the patronage which additional funds for canal enlargement and an alliance with the Polk administration would bring. The Hunkers opposed any stand on slavery which would antag-

ANTIRENTISM IN POLITICS

onize the Southern leaders of their party. After 1846 the quarrel became more intense. The Barnburners charged the Hunkers with knifing Governor Silas Wright's campaign for re-election in 1846. The controversy over the Wilmot Proviso tore the Democracy asunder in 1847. The Barnburners bolted the state convention and began to woo the Free-Soilers. So ardently did they pursue the courtship that in 1848 Martin Van Buren became the candidate for President on the Free-Soil ticket.[1]

The Whig party likewise suffered from factional disputes. The slavery issue divided the party by 1850 into two irreconcilable groups. Seward's strong stand against slavery led to an open break with those Whigs who followed President Millard Fillmore. Furthermore, Whigs had to put up with Horace Greeley and his *Tribune*. Like a burr Greeley goaded conservative Whigs to fury with his penchant for fads and his crusades for reform. They denounced him as an anarchist and a demagogue. Nevertheless, Greeley loathed Democrats and vigorously promoted high tariffs and internal improvements. Other Whigs disliked the slippery tactics of that arch manipulator Thurlow Weed, who dominated the inner councils of the Whig party.

A contemporary analysis of political parties by a conservative Whig makes it abundantly clear how similar the two major parties were in composition and how easy it was for crucial issues to divide them into warring groups.[2] Conservatives in both parties had to fight the reformers who took an advanced stand on slavery and on social reform. These bitter rivalries between and within the two major parties enabled the antirenters to exert more influence than their numbers would otherwise have warranted. By throwing their votes first to one candidate and then to another, the antirent leaders forced both parties to bid for their support.

Governor Seward's recommendation in 1840 that the legislature investigate the possibility of remedial legislation had caused the

---
[1] H. D. Donovan, *op. cit., passim.*
[2] *New York Express*, Aug. 25, 1846.

LANDLORDS AND FARMERS

tenants of the Van Rensselaer family to look hopefully to the legislature. When relief was not forthcoming and when the judiciary report of 1844 bluntly ridiculed their grievances, the tenants realized that they must bring more direct pressure on the lawmakers. They early hit upon the strategy of throwing their strength behind one of the regular candidates of the major parties. In several counties, notably Albany, Rensselaer, Delaware, Columbia, and Schoharie, the antirenters held the balance of power.[3] Canny politicians began to curry favor with the tenants in much the same way that politicians during the early decades of the twentieth century sought the support of the Anti-Saloon League.[4]

During the years 1844–1848 the antirenters found the Whigs in the leasehold area more receptive than the Democrats to the idea of coalition. To many conservative Whigs this was a *mésalliance* of the most odious kind. Others excused it on the ground of expediency. Since the Whigs had usually been in the minority in the Hudson Valley counties as well as in the state at large, their leaders were naturally eager to win new allies. Moreover, certain outstanding Whigs such as Horace Greeley, Ira Harris, later United States senator and jurist, and John Young, Whig governor in 1846, were conspicuous in their support of antirentism. On the other hand, the Democratic leader Governor Silas Wright had to assume the unpopular task of suppressing the disturbances in Columbia and Delaware counties.

In 1844 the Van Rensselaer tenants made their first organized attempt to influence the elections for the Assembly and the State Senate. Already in March, 1844, a select committee composed of the joint delegation from Albany and Rensselaer counties pro-

---

[3] A letter by "W." in the *Freeholder*, Oct. 13, 1847, notes that although only 1,000 people out of 6,000 on the manor would support an antirent nomination, this group held the balance of power.

[4] In the course of a debate in the Senate, July 1, 1847, Mr. Clark declared, "Again and again had the spectacle been presented of this truckling to Anti-Rentism for a nomination—and by both parties". (*Argus*, July 3, 1847).

ANTIRENTISM IN POLITICS

posed that the landlords should establish their titles. They further urged the right of each tenant to buy out the cash value of the rents. The signers of this report were Whigs, and the *Troy Whig* distributed the report throughout the county. The Whigs swamped the Democrats in the spring elections.[5]

Later in the year the antirent associations submitted two planks to the candidates for the Assembly. The first required persons deriving income from leases over twenty years in length to prove the validity of their titles. The second permitted the holders of leases to have the value of the rents appraised, after which they could buy out the rights of the landlord. Ira Harris of Albany endorsed both planks, although he considered the second proposal unconstitutional.[6] Once the fall election was over and after the murder of two citizens by the Indians had temporarily discredited the antirent cause, the politicians felt freer to criticize the movement. Both the *Argus* and the *Evening Journal* found delight in charging its rival with a too close association with antirentism.[7]

The outbreak of violence in Rensselaer and Columbia counties forced Governor Wright to submit the problem to the legislature. He vigorously condemned violence, declaring that until the antirenters abandoned all illegal methods he would not entertain any plans for compromising the controversy. He also recommended that the legislature tighten law enforcement by passing two new laws.[8] The legislators acted with alacrity. They forbade the use

---

[5] *New-York Weekly Tribune*, April 13, 1844.
[6] *Argus*, Nov. 1, 4, 1844.
[7] *Argus*, Dec. 23, 24, 30, 1844; *Albany Evening Journal*, Dec. 21, 1844.
[8] *Messages from Governors*, IV, 148–150. Christman accepts without qualification the bitter charges which the angry tenants made against Wright. He accuses the governor of hypocrisy, specious reasoning, interference with the judiciary, and tacit support of the dispatch of thugs to break up antirent meetings (*op. cit.*, pp. 124, 130–131, 247). His hatred of "King Silas" leads him to state that Wright's solution to the tenant system "was indeed the extermination of the tenants" (p. 195). Such criticism is unfair. Wright was conspicuous in his generation for integrity of character and devotion to liberal causes. He was no tool of the landlord class. Rather the answer to

LANDLORDS AND FARMERS

of disguises. They also authorized the governor to loan arms to sheriffs and to send troops to counties where officials were unable to cope with disorder. Wright's uncompromising attitude earned for him the hatred of the antirenters. Governors William H. Seward in 1839 and William C. Bouck in 1844 had shown much more willingness to appease the tenant farmers. But in early 1845 Wright faced a condition akin to open rebellion. The epidemic of outrages shocked him. The virtual breakdown of state authority in the antirent counties caused him alarm. The stern-minded governor resolved to restore law and order.

In the spring of 1845 those candidates who had received the blessing of antirent associations swept the local elections in the counties of Albany, Rensselaer, and Schoharie, and the town of Duanesburg, Schenectady County.[9] Most of the supervisors in these counties endorsed the antirent program. The antirent candidates showed impressive strength in the fall of 1845, despite the fact that the killing of Steele had stirred up a wave of opposition to antirentism. The exact number of assemblymen and senators who called themselves Antirenters is difficult to determine. Local associations sometimes nominated and elected their own candidates for supervisor, justice of the peace, and road commissioner. But most so-called Antirenters were Whigs or in some instances Democrats endorsed by the Antirent conventions. In 1845 the *Freeholder* claimed that the tenants had elected three assemblymen from Albany County, two from Delaware, three from Rensselaer, and one from Schoharie.[10] Other members from Schenectady, Montgomery, Columbia, and Greene counties were considered friendly. Perhaps the greatest upset was the election of Wil-

---

his attitude to antirentism lies in his unbending determination to perform his duty of enforcing the law. Perhaps he interpreted his oath of office too narrowly, but the disorders of 1845 would have forced any governor to take drastic steps.

[9] *Freeholder*, April 16, 1845. See the *Argus*, April 4, 1845, for the results in Rensselaer County.
[10] Nov. 12, 1845.

liam H. Van Schoonhoven, a Troy Whig, to the Senate in the traditionally Democratic third district. Van Schoonhoven won by a handsome majority despite the opposition of the *Delaware Express*, a Whig paper, which had joined the law and order camp in opposing all candidates backed by antirenters.[11] His election was a direct rebuke to Governor Wright and the Democratic party, whose press and conventions had openly praised the policy of suppressing the Indians.[12]

Antirent victories at the polls caused an immediate change in attitude on the part of the legislature. Prior to 1846 the lawmakers had largely ignored the petitions of the tenants except for an occasional minority report. Early in 1846 they showed, in the words of the correspondent of the *New-York Weekly Tribune*, "a wonderful anxiety . . . to give the Anti-Renters all they ask." [13] Even Governor Silas Wright in his message to the legislature displayed a more conciliatory tone. He urged the legislature to abolish distress for rent, to prohibit any more long-term leases, and to tax the income which the landowners received from their rents.[14]

Scarcely had the legislature met before it plunged into a partisan debate. The issue was whether that part of the governor's message referring to leasehold tenures should be handed to a select committee or to a committee of the whole.[15] Ira Harris and the antirent Whigs wanted a select committee composed of members from the disturbed counties to handle the matter, but the Democrats were determined that they should gain the honor and profit of aiding the tenants. Assemblyman Watson of Albany declared that the contest seemed to be over who was to do the most

---

[11] *Delaware Express*, Oct. 8, 1845, cited in *Oneida Whig*, Nov. 18, 1845. See also *New-York Weekly Tribune*, Nov. 12, 1845.

[12] *Freeholder*, Oct. 29, 1845, contains a long list of Democratic county meetings which endorsed Wright.

[13] Jan. 19, 1846.

[14] *Messages from Governors*, IV, 240–244.

[15] For speeches in this debate, see *Argus*, Jan. 12, 19, 31, Feb. 4, 5, 6, 1846.

for the tenants.[16] Most legislators were in full agreement with the governor's recommendations. Some of the more radical wished to examine the titles of the landlords.

During this debate both Whigs and Democrats tried to fasten the blame for the antirent uprising upon each other. The Democrats repeated the old accusation that Governor Seward had aroused false hopes among the tenants, hopes which the Whigs had failed to satisfy. The Whigs defended Seward's record. They denounced the judiciary report of 1844, which had been issued under a Democratic administration, as a capitulation to landlord influence. Practically all speakers opposed leasehold tenures as inconsistent with the democratic spirit of the age and detrimental to the agricultural and industrial development of eastern New York. Obviously politicians of both parties were trying to win the support of the antirent societies, which held their state conventions at Berne on January 15, 1845, and again on February 27, 1846. The conventions laid down a specific program of demands and promised to support any candidate who would favor their cause.[17]

Finally the Assembly appointed a select committee of which Samuel J. Tilden was chairman. This committee made several recommendations in its report of March 28, 1846, which thoroughly examined the history of the land grants and the social effects of the leasehold system. The committee held public hearings at which counsel for the proprietors of Rensselaerswyck were present as well as representatives of the tenants from the counties of Albany, Rensselaer, Columbia, Schoharie, Schenectady, Montgomery, Greene, and Delaware.[18]

The committee unequivocably agreed with the general conclusions of the tenants that leasehold tenures had a depressing effect on the "agricultural prosperity and social condition of the communities where they exist." Admitting that the free years and the

---

[16] *Argus*, Feb. 4, 1846.
[17] *Argus*, Feb. 10, 1845; *Freeholder*, March 4, 1846.
[18] N.Y. *Assembly Documents*, no. 156 (1846).

ANTIRENTISM IN POLITICS

light rent had eased the settler's burdens during the first years, the committee, however, felt that the rent burden later turned out to be a drag on his enterprise. The lack of full ownership and the feeling of dependence tended to blunt the spirit of initiative. Furthermore, the restraints on alienation such as the quarter sales and the water and mineral reservations prevented the free exchange of property and frightened away potential immigrants. Particularly disastrous was the effect of the leases upon agricultural practices. This was especially noticeable in those regions where the farms fell back to the landlord at the expiration of lives or a period of years.

The committee then took up the plea that the landlords should pay a tax on the interests they reserved in leases. Pointing out that a lease of land in perpetuity was in substance a form of sale with the interest payable as rent, the committee argued that to tax such debts secured on land would be an equitable distribution of the common burden of supporting public functions. Otherwise the exemption would encourage capital to invest in leaseholds which were socially undesirable. Since nonresidents held large tracts, the committee contended that the tax should be laid on the land and not the individual's residence.

The report favored the abolition of remedy by distress. Admittedly this right of the landlord to take and hold the goods of the tenant until the rents were paid had been seldom used. Nevertheless, it did give the landlord a preferred position in regard to debts as compared with other creditors. The committee likewise proposed a bill forbidding the future lease of agricultural land for periods exceeding ten years.

The suggestion that tenants be permitted to challenge the titles of their landlords received careful consideration. Tilden examined the various acts which guaranteed the possession of property against all claims after it had been held for twenty years or more. Tilden upheld the contention that such laws were necessary to quiet titles. Fire, flood, theft, and accident were continually destroying essential records. Furthermore, the Constitution forbade any state from impairing the obligation of contracts. Consequently, the covenants in the lease could not be abrogated by so changing the remedies to recover the possession of the land as to impair the right. The proposed bill would deny the remedy altogether except on a condition which had no relation to the nature or operation of the remedy. It meant that if a party entitled by the express words of the contract to the remedy could not definitely prove his title at the time the original contract was made, he could not have the remedy. The committee predicted that the Supreme Court would certainly outlaw such legislation.

Samuel Tilden possessed a keen legal mind which went straight to the heart of a problem. He noted that the legal instrument conveying the whole quantity of the grantor's estate was not a lease but a freehold. Thus the Van Rensselaer lease included the words "grant," "bargain and sell," "remise and release," and "to have and to hold."

> It is, in a word, a warrantee deed. The fee of the land is conveyed to the person who is called the tenant, but who in truth is the owner. The reservations, conditions and covenants are in the nature of a grant by the buyer to the seller, of an annuity secured on the land, or mortgage for the purchase money.[19]

Tilden felt that the only relief that could be given the tenant was through a change in the laws regulating devices and descents. He would attach a condition to the future transfer of property by devise or descent whereby the tenant could petition the court of chancery to have the rent converted into a principal sum which at legal interest would produce the annual rent.[20] Interestingly enough, the committee excluded the quarter sales from this amount by flatly denying the validity of all restraints on the lessee's right to dispose of the land in any way he saw fit.

---

[19] *N.Y. Assembly Documents,* no. 156 (1846), p. 23.
[20] For a copy of the proposed bill, see *ibid.,* no. 223 (1846).

ANTIRENTISM IN POLITICS

This report took a sound statesmanlike approach to a delicate problem. Of course, the tenants felt disappointed that it did not call upon the landlords to prove their titles in court. On the other hand, the landlords opposed the recommendations made by Tilden's committee.[21] The abolition of distress, the taxation of ground rents, and the proposed right of the tenant to buy out the landlord's interest were reforms flatly opposed by the landlords. Nevertheless, the legislature agreed to frame statutes providing for two of the three recommended changes. A bill abolishing distress and one permitting town assessors to ascertain the amount of any rents reserved in fee or in one or more lives and to tax these rents passed both the Assembly and the Senate. Governor Wright affixed his signature at once. The third proposal, which allowed the tenant to buy out the landlord's interest whenever the landlord died, failed to get the approval of the Senate.[22]

During the early part of the 1840's there arose a demand for several political reforms. Stricter control of the legislature's power to contract debts, a reorganization of the judiciary, elimination of the property qualification for holding office, and changes in the land law were among these reforms. Year after year attempts to submit amendments before the people failed to get through the legislature, where conservative forces blocked the proposed changes. As a result the liberal wings of both parties began to agitate for a constitutional convention in order to circumvent the opposition of the legislature. After a furious struggle John Young piloted a resolution through the Assembly calling for a convention. An eminent historian declares that the antirent crusade com-

---

[21] For the arguments used by landlords, see *N.Y. Senate Documents*, no. 92 (1846). Gulian C. Verplanck wrote to Samuel Tilden on April 2, 1846, objecting to the proposed change in the laws regulating Devises and Descents. He declared that the method of computing the commutation ignored other reservations such as mines (Box VIII, Verplanck Papers).

[22] *Argus*, May 14, 1846.

ing at that particular time gave the final push to the public pressure for a constitutional convention.[23]

The antirenters as well as the National Reformers saw the value of the convention as a sounding board for their ideas. They were very active in electing delegates who would be friendly to their program.[24] The antirenters claimed that thirteen delegates owed their seats to the votes of the tenants.[25] They succeeded in electing such staunch protagonists of their cause as Ira Harris and William Van Schoonhoven. Horace Greeley was eager to attend the convention but he was unable to secure a nomination from the Whigs. Shortly after the convention opened the great editor addressed an open letter to the delegates urging them to abolish land monopoly.[26] Greeley endorsed unreservedly the program of the National Reformers. He urged the convention to prohibit anyone from acquiring more than 160 or 320 acres after July 4, 1847. The practical grievances of the tenants and the agitation of the National Reformers kept the cause of antirentism before the minds of the delegates.

The convention, however, spent most of its time reorganizing the judiciary and providing for a greater amount of popular representation. Not until the last week did the convention take up the question of land tenures. The delegates were not dodging the issue. In fact, they were in general agreement as to what they could do about the problem. Nothing was done about existing leases. They were inviolate contracts. But the convention inserted certain safeguards to prevent the extension of the leasehold. The new constitution stated that all lands in the state were allodial. All fines, quarter sales, or other restraints on alienation were invalid for any lease made after 1846. Furthermore, it forbade any

---

[23] Edward P. Cheyney, "The Antirent Movement and the Constitution of 1846," in Flick, *History of N.Y.*, VI, 308 ff.
[24] *Freeholder*, March 4, 1846; *Semi-Weekly Courier and Enquirer*, Sept. 16, 1845.
[25] *Freeholder*, May 6, 1846.
[26] *New-York Weekly Tribune*, June 29, 1846.

ANTIRENTISM IN POLITICS

future lease of agricultural land which contained a reservation of rent or service for a longer period than twelve years. The constitution reasserted the law of 1787 abolishing all feudal tenures except rents and services lawfully created and reserved. Obviously the delegates were unwilling to disturb the existing legal pattern of land ownership.[27]

These provisions gave no relief to tenants chafing under the leasehold. Of course, the tenants won a moral victory since the representatives of the people had stamped leasehold as against the public interest. Moreover, it was a tactical victory in the war of nerves which the tenants were waging against the landlords. Landholders became much more willing to sell their rights in the land at a low figure. While the antirent leaders were happy at the changes, they did not overlook the fact that their followers were demanding relief from existing and not prospective leases. They began to marshal their forces for the state elections of 1846. The prize was the governorship. Delegates to the constitutional convention had already charged that the solicitude shown the tenants was partly inspired by the hope of securing antirent support in the coming campaign.[28]

A thorough understanding of the election of 1846 would require a more detailed analysis of factional disputes within the Democratic and Whig parties than is necessary or profitable in this study. It would be easy to interpret the defeat of Governor Silas Wright by John Young, his Whig rival, as proof of the political power of antirentism. The fact that Addison Gardiner, Democratic candidate for lieutenant governor, defeated his Whig opponent would seem to prove the case conclusively. Such an explanation, however, fails to take account of the internecine warfare which bedeviled the Democracy in 1846.

---

[27] For the new clauses concerning land tenure in the Constitution, see S. Croswell and R. Sutton, *Debates and Proceedings in the New York State Convention for the Revision of the Constitution* (Albany, 1846), p. 841.
[28] *Ibid.*, p. 816.

LANDLORDS AND FARMERS

John Young was an exceptionally strong candidate. He had achieved political fame because of the skill with which he had outwitted the Democratic majority in the Assembly in 1845. Furthermore, he was more responsible than anyone else for the calling of the constitutional convention, despite the opposition of the conservatives in both parties. For conservative Whig papers such as the *New York Express* and the *Semi-Weekly Courier and Enquirer*, his nomination for governor on the Whig ticket was a bitter pill to swallow.[29] Young was accused of being friendly with the antirenters and of having supported the Tilden program. When the Anti-Rent State Convention endorsed Young, J. Watson Webb was furious. He addressed a letter to Young asking "whether you are or are not, in favor of any Legislation intended, directly or indirectly, to interfere with the vested rights of landlords as now existing in this state." Young's refusal to reply caused Webb to declare that he would not vote for Young.[30]

A combination of circumstances made it possible for Young to win the support of the Antirent State Convention.[31] First of all, Young had distinguished himself as a friend of the tenants by backing Tilden's legislative program whereas Silas Wright had alienated most of the antirenters by his harsh strictures and his enforcement of the law. Furthermore, it is clear that Young and his friends promised the antirent leaders that in the event of his election he would pardon those antirenters who had been convicted for various crimes arising out of the disturbances of 1845.[32]

---

[29] The *New-York Tribune* (Aug. 27, 1846) carried editorials from many Whig papers denouncing the *Express* and the *Courier and Enquirer* for trying to disorganize the Whig party. See also the *New-York Weekly Tribune*, Sept. 28, 1846, which deplored the attacks of the *Courier and Enquirer* and the *Express*.

[30] *Semi-Weekly Courier and Enquirer*, Oct. 14, 1846.

[31] *Freeholder*, Oct. 14, 1846.

[32] Christman (*op. cit.*, p. 271) asserts that Wright offered pardons to Dr. Boughton and the Delaware County leaders if they would support his ticket (pp. 269–270).

ANTIRENTISM IN POLITICS

Since Ira Harris, a close political ally of John Young, was presiding at the antirent convention, he could easily give such assurances. The antirent convention, meeting in Albany in 1846, indulged in the usual round of oratory and resolutions. Behind this facade shrewd politicians were engaged in horse trading and wirepulling. George Henry Evans and Thomas Devyr were unable to persuade the antirenters to back Bradley, the candidate of the Liberty party. Bradley alone among the candidates had taken a stand acceptable to the National Reformers.[33] Horace Greeley and Thurlow Weed, powerful figures in the Whig party, were actively lobbying at the convention. Greeley later insisted that he and Weed had begged the delegates to support Hamilton Fish for lieutenant governor instead of Addison Gardiner, the Democratic candidate.[34] A year later Greeley, smarting under the taunts of his rivals, insisted that he had even tried to prevent the endorsement of John Young by the antirenters unless they would also support Young's running mate, Hamilton Fish.[35]

The defeat of Wright still further exacerbated the feelings of both Barnburners and Hunkers. Charges of treachery by Wright's followers led to recriminations by the Hunker press. In fact, the quarrel became so bitter that within a year the Democratic party was split wide open. In December, 1846, the *Albany Atlas*, the organ of the Barnburners, carried a series of articles analyzing the causes of Wright's defeat.[36] The author was obviously familiar with the devious crosscurrents of New York politics. He examined the

---

[33] Jabez Hammond, *Life and Times of Silas Wright* (Syracuse, 1848), p. 683. Strangely enough Thomas Devyr, who hated Ira Harris, urged his followers to vote for Wright (Christman, *op. cit.*, p. 274).

[34] *New-York Weekly Tribune*, Nov. 11, 1846. Fish wrote to a political ally that he did not believe Ira Harris, Thurlow Weed, and John Young sought the endorsement of the antirent convention (Hamilton Fish to A. G. Johnson, Oct. 23, 1846; Hamilton Fish to Thurlow Weed, Oct. 23, 1846, Correspondence of Hamilton Fish, Library of Congress).

[35] *New-York Weekly Tribune*, Aug. 9, 1847.

[36] It was later charged that Wright was the author (H. D. Donovan, *op. cit.*, p. 78). See the *Albany Atlas*, Dec. 4, 5, 7, 8, 10, 1846.

importance of the antirent vote, he tried to weigh the effect of Wright's veto of canal and bank bills, and he investigated the voting record of Hunker townships. This anonymous writer concluded that the "conservative [Hunker] defection was the cause" of Wright's defeat. He singled out the *Argus* in particular as a covert enemy of Wright. By comparing the Governor's vote in 1844 with that of 1846 in such strong Hunker counties as Oneida, Onondaga, Cayuga, and Chenango, the writer asserted that the Hunkers had either failed to vote or else had voted for the Whig candidate.[37]

The election results substantiate the boast of the antirenters that they held the balance of power and had put Young into the governorship.[38] His majority over Silas Wright was 11,572, whereas Fish trailed Gardiner by 13,357. The same split took place in the vote for canal commissioners. Thomas Clownes, Whig, and John T. Hudson, Democrat, were the victors. Both had received antirent endorsement. Obviously politicians in both parties could see that the friendship of the antirenters was worth cultivating.

The feud between Hunkers and Barnburners was unquestionably a factor in preventing the re-election of Silas Wright. But antirent votes were even more important. The following official count of the Albany County returns shows clearly the power of

[37] Dr. Donovan leans to the belief that the Hunkers were largely responsible for Wright's defeat (*op. cit.*, p. 80). A partisan biography of Wright likewise blames the conservative Democrats (R. H. Gillet, *The Life and Times of Silas Wright* [Albany, 1874], II, 1793). Jabez Hammond, a friend of Wright but withal a careful observer, notes that the Hunkers and their allies in the Polk administration injured the Governor's cause (*Silas Wright*, pp. 694–698). The main argument used by the Hunkers in refutation was that the antirent vote had beaten Wright (*Argus*, Nov. 9, 18, 21, 1846).

[38] *Freeholder*, Nov. 4, Dec. 9, 1846. The official figures were: Young (W), 198,878; Wright (D), 187,306; Fish (W), 187,613; Gardiner (D), 200,970. Fish stated that the antirenters "have the right to claim the victory" (Hamilton Fish to Daniel Dewey Barnard, Nov. 26, 1846, Correspondence of Hamilton Fish).

ANTIRENTISM IN POLITICS

the tenants.[39] Young, Gardiner, Hudson, and Clownes received antirent backing.

	DEMOCRATS			WHIGS	
Governor:	Wright	4,841		Young	7,659
Lieu.-Gov.:	Gardiner	7,430		Fish	5,290
Canal	Hudson	7,445		Clownes	7,679
commissioner	Allen	4,693		Cook	5,359

Young was able to change the Whig majority of twenty-five in 1844 to 2,818 in 1846. Similarly Young carried Delaware County, a Democratic stronghold, by over 1800 votes. These gains in the antirent counties were partially offset by the defection of conservative Whigs in New York City. Hundreds of Whigs either failed to vote for Young or else voted for Wright.[40]

The feuds within the Democratic and Whig parties make it hard to estimate the strength of the antirent vote. This is particularly true of the race in 1846 for governor and lieutenant governor. Much more significant and less subject to outside factors was the vote for canal commissioners. John T. Hudson, a Democrat, defeated his Whig opponent by 10,475 votes. Thomas Clownes, a Whig, won over his Democratic opponent by 10,136 votes.[41] Approximately ten thousand voters were willing to split their ticket in order to back candidates endorsed by the antirent convention. The antirent vote varied with each candidate and with each election. Never did it exceed 20,000 votes. The conservative *Journal of Commerce* stated that the antirenters had 20,000 votes which gave the tenants a whip hand over both parties.[42] The *Freeholder* in 1847 claimed 15,000 to 20,000 votes.[43] Nevertheless most tenants clung to the old party standards. For

---

[39] *Argus*, Nov. 1, 1846.
[40] *New-York Weekly Tribune*, Nov. 9, 1846.
[41] Official figures can be found in *ibid.*, Dec. 5, 1846.
[42] Quoted in *Freeholder*, Oct. 23, 1850.
[43] Oct. 20, 1847.

example, the *Freeholder* in 1849 sadly admitted that there were only 500 votes in Albany County definitely committed to the antirent cause.[44] Between 1846 and 1850 the antirenters used their strength to cajole and threaten the politicians of both parties. Well might the Democratic General Committee of Tammany in 1850 pass the resolution:

> Whereas, a small portion of the electors of this state, associated as a political faction, designated and known as "Anti-Renters," have uniformly, for several years past, selected from the names put in nomination by the whig and democratic organizations a third, or split ticket, and have thereby controlled our state elections, the individuals selected by them, from the respective tickets being almost invariably elected.[45]

Soon after he entered office Governor John Young issued a proclamation pardoning the eighteen antirent prisoners in the state prisons. Pointing out that their crimes were political in nature and that the agitation had almost subsided, Young declared that further punishment would serve no good purpose and would tend to keep alive the spirit of unrest.[46] His failure to restore citizenship to Dr. Boughton and three other prisoners annoyed the antirenters.

The Anti-Rent State Convention endorsed twelve men for various state offices in 1847. Eight of this number were Whigs, a fact which annoyed several Democratic antirenters.[47] The Whigs swept the election. Defeat deepened the split in the Democracy. The Hunkers angrily fastened the blame on the Barnburners, who were accused of ignoring the Hunker nominations.[48]

In 1848 the Barnburners bolted the Hunker-dominated convention of the Democratic party and nominated John Dix to run for governor on the Free-Soil ticket, along with Martin Van Buren who was making his last bid for the presidency. The third party

---

[44] Nov. 14, 1849. See also issues for Oct. 13, 1847, and Nov. 21, 1849.
[45] Quoted in *Freeholder*, Oct. 23, 1850.
[46] *Argus*, Jan. 28, 1847.
[47] *Freeholder*, Oct. 20, 1847.
[48] *Argus*, Nov. 8, 1847.

ANTIRENTISM IN POLITICS

guaranteed victory for the Whigs. The Whigs sidetracked John Young partly because he had pardoned the antirenters. They nominated the conservative Hamilton Fish in his stead.[49] The state convention of the antirent delegations refused to support Fish, but it did endorse Patterson, Whig candidate for Lieutenant Governor. The difference in the vote between Fish and Patterson in eleven counties where tenancy was an issue gives us another rough index of antirent strength. Patterson ran 3,545 votes ahead of Fish in these counties.[50]

In the following year antirentism gave a striking demonstration of its political power. The four candidates from each party which the antirent convention endorsed were successful.[51] An examination of the vote in Delaware County reveals that the four candidates of each party enjoying antirent support ran about 2,200 votes ahead of their fellow candidates. The tenant farmers likewise influenced the election results in Albany and Rensselaer counties.[52]

Again in 1850 the antirenters claimed that they had elected their entire slate with but one minor exception.[53] Coincidence alone cannot explain the victories of those candidates endorsed by the antirent convention. Of course, several other factors helped to defeat Horatio Seymour, the lone Democratic candidate not endorsed by the antirent convention. Nevertheless, the fact that Seymour lost the governorship by less than 300 votes makes it safe to state that antirent opposition caused his defeat in 1850.

Factionalism racked both parties as in 1846. The wounds of the disastrous split of 1848 had not yet healed within the Democratic party. Hunker newspapers were quick to blame the defeat of Seymour on the defection of the Barnburners, although the

---

[49] De Alva Stanwood Alexander, *Political History of the State of New York* (New York, 1906–1923), II, 139.
[50] *Argus*, Nov. 21, 1848.
[51] *New-York Weekly Tribune*, Nov. 19, 1849.
[52] *Argus*, Nov. 13, 1849.
[53] *Freeholder*, Nov. 20, 1850.

importance of the antirent vote was readily acknowledged.[54] The conservative Fillmore Whigs covertly sabotaged the campaign of Washington Hunt for the governorship. At the famous meeting in Castle Garden a group of Fillmore Whigs openly advocated the defeat of Hunt and the election of Seymour. It was estimated that Seymour received the votes of 3,000 Whigs in New York City and 1,500 in Brooklyn.[55] The fact that Hunt received the blessing of the antirenters added to the anger of the capitalists. Hunt did not openly disavow tenant support. He merely stated that he was the Whig candidate and could not accept any arrangement which would increase his vote over his running mates.[56]

Obviously these intra-party fights played an important part in the 1850 election. But the decisive character of the antirent endorsement cannot be denied. It was worth about 2,200 votes in Delaware County alone.[57] If Seymour had not been the special target of tenant wrath, he would have won the election. The antirenters, however, could not forgive his opposition to their legislative program in 1844 and 1845 and his close personal ties with prominent landlords. They had the satisfaction of defeating their old enemy in his bid for the governorship.

In 1851 the antirenters made their last attempt to influence the election of state officials. Their convention endorsed the entire Democratic ticket, much to the disgust of Whig delegates who bolted the convention and set up a rival slate composed of an equal number of Democrats and Whigs.[58] During the campaign speakers from the rival camps toured the countryside urging support for their ticket.[59] Again the election was close, with the result

---

[54] *Argus*, Nov. 15, 1850. See also Stewart Mitchell, *Horatio Seymour* (Cambridge, 1938), pp. 117 ff.
[55] *New-York Weekly Tribune*, Nov. 20, 21, 1850.
[56] The *Weekly Tribune* denounced the *Journal of Commerce* for assailing Hunt as an antirenter (Oct. 31, 1850).
[57] *Ibid.*, Nov. 23, 1850.
[58] *Argus*, Sept. 29, 1851; *New-York Weekly Tribune*, Oct. 4, 1851.
[59] *Argus*, Oct. 25, 1851.

ANTIRENTISM IN POLITICS

long in doubt. The Democrats won six state offices while the Whigs managed to secure two. The *Tribune* blamed the conservative Whigs for driving many Whig antirenters away from their own ticket.[60] The split among the antirenters in 1851 weakened the organization and virtually ended its political importance. By 1851 the controversies over the slavery question and rapid elimination of many leaseholds caused many tenants to return to the old party standards.

The question naturally arises, what benefits did tenant farmers receive as a result of their victories at the polls? First of all, the election of friendly sheriffs and local officials virtually paralyzed the efforts of landlords to collect the rents. This fact, coupled with the extralegal acts of the antirent associations, was extremely important in speeding up the process whereby hard pressed and disgusted landlords agreed to sell the fee at a low valuation. Secondly, the creation of a small but determined bloc in both houses of the legislature kept the grievances of the tenants continually before the eyes of the legislators and threatened the adoption of laws designed to challenge the titles of the landlords. The election of their favorite, John Young, as governor not only secured the pardon of antirent prisoners but also led to an investigation of land titles by the attorney general.

It is an amazing commentary on the shift of political power that the Whig and Democratic party leaders paid more attention to the demands of the tenant farmers than to the old landowning families. Of course the commercial, industrial, and financial interests associated with the growth of the port of New York and the commercial cities of the upstate region, in combination with the small-farmer society of central and western New York, had really grasped the sceptre of economic and political power. Nevertheless the solicitude with which politicians treated antirent appeals was a far cry from the days when the Livingstons, Duanes, Van Rensselaers, and Schuylers held undisputed sway over the

[60] *New-York Weekly Tribune*, Dec. 31, 1851.

LANDLORDS AND FARMERS

government. The fears expressed by Chancellor Kent and Jacob Van Rensselaer in 1821 that universal manhood suffrage would bring leveling ideas and agrarianism in its train were partly realized in the antirent movement only two decades later.

The landholding aristocracy, however, had many friends in the press, the legislature, and the courts. In fact, the weight of tradition, social prestige, and wealth undergirded by the framework of legal precedents was theirs from the start. What the landlords lacked in number they made up in power and influence. In all previous clashes between landlords and tenants the former had been able to smother the latter through their control of the government. But in the 1840's the opposing forces were more evenly matched. Toward the end of the decade the landlords were clearly on the defensive.

The tenants and landlords used the same weapons in this struggle. After the tenants had organized antirent associations the landholders formed the Freeholders Committee of Safety. Deputations of antirenters appearing before hearings of the legislature found agents of the landlords already on the scene. Editorials in the conservative press matched in vigor and violence the denunciations of the antirent press. When tenants organized bands of Indians to block the collection of rents, their foes organized law and order societies to aid harassed officials. When antirent lawyers and after 1848 the attorney general of the state brought suits against landlord titles, a galaxy of legal talents rose up to defend them. Charges that members of the landed gentry were the beneficiaries of corrupt land deals and that the leaseholds were feudal vestiges abhorrent to our democratic institutions provoked countercharges that the tenants were the dupes of wily agitators and that antirentism stemmed directly from agrarianism, communism, and infidelity. Appeals to the principles of the Declaration of Independence inspired the landlords to quote the constitutional provisions guaranteeing the sanctity of contracts. Legislators anxious to sponsor laws to reform the leasehold met the obstruction

ANTIRENTISM IN POLITICS

of other members equally determined to protect property rights. The rhetoric of antirent orators declaiming the iniquities of the leasehold system was no less turgid than the prose of James Fenimore Cooper, who wrote three novels called, as a whole, the *Littlepage Manuscripts*.[61] Cooper attempted with indifferent success to idealize the role of the landlord class in the development of New York.

The landlords had a strong case if one studies the antirent problem from the legal point of view. Perhaps no one drew up as elaborate and convincing a defense of the leasehold as Daniel D. Barnard, Albany lawyer and landlord apologist. His arguments deserve attention since they were frankly designed to present to the public the landlords' case.[62]

Barnard noted first of all that the landlords had permitted landless immigrants to settle on their farms without requiring any down payments. Usually the tenants paid no rent for the first five years. Thus in the case of the farmers on Rensselaerswyck, they became freeholders at the end of seven years without making any payment whatsoever. Thereafter the settlers had to pay an annual rent, but Barnard considered the yearly payment of approximately $32 as trifling. The fact that settlers took up farms so quickly on these conditions was additional evidence that the terms were not burdensome. Furthermore, Barnard stated that the landlords as a group had treated their tenants with generosity. They often waived the rent in hardship cases. They had contributed to the support of churches, schools, and roads. To deny the landlord his rent would be a repudiation of all debts.

Barnard was on solid ground when he asserted that the real issue was not rent but "indebtedness for land in any and every form." The antirent controversy was in effect a variation of the perennial struggle between debtor and creditor, although in this instance the semifeudal trappings associated with the leasehold

---

[61] *Satanstoe, The Chainbearer, The Redskins.*
[62] "Anti-Rent Movement," pp. 577–598.

became the main target of the tenants. Barnard, of course, insisted that the perpetual lease was in reality a freehold over which the farmer had sole ownership except that he must pay a small sum annually to the person from whom he acquired the land. This debt was secured by the personal effects of the farmer and also by his land. Barnard denied the allegation that leaseholds were not democratic. He deplored the use of the name tenant, insisting that the farmers were "substantial freeholders" and "absolute owners" who held the land "independently of the will and caprice of a feudal lord or landlord, or anyone else." He ridiculed the description of the leases as "feudal tenures" and described the Van Rensselaer leaseholds as almost identical with those under which thousands of citizens paid rent in New York City. As for the water and mineral reservations, Barnard minimized their importance. In similar fashion he disposed of the provision for quarter sales. The original purpose was to prevent speculation in farms and to keep out undesirables. Furthermore, the landlord should derive some benefit from the increased value of the land. As a matter of fact, the Van Rensselaer family had never exacted the full amount. For the farms located in the lowland towns only one eighth of the sale price had ever been paid. For the farms located in the Helderberg townships only a trifling amount had been exacted. After 1832, farmers in these townships enjoyed the right to commute the quarter sales for the small sum of $30. Finally, Barnard asserted that the Van Rensselaers were willing to sell out their rights at any time on liberal terms.

Barnard's defense of the landlords and his severe strictures on the violence and disorder caused by the antirenters naturally aroused a storm of criticism. The antirenters called him a hireling of the patroons.[63] Thurlow Weed's *Evening Journal* made a calm, reasoned reply to Barnard, challenging his assertion that the tenants were actually freeholders by pointing out that they still owed feudal services. It blamed the water and mineral reservations as responsible for the slow growth of industry in the region. It par-

[63] *Freeholder*, Jan. 28, 1846.

ANTIRENTISM IN POLITICS

ticularly condemned quarter sales as making the sale of lands difficult and thus discouraging new settlers. As for the argument that the landlords should derive some of the unearned increment, the editor stated that it was the labor of the tenants that had increased land values.[64]

The landowners enjoyed strong support in most of the press. Certain journals took a special interest in championing the cause of law and order and in attacking the tenants. Probably the most vitriolic and persistent foe of antirentism was James Watson Webb's *Courier and Enquirer*. As early as 1841 it described the tenants as so "debased and too dark in intellect to possess necessary knowledge to keep out of the fire." [65] The bloody events of 1845 stirred Webb to new heights of denunciation. One editorial urged the shooting down of a thousand rather than having the laws ignored.[66] The *New York Express* rivaled Webb in its attacks on Greeley's sympathy for the tenants.[67] Other papers also incurred the wrath of the antirenters. In 1850 the official organ of the antirenters listed the *Albany State Register*, the *New York Herald*, the *Journal of Commerce*, and the *Express* as the worst foes of their cause.[68]

Throughout this period the antirent press accused the landlords of maintaining a lobby at Albany and of bringing improper influence to bear on the legislators. Whether the second accusation is true is still hard to say, but there is no doubt as to the truth of the first. Fortunately the records of the Freeholders Committee of Safety are still available.[69] They provide interesting information concerning the activities of the landlords.

In November, 1844, a group of large landowners organized a

---

[64] *Albany Evening Journal*, Dec. 9, 1845.

[65] Quoted in *Argus*, May 13, 1841.

[66] *Semi-Weekly Courier and Enquirer*, Sept. 13, 1845. See also *ibid.*, May 30, 1845.

[67] For reprints of its editorials, see the *New-York Weekly Tribune*, April 20, May 6, 1846.

[68] *Freeholder*, Oct. 30, 1850.

[69] Vols. VI, X, XIII, XIV, F. De Peyster Collection.

LANDLORDS AND FARMERS

committee in order to "oppose the illegal efforts of the Anti-Renters." [70] Prior to that time William P. Van Rensselaer, heir to the east manor, had borne the brunt of the antirent attack. As long as unrest was confined to Rensselaer Manor, the rest of the landholders had been content to permit the Van Rensselaer family to shoulder the burden. But when in 1844 tenants in neighboring counties embraced such dangerous antirent doctrines as nonpayment of rent, the landowners found it necessary to band together in self-defense. Frederic De Peyster, scion of an old Dutch family and allied by marriage to the Watts and the Livingston families, became the treasurer of the committee.

The roster of the contributors to the war chest of $1,060 which the committee collected in 1845 and 1846 includes many of the famous families of New York.

RECEIPTS

Feb.	27,	1845	Robert Ray	$25.00
"	"		Campbell P. White	25.00
"	"		William Crosby	20.00
March	5		Mr. J. Watts De Peyster	35.00
	6		New York Life Insurance and Trust Co.	250.00
	25		James S. Wadsworth	25.00
	25		John Hunter	100.00
	25		Heirs of E. P. Livingston (deceased)	75.00
April	5		Maturin Livingston	25.00
	5		Mrs. Ed. Livingston	35.00
Nov.	4		Wm. S. Johnson and R. C. Johnson	75.00
	4		R. H. Nevius by W. S. Johnson	45.00
	7		Col. Henry Armstrong and brother	50.00
	11		John A. King	50.00
	13		R. H. Ludlow	25.00
March	7,	1846	G. C. Verplanck	100.00
April	21,	1846	John Hunter	100.00
				$1,060.00

The attempt of the committee to lay an assessment of $250 on William P. Van Rensselaer brought forth an angry retort. In

---

[70] Frederic De Peyster to Henry Hogeboom, March 17, 1845, in vol. VI, H, 1728–1856, F. De Peyster Collection.

ANTIRENTISM IN POLITICS

scathing terms he denounced the lack of support during the years when he was battling the antirenters singlehanded. He had employed a "professional gentleman" to get certain laws passed. He had paid out large sums to put down resistance and to induce "passage of other laws." Far from owing the committee anything, he testily declared that it should pay him $250 to compensate him for expenses incurred in a common cause.[71]

The Freeholders Committee hired several agents to watch over its interests in Albany. In November, 1844, Charles Hathaway, an attorney, was dispatched to the capitol. When he submitted his bill for $600 on May 20, 1845, he reviewed with satisfaction the steps taken by the legislature during the winter. He hailed the passage of the law forbidding persons from appearing disguised and armed and its companion piece of legislation granting additional power to the sheriff and the governor to call out military force whenever an emergency arose. On the other hand, every effort of the antirenters to pass laws interfering with the obligation of contract or taxing leasehold property had been squashed. In addition, Hathaway reported that he had spent about $200 in Delaware County aiding the sheriff to restore order. He had personally paid the cost of sending a special messenger to Albany to secure arms from the arsenal. Furthermore, he had served as counsel for two weeks in the spring trials which had convicted four disguised men.[72]

James Powers, Catskill attorney, likewise became an agent for the committee in the corridors of the capitol. Besides the retainer of $500 for his "attendance at Albany," he submitted a bill for several other items showing rather clearly some of the publicity

---

[71] W. P. Van Rensselaer to Messrs. G. C. Verplanck and W. S. Johnson, Dec. 6, 1845; W. P. Van Rensselaer to Sam Johnson, Dec. 5, 1845, in vol. XIII, S, 1827–1846, F. De Peyster Collection.

[72] For a statement of his expenses, see vol. VI, H, 1728–1856, F. De Peyster Collection. See also letter of Hathaway to W. S. Johnson, May 20, 1845 (*ibid.*).

LANDLORDS AND FARMERS

methods of the committee.[73] He had paid the editor of the *Catskill Recorder* $50 for publishing one thousand extra copies of the report of the judiciary committee of 1844. The same editor received another $15 for publishing four hundred copies of Governor Wright's message on antirent, and the editor of the *Catskill Messenger* received $16 for the same job. Both Hathaway and Powers experienced great difficulty in securing full payment for their services.

The committee employed other lawyers, including John Kiersted, Catskill attorney.[74] Frederic De Peyster offered Henry Hogeboom $100 to assist the district attorney of Columbia County at the trial of Big Thunder.[75] Killian Miller also received $100 for legal services.

In the light of these disclosures it is easy to believe the statements of the antirenters in the period following 1846 that the landlords were lobbying at Albany. Thus in 1848 the *Freeholder* denounced the dinners at which Stephen Van Rensselaer was entertaining members of the legislature.[76] Whether the tenants ever heard of the Freeholders Committee is very doubtful, but the antirenters knew full well that William S. Johnson, a state senator, was the champion of the landlords.[77] They realized that if they expected to push through their program, they must convince the politicians that opposition would result in certain defeat at the polls.

Landlord influence penetrated not only the legislature and press but also such organizations as agricultural societies and churches.[78]

---

[73] Vol. X, p. 100, F. De Peyster Collection.

[74] Vol. VIII, F. De Peyster Collection; *John Kiersted Acc't Book*, p. 178, Kingston Papers.

[75] Frederic De Peyster to Henry Hogeboom, March 17, 1845, in vol. VI, H, 1728–1856, F. De Peyster Collection.

[76] Jan. 19, Feb. 2, 1848.

[77] *Freeholder*, Feb. 23, 1848.

[78] The *Freeholder* (Sept. 17, 1845) denounced the Methodist and Presbyterian churches of Delaware County for calling antirentism a crime.

ANTIRENTISM IN POLITICS

The annual meeting of the state agricultural society dodged the issue in 1846. County and state societies never gave a word of sympathy to the tenants.[79] Considering the widespread interest in antirentism, it is significant that the agricultural journals uniformly avoided any comment.[80] That landlords and their allies were active in supporting law and order societies and meetings was but to be expected. That they hired bullies to browbeat tenants and subsidized Indians in order to discredit antirentism are charges more difficult to believe without further evidence.[81]

An unexpected and perhaps unwelcome ally in the person of James Fenimore Cooper rallied to the support of the landlords. Although the choleric creator of Natty Bumppo professed to be an ardent republican and a fervent adherent of the Democratic party, he was by no means a leveler or a believer in social democracy. Cooper had been born to the purple. His father, Judge William Cooper, had owned vast tracts of land and had erected a bastion of Federalism in the wilderness. It was perhaps inevitable that Cooper should absorb some of the social and political views of the landlord class in which he was reared.

During the years 1845 and 1846, when the antirent agitation was at its height, Cooper published the *Littlepage Manuscripts*. His purpose was to justify the role of the landed aristocracy and to expose the nefarious designs of the antirenters. The first novel in the series of three was called *Satanstoe*. It is a sympathetic portrayal of genteel life in the middle of the eighteenth century when the fringe of settlement had barely advanced back from the river. The second novel, *The Chainbearer*, described the Littlepage family some fifty years later. The Revolution is over and the young son of the family is sent into the wilderness to open up the family

---

[79] *Freeholder*, June 23, 1848.

[80] The only reference which the writer has seen is a letter opposing leaseholds in the *Cultivator*, n.s. I (May, 1844), 151.

[81] Antirenters made such charges (*Freeholder*, Sept. 15, 1847; May 17, July 5, 1848).

lands for settlement. The responsibilities and the difficulties involved in the task, especially the struggle with the Yankee squatter Thousandacres, are carefully depicted by Cooper. His third novel, *The Redskins,* described the clash between the antirenters and the landowners.

In the preface of this work Cooper elaborated his social theory that the landlord class must remain as the "capital" of the "column of society." Far from yielding to the rather widely held opinion even among the friends of the landlords that the leasehold was an outmoded institution, Cooper boldly asserted that "the relation of landlord and tenant is one entirely natural and salutary, in a wealthy community." [82] He summarily dismissed the argument that leases were inconsistent with American traditions. He maintained that the leaseholds had been an integral part of our institutions recognized from the outset by state law and guaranteed by the Federal Constitution. The laws proposed by the Tilden report of 1846 whereby the state would prohibit future leases, tax the rents, and permit the tenant to buy out the landholder's interests, Cooper denounced as a diabolical "outrage on liberty." Throughout these novels he depicted the landlords as well-educated and humanitarian gentlemen. He portrayed the tenants, except those loyal to the landlords, as coarse and ignorant boors. The particular object of his wrath was the Yankee farmer, whom he held largely responsible for the pernicious doctrine that every man should be a freeholder.[83]

In the years following 1847 the landlords found themselves on the defensive in the arena of the courts. Sobered by the public reaction to the bloody events in Delaware County but heartened by their political victories, the antirenters concentrated their fire on the validity of landlord titles. Resolutions adopted at antirent meetings, petitions to the legislature, and editorials in their news-

---

[82] Preface of *The Redskins,* xvi.
[83] *Ibid.,* pp. 457–459.

ANTIRENTISM IN POLITICS

papers all demanded an investigation of land titles.[84] The corrupt land transactions of colonial New York were once more exposed to the public gaze. Unfortunately for the tenants they could not bring suit in their own right. The very act of signing a lease automatically estopped the signer from challenging its validity. Consequently, the tenants demanded that the state should either grant them this right or else should bring suit itself to recover the lands. If the landlord's title were invalid, then the land would revert to the state.

The chorus for an investigation of titles grew louder. In 1847 a committee of the Assembly recommended that the state authorize tenants to dispute titles.[85] Private attempts to arrange a test case between landlord and tenant proved abortive.[86] Finally Governor Young in his message to the legislature in 1848 urged the lawmakers to authorize the attorney general to investigate certain titles and to bring action against them.[87] In response to this plea the legislature passed a joint resolution authorizing the attorney general to bring suit for ejectment against a landholder if after inquiry he found the title might be justly questioned. All the protests of William S. Johnson and a few others were unable to stem the resolution.[88] Throughout the late spring and summer of 1848 the tenants were holding meetings and appointing committees to wait upon Ambrose Jordan, the attorney general.[89]

Despite the impatience of the tenants it was not until the spring of 1849 that Jordan felt ready to take action. On April 12, 1849, he brought suit against Henry Overing and John Garmel, who owned land in the Hardenburgh Patent. On May 1, 1849, he delighted the tenants of Rensselaerswyck by bringing suit against William

---

[84] *Freeholder,* Jan. 19, March 15, 1848; *New-York Weekly Tribune,* March 29, May 17, 1847; Calvin Pepper, *Manor of Rensselaerwyck* (Albany, 1846).
[85] *N.Y. Assembly Documents,* no. 162 (1847).
[86] *New-York Weekly Tribune,* April 12, 1847.
[87] *Messages from Governors,* IV, 412.   [88] *Argus,* Feb. 12, 1848.
[89] *Freeholder,* June 7, 21, July 5, Sept. 20, 1848.

P. and Stephen Van Rensselaer. It seemed that at last the farmers were to throw off the shackles of the leasehold.

A spirit of enthusiasm swept through the townships on both sides of the Hudson. Meetings were held in almost every township in Albany and Rensselaer counties.[90] The Rensselaer County convention petitioned the courts to grant a stay on all collections until the courts had decided the validity of the title. The members pledged themselves to pay $1.00 each to the treasury, to refuse to pay rent, and if prosecuted to pay a ratable proportion of costs arising from such prosecution.[91] From Delaware County came reports that antirent associations were assessing their members in order to secure funds whereby they might employ counsel to assist the attorney general in his prosecutions.[92] The tenants in Duanesburg asked the state to examine the title of the Duane family.[93] The tenants of George Clarke, Jr., who had attempted unsuccessfully in 1812 to test his title, yielded to the popular clamor. In Charleston, Montgomery County and in Oneida County antirent associations were formed to bring to the attention of the public and the attorney general the fraudulent features of the Corry and Oriskany patents respectively.[94]

Annoying delays postponed an early decision in the courts. In the meantime the antirenters demanded that they should be relieved of the burden of rent payments until the final decision had been handed down. The refusal of the courts to issue stays on proceedings forced the tenants to turn once again to the legislature for relief.[95] Their plea for a suspension of rent collections while the trials were going on received support in the report of Mr.

---

[90] *Freeholder,* March 21, 28, April 18, 1849.

[91] *Ibid.,* March 7, 1849.

[92] *Argus,* May 17, 1849.

[93] *Freeholder,* Feb. 27, 1850.

[94] *Ibid.,* Sept. 5, Oct. 3, 1849; Jan. 16, 23, 1850; *Utica Daily Gazette,* Jan. 18, Oct. 30, 1850.

[95] The *Argus* of June 4, 1849, reports the decision of Judges Harris and Wright.

ANTIRENTISM IN POLITICS

Chatfield, who succeeded Jordan as attorney general.[96] Early in 1850 the issue precipitated a furious debate in the legislature. A report of the majority of the Senate judiciary committee found the proposal unconstitutional, but it did offer an alternative plan. The state was to confirm lands in all cases where they had been held under leases for more than twenty years on condition that the landlords would consent to sell rights to the rents reserved.[97]

The landlords petitioned for a hearing before the judiciary committee of the Assembly. John C. Spencer, eminent lawyer who had served on the committee to revise the state laws, Samuel Beardsley, late Chief Justice of the State Supreme Court, and several other legal luminaries and agents testified that the proposed stay was unconstitutional.[98] Despite these protests the bill passed through the Senate by the vote of 18 to 10, each party contributing an equal share to each total. In the Assembly the opponents were able to place many obstructions in the path of the bill. Its proponents, however, circumvented these obstacles and forced a vote. They mustered 56 votes as compared to only 36 opposing votes. But because thirty-four members failed to vote, the bill lacked nine of securing a constitutional majority, i.e., a majority of all the members elected.[99] Certain members did not want to antagonize landlords or tenants by their vote.

In 1851 the same struggle took place although on a smaller scale. A select committee of the Assembly recapitulated all the arguments against the leasehold. It specifically denounced the landlords for switching their defense from titles based on patents to titles based on possession. They likewise charged that the landholders were causing court delays in order to tire out the tenants.[100] The minority submitted another report which took the view that

---

[96] *N.Y. Senate Documents*, no. 26 (1850).
[97] *Ibid.*, no. 96 (1850).
[98] *Freeholder*, April 3, 1850.
[99] *Argus*, April 12, 1850.
[100] *N.Y. Assembly Documents*, no. 132 (1851).

a suspension of rent collections was unconstitutional and improper class legislation. It caustically noted that the case against the landlord was so weak that the attorney general had already discontinued several actions. It warned the tenants not to follow scheming politicians. Instead it urged them to buy out the rights of the landlords.[101] Apparently the report of the attorney general that he was not continuing several actions as well as the decline in tenant agitation persuaded many legislators that the bill was unnecessary.[102] At any rate only twelve members of the Senate voted for its passage.

The quarter sales provision was the most vulnerable in the leasehold. Such essentially conservative lawyers as Samuel Tilden considered it an illegal restraint on alienation. The refusal of the tenants to pay the quarter sales led to actions for ejectment and to a judicial review of their legality. In Albany County John Overbaugh brought action against John Patrie of Westerlo for failure to pay Overbaugh one fourth of the purchase money when the latter sold his farm. The antirenters immediately rallied to Patrie's defense. They sent out an appeal for funds to pay for counsel.[103] Azor Tabor headed their legal staff and in 1850 he persuaded the Supreme Court of the state to outlaw the quarter sales.[104] In the meantime John Watts De Peyster was suing Anthony Michael of Claverack for the same offense. This case eventually reached the Court of Appeals in 1852. Judge Ruggles speaking for the court declared that since leases in perpetuity were in reality estates in fee, they could not contain any conditions restraining the right to alien the land. In other words the grantees were owners and not tenants.[105]

The antirenters hailed this decision as a tremendous victory. In

---

[101] *N.Y. Assembly Documents,* no. 133 (1851).
[102] *N.Y. Senate Documents,* no. 27 (1851).
[103] *Freeholder,* Oct. 20, 1847.
[104] *Report of the Argument of Azor Taber* (Albany, 1850).
[105] *De Peyster* v. *Michael,* 6 *N.Y.* 467.

the future they were to rest most of their position on the ruling that they were freeholders. They argued that the right of reversion was in the state and not the grantor. Unless the landlord could show title to the land, he could not begin suits for re-entry. Of course the landlords refused to accept this contention. They insisted that although the rent was not an estate in land, it was a hereditament, devisable and assignable. Furthermore, they did not need the right of reversion to sustain actions to recover the rent.

The antirenters were not to realize their hopes that the attorney general would overturn the titles of the Livingstons, Clarkes, and Van Rensselaers. The action against Hermon Livingston attracted widespread interest.[106] The state, represented by dashing John Van Buren, attempted to circumvent the argument of adverse possession by selecting a parcel of land not under actual occupation. Finally 150 acres of waste land were found on Livingston Manor. Van Buren attacked the title of the Livingston family as tainted with fraud. The defense, headed by Josiah Sutherland, denied this charge, but it relied very largely on title by possession which the various statutes of limitations had made unimpeachable. Judge Wright handed down his opinion in November, 1850. He upheld the paper title of the Livingstons.[107]

The tenants on Van Rensselaer Manor watched with keen interest the progress of the suit against the Van Rensselaer title. They were jubilant when Justice Ira Harris, long a champion of their cause, examined the title and found the original patents void. But only one year later the Court of Appeals reversed this opinion, holding that the Statute of Limitations effectively barred the state from questioning the imperfections of the paper title.[108] The at-

---

[106] See *Argus*, April 20, 22, 26, 29, 1850.

[107] *Mr. [John] Van Buren's Argument Delivered at Hudson, May 28, 1850* (n.p., n.d.); Josiah Sutherland, *Supreme Court: the People of the State of New-York agst. Herman Livingston . . . Points and Arguments of Josiah Sutherland* (Hudson, 1850).

[108] *People v. Van Rensselaer*, 9 N.Y. 317.

LANDLORDS AND FARMERS

tempt to question the title of George Clarke, Jr., met a similar fate at the hands of Judge Cady of the Supreme Court.[109]

In Sullivan County the antirenters attempted to set up a rival title to part of the Hardenburgh Patent. They declared that about 100,000 acres belonged to the town of Rochester. The original transaction whereby the trustees of the town had deeded the lands west of the "settlement line" to several individuals owning lands in the Hardenburgh Patent was invalid.[110] In both the state and the federal courts the landlords defeated this attack.[111]

The publication of the De Peyster decision holding that the title deeds were not deeds of lease but deeds of assignment in which the landholder had no reversion convinced the antirenters that they owed no service of any kind to anyone. No doubt the prospect of fighting interminable court battles and ejecting hundreds of recalcitrant tenants was the decisive factor persuading Stephen Van Rensselaer of the west manor to sell out his rights. At any rate in 1853 and 1854 Walter Church and Oscar Tyler, speculators in land, were able to buy all his leases at from 50 to 60 cents on the dollar. Wheat was computed at $1.00 a bushel, a day's labor at $2.00, and fat fowl at 12½ cents each. The rent, including the arrears, was capitalized at a sum which at 6 per cent would produce a revenue equal to the annual rent at the prices cited above. The nominal value of the leases in Albany County was estimated at $550,000, but Church was to pay only $210,000. Because of the heavy expenses incurred in court actions, Church was unable to meet the payments due Stephen Van Rensselaer and was forced to borrow from Peter Cagger and James Kidd in 1861.[112]

---

[109] *Opinion of Hon. Judge Cady in Supreme Court. The People of the State of New York* vs. *George Clarke* (Albany, 1851).

[110] *Freeholder*, Oct. 23, 1850; *Argus*, May 6, 8, 20, 1850.

[111] A. C. Niven, "A Chapter of Anti-Rent History," *Albany Law Journal*, XXIV (1881), 127.

[112] Walter Church testified before a committee of the Assembly as to his business deals (*N.Y. Assembly Documents*, no. 237 [1862], pp. 6–10).

ANTIRENTISM IN POLITICS

In 1857 Walter Church, along with Cagger and Kidd, made a similar agreement with William P. Van Rensselaer for the east manor. They agreed to pay approximately $100,000 for leases which if capitalized at the face value would have been worth $200,000 to $300,000. Church was unable to make the required payments. As a result Van Rensselaer sold all his remaining rents in Rensselaer for $41,983.64. In 1863 there were twenty-three different individuals or banks claiming rent in Rensselaer County.[113]

Colonel Walter Church soon won the enmity of the farmers in Albany and Rensselaer counties. He was regarded as an interloper who was battening on the spoils of the Van Rensselaer manor. Colonel Church rode at the head of the posses which served notices and protected auctions. The vigor with which he prosecuted the tenant farmers and the reputed skill with which he influenced public officials made him a veritable ogre to the farmers.[114] Church's power in the Democratic machine and his sumptuous dinners for politicians and judges aroused still more the suspicion and hatred of the antirenters. Church did not brook any delay in payment. On one occasion he testified that he had been interested in some two thousand suits.[115]

In 1858 the Court of Appeals handed down the important ruling that the landholder could still collect rents even though he had no reversion in the estate.[116] The statute of 1805 conferred this power to the landholder. This decision aroused so much opposition that the legislature in 1860 repealed the act of 1805. The Court of

---

[113] See list in A. G. Johnson, *A Chapter of History, or, the Progress of Judicial Usurpation* (Troy, 1863), pp. 20–21; Cheyney, *Anti-Rent Agitation*, p. 50.

[114] G. R. Howell and Jonathan Tenney, *History of the County of Albany, 1609–1886* (New York, 1886), pp. 277 ff.; *Landholders' Convention* (n.p., n.d.), pp. 1–4.

[115] Simon W. Rosendale, "Closing Phases of the Manorial System in Albany," *Proceedings of the New York State Historical Association*, VIII (1909), 240–242.

[116] *Van Rensselaer v. Ball*, 19 N.Y. 100.

LANDLORDS AND FARMERS

Appeals in 1863 declared that landholders could forfeit farms held on perpetual lease when the rent was not paid because the common law carried with it this right.[117]

We can do little more than sketch the sporadic outbreaks arising out of the leaseholds during the second half of the nineteenth century. Thus in 1878 an observer noted that many tenants were being ejected from the Clarke estate in Montgomery County for refusal to pay the rent. In retaliation the tenants were burning down their houses, throwing down the fences, and exhausting the soil.[118]

The mountain towns back of the Helderberg escarpment in western Albany County remained the stronghold of antirentism. The militia trudging through the deep snow in December, 1839, had failed to crush the spirit of resistance. For more than a quarter of a century the farmers resisted the landholders in every possible way. The Van Rensselaer family finally gave up the struggle. In Walter Church, who bought their claims, the antirenters found a fearless and skillful foe. Inevitably Church's vigorous methods provoked reprisals. On February 17, 1860, the sheriff's posse accompanied by Colonel Church raided the farm of Peter Ball in the town of Berne. Ball had failed to pay the back rents. Consequently he and his family were turned out into the winter night. Across the river in the town of Greenbush William Witbeck faced a similar threat. Witbeck, however, killed the deputy sheriff who tried to take possession of his farm.[119]

In 1865 and 1866 the Helderberg War flared up again on a large scale. Colonel Church was pressing his suits with great vigor. Antirent efforts to take away the right of ejectment by repealing the Statute of 1805 had proved futile. In desperation the farmers began to reorganize their associations. In May, 1865, Indians re-

---

[117] *Van Rensselaer v. Read*, 26 N.Y. 558.

[118] *History of Montgomery and Fulton Counties, New York* (New York, 1878), p. 72.

[119] Howell and Tenney, *op. cit.*, pp. 283 ff.; Christman, *op. cit.*, pp. 294–297, 301–302.

ANTIRENTISM IN POLITICS

appeared in the town of Berne. They ousted a man who had bought the property of an evicted farmer and they resisted unsuccessfully the sheriff's effort to reinstate the man. In July, 1866, a mob of seventy-five men armed with clubs met Sheriff Fitch and his deputies who had broken into the house of Peter Warner. Fitch immediately sent for reinforcements as his predecessor had done in 1839. The militia, well-supplied with ammunition, marched along the dusty roads which crawled up the steep slopes of the Helderbergs. The sun beat down upon them, but no farmhouse along the road would give them water. Indian scouts watched the expedition from vantage points. Finally the militia reached the home of Peter Warner in the town of Knox. An angry crowd of farmers surrounded Colonel Church, cursing him and thrusting their fists in his face. Sheriff Fitch carried out his orders with dispatch. Warner's furniture was put in the road, as were the books of Pastor Daniels, who lived in the same house. The next few days the sheriff proceeded to evict other defaulting farmers. To protect his property Colonel Church hired a dozen men at $3.00 a day. Such precautions were necessary because Indians interfered with the sheriff for several months.[120]

The antirenters of Albany County revived the old methods which had proved so successful during the 1840's. The Indians intimidated the sheriff and molested anyone who bought property from Church. The antirenters organized town and county committees. They sent petitions to the legislature asking for redress of grievances. The antirent county convention endorsed several candidates for local offices.[121] Since Colonel Church was a prominent Democrat they supported Republican candidates. Finally on October 20, 1866, a special landholder's convention met in the Assembly chamber to draw up resolutions for the lawmakers and the public to read.[122]

---

[120] *Albany Evening Journal*, July 17, 19, 20, 22, 25, Sept. 11, 1866.
[121] *Ibid.*, Sept. 24, Oct. 4, 1866.
[122] *Landholders' Convention*, p. 4.

LANDLORDS AND FARMERS

The outbreak of 1865–1866 failed to check Colonel Church. He systematically and ruthlessly brought suit against all delinquent farmers and evicted scores of them. For years the court calendars were congested with antirent cases. Invariably the courts upheld the right to recover property from farmers in arrears. In 1882 several cases arose in the Delaware County courts. These courts likewise upheld the right of the landholder to evict farmers who owed rent.[123]

This mass of litigation was the death struggle of the leasehold. Obviously a venerable institution so deeply rooted in the bedrock of New York life could not be uprooted painlessly. By 1845 the landholders had reconciled themselves to the gradual and eventual destruction of the leasehold. Thereafter their main effort was to salvage as much as possible.

Several factors prompted the large proprietors to sell. First and foremost was the effective work of antirent associations in preventing rent collections. Even if the landholder could recover possession of the farm, he found it virtually impossible to persuade anyone to buy or lease the property. Antirent victories at the polls foreshadowed a hostile attitude by the local and state governments. The laws of 1846 such as the tax on the landlord's interests in the land seemed to threaten his equity. The De Peyster decision declaring that holders of perpetual leases were freeholders convinced many proprietors that the leasehold system could never be restored in its original vigor. These reasons and many others, such as public disapproval of tenancy, persuaded many proprietors to sell out their interests.[124]

In August, 1845, seventeen landholders in Greene, Ulster, Columbia, Rensselaer, and Dutchess counties announced that they were ready to make sales on reasonable terms. Among the signers were John Hunter, Henry Overing, four members of the Verplanck

---

[123] Simon W. Rosendale, *op. cit.*, pp. 240 ff.

[124] In 1851 (June 11) the *Freeholder* noted that landholders were willing to sell at low prices.

ANTIRENTISM IN POLITICS

family, Frederic De Peyster, John A. Livingston, Robert Ludlow, and Goldsboro' LeRoy Banyar.[125]

In September of the same year Stephen Van Rensselaer made a definite offer to his tenants in the Helderberg townships.[126] On the condition that the tenants paid up all arrears and $30.00 for the quarter sales, he would sell the fee on the following terms: Wheat would be estimated at $1.00 a bushel, a day's service at $2.00, and four fowl at 50 cents. Thus the rent of a farm of 160 acres owing 14 bushels of wheat per hundred acres would amount to $25.00.[127] If the farmer paid a sum which at 6 per cent yielded this amount, he would receive the fee. By March 12, 1846, some eighty to ninety farms were released from rent burdens, some by cash and the rest by mortgage.[128] The antirenters attacked this offer as inadequate. They pointed out that it applied only to the Helderberg townships and that it required the tenants to pay the arrears at the old rate.[129] In 1848 William P. Van Rensselaer offered similar terms for all leases in Stephentown.[130] The *Freeholder* reported in 1848 that it had heard that about five hundred bonds had been executed between William Van Rensselaer and his tenants.[131]

The statute of 1846 authorized the assessors of each town to ascertain the amount of rents reserved in fee or in leases for lives and over twenty-one years. Such rents were to be assessed as personal estate at a sum the interest of which would produce an amount equal to such annual rents. The antirenters naturally seized upon this law as a weapon to intimidate the landholders.

---

[125] *Argus*, Aug. 18, 1845.

[126] *Ibid.*, Sept. 18, 1845.

[127] This figure corresponds closely with the second offer of the antirenters in 1839. It did not provide, however, for a comparable reduction in the arrears.

[128] *N.Y. Senate Documents*, no. 92 (1846).

[129] *Freeholder*, Sept. 24, 1845.

[130] *Freeholder*, July 26, 1848.

[131] *Freeholder*, Feb. 9, 1848.

LANDLORDS AND FARMERS

In 1847 Stephen Van Rensselaer sent a memorial to the legislature charging that the law was unfair and subject to abuse. He complained that he had been assessed in seven towns for personal estate to the amount of $296,979, whereas the total amount of assessed personal estate in these towns was only $574,559. He denounced the assessors for valuing his lands at a rate three times that of ordinary land. In fact, the amount of taxes levied exceeded the whole amount of rent voluntarily paid during the previous three years.[132] From Columbia County came reports that Henry Livingston was also complaining of excessive assessments.[133] In Rensselaer County the antirenters accused the assessors in several towns of being the tools of William P. Van Rensselaer. The assessors had listed his property at the low figure of $145,737.71.[134]

Assailed on one hand by a concerted conspiracy not to pay rent and attacked on the other hand by heavy taxes and investigations of title by the state, the landed proprietors were only too happy to sell. Amicable settlements were reached by committees representing both parties in a few instances.[135] Throughout the leasehold area came reports of the liquidation of the old estates. In 1846 the Tilden committee noted that the sale of the fee to the tenants was progressing at a rapid rate on Livingston Manor. The lawyer for the family declared to the court in 1850 that of the original 160,000 acres in the manor, only 35,000 acres were still held under lease. The rest had been sold.[136] The historian of Delaware County noted the "almost universal sale of the fee-simple" to the farmers.[137]

During the period of antirent agitation many of the leases for

---

[132] For hostile comments on the memorial, see the *Freeholder*, March 31, 1847.

[133] *Ibid.*, Aug. 5, 1849.

[134] *Ibid.*, Dec. 22, 1847, Jan. 19, 1849.

[135] The tenants of Commodore Ridgely in Neversink, Sullivan County, made such an arrangement (*Newspaper Clippings*, p. 26).

[136] Josiah Sutherland, *Deduction of the Title to the Manor of Livingston* (Hudson, 1850).

[137] Murray, *Delaware County*, pp. 96–97.

ANTIRENTISM IN POLITICS

three lives on the land of George Clarke, Jr., in Montgomery County were expiring. Compared with the farmers on Rensselaerswyck these tenants were in an unenviable position. All the improvements they had placed on the farm now reverted to Clarke, who was under no obligation to compensate the tenants. The suggestion of Assemblyman Bowdish that the state pass a law securing to the tenants a fair remuneration for permanent improvements made no headway.[138] George Clarke, Jr., adopted the policy of issuing annual leases. For example, the terms of a lease signed by Nathan Kimball in 1843 called for an annual rent of $50, a sum approximately four times the former rent. In addition, Kimball agreed to keep all the manure on the farm, make and repair all necessary fences, and repair the barns and house.[139] That the Clarke policy of handling tenants was unpopular became evident in the decade of the 1870's, when another uprising took place.

The provision in the constitution of 1846 prohibiting the signing of new leases for periods of over twelve years meant the eventual elimination of all but short-term leases. Of course, it did not affect leases in perpetuity such as those on Van Rensselaer Manor. Nevertheless, the number of farms owing rent steadily declined. Whether by eviction or by purchase most of the farms were being released from the annual rent burdens. Thus in 1858 one report estimated the proportion of leased land in Rensselaer County as follows: in Stephentown, nearly all leased; in Grafton, Nassau, Schodack, East Greenbush, North Greenbush, and Brunswick, about two thirds leased; in Berlin and Petersburg, about one half leased; in Sandlake, one third leased; in Poestenkill nearly all freehold.[140] Across the river in Albany County it was estimated that practically all of Watervliet, three fourths of Guilderland, and two

---

[138] *N.Y. Assembly Documents*, no. 261 (1847).
[139] *Freeholder*, Dec. 29, 1847, Jan. 3, 1849. The *Freeholder* (May 16, 1849) noted that Clarke was trying to sell his farms. Between 1840 and 1880 the population of Charleston, where Clarke's lands were located, dropped from 2,103 to 1,334.
[140] French, *op. cit.*, p. 553 n.

LANDLORDS AND FARMERS

thirds of Bethlehem, Coeymans, and New Scotland were held in fee. The proportion of leased land in the Helderberg townships was higher. Only one half of Knox, Rensselaerville, and Westerlo and one third of Berne were held in fee.[141] Already by 1858 much of the land on the manor had been freed of the rent burden. The wave of ejectment suits in the 1860's culminating in the outbreaks of 1865 and 1866 speeded up the process. One observer stated in 1884 that three fourths of the manor was entirely free from any rent charges.[142]

The antirent struggle left deep scars on the agricultural communities of the Hudson-Mohawk Valley. To the admittedly evil effects of tenancy were now added the excitement, uncertainty, and bitterness of the antirent agitation. Many farmers in the hill towns where the exhausted soils, transportation difficulties, and full impact of western competition had already set in motion the forces of rural decline became discouraged and gave up their farms. Even if they had been willing to pay the annual rent to Colonel Church, some were unable to pay the accumulation of back rents. No doubt the 27 per cent decline in the population of the Helderberg townships in the forty years following 1840 reflects in part the social disorganization caused by the fight against the Van Rensselaers.

	1840	1880
Berne	3,740	2,616
Knox	2,143	1,694
Rensselaerville	3,705	2,488
Westerlo	3,096	2,324
	12,684	9,122 [143]

The question arises whether there was any connection between the leasehold and the growth of modern tenant farming. The

---

[141] French, *op. cit.*, p. 157 n.

[142] Henry Pitt Phelps, *The Albany Hand-Book* (Albany, 1884), p. 11.

[143] United States, Census Office, *Statistics of the Population of the United States at the Tenth Census (June 1, 1880)* (Washington, 1883).

ANTIRENTISM IN POLITICS

scanty evidence on this point seems to indicate a negative answer. Thus the census figures of 1880 reveal that the percentage of tenant-operated farms in Columbia, Albany, and Rensselaer counties was not significantly different from that for the entire state.[144] The landholders were only too happy to get rid of their farms. The farmers naturally had built up a strong prejudice against leases. Without further study of the county records it would be difficult to ascertain whether the percentage of mortgaged farms was higher in the leasehold region than in the state as a whole.

The institution of leasehold tenure died hard. For over two hundred years sporadic revolts against the landlords punctuated the history of eastern New York. Despite their defeats in the 1760's, 1790's, and in 1812 and 1813, the tenant farmers refused to give up the hope that eventually they would free themselves from the rent. As the decades rolled by and as the tide of democratic thought and action rose to new levels, they found the provisions of the leasehold more and more galling and incongruous. The uncertainties accompanying the growth of commercial agriculture intensified the spirit of unrest. Only a spark was needed to touch off the powder keg of accumulated grievances and frustrated hopes.

The death of Stephen Van Rensselaer in 1839 gave the signal for a renewal of the struggle between landlord and tenant. But this time the farmers were better prepared to do battle. Armed with the weapon of the ballot, inspired with the crusading fervor so characteristic of contemporary reform movements, and skillfully employing many of the techniques of modern pressure groups, the leaseholders outgeneraled their foes in political campaigns and forced most of them to surrender their interests at a

---

[144] The percentage of owner-operated farms in Albany County was 79; Rensselaer County, 84; Columbia County, 79. The percentage for the state was 83 (*ibid.*).

LANDLORDS AND FARMERS

sacrifice. It is true that by retreating to the courts the landholders were able to secure judicial support for most of their rights. Such legal victories, however, were of doubtful value in the face of tenant resistance which sometimes took the form of violence and practically paralyzed the agencies of law enforcement. Colonel Church, to be sure, forced the farmers to recognize his claims but only at the cost of endless litigation and tireless activity. Even Church, however, did not try to revive the old order to which the antirenters had given the deathblow.

By 1860 the tenant farmers in the Hudson-Mohawk region had largely succeeded in breaking up the leasehold. Their long and gallant struggle to eliminate the vestiges of feudal land tenure had been crowned with success. But the individual tenant farmer might well have wondered whether his side had actually won. The title of the landlords to the original grants withstood every test. The rent burden remained until the tenant farmer bought out the landlord's rights. For hundreds of tenant farmers who were evicted by Colonel Church, there was no victory. For those who were willing and able to purchase the reversionary rights of the landlord, there was no sense of elation—only a grim satisfaction that they would no longer have to pay annual rents smacking of feudal obligations.

The antirent movement was more than a mere economic struggle, a selfish desire to escape the payment of some thirty dollars or more of rent. It was also a ringing protest by democratic farmers against the aristocratic clique which had dominated New York for so many decades. Moreover, the movement had more than local significance. By dramatizing the evils of land monopoly and by identifying their cause with the demand for more democracy, the antirenters helped to arouse the nation to the importance of land reform. Within less than twenty years Congress was to enact the famous Homestead Act which despite its many faults was an important milestone in furthering Jefferson's dream of a nation of small independent farmers.

APPENDIX A

NOTES ON THE PREPARATION OF MAPS

THE FACTS upon which the population maps are based are furnished by the *Census of the State of New York for 1855* (Albany, 1857). Dr. Franklin Hough, Superintendent of the Census, has included in the Introduction extensive tables showing the comparative population of towns and counties from 1790 to 1855. These statistics are drawn from both the federal and state census figures. Furthermore, the towns are considered as part of the counties in which they existed in 1855. Because of the subdivision of towns and in some cases the transfer of parts of towns to other counties, these tables cannot be strictly accurate. It must also be remembered that the haphazard methods of taking the census in this period led to many errors. Nevertheless, the errors cancel each other in many cases and the figures give us valuable evidence as to major trends in the population of eastern New York.

In computing gains and losses in population whenever new townships have been created, it has been necessary to adopt a rather arbitrary procedure. Thus when a town such as Root in Montgomery County was created out of Canajoharie and Charleston in 1823, I have assumed that each of the latter townships lost the same amount of population. Such a practice admittedly may be far from the truth. Similarly, when the shifts in population have been computed, I have arbitrarily included half of the population of the town of Root in the total for Canajoharie in 1830. Inevitably errors have crept in but not to the point of making invalid the general picture of population growth and decline.

It will be noted that, except for the map showing changes between 1790 and 1800, Westchester County has been left blank. The reason for this omission has been twofold. First, the townships are so small and the lines are so indistinct that it would be difficult to show the changes on the map. Second, the expansion of the metropolitan population into the lower half of the county makes it of less interest for our purpose. Northern Herkimer County has also been left blank because it was and remains a wilderness.

In preparing the map showing the population changes between 1790 and 1800, the writer immediately noticed that Montgomery County was credited with only 13,015 inhabitants in 1800 as compared with 18,261 in 1790. Such a loss coming at a period of immigration seemed unusual and highly improbable. Upon further examination, it was found that the loss was actually a substantial gain. The act of March 7, 1788, defining the bounds of Montgomery County, set up nine towns. These nine towns contained all of New York State west of the counties of Ulster, Albany, Washington, and Clinton. By 1800 Montgomery County had shrunk to roughly the area comprising the present counties of Montgomery and Fulton. If we subtract 3,078, which equals the population of the towns lying wholly outside the county of Montgomery in 1800 and one half of the population of Canajoharie (3,078), which by 1800 had been parceled out to Montgomery, Schoharie, and Otsego counties, we get a lower total for the population of Montgomery County in 1790. The new figure is 15,183. On the other hand, we must add to the total for the year 1800 the population of Fulton County. In this map Fulton and Montgomery counties are taken as one unit, largely because it would be impossible to determine the population of either county in 1790 and in 1800 with any degree of accuracy. In addition, we must add 1,753 to the total in order to take account of the people which Montgomery County lost to

APPENDIX A

Herkimer County between 1790 and 1800. The new total is 21,699, or a percentage gain of approximately 43 per cent over 1790.

The map "Turnpikes of Eastern New York" is based on information contained in Benjamin De Witt's article, "Sketch of the Turnpike Roads in the State of New York," which appeared in 1807 in *Transactions of the Society for the Promotion of Useful Arts in the State of New York* (II, 192). Information for the map "Sheep in Each Town in 1836" was taken from Benton and Barry's *Statistical View of the Number of Sheep*. . . . *Hunt's Merchants' Magazine* and other contemporary sources supplied information for the map of "Railroads and Canals of 1855."

APPENDIX B

TEXTILE INDUSTRY OF ONEIDA COUNTY, 1827

Name of Factory	Location	Date Founded	Orig. Capital	Pres. (1827) Value	Spindles	Employees	No. yds. cloth per annum
New York Mills	Whitestown	1825	$100,000	$100,000	4,000	135	430,384
Oneida Mfg. Co.	"	1809	44,000	30,000	925	63	238,000
Hovey & Co.	"	1824	7,000	6,000	250	11	
New Hartford Mfg. Soc.	New Hartford	1812	50,000	30,000	1,000	60	250,400
Eagle Cotton Fact.	"	1816	25,000	15,000	750	29	115,000
Utica Cotton Fact.	"	1815	45,000	45,000	1,500	103	313,000
Whitestown Cotton & Wool Mfg. Co.	"	1812	35,000	35,000	1,664	75	275,440
Mechanics Factory	"	1812	12,000	6,000	330	17	
Half Cent. Mfg. Co.	"	1826	5,000	5,000	216	12	
Franklin Factory	Paris	1826	25,000	25,000	950	36	158,000
Farmer's Wool & Cotton Mfg. Co.	"	1812	43,000	30,000	700	44	143,980
Sangerfield Mfg. Co.	Waterville	1816	25,000	15,000	700	27	115,000
Manchester Cotton Mfg. Co.	Kirkland	1815	25,000	15,000	660	38	122,000
Rome Cotton Factory	Rome	1816	16,000	16,000	952	32	92,352
Schenando Cotton Mfg.	Verona	1814	10,000	5,000	250	17	37,580
Oriskany Woolen Factory	"	1810	74,000		950	80	

There were other small woolen factories in Clinton, Manchester, New Hartford, Vernon, Trenton, and Rome, but they were in "languishing condition."

Several cotton factories were expanding rapidly and improving buildings and machinery. They used about 625,000 pounds of cotton worth $68,750. Gross value of cloth amounted to $301,750. They also made a large quantity of yarn, which was made into various goods by hand looms.

This table is primarily taken from *Utica Intelligencer* of July 3, 1827, quoting from the *Utica Sentinel and Gazette*. John Donovan, *Textile Manufacture in New York Before 1840*, p. 60, contains approximately the same material, taken from the *Utica Directory* for the years 1828–1829.

APPENDIX C

NUMBER OF SHEEP IN EASTERN NEW YORK

	1845	1855
Albany County	66,536	37,054
Columbia	172,579	87,549
Delaware	135,633	71,315
Dutchess	199,993	73,687
Fulton	38,546	16,969
Greene	48,541	19,382
Herkimer	75,964	17,706
Montgomery	56,260	29,661
Oneida	194,589	50,841
Orange	45,819	21,377
Otsego	270,564	109,937
Putnam	14,062	5,804
Rensselaer	170,552	64,609
Rockland	2,830	926
Saratoga	99,706	46,018
Schenectady	19,461	10,759
Schoharie	75,131	45,596
Sullivan	19,545	12,591
Ulster	46,522	29,841
Washington	254,866	118,533
Westchester	21,567	11,321
Total	2,029,266	881,476

BIBLIOGRAPHY

PRIMARY SOURCES

MANUSCRIPT MATERIALS

Library of Congress
  Correspondence of Hamilton Fish
New York Historical Society
  Frederic De Peyster Collection. Volume VI, VIII, X, and XIII contain information concerning the Freeholders Committee of Safety, an organization formed to protect the interests of the landlords against anti-rentism.
  James Duane Manuscripts, 1752–1796, 10 boxes. Valuable for information on the founding and settlement of Duanesburg.
  Philip Livingston Papers.
  Robert R. Livingston's Account Book, Clermont, 1780–1807, New York.
  Livingston's Great Patent Account Book, Middletown, N.Y.
  Verplanck Papers.
New York Public Library
  James Duane Estate Land Papers, 1750–1867, 4 vols.
  Fairchild Collection. *Extracts from Blockley Farm Journal* (1816–) written by Paul Busti, general agent for the Holland Land Company.
  Gansevoort-Lansing Collection.
  Gilbert Livingston Land Papers and Correspondence.
  Philip Schuyler Papers.
    Schuyler Account Book, 1758–1798.
    Ledger of Rents at Saratoga, 1760–1805.
New York State Library
  Goldsbrow Banyar Papers. This large collection includes maps, leases, and surveys relating to land in the Banyar, Lott and Low, Magin, Schuyler,

BIBLIOGRAPHY

Staley, and Stewart patents. Ledgers, rent books, and memorandum reports contain information about the management of the Banyar estate. Particularly valuable is *John Wigram's Proceedings on Goldsbrow Banyar Business, 1812.*

George Clarke, Jr., Leases.

James Cockburn Papers. Maps, leases, and a few letters.

Hardenbergh Papers, 5 boxes. Deeds, wills, maps, etc.

Kingston Papers, 14 boxes.

John Kiersted's Acc't Book, 1807–1862.

Samuel A. Law Papers, 1795–1887, 10,000 items. Law kept meticulous accounts of all his varied activities as a land agent, farmer, and businessman in Delaware County.

"Livingston Manor Memoranda."

"Robert L. Livingston's Account with Tenants, 1812–1813."

William North Papers, 1783–1820.

Scriba Papers.

Seventh Census of the United States, Original Returns of the Assistant Marshalls: Agricultural Production (N–O).

Thomson Collection, 1786–1846.

Van Rensselaer Manor Papers. Leases, maps, and legal documents. The rent books begun by Stephen Van Rensselaer and continued by W. S. Church show the annual payments of the tenants.

Van Vechten Collection.

Oneida County Clerk's Office, Utica, New York
  Deeds, Libri I–XX.

Oneida Historical Society, Utica, New York
  Baron Steuben Papers, 1778–1794. 200 pieces.
  Correspondence of Benjamin Walker, 1792–1818.

Schuyler Mansion, Albany, New York
  Address of Gen. Philip Schuyler to the Tenants of Lands at Hillsdale, Derived Through His Wife from Her Father, John Van Rensselaer, Nov. 12, 1790.

Syracuse University Library
  Gerrit Smith Miller Collection.

William L. Clements Library, Ann Arbor, Michigan
  William H. Seward Letters.

NEWSPAPERS

The dates given indicate the extent of the files used. Some of the files consulted have been irregular.

Albany Argus. The title varied both in the weekly and daily editions.
  The weekly edition carried titles such as *Argus, Weekly Argus,* etc. I have used this file for the following periods: 1813–June, 1815; 1816–1820; 1822–1826.

LANDLORDS AND FARMERS

The *Daily Albany Argus* carried titles such as *Albany Argus, Albany Argus and Daily City Gazette,* etc. I have used this file from 1828 to 1851.
Albany Atlas, Nov. 8–Dec. 26, 1846.
Albany Balance, 1809–1811.
Albany Evening Journal, 1839–1840; 1844–1845.
Albany Freeholder, April, 1845–April, 1847; Sept., 1847–June 11, 1851. This file is indispensable for a study of antirentism.
Albany Gazette, 1785–1820.
Albany Journal, 1788–1789.
Albany Register, 1795–1802; Oct., 1804–Oct., 1805; Oct., 1806–Dec., 1808; 1810.
Anti-Renter (Albany), Sept. 13, 1845–Oct. 24, 1846. A scattered file is in the New York State Library.
Hudson Balance, 1802–1808.
Lansingsburgh Gazette, 1808; 1811–1813.
New York Express, July 30, Aug. 2, 21, 1845.
New-York Herald, 1845.
New-York Spectator, 1812.
New-York Tribune:
    Daily, 1841; 1844; 1846; 1847.
    Semi-Weekly, 1845.
    Weekly, 1842–1852.
Newspaper Clippings Relating to Anti-Rent Disturbances in New York State with Some Account of the Resulting Legal Trials. Bound by the New York State Library, 1923.
Northern Whig (Hudson), 1815–1816.
Oneida Whig (Utica), 1834–1838.
Orange County Patriot, 1809–1815; 1820–1823.
Political Reformer, May, 1838–May, 1839.
Schoharie Republican, 1839–1840; 1843–1849.
Semi-Weekly Courier and Enquirer (New York), 1845.
Troy Daily Budget, 1842.
Troy Sentinel, 1825.
Ulster Republican, May, 1835–May, 1839; 1845–1848.
Utica Daily Gazette, 1850.
Utica Daily News, 1842.
Utica Democrat, 1836–1839.
Utica Intelligencer, 1827–1830.
Utica Observer, 1842–1843.
Utica Patriot, Oct. 24, 1820.
Utica Sentinel and Gazette, June, 1825–June, 1827; June, 1828–1834.
Working Man's Advocate (New York), second series, 1844–1845.
Young America (New York), March, 1845–March, 1847.

BIBLIOGRAPHY

OTHER CONTEMPORARY PERIODICALS AND SERIALS

(Dates indicate the extent of the files used.)
American Agriculturist, 1842–1855 (New York).
American Quarterly Journal of Agriculture and Science, 1845–1848 (Albany and New York).
Central New-York Farmer, 1842–1844 (Rome and Oneida).
Country Gentleman, 1853–1856 (Albany).
Cultivator, The, 1834–1856 (Albany).
Genesee Farmer, 1833–1836 (Rochester).
Hunt's Merchants' Magazine, 1847–1852 (New York).
Memoirs of the Board of Agriculture of the State of New York, 1821–1826 (Albany).
New-York Farmer, 1828–1839 (New York).
New York Farmer and Mechanic, 1844–1852 (New York). Title varies.
Niles' Weekly Register, 1814–1849 (Baltimore).
Plough Boy, 1809–1823 (Albany).
Plough, the Loom, and the Anvil, 1848–1852 (Philadelphia and New York).
Rural New-Yorker, 1849–1855 (Rochester). During the first years the title was Moore's Rural New-Yorker.
Transactions of the Albany Institute, 1864 (Albany).
Transactions of the New York State Agricultural Society, 1841–1870 (Albany). Footnote abbreviation is Trans.
Transactions of the Society for the Promotion of Agriculture, Arts, and Manufactures, 1791–1798 (New York).
Transactions of the Society for the Promotion of Useful Arts in the State of New York, 1807–1814 (New York). This journal and the preceding one are cited in the footnotes as Trans. for Promotion of Arts.

GOVERNMENT PUBLICATIONS

New York (State), Franklin B. Hough, Superintendent of the Census, Census of the State of New-York for 1855. Albany, 1857.
——, New York Planning Board, A Graphic Compendium of Planning Studies. Albany, 1935.
——, Assembly Documents, 1831–1855.
——, Census of the State of New-York for 1835. Albany, 1836.
——, Census of the State of New-York for 1845. Albany, 1846.
——, Journals of the Assembly of the State of New-York. Albany, 1795–1855.
——, Journals of the Senate of the State of New-York. Albany, 1798–1855.
——, Laws of the State of New-York Passed at the Sessions of the Legislature Held in the Years 1777 . . . 1801. Albany, 1887. 5 vols.
——, Messages from the Governors, Comprising Executive Communications to the Legislature and Other Papers . . . , 1683–1906. Ed. by Charles Z. Lincoln. Albany, 1909. 11 vols.

LANDLORDS AND FARMERS

New York (State), *New York Reports.*
——, *Report of the Commission of Housing and Regional Planning to Governor Alfred E. Smith, May 17, 1926.* Albany, 1926.
——, *Senate Documents,* 1832–1855.
——, *Supreme Court, Reports of Cases Argued and Determined in the Supreme Court of Judicature.* Ed. by R. Johnstone. Albany, 1859–1860. 26 vols.
United States, Bureau of the Census, *Heads of Families at the First Census of the United States Taken in the Year 1790, New York.* Washington, 1908.
——, Bureau of the Census, *Sixteenth Census of the United States: 1940. Population,* II. Washington, 1943.
——, Census Office, *First Census, 1790, Return of the Whole Number of Persons Within the Several Districts of the United States.* Philadelphia, 1791.
——, Census Office, *Statistics of the Population of the United States at the Tenth Census (June 1, 1880).* Washington, 1883.
——, Joseph C. G. Kennedy, Superintendent of the Census, *Agriculture of the United States in 1860; Compiled from the Original Returns of the Eighth Census.* Washington, 1864.
——, *American State Papers, Finance,* II. Washington, 1832.
——, *Annual Reports of the Commissioners of Patents.* 1839–1862.
——, *Statistics of the United States of America . . . The Sixth Census; Corrected at the Department of State June 1, 1840.* Washington, 1841.

MISCELLANEOUS WORKS (Journals, Travels, Pamphlets, Letters)

Abdy, Edward S., *Journal of a Residence and Tour of the United States.* London, 1825.
Allardice, Robert Barclay, *Agricultural Tour in the United States and Upper Canada.* London, 1842.
American Husbandry. London, 1775. 2 vols.
Beardsley, Levi, *Reminiscences.* New York, 1852.
Belknap, Jeremy, *Journal of a Tour from Boston to Oneida, June, 1796.* Cambridge, 1882.
Bigelow, John, *Retrospections of an Active Life.* New York, 1909–1913. 5 vols.
Bigelow, Timothy, *Journal of a Tour to Niagara Falls in 1805.* Boston, 1876.
Bond, Phineas, "Letters of . . . ," ed. by J. Franklin Jameson, in *Annual Report of the American Historical Association for the Year 1896.* Washington, 1897.
Burroughs, John, *My Boyhood.* Garden City, New York, 1922.
Campbell, William W., *The Life and Writings of De Witt Clinton.* New York, 1849.
Carroll, Charles, *Journal of Charles Carroll of Carrollton During His Visit to Canada in 1776.* Baltimore, 1845.

BIBLIOGRAPHY

Chastellux, François Jean, *Travels in North America in the Years 1780, 1781 and 1782.* New York, 1827.
Cobbett, William, *A Year's Residence, in the United States of America.* 3d ed. London, 1828.
Colvin, Andrew J., and Anson Bingham, *Slavery, or Involuntary Servitude: Does It Legally Exist in the State of New York?* Albany, 1864.
Combe, George, *Notes on the United States of North America During a Phrenological Visit in 1838–40.* Edinburgh, 1841. 2 vols.
Cooper, Thomas, *Some Information Respecting America.* London, 1794.
Cooper, William, *A Guide in the Wilderness, or the History of the First Settlements in the Western Counties of New York, with Useful Instructions to Future Settlers.* Dublin, 1810. Reprinted in Rochester in 1897 with an introduction by James Fenimore Cooper.
"Corrector," *Letters Addressed to Martin Van Buren, Esq.* New York, 1830.
Coxe, Tench, *A View of the United States of America.* Philadelphia, 1794.
Crèvecoeur, Michel Guillaume Jean de ("Hector St. John de"), *Letters from an American farmer.* London, 1783.
———, *Sketches of Eighteenth Century America.* Ed. by Henri Bourdin, Ralph H. Gabriel, and Stanley T. Williams. New Haven, 1925.
———, *Voyage dans la haute Pensylvanie et dans New-York; par un membre adoptif de la nation Oneida.* Paris, 1801.
Crosswell, S., and R. Sutton, *Debates and Proceedings in the New York State Convention for the Revision of the Constitution.* Albany, 1846.
Darby, William, *A Tour from the City of New York, to Detroit, in the Michigan Territory.* New York, 1819.
Davis, John, *Travels in the United States of America.* London, 1803.
Devyr, Thomas Ainge, *Odd Book of the 19th Century, or "Chivalry" in Modern Days, a Personal Record of Reform—Chiefly Land Reform, for the Last 50 Years.* New York, 1882.
Duncan, John M., *Travels Through Part of the United States and Canada in 1818 and 1819.* London, 1823. 2 vols.
Dwight, Timothy, *Travels in New-England and New-York.* New Haven, 1821–1822. A fine source on frontier farming and life by an accurate observer.
Edmonds, John W., *Reports of Select Cases Decided in the Courts of New York.* New York, 1868–1883. 2 vols.
Emmons, Ebenezer, *Agriculture of New-York: Comprising an Account of the Classification, Composition and Distribution of the Different Geological Formations.* Albany, 1846–1854. 5 vols.
Fowler, John, *Journal of a Tour in the State of New York in 1830.* London, 1831.
Grant, Anna, Mrs., *Memoirs of an American Lady.* London, 1808. 2 vols.
Hadfield, Joseph, *An Englishman in America, 1785, Being the Diary of. . . .* Ed. by Douglas Robertson. Toronto, 1923.
Harriott, John, *Struggles Through Life, Exemplified in the Various Travels*

LANDLORDS AND FARMERS

and *Adventures in Europe, Asia, Africa, and America*. 2d ed. London, 1808. 2 vols.

Historical Records Survey, *Records of the Road Commissioners of Ulster County, 1722–1795*. Albany, 1940. 2 vols.

Hone, Philip, *The Diary of* . . . , *1828–1851*. Ed. by Allan Nevins. New York, 1927. 2 vols.

Horton, John T., "The Mohawk Valley in 1791," *New York History*, XXXIX (April, 1941), 208–213.

Hosack, David, *Memoir of De Witt Clinton*. New York, 1829.

Jay, John, *The Correspondence and Public Letters of* . . . , *1763–1826*. Ed. by H. P. Johnston. New York, 1890–1893. 4 vols.

Johnson, A. G., *A Chapter of History, or the Progress of Judicial Usurpation*. Troy, 1863. A pamphlet put out by the antirenters.

Johnston, James Finlay Weir, *Notes on North America*. Boston, 1851. 2 vols.

Kalm, Per, *Travels into North America*. Tr. by John Forster. 2d ed. London, 1772. 2 vols.

Kent, James, "Judge Kent's 'Jaunt' to Cooperstown in 1792," ed. by Edward Porter Alexander, in *New York History*, XXII (Oct., 1941), 45–56.

Landholders' Convention [n.p., n.d.]. A pamphlet describing a meeting of antirenters in Albany in 1866.

La Rochefoucauld-Liancourt, François Alexandre Frédéric de, *Voyage dans les Etats-Unis d'Amérique fait en 1795, 1796 et 1797*. Paris, 1799. 8 vols.

La Rochefoucault Liancourt [*sic*], [François Alexandre Frédéric de], *Travels Through the United States of North America*. 2d ed. London, 1800. 2 vols.

Lincklaen, Jan, *Travels in the Years 1791 and 1792 in Pennsylvania, New York, and Vermont; Journals of John Lincklaen, with a Biographical Sketch and Notes*. New York, 1897.

Livingston Manor Case. Opinion of Mr. Justice Wright in the Case of The People v. Hermon Livingston. Hudson, 1851. This and other antirent pamphlets are bound together in a volume titled *Manorial Pamphlets* at the Cornell University Library.

Livingston, Robert R., "American Agriculture." In *Edinburgh Encyclopaedia*. 1st Amer. ed. Philadelphia, 1832. 18 vols.

———, *Essay on Sheep*. New York, 1809.

Lloyd Family, *Papers of the Lloyd Family of the Manor of Queens Village, Lloyd's Neck, Long Island, New York, 1654–1826*. In *Collections of the New York Historical Society*. New York, 1926–1927. 2 vols.

Maude, John, *Visit to the Falls of Niagara in 1800*. London, 1826.

Mr. [John] Van Buren's Argument Delivered at Hudson, May 28, 1850 [n.p., n.d.]. In *Manorial Pamphlets*, Cornell University Library.

O'Callaghan, Edmund Burke, ed., *Documentary History of the State of New-*

BIBLIOGRAPHY

York. Albany, 1849–1851. 4 vols. A mine of source material, particularly useful for a study of early settlement and land history.

———, ed., *Documents Relative to the Colonial History of the State of New-York.* Albany, 1853–1887. 15 vols.

Opinion of Hon. Judge Cady in Supreme Court. The People of the State of New York vs. George Clarke. Albany, 1851.

Power, Tyrone, *Impressions of America During the Years 1833, 1834 and 1835.* London, 1836. 2 vols.

Priest, William, *Travels in the United States of America, Commencing in the Year 1793 and Ending in 1797.* London, 1802.

Smith, Richard, *A Tour of Four Great Rivers: the Hudson, Mohawk, Susquehanna, and Delaware in 1769.* Ed. by Francis W. Halsey. New York, 1906.

Strickland, William, *Observations on the Agriculture of the United States of America.* London, 1801.

Stuart, James, *Three Years in North America.* Edinburgh, 1833. 2 vols.

Sutherland, Josiah, *Deduction of the Title to the Manor of Livingston.* Hudson, 1850.

———, *Supreme Court: the People of the State of New-York agst. Herman Livingston . . . Points and Arguments of Josiah Sutherland.* Hudson, 1850.

Taber, Azor, *Report of the Argument of . . . .* Albany, 1850. This pamphlet and the two preceding items are found in *Manorial Pamphlets,* Cornell University Library.

Van Buren, Martin, *The Autobiography of . . .*, ed. by John Fitzpatrick, in *Annual Report of the American Historical Association for the Year 1918.* Washington, 1920.

Watson, Elkanah, *History of the Rise, Progress, and Existing Condition of the Western Canals in the State of New York.* Albany, 1820.

———, *Men and Times of the Revolution; or, Memoirs of Elkanah Watson . . . 1777–1842.* Ed. by Winslow C. Watson. New York, 1856.

———, *Rise, Progress, and Existing State of Modern Agricultural Societies on the Berkshire System.* Albany, 1820.

Washington, George, *The Writings of . . . .* Ed. by John Fitzpatrick. Washington, 1931–. Vol. XXVII.

Wraxall, Peter, *An Abridgement of the Indian Affairs, 1678–1751.* Ed. by Charles H. McIlwain. Cambridge, 1915.

SECONDARY SOURCES

Albion, Robert, *The Rise of New York Port.* New York, 1939.

Alexander, De Alva Stanwood, *Political History of the State of New York.* New York, 1906–1923. 4 vols.

LANDLORDS AND FARMERS

Alexander, Edward Porter, *A Revolutionary Conservative, James Duane of New York.* New York, 1938.

Alexander, Holmes Moss, *The American Talleyrand; the Career and Contemporaries of Martin Van Buren, Eighth President.* New York, 1935.

Anderson, George Baker, *Landmarks of Rensselaer County, New York.* Syracuse, 1897.

Anderson, Russell H., "New York Agriculture Meets the West, 1830–1850," *Wisconsin Magazine of History*, XVI (Dec., 1932; March, 1933), 163–198, 285–296. This article is full of suggestive ideas and valuable data.

Bagnall, W. R., *The Textile Industries of the United States, 1609–1810.* Cambridge, 1893.

Barnard, Daniel Dewey, "The 'Anti-Rent' Movement and Outbreak in New York," *The American Review*, II (Dec., 1845), 547–598.

———, *Discourse on the Life, Services, and Character of Stephen Van Rensselaer.* Albany, 1839.

Bayne, Martha C., *County at Large.* Poughkeepsie, 1937.

Becker, Carl L., *The History of Political Parties in the Province of New York, 1760–1776.* Madison, 1909.

Benton, C., and Samuel Barry, *Statistical View of the Number of Sheep in the Several Towns and Counties in Maine, New Hampshire, Vermont, Massachusetts, Rhode Island, Connecticut, New York, Pennsylvania, and Ohio . . . in 1836 and an Account of the Principal Woolen Manufactures in Said States.* Cambridge, 1837.

Benton, Nathaniel S., *History of Herkimer County, Including the Upper Mohawk Valley.* Albany, 1856.

Bidwell, Percy W., "The Agricultural Revolution in New England," *American Historical Review*, XXVI (July, 1921), 683–702.

———, "Rural Economy in New England at the Beginning of the Nineteenth Century," *Transactions of the Connecticut Academy of Arts and Sciences*, XX (April, 1916), 241–399.

———, and John Falconer, *History of Agriculture in the Northern United States, 1620–1860.* Washington, 1925.

Bien, Joseph R., *Atlas of the State of New York.* New York, 1895.

Birdsell, Ralph, *The Story of Cooperstown.* Cooperstown, 1917.

Bishop, J. L., *A History of American Manufactures from 1608 to 1860.* Philadelphia, 1861–1868. 3 vols.

Blake, William J., *The History of Putnam County, N.Y.* New York, 1849.

Bolton, Robert, *A History of the County of Westchester from its First Settlement.* New York, 1848. 2 vols.

Bond, Beverly, *The Quit-Rent System in the American Colonies.* New Haven, 1919.

Brown, Ralph Adams, *The Lumber Industry in the State of New York, 1790–1830.* Unpublished master's thesis in the Columbia University Library, 1932.

BIBLIOGRAPHY

Buck, Solon J., and Elizabeth Buck, *The Planting of Civilization in Western Pennsylvania.* Pittsburgh, 1939.
Campbell, William W., *The Annals of Tryon County: or the Border Warfare of New York during the Revolution.* New York, 1924.
Carman, Harry, "Jesse Buel, Albany County Agriculturist," *New York History,* XXXI (July, 1933), 241-249.
Carrier, Lyman, *The Beginnings of Agriculture in America.* New York, 1923.
Channing, Edward, *A History of the United States.* New York, 1912. Vol. III.
Cheyney, Edward Potts, *Anti-Rent Agitation in the State of New York, 1839-1846.* ("University of Pennsylvania Political Economy and Public Law Series," No. 2.) Philadelphia, 1887. Mr. Cheyney wrote almost half a century later another study of the antirent war. It is the chapter entitled "The Antirent Movement and the Constitution of 1846," in A. C. Flick, ed., *History of the State of New York,* VI, 283-321. New York, 1934.
Christman, Henry, *Tin Horns and Calico.* New York, 1945.
Clearwater, A. T., *The History of Ulster County.* Kingston, 1907.
Cochran, Thomas C., *New York in the Confederation: an Economic Study.* Philadelphia, 1932.
Cole, Arthur, "Agricultural Crazes," *American Economic Review,* XVI (Dec., 1926), 622-639.
———, *The American Wool Manufacture.* Cambridge, 1926. 2 vols.
Cole, David, *History of Rockland County, New York.* New York, 1884.
Collier, Edward A., *A History of Old Kinderhook.* New York, 1914.
Columbia County at the End of the Century. Hudson, 1900. 2 vols.
Connor, L. C., "Brief History of the Sheep Industry in the United States," *Annual Report of the American Historical Association for the Year 1918,* I, 110-149. Washington, 1921.
Cooper, James Fenimore, *The Chainbearer.* New York, 1892.
———, *Chronicles of Cooperstown.* Cooperstown, 1838.
———, *The Redskins, or Indian or Injin.* New York, 1892.
———, *Satanstoe.* New York, 1892.
Cooper, James Fenimore, 1858-. *The Legends and Traditions of a Northern County.* New York, 1921.
Cowan, Helen, *Charles Williamson.* Rochester, 1942. ("Rochester Historical Society Publication Fund Series," vol. XIX.)
Craven, Avery, *Soil Exhaustion as a Factor in the Agricultural History of Virginia and Maryland, 1606-1860.* Urbana, 1926.
De Lancey, Edward Floyd, "Origin and History of Manors in the County of Westchester." In J. T. Scharf, *History of Westchester County, New York.* Philadelphia, 1886. 2 vols.
Delaware and Hudson Company, *A Century of Progress, A History of the Delaware and Hudson Company.* Albany, 1929.
Demaree, Albert, *The American Agricultural Press, 1819-1860.* New York, 1941.

LANDLORDS AND FARMERS

De Voe, Thomas F., *The Market Book*. New York, 1862. Vol. I.
Diefendorf, Mary, *The Historic Mohawk*. New York, 1910.
Donovan, Herbert D., *The Barnburners*. New York, 1925.
Donovan, J. L., *Textile Manufacture in New York Before 1840*. Unpublished master's thesis in Columbia University Library, 1932.
Durrenberger, Joseph Austin, *Turnpikes; a Study of the Toll Road Movement in the Middle Atlantic States and Maryland*. Valdosta, Georgia, 1931.
Eager, Samuel, *An Outline History of Orange County*. Newburgh, 1846–1847.
East, Robert, *Business Enterprise in the American Revolutionary Era*. New York, 1938.
Ellis, David Maldwyn, "Albany and Troy—Commercial Rivals," *New York History*, XXIV (Oct., 1943), 484–511.
———, "Land Tenure and Tenancy in the Hudson Valley, 1790–1860," *Agricultural History*, XVIII (April, 1944), 75–82.
Ellis, Franklin, *History of Columbia County, New York*. Philadelphia, 1878.
Etling, Irving, *Dutch Village Communities on the Hudson River*. Baltimore, 1886. ("Johns Hopkins University Studies in Historical and Political Science.")
Evans, Paul Demund, *The Holland Land Company*. Buffalo, 1924.
———, *The Welsh in Oneida County*. Unpublished master's thesis in the Cornell University Library, 1914.
Fippin, Elmer, *Rural New York*. New York, 1921.
Flick, Alexander C., *Loyalism in New York During the American Revolution*. New York, 1901. ("Columbia University Studies in History, Economics, and Public Law," vol. XIV.)
———, ed., *History of the State of New York*. New York, 1933–1937. 10 vols.
Fox, Dixon Ryan, *The Decline of Aristocracy in the Politics of New York*. New York, 1919. ("Columbia University Studies in History, Economics, and Public Law," vol. LXXXVI.)
———, *Yankees and Yorkers*. New York, 1940.
Fox, William F., *A History of the Lumber Industry in the State of New York*. Washington, 1902. (Department of Agriculture, Bureau of Forestry, Bulletin no. 34.)
French, John H., comp., *Gazetteer of the State of New York: Embracing a Comprehensive View of the Geography, Geology, and General History of the State*. Syracuse, 1860.
Frothingham, Washington, *History of Montgomery County*. Syracuse, 1892.
Gabriel, Ralph Henry, *The Evolution of Long Island*. New Haven, 1921.
Garff, Ralph Lovell, *Social and Economic Conditions in the Genesee Country, 1787–1812*. Unpublished doctoral thesis in the Northwestern University Library, Evanston, 1939.

BIBLIOGRAPHY

Gebhard, Elizabeth Louisa, *The Parsonage Between Two Manors; Annals of Clover-Reach.* 3d ed. Hudson, 1925.

Gillet, R. H., *The Life and Times of Silas Wright.* Albany, 1874. 2 vols.

Goodenow, Sterling, *A Brief Topographical and Statistical Manual of the State of New York.* 2d ed. New York, 1822.

Gordon, Thomas F., *Gazetteer of the State of New York.* Philadelphia, 1836.

Gould, Jay, *History of Delaware County and the Border Wars of New York.* Roxbury, 1856.

Green, Frank B., *The History of Rockland County, New York.* New York, 1886.

Greene, Nelson, ed., *History of the Mohawk Valley, Gateway to the West, 1614–1925.* Chicago, 1925. 4 vols.

Gregg, Arthur B., *Old Hellebergh.* Altamont, 1936.

Gridley, A. D., *History of the Town of Kirkland, New York.* New York, 1874.

Halsey, Francis W., *The Old New York Frontier: Its Wars with Indians and Tories; Its Missionary Schools, Pioneers and Land Titles, 1614–1800.* New York, 1913.

Hammond, Jabez D., *History of Political Parties in the State of New York.* Syracuse, 1852. 3 vols.

——, *Life and Times of Silas Wright.* Syracuse, 1848.

Handlin, Oscar, "The Eastern Frontier of New York," *New York History,* XXXV (Jan., 1937), 50–75.

Hansen, Millard, "The Significance of Shays' Rebellion," *The South Atlantic Quarterly,* XXXIX (July, 1940), 305–317.

Harrington, Virginia D., *The New York Merchant on the Eve of the Revolution.* New York, 1935.

Hasbrouck, Frank, ed., *The History of Dutchess County, New York.* Poughkeepsie, 1909.

Hayner, Rutherford, *Troy and Rensselaer County: A History.* New York, 1925.

Hedrick, Ulysses P., *A History of Agriculture in the State of New York.* Albany, 1933. An excellent history of rural life in New York.

Higgins, Ruth, *Expansion in New York with Especial Reference to the Eighteenth Century.* Columbus, Ohio, 1931. This book is the most thorough study of the expansion of New York.

History and Biography of Washington County and the Town of Queensburg. Richmond, Indiana, 1894.

History of Greene County, New York. New York, 1884.

History of Montgomery and Fulton Counties, New York. New York, 1878.

Holmes, Oliver, "The Stage-Coach Business in the Hudson Valley," *Quarterly Journal of the New York State Historical Association,* XII (1931), 231–250.

Horton, John, *James Kent, A Study in Conservatism.* New York, 1939.

LANDLORDS AND FARMERS

Howe, Frank B., *Classification and Agricultural Value of New York Soils.* Ithaca, 1934. (Cornell University Experiment Station, Bulletin no. 619.)

Howell, George Rogers, *Bi-Centennial History of Albany. History of the County of Albany, N.Y., from 1609 to 1886.* New York, 1886. Andrew J. Colvin has contributed an informative chapter on the antirent disturbances.

——, *History of the County of Schenectady, N.Y., from 1662 to 1886.* New York, 1886.

Hulbert, Archer B., *The Great American Canals. The Erie Canal.* Cleveland, 1904. 2 vols. ("Historical Highways of America Series.")

Huntting, Isaac, *History of Little Nine Partners, of North East Precinct and Pine Plains, New York, Dutchess County.* Amenia, 1897.

Hutchinson, William, *Cyrus H. McCormick.* New York, 1930–1935. 2 vols.

Jameson, J. Franklin, *The American Revolution Considered as a Social Movement.* Princeton, 1926.

Jennings, Walter W., *The American Embargo, 1807–1809, with Particular Reference to Its Effect on Industry.* Iowa City, 1921. ("University of Iowa Studies in Social Sciences," VIII.)

Johnson, Emory, *et al., History of the Domestic and Foreign Commerce of the United States.* Washington, 1915. 2 vols.

Jones, Pomroy, *Annals and Recollections of Oneida County.* Rome, 1851.

Kelsay, Isabel Thompson, "The Trial of Big Thunder," *New York History,* XXXIII (July, 1935), 266–277.

Kuhlmann, Charles Bryon, *The Development of the Flour-Milling Industry in the United States.* Boston, 1929.

Lane, Wheaton J., *From Indian Trail to Iron Horse, Travel and Transportation in New Jersey, 1620–1860.* Princeton, 1939.

Le Fevre, Ralph, *History of New Paltz, New York and its Old Families,* 2d ed. Albany, 1909.

Livingston, J. H., *Minor Manors of New York.* Baltimore, 1923.

Macauley, James, *The Natural, Statistical, and Civil History of the State of New York.* New York, 1829. 3 vols.

MacGill, Caroline, *et al., History of Transportation in the United States Before 1860.* Washington, 1917.

McMaster, John Bach, *A History of the People of the United States.* New York, 1883–1913. 8 vols. Volumes II and VII were particularly useful.

McNall, Neil A., "The Landed Gentry of the Genesee," *New York History,* XXVI (April, 1945), 162–176.

Mark, Irving, *Agrarian Conflicts in Colonial New York, 1711–1775.* New York, 1940. An excellent introduction to this study.

Mathews, Lois K., *The Expansion of New England.* Boston, 1909.

Mayham, Albert C., *The Anti-Rent War on Blenheim Hill, an Episode of the 40's.* Jefferson, 1906.

BIBLIOGRAPHY

Miller, William J., *The Geological History of New York State*. Albany, 1914. (New York State Museum, Bulletin no. 168.)
Mitchell, Stewart, *Horatio Seymour*. Cambridge, 1938.
Mordoff, R. A., *The Climate of New York*. Ithaca, 1925. (Cornell University Agriculture Experiment Station, Bulletin no. 444.)
Morse, Jedidiah, *The American Universal Geography*. Boston, 1805. 2 vols.
[Munsell, Joel], *Collections on the History of Albany from Its Discovery to the Present Time*. Albany, 1865–1871. 4 vols.
——, comp., *The Annals of Albany*. Albany, 1850–1859. 10 vols.
Murray, David, "The Antirent Episode in the State of New York," *Annual Report of the American Historical Association for the Year 1896*, I, 137–173.
——, *Delaware County, New York, History of the Century, 1797–1897*. Delhi, 1898.
Niles, Grace G., *The Hoosac Valley, Its Legends and Its History*. New York, 1912.
Nissenson, S. G., *The Patroon's Domain*. New York, 1937.
Niven, A. C., "A Chapter of Anti-Rent History," *Albany Law Journal*, XXIV (1881), 125–127.
Palmer, John M., *General Von Steuben*. New York, 1939.
Pelletreau, William S., *History of Putnam County, New York*. Philadelphia, 1886.
Pepper, Calvin, *Manor of Rensselaerwyck*. Albany, 1846. A pamphlet put out by the antirent associations of Albany and Rensselaer counties.
Phelps, Henry Pitt, *The Albany Hand-Book*. Albany, 1884.
Pitkin, Timothy, *A Statistical View of the Commerce of the United States of America*. 2d ed. New York, 1817.
Pomerantz, Sidney, *New York: An American City, 1783–1803*. New York, 1938.
Porter, Kenneth, *John Jacob Astor, Business Man*. Cambridge, 1931. 2 vols.
Potter, Elsie, *The Influence of the Champlain Canal on Eastern New York and Western Vermont, 1823–1860*. Unpublished master's thesis in Cornell University Library, 1939.
Powell, Frederick, "Two Experiments in Public Ownership of Steam Railroads," *Quarterly Journal of Economics*, XXIII (Nov., 1908), 137–150.
Quinlan, James Eldridge, *History of Sullivan County*. Liberty, 1873.
Rensselaerville Reminiscences and Rhymes. Albany, 1890.
Report of the Committee on Linguistic and National Stocks in the Population of the United States. In *Annual Report of the American Historical Association for the Year 1931*. Washington, 1932.
Rezneck, Samuel, "Samuel A. Law: Delaware County Entrepreneur, 1798–1845," *New York History*, XXXI (Oct., 1933), 382–401.
Richards, Augustus, *Steuben, the Pioneer*. [n.p.], 1936. An address given before the Steuben Old Home Day Association, August 24, 1935.

LANDLORDS AND FARMERS

Rife, Clarence W., "Land Tenure in New Netherland," in *Essays in Colonial History Presented to Charles McLean Andrews*. New Haven, 1931.

Roberts, Millard, *A Narrative History of Remsen, New York*. Syracuse, 1914.

Rockwell, Charles, *The Catskill Mountains and the Region Around*. New York, 1867.

Rogers, Henry C., *History of the Town of Paris*. Utica, 1881.

Roscoe, William S., *History of Schoharie County*. Syracuse, 1882.

Rosendale, Simon W., "Closing Phases of the Manorial System in Albany," *Proceedings of the New York State Historical Association*, VIII (1909), 234–245. The best account of the legal issues arising from the antirent cases.

Ruttenber, Edward, *History of the County of Orange, with a History of the Town and City of Newburgh*. Newburgh, 1875.

Sawyer, John, *History of Cherry Valley from 1740 to 1898*. Cherry Valley, 1898.

Schafer, Joseph, *A History of Agriculture in Wisconsin*. Madison, 1922.

Scharf, J. Thomas, *History of Westchester County, New York*. Philadelphia, 1886. 2 vols.

Schoolcraft, Henry Rowe, *Helderbergia; or, The Apotheosis of the Heroes of the Antirent War*. Albany, 1855.

Schoonmaker, Marius, *The History of Kingston, New York*. New York, 1888.

Shryock, Richard, "The Pennsylvania Germans in American History," *Pennsylvania Magazine of History*, LXIII (July, 1939), 261–281.

Simms, Jeptha R., *History of Schoharie County and Border Wars of New York*. Albany, 1845.

Smith, George A., *The Cheese Industry of the State of New York*, New York Department of Agriculture Bulletin 54, pp. 195–222. Albany, 1913.

Smith, James H., *History of Dutchess County, New York*. Syracuse, 1882.

Smith, Philip Henry, *General History of Dutchess County, from 1609 to 1876, Inclusive*. Pawling, 1897.

Smith, William H., *The History of the Late Province of New York from Its Discovery to the Appointment of Governor Colden in 1762*. New York, 1829. 2 vols.

Spafford, Horatio Gates, *A Gazetteer of the State of New York*. Albany, 1813. This gazetteer was reissued in 1824.

Spaulding, E. Wilder, *New York in the Critical Period, 1783–1789*. New York, 1932. A basic study of New York life in all its phases.

Special Report on the History and Present Condition of the Sheep Industry of the United States. Ed. by D. E. Salmon. Washington, 1892.

Spencer, Charles Worthen, "The Land System of Colonial New York," *Proceedings of the New York State Historical Association*, XVI (1917), 150–164.

BIBLIOGRAPHY

Stevens, Frank, *The Beginnings of the New York Central Railroad*. New York, 1926.
Stillwell, Lewis, "Migration from Vermont (1776–1860)," *Proceedings of the Vermont Historical Society*, V (1927).
Stone, William Leete, *Washington County, New York*. New York, 1901.
Sutherland, Stella, *Population Distribution in Colonial America*. New York, 1941.
Sylvester, Nathaniel B., *History of Saratoga County, New York*. Philadelphia, 1878.
Tarr, Ralph, *The Physical Geography of New York State*. New York, 1902.
Torrance, Mary Fisher, *The Story of Old Rensselaerville*. New York, 1939.
True, Alfred Charles, *A History of Agricultural Education in the United States, 1785–1925*. Washington, 1929. (U.S. Dept. of Agr., Misc. Publications no. 36).
Tryon, Rollo, *Household Manufacture in the United States, 1640–1860*. Chicago, 1917.
Turner, Frederick Jackson, "The Old West," *Proceedings of the Wisconsin Historical Society* (1908).
Turner, Orsamus, *History of the Pioneer Settlement of Phelps and Gorham's Purchase and Morris' Reserve*. Rochester, 1852.
———, *Pioneer History of the Holland Purchase of Western New York*. Buffalo, 1849.
Van Wagenen, Jared, *The Golden Age of Homespun*. Albany, 1927. (New York State Dept. of Agr., Bulletin no. 203).
Volwiler, Albert T., "George Croghan and the Development of Central New York, 1763–1800," *Quarterly Journal of the New York State Historical Association*, XXI (Jan., 1923), 21–40.
Warren, George, and Frank Pearson, *Prices*. New York, 1933.
Weise, Arthur James, *Troy's One Hundred Years, 1789–1889*. Troy, 1891.
Wertenbecker, Thomas J., *The Founding of American Civilization, The Middle Colonies*. New York, 1938.
White, Bouck, *The Book of Daniel Drew*. New York, 1910.
Whitford, Noble, *History of the Canal System of the State of New York*. Albany, 1906. 2 vols.
Wilson, Harold, *The Hill Country of Northern New England*. New York, 1936.
Wilson, Warren H., *Quaker Hill, A Sociological Study*. New York, 1907. ("Columbia University Dissertations," 1907–1908, vol. LXXIX.)
Winden, Julius, *The Influence of the Erie Canal upon the Population Along Its Course*. Unpublished master's thesis in the University of Wisconsin Library, 1901.
Woodward, Carl R., *The Development of Agriculture in New Jersey, 1640–1880, A Monographic Study in Agricultural History*. New Brunswick, New Jersey, 1927.

LANDLORDS AND FARMERS

Woodworth, John, *Reminiscences of Troy from Its Settlement in 1790 to 1807.* 2d ed. Albany, 1860.
Worth, Gorham, *Random Recollections of Albany, from 1800 to 1808.* 3d ed. Albany, 1866.
Wright, Chester W., *Wool-Growing and the Tariff.* Boston, 1910.
Yoshpe, Harry B., *The Disposition of Loyalist Estates in the Southern District of the State of New York.* New York, 1939.
Zahler, Helene S., *Eastern Workingmen and National Land Policy, 1829–1862.* New York, 1941.

INDEX

Act of 1805, 303, 304
Adams, Sheriff Amos, 238, 242
Adgate Patent, 26, 52, 53, 54, 114
Adirondack Mountains, 44, 209
Agricultural education and schools (*see also* Agricultural societies), 213-214, 222, 223
Agricultural fairs, 137-142
Agricultural improvements and reform, 92-94, 98-99, 214-217
Agricultural labor, 15, 74-75, 102-104
Agricultural machinery, 15, 216-218
Agricultural profits, 99-102, 157-158
Agricultural societies, 92, 93, 94, 98, 138-142, 211-214
Agriculture (*see also* Cattle, Dairying, Frontier farming, Sheep raising, Wheat, *and special topics*):
  Colonial period: 13-15
  Period, 1790–1808: frontier farming, 66-76; general condition, 76-77; influence of exports, urban growth, and transportation, 77-88; credit and currency, 88-90; husbandry, 90-91; fertilizers, 92-94; racial differences in farming, 94-98; landlord leadership, 98-99; profits, 99-102; labor, 102-104; wheat, 91, 105-106; corn, 106-107; minor grains, 107;

hemp and flax, 107-108; cattle, 108; dairying, 109; sheep raising, 109-110; household manufacture, 110-112; lumbering, 112-113; maple sugar, 114; village industries, 115
  Period, 1808–1825: general description, 118, 126-127, 135-137; export and price fluctuations, 120, 122-126; industrial and urban markets, 127-130; household manufacture, 128, 129, 148-149; effect of transportation development, 130-135; wheat supremacy, 136-137; county fair movement, 137-142; sheep raising, 142-148; dairying, 149-151; tenant uprising, 151-155; landlord agriculture, 155; emigration from farm, 155-157; profits, 157-158
  Period, 1825–1850: prices, 184-185; soil depletion, 186-187; wheat decline, 187-189; minor grains, 189-190; potatoes, 190-191; flax and hops, 192; vegetables and fruit, 193-194; sheep and woolen manufacture, 194-199; cattle, 199-200; dairying, 201-208; lumbering, 209-211; reformers and societies, 211-214; improved methods, 214-218;

335

INDEX

Agriculture (*Continued*)
  machinery, 216-218; rural decline, 218-223; specialization, 223-224
Agriculture of aristocracy, 69-71, 98-99, 155
Agriculture of frontier, 66-76, 116
Agriculture of racial groups: Yankee, 76, 95, 96, 97; Dutch, 95, 96, 97, 98, 103, 104; German, 95, 96, 97, 98, 142
Agriculture of tenants, 77, 155, 187, 230-231
Albany, 6, 21, 78, 79, 80, 81, 82, 84, 85, 87, 89, 101, 102, 108, 112, 115, 123, 133, 134, 160, 170, 171, 175-180, 200, 239, 240
Albany and Schenectady Turnpike Company, 87
Albany and West Stockbridge Railroad, 177, 178
Albany *Argus*, 212, 213, 259, 271, 282
Albany *Atlas*, 281
Albany bridge, 179, 180
Albany County, 4, 17, 40, 163, 173, 187, 188, 227, 230, 234, 242, 252, 270, 272, 274, 284, 285, 298, 300, 302, 304-306, 309, 311
Albany *Evening Journal*, 259, 271, 290
Albany *Freeholder*, 251, 254, 255, 256, 257, 272, 283, 284, 294, 307
Albany Register, 39
Albany State Register, 291
Alexander, Edward Porter, 42 n., 43 n.
American Husbandry, 75, 90
Amsterdam, 115
Andes (Delaware Co.), 265
Antirent and antirenters (*see also* Landlords, Leasehold, Leases, Livingston Manor, Rensselaerswyck, *and* Stephen Van Rensselaer, IV):
  Movement, 1832–1845: part of reform era, 225-227; leasehold extent and burden, 227-231; Helderberg War, 232-246; antirent organizations and practices, 246-252; relations with National Reform, 252-258; antirentism in 1844–1845, 258-267
  Periods: colonial, 10-12; from 1790 to 1800, 34-35; from 1800 to 1810, 151-155; from 1832 to 1845, 225-267; from 1845 to 1860, 268-303, 306-309; from 1860 to 1878, 304-305, 310-311
  Politics (*see also* New York State politics): background of parties, 268-270; elections in 1844–1845, 270, 271, 272; laws and debates, 271-274; Tilden report, 274-277; Constitutional convention, 277-279; election of 1846, 279-283; elections, 1847–1851, 284-287; political benefits, 287; landlord defense, 288-296; title investigations, 296-302, 303, 304; Van Rensselaers sell, 302-303; outbreaks of 1860's, 304-306; landlords sell, 306-308; results of antirentism, 308-312
Antirent organizations and practices: societies, 246-247; "Indians," 248-249; meetings and orators, 249-250; press, 251-252; conventions, 252
Antirent outbreaks in 1844–1845: Rensselaer Co., 260; Columbia Co., 260-262; Greene Co., 262; Ulster Co., 262; Otsego Co., 262; Schoharie Co., 263-265; Delaware Co., 265-267
Antirent state conventions, 252, 280, 281, 284
Anti-Renter, 251, 255
Apples, 108, 193, 194
Archer, Sheriff Michael, 238, 239
Aristocracy (*see* Landlords)
Armstrong, Henry, 292
Astor, John Jacob, 58, 129

Ball, Peter, 304
Banyar, Goldsboro' LeRoy, 307
Banyar estate, 41, 44-45, 46, 56, 57, 64, 69 n., 187, 229, 307

INDEX

Barclay, Colonel, 144
Bard, Samuel, 92
Barley, 107, 190
Barnard, Daniel D., 289-290
Barnburners, 268, 269, 281, 282, 284, 285
Batterman, Sheriff Christopher, 249
Beardsley, Samuel, 108 n., 115 n., 299
Beekman, John, 104
Bellomont, Gov. Richard Coote, 9, 30
Belvidere Patent, 57
Berkshire Agricultural Society, 138
Berne (Albany Co.), 235, 237, 238, 241, 252, 253, 304, 310
Bethlehem (Albany Co.), 37
Big Thunder, 250, 260, 261
Black River Canal, 167
Bleeker, J. R., 38 n.
Bleeker, Rutger, 47-48
Blenheim (Schoharie Co.), 264
Blenheim Hill, 249, 264
Blenheim Patent, 57, 58, 263
Bluebeard, 265
Bond, Phineas, 112
Boon, Gerrit, 26, 52-53, 114
Bouck, Gov. William, 247, 259, 261
Boughton, Dr. Smith A., 244 n., 250, 260-262, 280 n., 284
Bouton, Charles, 251, 254
Bouton, Palmer, 242
Bovay, Alvan, 250, 253, 256-257
Bowdish, Assemblyman, 309
Brett, Madam, 28
Brodhead, Charles, 59
Broomcorn, 189
Brown, Sheriff John S., 264
Brunswick (Rensselaer Co.), 309
Buckwheat, 190
Buel, Jesse, 139, 142, 157, 188, 211-213, 216, 217, 224
Busti, Paul, 155
Butter, 109, 150, 204-205

Cady, Judge, 302
Cagger, Peter, 302, 303
Cambridge (Washington Co.), 199
Cambridge Patent, 41
Canada thistle, 136

Canajoharie, 113
Canals (*see also* Champlain, Delaware and Hudson, *and* Erie canals), 83, 130-131, 166-173, 210
Capital, lack of, 67, 71, 102, 223
Capron, Dr. Seth, 146
Carroll, Charles, 41
Catskill, 31, 79, 82, 89, 115, 130, 172, 262
Catskill and Canajoharie Railroad, 169, 178
Catskill Messenger, 294
Catskill Mountain region, 120, 134, 160, 209, 210
Catskill Recorder, 294
Cattle (*see also* Dairying), 108, 199-200, 202, 203
Cazenove, Theophile, 52, 53
Census of the State of New-York for 1855, 17 n.
Central New-York Farmer, 213
Chainbearer, 101, 295
Champlain Canal, 131
Champlain Valley, 6, 120
Charleston (Montgomery Co.), 298, 309
Chatfield, Attorney General, 299
Cheese, 109, 151, 202-204
Chenango Canal, 167
Cherry Valley Turnpike, 87, 133, 163, 181
Cheyney, Edward Potts, 242 n.
Christman, Henry, 226 n., 271 n., 280 n.
Church, Walter: buys Van Rensselaer leases, 302-303; ousts tenants, 303-306, 310, 312
Cider, 108, 193
Clarke, George, Jr., 28, 45, 46, 47, 88, 104 n., 187, 298, 302, 304, 309
Claverack, 260
Claverack tract of Van Rensselaers, 33
Clearing the land, 66, 73-75
Clinton, De Witt, 88 n., 99, 109, 113, 128, 131, 137, 140, 141, 166, 167, 168
Clinton, George, 2, 3, 13, 29, 40, 48, 49, 51 n., 83, 114 n.

337

INDEX

Clover, 93, 137
Clownes, Thomas, 282, 283
Clymer, George, 62, 63
Cobbett, William, 158
Cobus Kill Patent, 57
Cockran, James, 48
Coeymans (Albany Co.), 40, 310
Colbrath, Colonel, 51
Colden, Cadwallader, 10
Coleman, Henry, 98 n.
Colonial agriculture, 13-15
Colonial land grants, 7-10
Columbia County, 8, 17, 32-33, 36, 89, 96, 152, 163, 187, 189, 197, 206, 208, 227, 232, 246, 252, 260-262, 270, 272, 274, 306, 308, 311
Colwell, J. R., 208
Commerce (see Country store and Exports)
Commercial Advertizer, 257
Conesville (Schoharie Co.), 264
Connecticut, 5, 22, 206
Cooper, James Fenimore, 21 n., 36 n., 66, 69 n., 101, 102, 289, 295-296
Cooper, William, 55-56, 75 n., 87, 104 n., 108, 110, 114, 163
Cooperstown, 113
Corn, 76, 106, 107, 124, 189
Cornbury, Gov. Edward Hyde, 9
Corry Patent, 45
Cortlandt Manor, 8, 27
Cosby Manor, 47-49
Country Gentleman, 213
Country store, 88-89, 220
County fairs, 137-142
Coxe, Tench, 114
Coxe Patent, 49
Craigie, Andrew, 49
Credit, 88, 89, 90
Crèvecoeur, Guillaume Jean de, 15, 66, 103
Croghan, George, 55
Crosby, William, 292
Crosswell, Archibald, 148
Cultivator, 191, 211, 212, 213, 218 n., 221
Currency, 88, 90

Dairy products (see Butter, Cheese, and Milk)
Dairying, 108, 109, 149-151, 181, 193, 194, 201-208
Dairymen's Board of Trade, 204
Day, Stephen, 31, 32
De Chaumont, Le Ray, 211
Delaware and Hudson Canal, 167-168, 172, 210
Delaware County, 3, 4, 17, 26, 59-64, 124, 125, 126, 137, 150, 151, 163, 166-167, 173, 204, 209, 210, 211, 220-221, 223, 227, 246-247, 252, 265-267, 270, 272, 274, 283, 285, 286, 298, 306
Delaware County Equal Rights Anti-Rent Association, 246, 257
Delaware Express, 273
Delaware River, 3, 83, 209
Delaware Valley (headwaters), 54-56
Democratic Party, 268, 269, 270
De Peyster, Frederic, 292, 294, 307
De Peyster, John Watt, 292, 300
De Peyster decision, 302, 306
Desbrosses, James, 61
Devyr, Thomas Ainge, 226 n., 250, 251, 253-255, 281
De Witt, Simeon, 98, 213
Dexter, James, 229
Distillery milk, 206
Dix, John, 284
Domestic manufacture (see Household manufacture)
Donovan, Herbert D., 282 n.
Downing, Samuel, 194
Draining, 216
Drew, Daniel, 200
Drinker, Henry, 62, 63
Duane, James, 42-43, 88, 135
Duanesburg, 42-43, 272, 298
Durham boat, 83
Durham cattle, 202
Dutch, 4, 22, 95, 96, 97, 98, 103, 104
Dutch agriculture, 95-98, 103, 104
Dutch land speculators, 52-54
Dutchess County, 17, 27, 28, 29, 111 n., 129, 160, 163, 173, 184 n., 187, 189, 191, 196, 197, 206, 208, 221, 227, 306

INDEX

Dwight, Timothy, 20 n., 21, 22 n., 29 n., 32, 54, 68 n., 82 n., 84 n., 95, 97, 115 n., 126

Earle, Moses, 265, 266
East Greenbush (Rensselaer Co.), 309
Edmeston, Mr., 57
Edmonds, Judge John Worth, 261-262
Embargo Act, 112, 118, 120, 122
Emmet, Thomas A., 154
English stock, 4
Erie Canal, 129, 130, 131, 163, 170-173, 175, 202, 220
Erie Railroad, 169, 180-181, 193, 207, 208, 210, 221
Essay on Sheep, 144
Evans, George Henry, 225, 252, 253, 254, 256, 258, 281
Evans, Paul Demund, 52 n., 54
Exports, 14, 77-79, 120, 122-123, 170, 171

Fairfield (Herkimer Co.), 202, 219
Fairs (*see* County fairs)
Fallow crops, 216
Faneuil, Peter, 59
Farm labor, 102-104, 217-218
Farm size, 104-105, 219
Featherstonhaugh, George W., 135, 140, 147 n., 176
Fertilizers, 92, 93, 94, 215
Feudal tenure (*see also* Leases and Quarter sales), 11, 11 n., 12, 13
Fevers, 20
Fink's Tavern (North Blenheim), 264
First Great Western Turnpike Road Company, 87
Fish, Hamilton, 281, 282, 283, 285
Fisher, Charles, 147
Fisher, James C., 62, 63
Fitch, Sheriff Henry, 305
Flax, 107, 192
Fletcher, Gov. Benjamin, 9
Flour, 14, 106, 137
Floyd, Gen. William, 48, 49
Fonda Patent, 48
Fordham Manor, 8

Forests, 73, 112, 114; cost of clearing, 73-75
Fort Edward, 209
Fox, Dixon Ryan, 2 n., 13 n.
Franklin Patent, 62, 63, 64
Freeholder (*see* Albany *Freeholder*)
Freeholders Committee of Safety, 245, 288, 291-294
Free-Soil Party, 269
French, 5, 6
Frontier farming, 66-76
Fruits, 108, 193-194
Fulton County, 44
Furs and fur trade, 6, 14, 80 n.

Gage, Henry, Lord Viscount, 49
Gallup, John, 245 n., 253
Gallup, William, 251
Gansevoort, Herman, 218 n.
Gardiner, Addison, 279, 281
Garmel, John, 297
Gaylord, Willis, 212
Genesee County, 188
Genesee Farmer, 212
German Flats, 97
Germans, 5, 18, 20, 22, 44, 57, 82, 93, 95, 96, 97, 98, 142
Glens Falls, 209
Gold, Thomas, 122
Goshen butter, 150, 204
Grafton (Rensselaer Co.), 309
Granville (Rensselaer Co.), 199
Grazing (*see also* Cattle *and* Sheep raising), 108-110, 194-196, 199-200
Greeley, Horace, 34 n., 209, 216 n., 225, 230, 231, 251, 257-258, 269, 270, 278, 281
Greenbush, 177, 178, 179
Greene County, 17, 31, 163, 204, 205, 210, 211, 262, 272, 274, 306
Guano, 215
Guardian of the Soil, 251
Guide in the Wilderness, 56
Guilderland (Albany Co.), 37, 309
Gypsum, 93-94, 106, 137, 138, 215

Halsey, Francis, 22 n.
Hamilton, Alexander, 2

INDEX

Hammond, Jabez, 282 n.
Hardenbergh, Abraham, 59
Hardenbergh, Gerald, 62
Hardenbergh, Isaac, 61
Hardenbergh, Johannes, 59
Hardenburgh Patent, 9, 32, 59-62, 87, 265, 297, 302
Harris, Ira, 29 n., 250, 251, 270, 271, 273, 278, 281, 301
Hartwick Patent, 57
Hathaway, Charles, 293-294
Hay, 208-209, 217
Hedrick, Ulysses P., 74 n.
Helderberg Advocate, 251, 253
Helderberg townships (Albany Co.), 37, 230, 243, 307, 310
Helderberg War, 232-246, 304-306
Hemp, 107
Herkimer County, 17, 44, 93, 95, 96, 109, 120, 123, 151, 173, 188, 192, 202-204, 217, 223
Hessian fly, 105, 106, 136
Highland Patent, 8, 28-29, 227
Hill farming, 72
Hillsdale (Columbia Co.), 155
Hogeboom, Sheriff Cornelius, 34-35
Hogeboom, Henry, 294
Hogs, 200-201
Holland, Henry Richard, 49
Holland Land Company, 126
Hone, Philip, 129, 168
Hoosic Valley, 192
Hops, 192
Horses, 108, 109
Household manufacture, 110-112, 127, 128, 148-149, 182, 198
Hudson, John T., 282, 283
Hudson, 79, 82, 87, 112, 130, 172, 261
Hudson *Advocate*, 153
Hudson and Berkshire Railroad, 169
Hudson-Mohawk region: defined, 3-4
Hudson River, 14, 79, 112, 130, 134-135
Hudson River Railroad, 179, 208
Hudson Valley, 1, 3, 5, 186, 194
Humphreys, David, 144, 145
Hungerford, Isaac, 238
Hunkers, 268, 269, 281, 282, 284, 285

Hunt, Washington, 286
Hunter, John, 61, 292, 306
Hussey reaper, 217

Indians, 2, 6
"Indians" (antirent), 242, 247, 248, 250, 260, 261, 304-305
Irish, 5
Iroquois, 2, 6
Ithaca, 87, 133

Jarvis, William, 144
Jay, John, 35, 36 n., 92, 94, 99, 105
Jefferson (Schoharie Co.), 264
Jessup, Edward, 45
John Morin Scott Patent, 57, 58
Johnson, Guy, 45
Johnson, Horace, 49
Johnson, Sir John, 45
Johnson, Sir William, 7, 14, 44, 96
Johnson, William S., 245 n., 292, 294, 297
Johnston, James Finlay Weir, 25 n., 214
Jordan, Ambrose, 261, 297
Journal of Commerce, 283, 291

Kane brothers (Canajoharie), 113
Kayeraderosseras Patent, 9 n., 41
Kemble, Robert, 49
Kent, James, 113, 288
Kidd, James, 302, 303
Kiersted, John, 61, 294
Kimball, Nathan, 309
Kinderhook, 89
Kinderhook Patent, 33
King, John A., 58 n., 263, 292
Kings County, 206
Kingston, 30 n., 79, 87, 130, 168, 172, 262
Kirkland (Oneida Co.), 47 n.
Knox (Albany Co.), 237, 310
Kortright Patent, 64

Laight, William, 58
Lake Champlain, 83, 112, 131
Lake Ontario, 83
Land pattern: Westchester Co., 27; Dutchess Co., 27-29; Rockland

340

INDEX

Co., 29; Orange Co., 30; Ulster Co., 30-31, 60; Greene Co., 31-32; Columbia Co., 32-36; Albany and Rensselaer cos., 36-40; Washington Co., 40-41; Saratoga Co., 41-42; Schenectady Co., 42-43; Montgomery Co., 44-46; Herkimer Co., 44-46; Oneida Co., 46-54; Otsego Co., 54-57; Schoharie Co., 57-59; Hardenburgh Patent, 59-62; Delaware Co., 62-64

Land tenure (see Leasehold and Leases)

Land values and land speculation, 23-26, 44, 45, 49, 51-54, 62-64, 122, 126, 166, 167, 173, 220, 221

Landlords: colonial power, 2, 7, 11; as pioneers, 69-71; as agricultural leaders, 98-99, 155; opposition to antirentism, 288-296; newspaper support, 291; titles challenged, 296-302, 303, 304, 306

Lansingburg, 79, 81

La Rochefoucauld-Liancourt, François Alexandre Frédéric de, 29 n., 81, 96, 102 n., 104 n., 109 n.

Law, Samuel A., 23 n., 26 n., 62-64, 70, 75, 115, 124-126, 147, 195, 218 n., 246, 263 n.

Law of February 20, 1787, 13 n.

Leake, Robert, 45

Leasehold: extent, 3, 4, 227; Westchester Co., 27; Dutchess Co., 28-29; Ulster Co., 31; Columbia Co., 32-36; Rensselaerswyck (Albany and Rensselaer cos.), 36-40; Saratoga Co., 41-42; Washington Co., 41; Duanesburg (Schenectady Co.), 42-43; Clarke estate (Montgomery Co.), 46; Oneida Co., 47-54; effect on farming, 54, 77, 155, 187, 230-231; Otsego Co., 56-57; Schoharie Co., 57-58; Hardenburgh Patent, 60-62; Delaware Co., 64

Leases (see also Leasehold, Rensselaerswyck, and Quarter sales), 11, 33 n., 37, 38, 39, 105, 227, 228, 276, 289-291

Lebanon Springs, 87

Leonard, Daniel, 238

Lewis, Leonard, 59

Lewis, Morgan, 60, 99, 104 n.

L'Hommedieu, Ezra, 92

Lincklaen, Jan, 25 n., 52, 56 n.

Little Falls, 82, 83

Little Nine Partners, 9 n., 28

Littlepage Manuscripts, 289, 295

Livingston, Mrs. Edward, 292

Livingston, Gilbert, 89, 90

Livingston, Henry, 33 n., 308

Livingston, Henry A., 45 n.

Livingston, Henry L., 89-90

Livingston, Hermon, 301

Livingston, Gen. Jacob, 263

Livingston, John, 57

Livingston, John A., 307

Livingston, John R., 60, 143

Livingston, Maturin, 292

Livingston, Robert, 59

Livingston, Robert L., 33 n., 60, 262

Livingston, Chancellor Robert R., 59, 60, 92, 93, 94, 98, 99, 100, 101, 102, 103, 108, 114 n., 142, 143, 144, 147 n., 216

Livingston estate in Schoharie County, 57, 243

Livingston Manor, 8, 12, 32-36, 153-155, 228, 234, 260, 301, 308

Livingston's great patent (Middletown, Delaware Co.), 60

Long Island, 3 n., 4, 5, 92, 103, 105, 158

Ludlow, R. H., 229, 292, 309

Lumber and lumbering, 14, 75, 112-113, 131, 209-211

Lynch, Dominick, 54 n.

McCormick reaper, 217

McEvers, Charles, 61

McIlwain, Charles H., 7 n.

McNish, Alexander, 145, 146

Macomb, Alexander, 24

Madison County, 192

Manufacturing (see also Household

341

INDEX

Manufacturing (*Continued*)
  manufacture), 112, 127-129, 146, 148, 195, 198-199, 316
Manures, 93, 215
Maple sugar, 114-115
Mappa, Mr., 53, 54
Marcy, William, 167
Mark, Irving, 7 n., 10 n., 11 n., 37 n.
Martin, Jacob, 242
Mattewan Manufacturing Company, 129
Mattice, Judge Frederick M., 263
Maude, John, 81 n.
Mayham, John, 249
Merchants (country), 88-89
Meredith, Samuel, 62, 63
Merino sheep, 138, 142-146
Michael, Anthony, 300
Milk, 181, 193, 205-208
Miller, Rev. John, 44 n.
Miller, Killian, 294
Minisink (Orange Co.), 205
Minisink Patent, 30 n.
Minor grains, 107, 189-190
Mitchell, Samuel L., 92, 96, 98, 99, 144
Mohawk and Hudson Railroad, 175-176, 177
Mohawk River traffic, 82, 83
Mohawk Turnpike and Bridge Company, 87, 180
Mohawk Valley, 5, 6, 43-45, 82, 87, 186, 188, 190, 191, 194, 200
Monroe County, 187, 188
Montgomery County, 44, 45, 151, 187, 192, 227, 252, 272, 274, 304
Moore, Sheriff Green, 265
Morris, Gen. Jacob, 57
Morris, Roger, 28
Morrisania Manor, 8
Morus multicaulis, 193
Mount Merino Association, 146
Mullaly, John, 207

Nassau (Rensselaer Co.), 309
National Advertizer, 133
National Reform and National Reformers, 252-258, 278
National Reformer, 254

Negroes: colonial population, 5; agricultural labor, 103-104
Nevius, R. H., 292
New England agriculture, 95, 96, 97
New England migration, 2, 4, 18, 20-23, 29, 44, 57
New Hartford, 199
New Jersey, 206
New Paltz, 30 n.
New Scotland (Albany Co.), 37, 310
New York, 3 n., 4, 5, 78, 90, 109, 122, 124, 150, 170, 171, 178, 206-207, 283
New York Academy of Medicine, 207
New York and Albany Railroad, 169, 179
New York and Harlem Railroad, 169, 178, 191, 208
New York Central, 1, 175, 200
New York colony: population, 2, 5; French and Indian attacks, 6-7; land system, 7-10; tenant unrest, 10-13; agriculture, 13-15
New York *Express*, 257, 280, 291
New York *Herald*, 291
New York Life Insurance and Trust Company, 292
New York State Agricultural Society, 211, 212, 213, 214
New York State Assembly (*see also* New York State legislature), 244-245, 273-277
New York State attorney general: challenges landlord titles, 297-298, 299, 301, 302
New York State Board of Agriculture, 136, 147
New York State Constitutional Convention: (1821), 3, 13; (1846), 277-279
New York State Court of Appeals, 300, 301-302, 303-304
New York State courts: uphold rent collection, 238, 303-304, 306; sentence antirenters, 261-262, 266-267; delays on title suits, 298; outlaw quarter sales, 300; uphold titles, 301-302; De Peyster decision, 302, 306

INDEX

New York State legislature (*see also* New York State politics): bans feudal tenure, 13; aids agricultural societies, 140-142, 214; aids household manufacture, 148; urges title examination in 1811-1812, 151-152, 154; considers tenant pleas in 1835, 234-235; sets up investigation in 1840, 240-241; committee reports, 243, 244, 245; influenced by anti-renters, 252, 270-273; forbids disguises, 271-272; debates Wright's program, 273-274; Tilden committee report, 274-277; taxes ground rents and abolishes distress, 277; calls constitution convention, 277-278; landlord influence in, 288, 291, 293, 294; debates stay of rent, 298-300; repeals act of 1805, 303

New York State politics: canal issue, 165, 168, 169; Seward's policy attacked, 240; intraparty factionalism, 268-270; elections of 1844-1845, 270-273; election of 1846, 279-283; election of 1847, 284; election of 1848, 284-285; election of 1850, 285-286; election of 1851, 286-287; church's power, 303

New York *Tribune* (daily and weekly), 251, 257, 258, 260 n., 269, 273, 280 n., 287

Newburgh, 79, 87, 112, 130, 134, 150

Newburgh and Cochecton Turnpike, 87

Niagara County, 188

Nissenson, S. G., 37 n.

Nobletown (Columbia Co.), 34

North Greenbush (Rensselaer Co.), 309

North, William, 40, 43, 50, 51, 52, 70, 77

Northern Inland Lock Navigation Company, 83

Nott, Eliphalet, 169

Noyes, John Humphrey, 225

Oats, 107, 189

O'Connor, Edward, 267

Oneida Community, 225

Oneida County, 17, 23, 26, 46-54, 109, 114, 122, 128, 129, 146, 151, 173, 186, 191, 192, 194, 197, 199, 202, 204, 218 n., 227, 298

Oneida Manufacturing Company, 128, 146

Ontario County, 126, 188

Orange County, 21, 29, 30, 107, 109, 150, 181, 186, 191, 204-206, 207, 223

Orchards, 193-194

Oriskany, 129, 199

Oriskany Manufacturing Company, 148

Oriskany Patent, 47

Oswego, 6 n., 120, 133

Otsego (Otsego Co.), 114

Otsego County, 4, 17, 55-57, 108, 139, 151, 160, 163, 173, 187, 189, 192, 194, 196, 204, 222, 252

Overbaugh, John, 300

Overing, Henry, 61, 297, 306

Palmer, John M., 51 n.

Paris (Oneida Co.), 47 n.

Parker, Judge Amasa, 262, 266, 267

Patrie, John, 300

Pelham Manor, 8

Pell, Robert, 194

Peters, Judge Richard, 99

Petersburg (Rensselaer Co.), 309

Philipsburgh Manor, 8, 27

Phillips, G. N., 149 n.

Pittstown (Rensselaer Co.), 40

Plough Boy (Albany), 138, 141, 156

Poestenkill (Rensselaer Co.), 309

Population: colonial, 4-5; changes from 1790 to 1800, 17, 18; from 1800 to 1810, 17, 19; from 1810 to 1820, 119-120; from 1820 to 1830, 120-121; from 1830 to 1840, 160-161; from 1840 to 1850, 160, 163, 164; from 1850 to 1860, 163, 165; urban growth,

343

INDEX

Population (*Continued*)
    79-82, 129-130, 156-157, 220;
    rural decline, 155-156, 164, 218-223
Porter, Kenneth, 28 n., 58
Potash, 14, 71, 75, 89, 91, 113
Potatoes, 107, 190-191
Powers, James, 293, 294
Pratt, Zadock, 205, 211
Prattsville (Greene Co.), 211
Prices, 122-126, 184-186
Prince, Robert, 145
Profits of farming, 67, 99-102, 147, 157-158
Putnam County, 27, 191, 200, 206, 208

Quaker Hill, 184 n.
Quarter sales (*see* Leases), 37, 39, 42, 152, 228, 230, 234, 276, 278, 290, 300, 307
Queens County, 206
Quitrents, 9, 13

Racial differences, 21, 22, 95-98
Railroads (*see also individual companies*), 173-181
Randall, Henry, 197, 201
Rapelye Patent, 64 n.
Ray, Robert, 292
Redskins, 36 n., 296
Reidsville (Albany Co.), 238, 239
Rensselaer and Saratoga Railroad, 176
Rensselaer County, 8, 128, 192, 227, 234, 235, 243, 252, 260, 270, 272, 274, 298, 303, 306, 309, 311
Rensselaer County Antirent Association, 260
Rensselaerswyck: extent and settlement, 8, 36, 38-40; colonial uprising, 12; leases, 37-39, 227-228, 276; rent burden, 230-231; Helderberg War, 232-246, 304-306; title disputed, 297-298, 301-302; sold, 302-303, 307, 309-310

Rensselaerville (Albany Co.), 38 n., 237, 238, 239, 249, 253, 310
Rent burden (*see* Leases), 227-231
Revolutionary War: effects, 2, 12
Reynolds, Sheriff Gideon, 259
Rifenburgh, William, 260
River transportation, 79, 82-84, 112, 130, 134, 135, 173
Roads (*see* Turnpikes), 84, 85, 166, 181-182
Robinson, Solon, 186, 208, 221
Rochester (Sullivan Co.), 302
Rockland County, 17, 29, 191
Rohan potato, 190-191
Rombout Patent, 28
Rome, 54, 131, 133
Root, Erastus, 195
Rosman, Jacob, lease, 33 n.
Rotation of crops, 91, 216
Roxbury (Delaware Co.), 265
Ruggles, Samuel, 169, 300
Rural decline (*see* Antirent and antirenters), 36, 155-156, 218-223
Rye, 107, 189

Salem (Washington Co.), 199
Saratoga and Schenectady Railroad, 176
Saratoga County, 40-41, 151
Saratoga Patent, 41
Satanstoe, 295
Saxon Merino sheep, 195-196
Scarsdale Manor, 8
Schaghticoke (Rensselaer Co.), 40
Schenck, Peter, 129
Schenectady, 6, 79, 80, 160, 176
Schenectady and Troy Railroad, 177
Schenectady County, 42-43, 188, 227, 252, 274
Schodack (Rensselaer Co.), 309
Schoharie County, 17, 57-58, 138, 163, 188, 210, 211, 243, 246, 249, 251, 252, 262-265, 270, 272, 274
Schoharie Valley, 5, 136, 142
Schultz, Christian, 84, 90
Schuyler, Elizabeth, 2
Schuyler, Philip, 34 n., 41-42, 47-48, 97, 228

INDEX

Scots, 5, 20
Scott, Hugh, 238
Scott (John Morin) Patent, 263
Scudder, Warren, 267
Second Great Western Turnpike Company, 87
Semi-Weekly *Courier and Enquirer* (New York), 247 n., 251, 257, 258, 280, 291
Seneca Lake, 83
Seneca Turnpike Company, 87
Servis Patent, 26, 52-54, 114
Seward, William H., 238-240, 244, 269, 272, 274
Seymour, Horatio, 285, 286
Sheep raising, 109-110, 127, 138, 142-148, 162, 194-199, 317
Sherburne, 87
Sinclair, John, 99
Smith, Elijah, 260
Smith, Gerrit, 225
Smith, Peter, 45, 58, 99
Society for the Promotion of Agriculture, Arts, and Manufactures, 92, 93, 94, 98
Society for the Promotion of Useful Arts, 98, 143
Soil, 73
Soil depletion, 15, 91-93, 102, 163, 186, 187, 188, 201, 215
Southwick, Solomon, 141
Spafford, Horatio, 29 n., 30 n., 33 n., 73 n., 81 n., 94, 105 n.
Spaulding, E. Wilder, 11 n.
Specie Circular, 185
Spencer, John C., 299
Squatters, 70
Squires, Daniel, 265
State roads (*see* Roads)
Steele, Osman N., 258, 265-266
Stephentown (Rensselaer Co.), 307, 309
Steuben, Baron, 48, 49-52, 71, 75, 88, 227
Steuben (Oneida Co.), 47, 150, 204, 205
Stimson, Earl, 157
Strickland, William, 91, 93
Stuart, James, 216 n.

Sullivan County, 4, 17, 59, 60, 209, 210, 211, 227, 252, 302
Susquehanna River, 3, 5
Susquehanna Turnpike, 87
Sutherland, Josiah, 301
Syluster, John, 245

Tabor, Azor, 300
Tammany Committee of 1850: deplores antirent influence, 284
Tanneries, 115, 210-211
Taxation of ground rents, 275, 277, 307-308
Taylor, John, 45, 128
Taverns, 115-116
Tenancy (*see* Leasehold)
Tenant farmers, 54, 77, 155, 187, 230-231
Textile industry, 128-129, 195-196, 198, 316
Thayer, Jared, 109
Thomson, J. A., 190
Tibbits, George, 128
Tilden, Samuel J., 274-277, 296
Tin Horns and Calico, 226 n., 271 n.
Tories: expelled, 2; lands confiscated, 13, 45
Transportation (*see also* Canals, Railroads, River transportation, Roads, *and* Turnpikes): river, 79, 82-84, 112, 130, 134, 135, 173; turnpikes, 80, 85-88, 132-134; canals, 83, 130-131, 166-173; roads, 84-85; 181-182; railroads, 173-181
Troy, 21, 79, 80, 81, 89, 108, 112, 115, 122, 130, 160, 170, 175-180
Troy and Greenbush Railroad, 179
Troy and Schenectady Railroad, 169
Troy Steamboat Company, 173
Troy Whig, 271
Tryon, Gov. William, 91
Tucker, Luther, 212, 213
Turner, Orsamus, 66, 68 n., 74 n.
Turnpikes: early promotion, 80, 85-88; "era" of, 132-134
Tyler, Oscar, 302

345

INDEX

Ulster County, 4, 29, 30, 31, 60, 103, 110, 173, 204, 227, 252, 262, 306
Ulster Irish, 5
Urban development, 79-82, 129-130, 156-157, 220
Utica, 47, 54, 80, 87, 90, 130, 133, 160
Utica and Schenectady Railroad, 180
Utica and Syracuse Railroad, 180

Van Buren, John, 261, 301
Van Buren, Martin, 152-154, 269
Van Deusen, Lawrence, 236
Van Hoesen, Jan, tract of, 33
Van Ness, William P., 152
Van Rensselaer, Jacob R., 152, 153, 154, 155, 288
Van Rensselaer, Jeremiah, 45
Van Rensselaer, John, 34 n.
Van Rensselaer, Maria, 39
Van Rensselaer, Stephen, III: develops Rensselaerswyck, 36-37; leases, 37-39, 227-228, 230, 231; political influence, 39-40; agricultural leadership, 98, 124, 140; interest in manufactures and railroads, 128, 176; death and will, 232-233
Van Renssealer, Stephen, IV: inherits west manor, 234-235; collection of rent provokes tenants, 235-239, 241; disposes of land, 243, 302, 307; influences legislature, 294; protests tax on ground rents, 308
Van Rensselaer, William P.: inherits east manor, 234; lobbies against antirenters, 245, 292-293; outrages on land, 259-260; disposes of land, 303, 307-308
Van Rensselaer leases (*see* Rensselaerswyck)
Van Rensselaer Manor (*see* Rensselaerswyck)
Van Schoonhoven, William H., 273, 278
Van Steenburg, John, 267
Van Vechten, Abraham, 154

Varick, Abraham, 54
Vegetables, 193
Vermont, 8, 12, 22, 122
Verplanck, Charlotte, 266
Verplanck, Daniel, 61
Verplanck, Gulian C., 59, 245 n., 277 n., 292
Verplanck family, 28, 306
Village industries, 115
Voice of the People, 252

Wadsworth, James, 100 n., 126, 185 n., 292
Walcott, Benjamin, 128
Walker, Benjamin, 20 n., 40, 43, 51, 52, 67 n., 70
Wallace Patent, 57
Wallkill River, 5
Warner, Peter, 305
Washington, George, 49, 82
Washington County, 40-41, 145, 160, 192, 194, 196, 197, 198, 199, 223
Watervliet (Albany Co.), 37, 170, 309
Watson, Assemblyman, 273
Watson, Elkanah, 22 n., 46, 83, 84, 96, 98, 126, 138-141, 144, 213, 223
Watts, John, 10 n.
Wawayanda Patent, 9 n.
Webb, J. Watson, 251, 258, 291
Weed, Thurlow, 259, 269, 281, 290
Welsh, 18, 20
Wenham, John, 59
Wertenbecker, Thomas Jefferson, 95
West Albany, 200
West Sand Lake, 259
Westchester County, 8, 13, 17, 27, 191, 193, 206, 207, 208
Westerlo (Albany Co.), 237, 238, 310
Western Inland Lock Navigation Company, 83, 131
Western Railway of Massachusetts, 177, 178, 179
Westward migration, 156, 219, 220-222
Wharton, Charles, 62, 63, 125

346

INDEX

Wharton, John, 220
Wharton, Samuel, 55
Wheat: exports, 14, 78, 122, 137; rents, 33, 37, 42, 227-230; cultivation of, 71, 76, 91, 101, 105-106, 124, 136-137; prices, 123, 185, 228-230; decline, 187-189, 230
Whig Party (*see also* New York State politics), 240, 268, 269, 270, 282, 283
White, Campbell P., 292
White, Henry, 45
White, Hugh, 23, 46, 51 n.
Whitehall, 112
Whitestown, 89, 113
Wigram, John, 64, 69 n., 74 n., 228 n.
Williams, Jessie, 203

Williams, Gen. John, 41
Williamson, Charles, 84 n.
Winden, Julius, 179
Witbeck, William, 304
Woods Creek, 83
Woodworth, John, 152
Wool depots, 199
Wool market, 198-199
Woolen manufacture, 146, 148, 198
Wright, Gov. Silas, 226 n., 248 n., 266-273, 277, 279
Wurtz, Maurice, 168

Yoshpe, Harry, 27 n., 45 n.
Young, Arthur, 98, 99
Young, John, 227, 270, 277, 280-283, 284, 287, 297
Young America, 267 n.

www.ingramcontent.com/pod-product-compliance
Lightning Source LLC
Chambersburg PA
CBHW021134230426
43667CB00005B/113